The Politics of Revenue Bargaining in Africa

The Politics of Revenue Bargaining in Africa

Triggers, Processes, and Outcomes

Edited by
Anne Mette Kjær
Marianne S. Ulriksen
and
Ane Karoline Bak

OXFORD
UNIVERSITY PRESS

OXFORD
UNIVERSITY PRESS

Great Clarendon Street, Oxford, OX2 6DP,
United Kingdom

Oxford University Press is a department of the University of Oxford.
It furthers the University's objective of excellence in research, scholarship,
and education by publishing worldwide. Oxford is a registered trade mark of
Oxford University Press in the UK and in certain other countries

Published in the United States of America by Oxford University Press
198 Madison Avenue, New York, NY 10016, United States of America

British Library Cataloguing in Publication Data

Data available

Library of Congress Control Number: 2023940510

ISBN 9780192868787

DOI: 10.1093/oso/9780192868787.001.0001

Printed and bound by
CPI Group (UK) Ltd, Croydon, CR0 4YY

Acknowledgements

The early ideas for this book emerged a decade ago. In 2013, Jalia Kangave, Mesharch Katusiimeh, Marianne Ulriksen, and Anne Mette Kjær were working on a contribution to an UNRISD research programme on domestic revenue mobilization for financing social policies. The programme was run by Katja Hujo at UNRISD. While doing this work, we realized there was a lack of systematic and comparative research into cases of micro-level revenue bargaining between specific groups of revenue providers and the state. In fact, we knew little of the political dynamics of revenue bargaining in Africa.

Jalia, Marianne, and Anne Mette pursued the idea over a couple of years and discussed it on several occasions in Aarhus and Johannesburg. Would aid dependence be further reduced and would this lead to increased efforts at raising domestic revenues and more domestic state–society reciprocity? A first unsuccessful proposal led to our narrowing in on revenue bargaining as the centre of attention in the analytical framework we then developed. This became the central focus in the proposal for the research programme 'Political Settlements and Revenue Bargains in Africa', which was granted funding in 2016 by Danida's Consultative Research Committee (16-03-AU). Consequently, the acknowledgements for this book would be incomplete without mentioning those that made the broader research project happen through commenting and inspiring discussions: Ole Therkildsen and the members of the comparative politics section at the Department of Political Science, Aarhus University. Also, Jalia Kangave, who was initially part of the proposal but who then got a position with the IDS in Sussex and had to leave us, offered valuable insights. Members of the research section of comparative politics at the Department of Political Science also offered generous comments on the proposal.

The research programme 'Political Settlements and Revenue Bargains in Africa' (PSRB) www.ps.au.dk/psrb developed into a truly collaborative effort and research on revenue bargaining in particular in Tanzania and Uganda but also Senegal, Togo, and Zambia. The project has also seen cross-country collaborations with important comparative contributions. Professor Bakibinga and Dr Jamal Msami as heads of south teams of the PSRB programme have been the best partners: thank you. All these projects have been discussed continuously at five incredibly engaging and inspiring project workshops in

Aarhus in 2016, Entebbe in 2017, Bagamoyo in 2017, Arusha in 2019, and then finally again in Aarhus in August 2022. Thank you to all the programme researchers for always being keen to provide comments and constructive feedback on early as well as later paper drafts. In these project workshops, we were also lucky enough to get inputs from the outside. Thank you to Odd-Helge Fjeldstad, who joined us in Entebbe and Aarhus; to Matilde Thorsen who was with us in Bagamoyo; and Per Tidemand, who hosted us in Arusha and joined us in Aarhus.

The importance of these PSRB workshops for this book cannot be emphasized enough. Quite concretely, the theoretical framework, which is carried through in this book, is largely built on a collaborative effort and sometimes strenuous conceptual and theoretical discussions at these workshops.

The book itself came into being when four reviewers provided excellent feedback on the initial book proposal sent to Oxford University Press. The comments were exceptionally thoughtful and made us think and work harder on the common framework as well as introductory and concluding chapters. Thank you also to the editors Adam Swallow and Vicki Sunter for their patience and belief in our work.

Anna Persson, Lise Rakner, and Anne Mette Kjær organized a panel about revenue bargaining at the ECPR joint sessions in Cyprus in 2018, and we thank participants at the panel, and Anna Persson and Christian von Haldenwang in particular. Several of the chapters here became a part of the book project in the wake of this workshop.

We presented different chapters at various events: the Effective States and Inclusive Development conference in Manchester in September 2019; the IPSA in Brisbane in 2018; the NoPSA in 2021; the annual meetings of the Danish Political Science Associations; and a workshop at the Centre for Emerging African Economies at Roskilde University in December 2019. We thank Sam Hickey, Lars Buur, Rasmus Hundsbæk Petersen, and Lindsay Whitfield for comments on these occasions. The Effective States and Inclusive Development programme at Manchester has been a special source of inspiration, and we thank in particular Sam Hickey and Tom Goodfellow for their willingness to discuss their own book projects and pass on experiences.

Furthermore, several annual meetings of the African Studies Association have provided the setting for presenting and discussing many of the book's empirical chapters, including in Boston in 2019 where Nic van de Walle acted as discussant on our book panel and gave insightful comments for which we are grateful, and at the Taxation in Africa panel in 2020 where Catherine Boone was another brilliant discussant.

For comments on many parts of the book project along the way, we would like to thank the Comparative Politics section at the Department of Political Science, Aarhus University, and the Danish Centre for Welfare Studies at the Department of Political Science, University of Southern Denmark.

Mia Woer provided excellent research assistance for the introductory chapter, for which we are thankful.

We thank 'the Bergen tax people' Odd-Helge and Lise Rakner for continuous discussions about the book project, and taxation and development issues in general. These conversations have been immensely important for the book, and we are thankful to Odd and Lise for your continuous support.

Mick Moore, always a hard but fair critic, has commented on various papers of ours which have developed into parts of the book, and we owe a lot to Mick's way of thinking about tax and the governance dividend.

We owe a special and heartfelt thanks to Ole Therkildsen for his always very clever and thoughtful inputs.

To the 'Tax Ladies'—Rachel Beach, Matilde Jeppesen, and Ane Edslev Jacobsen: Thank you for all our evenings of nerdy tax discussions, which have fed into this book and enriched it.

Finally, Annette Bruun Andersen and Natasha Elizabeth Perera have been efficient and patient with us in the language-revision phase and we are eternally grateful to you for bearing with us.

Contents

List of Figures

List of Tables

List of Contributors

Clayton Arinanye, independent consultant

Ane Karoline Bak, Danish Centre for Welfare Studies and Department of Political Science, University of Southern Denmark

Rachel Beach, United Nations Development Programme (UNDP)

Odd-Helge Fjeldstad, Chr. Michelsen Institute, and African Tax Institute, University of Pretoria

Constantine George, Research on Poverty Alleviation (REPOA) Tanzania

Ane Edslev Jacobsen, Department of Political Science, Aarhus University

Lucas Katera, Research on Poverty Alleviation (REPOA) Tanzania

Moses Khisa, School of Public and International Affairs, North Carolina State University

Anne Mette Kjær, Department of Political Science, Aarhus University

Jamal Msami, Research on Poverty Alleviation (REPOA) Tanzania

Flora Myamba, Women and Social Protection Tanzania

Dan Ngabirano, School of Law, Makerere University and Development Law Group

Lise Rakner, Department of Administration and Organization Theory, University of Bergen and Chr. Michelsen Institute

Armin von Schiller, German Institute of Development and Sustainability (IDOS)

Ole Therkildsen, Danish Institute for Development Studies

Marianne S. Ulriksen, Department of Political Science, University of Southern Denmark; Centre for Social Development in Africa, University of Johannesburg

1
Politicization of taxation and state–society reciprocity in Africa

Anne Mette Kjær, Marianne S. Ulriksen, and Ane Karoline Bak

1.1 Introduction

On 12 June 12 2014, the Ugandan Minister of Finance, Planning and Economic Development held her annual budget speech and, to the surprise of many, announced the annulment of VAT exemptions on input supply for agriculture, such as machinery, tools, seeds, fertilizers, and pesticides. The measure caused uproar among many civil society organizations who considered it harmful to agricultural productivity and to the poorest farmers. A civil society umbrella association (CSBAG) then organized a broad-based protest against the measure that immediately caught the media's attention and was debated in several news outlets. CSBAG initiated a petition and collected more than a million signatures. The farmers' associations had not really raised their voice, but they soon joined the protests organized by CSBAG, and together the associations created a petition to parliament. When the news reached the president, he was quoted in the media as saying: 'It is very sad that some people passed behind me and included those taxes into our budget. This is counterproductive and I Museveni who has been championing the growth of rural income through agriculture across the country cannot again be the one to put those taxes'. The president and the parliament then overruled the Ministry of Finance's decision to terminate the exemptions (see Chapter 7 in this volume for full references).

This example is a case of what we call micro-level revenue bargaining, which is an instance of implicit or explicit negotiations related to revenue provision between individual or groups of revenue providers and the ruling elite (or representatives hereof). The case represents one of several patterns of revenue bargaining found in this volume: here, the bargaining process is triggered by a decision in a line ministry (in this case the Ministry of Finance), followed by substantial mobilization and protest by groups in society, and

Anne Mette Kjær, Marianne S. Ulriksen, and Ane Karoline Bak, *Politicization of taxation and state–society reciprocity in Africa.* In: *The Politics of Revenue Bargaining in Africa.* Edited by: Anne Mette Kjær, Marianne S. Ulriksen, and Ane Karoline Bak, Oxford University Press. © Oxford University Press (2024). DOI: 10.1093/oso/9780192868787.003.0001 then politically overruled. In this case, as in many others, the bargaining process ends in (the continuation of) tax exemptions. We argue that this outcome represents a micro-level fiscal contract defined as explicit or implicit agreements between ruling elites (or representatives thereof) and individuals or groups of revenue providers related to revenue provision. While not an agreement concerning an exchange of taxes for goods or services, it is still an agreement in which the bargaining parties recognize their mutuality and interdependence. Tax exemptions may seem a poor choice from a revenue mobilization perspective, but they accommodate the demands of the farmers and the political concerns of Ugandan politicians. This tension between fiscal and political interests is at the heart of this book. Throughout the chapters, we present micro-level instances of revenue bargaining across five African countries to explore how and under what conditions revenue bargaining emerges, evolves, and leads to fiscal contracts.

Our theoretical framework (Figure 1.1) informs the case studies presented in the empirical chapters, Chapters 3–12. The bottom part of the framework illustrates how the revenue-bargaining processes unfold at the micro level. As we theorize in Chapter 2, whether and when revenue bargaining leads to micro-level fiscal contracts is conditioned by what triggered the bargaining, how and where the bargaining processes unfold, and in particular the relative bargaining positions of revenue providers vis-à-vis ruling elites.

We focus on the micro level to gain a nuanced and in-depth understanding of the politics of revenue bargaining. However, micro-level instances of revenue bargaining are formed by macro-level contexts and have macro-level implications (top part of Figure 1.1). Thus, we situate the microcosmoses of revenue bargaining within countries' political contexts, that is, the *political settlements*. The political settlement approach helps to disaggregate state and societal actors and to pay attention to revenue providers' resources and bargaining power within contexts dominated by informal clientelistic relations in resource-constrained economies. The political dynamics at play across the cases show, among other things, that ruling elites (i.e. individuals who have either formal or informal positions of governing power) often accept tax exemptions in order to maintain their positions of power. We assess whether the micro-level fiscal contracts entail some level of responsiveness and repeated interactions between the ruling elite or representatives hereof and revenue providers; what we term *state–society reciprocity*. Many of the case studies show that governments prove willing to negotiate with revenue providers—from big business to informal sector workers—and make concessions, although these are often in the form of reduced tax payments.

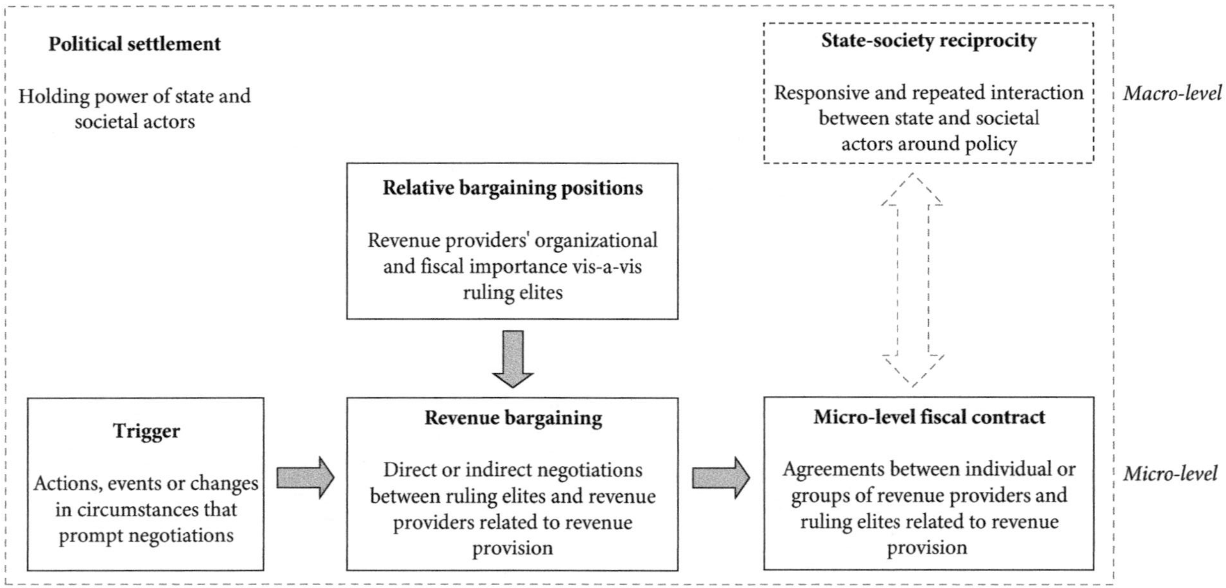

Figure 1.1 The book's theoretical framework.

While the concessions given by governments do not amount to increased political accountability or improvements in public service delivery, our empirical case studies show that negotiations can prompt responsiveness and repeated engagements. In some cases, these engagements became institutionalized within the formal state structures, thereby having the potential to move beyond informal processes of policymaking. Consequently, in this book, we contribute to knowledge about when and how expanding revenue mobilization may prompt institutionalization of state–society interactions around taxation.

In the following, we begin by describing the increased focus on domestic revenue mobilization, its effect on the politicization of taxation, and whether current research has found signs of the emergence of fiscal social contracts. Second, we look back at the early contributions on taxation and on state–society relations in Africa and argue that political changes since the 1990s have fertilized the grounds for a link between taxation and state–society reciprocity. Third, we outline our theoretical contributions to the fiscal contract and the political settlement theories (top part of Figure 1.1). Finally, we set the stage for studying revenue bargaining by presenting our comparative design, which includes case studies in Tanzania, Uganda, Mozambique, Senegal, and Togo. Chapter 2 will then detail the theoretical framework (bottom part of Figure 1.1), explain the methodological approach, and briefly introduce the empirical chapters in the volume.

1.2 Expanding taxation, politicizing taxation

Since the turn of the new millennium, the focus on the importance of domestic revenue mobilization in low or lower-middle income countries has increased immensely among academics, governments, and development practitioners alike. This is most importantly explained by increasing demands for the financing of development and public goods provision such as improved public infrastructure and better public services in health, education, and social protection (IMF, 2018; UN, 2021). The UN's ambitious Sustainable Development Goals (SDGs), agreed upon by all member states, are a manifestation of these demands and serve to reinforce the need for development financing, beyond what can be achieved by overseas development assistance (ODA).

While total net ODA has effectively increased in absolute terms in recent years, even reaching its highest-ever point (USD 162 billion) in 2020, it still only constitutes a very small proportion of the estimated amount needed to finance the SDGs, around USD 2.5 trillion (Doumbia and Lauridsen, 2019; Winckler Andersen and Therkildsen, 2019). The UN has acknowledged this critical gap in the financing of the SDGs, which led to the formulation of the Addis Ababa Action Agenda in 2015, and with it the intention to integrate financing into the work of reaching the SDGs. A designated UN Tax Committee was established to support, in particular, developing countries in strengthening tax systems and domestic revenue mobilization (see e.g. UN, 2021).

Increasing debt burdens have further heightened the pressure on governments to expand domestic revenue mobilization to balance debt stocks (Bak, Jeppesen, and Kjær, 2021; Smith, 2021; OECD, 2021), a demand which has become even more pronounced since the COVID-19 pandemic.

Attention to domestic revenue mobilization has increased and, since the turn of the millennium, so too has tax revenue across Africa. According to the IMF (2018), total revenue, excluding grants, increased from an average of 14% of GDP in the 1990s to about 18% in 2016, while total tax revenues increased from 11 to 15% in the same period (Moore, Prichard, and Fjeldstad, 2018, 32). The same trend is found in several newly developed datasets (UNU-WIDER, 2021; Cogneau et al., 2021; Jerven, 2022) which have sought to improve both data quality and measurement validity, as well as to bolster avenues for comparison of revenue trends across time and space. Albers and Suesse (2022) carefully calculate real tax revenue per capita from 1900 up until the present. They find that for the average African country, taxation has increased since the 1960s, but took a large jump at the turn of the millennium. Cogneau et al. (2021) find that in former French colonies, tax per GDP has increased by 5.9 percentage points of GDP between independence and today. They find that this increase is largely explained by natural resource revenue, but other researchers argue that the increase follows a rise in the capacity to tax society more broadly (Jerven et al., 2022; Moore, 2021). Many so-called modern taxes such as personal and company income taxation, and property taxes had already been introduced in colonial times (Genschel and Seelkopf, 2022). Beyond a sustained period of economic growth in the 2000s, recent expansions in domestic revenue mobilization can be explained at least partly by growing capacity in tax administrations, new technological opportunities, the adoption of tax instruments that target and accommodate challenges posed by the globalized economy, and the economic structures and realities on the ground (Moore, 2021).

The expectation among academics, donors, and development practitioners alike is that taxation could be the source of a 'healthy' conflict between citizens, bureaucrats, and politicians, and between state and society more broadly (Moore, 2004; Bräutigam, 2008; Prichard, 2015; Lucas, 2017). As individuals feel a higher fiscal burden, they could be expected to make demands for a return in the form of improved public goods and services and more political accountability from state actors. In theory, states will then seek to accommodate these demands because it is less administratively and politically costly to tax people if they are themselves more willing to pay. Over time, such interactions around taxation have been theorized to create an exchange-based macro-level fiscal social contract, whereby the state delivers public goods and services in return for tax compliance and revenue (Levi, 1988; Bräutigam, Moore, and Fjeldstad, 2008; Moore, Prichard, and Fjeldstad, 2018; Bak, 2019).

Looking across the continent, taxation has been source of some conflict, as individuals and taxpayers have reacted to new or increased taxes. To highlight a few examples from recent years: several African countries have sought to tax social media, which met with strong popular reactions in, for example, Uganda (Reuters, 2018) and Benin (Okunoye, 2019); or to tax mobile money transactions, which took people to the streets in Ghana and Tanzania in 2021 (*The East African*, 2021; BBC, 2022). In Kenya, the removal of VAT exemptions for fuel led to strikes and widespread protests on social media and in the streets in September 2018 (Miriri, 2018); and in Ethiopia, small business owners shut their businesses to protest against a tax hike (Africanews, 2017).

Such protests over specific taxes spur revenue bargaining between revenue providers and state actors, but they relatively rarely revolve around a new demand for public service delivery and accountability in exchange for the tax. Rather, the demand is that the proposed change in taxation is not adopted. The protests are sometimes successful in prompting governments to respond. In Benin, for example, the social media tax was never adopted; in Kenya the suggested VAT rate on fuel was halved from 16 to 8%; and in Ethiopia, the tax hike was abolished.

Tax grievances sometimes coincide with larger grievances and dissatisfactions with government. One oft-cited case from the 1990s is the protests against increases in VAT in Ghana, which led to large-scale anti-government protests (Prichard, 2015, ch. 3). In the 2017 case of Ethiopia, the so-called tax hike protests evolved into anti-government protests in Oromia state, largely explained by the Oromo people's already strained relations with the national government (Dahir, 2017). However, such cases are rare and the circumstances often quite specific, as in Oromia.

Summing up, there are signs of politicization of taxation in the wake of increasing domestic revenue mobilization on the African continent. But it is not clear what this politicization implies for the expectation of the emergence of fiscal social contracts between state and society, especially ones centred on the exchange of taxes for political accountability and public service delivery.

1.3 Signs of fiscal social contracts?

During the past two decades, the scholarly literature on taxation and fiscal contracts has grown immensely, seeking to answer whether taxation leads to fiscal social contracts and whether it has positive so-called governance dividends (Moore, 2004; 2015) such as political accountability and representation. It is fairly established that, on the macro level and across continents, higher taxation levels are positively correlated with certain political outcomes. Taxation has been linked statistically to levels of democracy (Ross, 2004; Baskaran, 2014), the quality of governance (Baskaran and Bigsten, 2013; Broms, 2015), and vertical accountability (Dom, 2018). Survey-based research examining the behavioural effects of taxation upon the individuals paying taxes have also found positive effects on various measures of political engagement or accountability demands (Paler, 2013; Broms, 2015; Sjursen, 2018). However, as Dom (2018, 31) notes, the observations of an average correlation on the macro level tells us little about whether and how taxation relates to such political outcomes in individual countries. Nor do individual-level survey experiments translate into implications about the potential for societal and political changes.

While it seems that taxation may have some effects on political outcomes, there are few signs of macro-level exchange-based fiscal social contracts whereby improved public service delivery is provided in return for tax payments (Moore, Prichard, and Fjeldstad, 2018, Guimaraes, Duca, and Ndlovu, 2018; Fjeldstad and Therkildsen, 2020). As Fjeldstad and Therkildsen (2020, 38) state, 'we do not know of any major political deals (fiscal contracts) in recent years involving an increase in broad-based taxes in exchange for the provision of public services (education, health, roads, etc.)'.

There is also a large strand of qualitative case-based research that aims to further explore the effects of taxation on political outcomes and state–society relations (Rakner and Gloppen, 2003; Eubank, 2012; Jibao and Prichard, 2015; Prichard, 2015; Rakner, 2017; Gatt and Owen, 2018; Goodfellow and Owen, 2018; Bak, 2019; Schneider, 2020). Most of this research demonstrates that taxation can prompt state–society interactions. However, they remain isolated case studies with few or no cross-country comparisons, and they do not systematically disaggregate the causal mechanisms between taxation and its political outcomes. One notable exception is Prichard's (2015) study of tax bargaining across the diverse political contexts of Ghana, Kenya, and Ethiopia. He finds that taxation can lead to changes in public service provision, tax policy, and administration and expansions in accountability, and he goes some way towards theorizing when governments' tax initiatives lead to tax bargaining, focusing on a limited set of institutional conditions.

The scholarly interest has been mainly focused on broad-based exchanges of taxation in return for something. As Prichard himself later observed (2019, 9), much of the original fiscal contract literature on the macro level has studied large, relatively dramatic shifts in tax collection and accordingly fiscal contracts. Perhaps we have been looking in the wrong places? There is growing evidence that changes in taxation do lead to revenue bargaining around tax policies, but as shown above, rarely at the macro level. Bargaining is confined to specific groups of taxpayers or to specific instances of tax reform or reactions to changes in tax administration. As Moore, Prichard, and Fjeldstad (2018, 182) have rightly argued, we need to explore not so much whether macro-level fiscal contracts are emerging, but rather 'what kinds of tax bargains are likely in different contexts'. Incremental yet significant changes and political effects are also likely to unfold at the micro level, where individuals or groups negotiate with state actors over taxes.

A critical and more recent strand of the literature has stressed the importance of contextualizing taxation to understand its effects below the macro level (Fjeldstad, 2001; Kjær, 2009; Bodea and Lebas, 2016; Broms, 2017; Prichard and van den Boogaard, 2017; Meagher, 2018; Bak, 2019; van den Boogaard, Prichard, Beach, and Mohiuddin, 2021). Specifically, this research shows that whether or not societal actors engage with state actors around tax-related issues is conditioned by their capacity for collective action, tax-collection methods, the presence of community-based service, and social circumstances such as gender, ethnic identity, and patronage ties. Local politics and societal structures condition the effects of taxation but, importantly, are also shaped, disrupted, or reinforced by taxation. Thus, when observing the effects of increases in taxation on state–society relations and political outcomes, we need to pay attention to the effects on social and political power structures.

Therefore, this book embeds the analysis of revenue bargaining within a theoretical framework cognisant of macro- and micro-level power structures. This implies that as we study revenue bargaining at the micro level, we pay particular attention to how the power positions of revenue providers vis-à-vis ruling elites shape the processes and potential outcomes. We heed Mick Moore's advice, and 'go beyond the initial reactions to taxation of each type of actor and take into account the ways in which they then interact, whether conflictual, cooperatively, or in more complex ways' (Moore, 2007, 16). This enables us to observe how negotiations related to revenue provision result from and feed into existing power structures, and thereby we can determine whether and when such moments could indeed be termed *reciprocal* interaction around taxation. We gain a deeper understanding of the potential effects of taxation on state–society reciprocity and, in turn, a new perspective on the implications of the recent increased politicization of taxation in Africa.

In the following, we further develop our understanding of state–society reciprocity and how it relates to taxation. We present a broader and older literature on state–society relations and disengagement in Africa and relate this to recent political progress on the continent. We argue that, in a context of regular elections, increased political competition, and strengthened civil society, the stage may be set for state–society reciprocity to develop through revenue bargaining.

1.4 Taxation and state–society reciprocity in Africa

The idea that expansions in taxation in less democratic developing countries could cause accountability and state–society engagement originates from European state-building experiences. The comparative historical accounts by Levi (1988) unfold the idea that taxation involves some kind of bargained exchanges between states and their citizens. Drawing specifically on the emergence of institutionalized representation and accountability in Britain and juxtaposing rentier states with fiscal states, Moore (2004) developed the proposition of a governance dividend of taxation in contemporary developing countries. Building on these seminal works, the edited volume by Bräutigam, Fjeldstad, and Moore (2008) cemented the potential links between taxation and the development of political institutions and state-building in developing countries through both theoretical and empirical chapters. Since then, the fiscal contract literature has flourished.

An older literature on state–society relations, state-building, and development in Africa had in fact touched on similar issues, although with a less systematic focus on taxation (Ekeh, 1975; Hyden, 1983; Rothchild and Chazan, 1988; Migdal, 1988; Boone, 1992; Bratton and Hyden, 1992; Guyer, 1992; Harbeson, Rothchild, and Chazan, 1994). In this literature, the concept of reciprocity featured centrally in the analysis of the African state. The state was often described as being detached from society, as citizens would withdraw from often repressive state actions. In Victor Azarya's (1988) words, they would 'disengage' from the state, seeking survival in the reciprocal relations existing in alternative realms. Such alternative realms have been defined in slightly different ways and given a variety of labels, including the 'economy of affection' (Hyden, 1983) or in Peter Ekeh's (1975) term 'the primordial realm'. Ekeh famously argued that real reciprocity existed in the primordial realm rather than in the formal 'civic realm'. In the former, citizens felt that their contributions, given in the form of tribute, time, labour, and loyalty, were truly reciprocated. They were willing to invest in the primordial realm because they recognized that here they had duties as well as rights.

Within this literature, Hyden (1980; 1983) formulated a negative link between taxation and reciprocity. Based on the concept of 'the peasant mode of production', he argued that the peasant economy with its limited technological advances and widespread subsistence production did not give grounds for the state to grow structural or functional roots in society. Rulers could not tax surplus production, which would emerge only out of productivity increases, and instead, they had to demand tributes from the existing stock. Consequently, taxation was seen as an imposition and the state an intruder, coercive in nature. Rather than opting fully into the formal system, peasants preferred to have an exit option and would therefore always keep one leg in the informal 'economy of affection'. Any taxation-induced reciprocity between state and society became difficult, precisely because genuine reciprocity effectively only existed within the economy of affection.

Hyden's contribution was criticized for exaggerating the extent to which peasants were able to exit the system (Bates, 1981), and it was questioned whether customary relations could indeed be reciprocal given the nature of highly hierarchical socio-economic structures. For example, René Lemarchand argued that reciprocation may arise as much from the fear of retaliation as from a 'structurally induced form of altruism' (1989, 38–40).

In a later contribution on concepts in the study of politics in Africa, Hyden (1992, 9f) develops his understanding of reciprocity, on which we rely here. He argues that state–society relations do not rest merely on immediate quid pro quo exchanges, and that we should bring into the analysis the concept of reciprocity. While reciprocity has much in common with exchange, it differs first and foremost in that it constitutes a continuous relationship, which is based as much on expectations of behaviour as it is on actual behaviour. Reciprocity requires broader agreement and a consensual underpinning. Examining how revenue bargaining and the politics thereof influence state–society reciprocity thus allows us to identify different and more nuanced effects of taxation and revenue bargaining than simple exchanges of taxation for public services and accountability.

As is evident from the thriving fiscal contract literature, Hyden's focus on the relationship between taxation and reciprocity remains relevant; however, there are reasons to subscribe to a more positive perspective than that which prevailed in the 1980s.

1.4.1 Fertilized ground for state–society reciprocity?

Since the publication of these important contributions on state–society relations in Africa in the 1980s and 1990s, the political and economic contexts have changed significantly, with implications for the dynamics of state–society reciprocity. Subsequent generations of political science research have highlighted, among other things, the significance of increased political competition and a strengthened civil society. This changed context may have fertilized the ground for the emergence of revenue bargaining as 'healthy' interactions between states and their citizens, which in turn build state–societal reciprocity.

Many African countries experienced democratic openings during the 1990s and with them a political competition that caused optimism for the development of state–society reciprocity (Bratton and van de Walle, 1997). Was this positive expectation realized? From one perspective, it can be argued that progress towards democratic consolidation has been disappointing, as most African regimes did not fully democratize. Indeed, recent scholarly contributions on African politics highlight the stability of hybrid regimes where formal democratic institutions, such as elections, parliaments, and courts, coexist with authoritarian features such as the concentration of power in the president who often prolongs term limits or uses the parliament as a rubber stamp in de facto one-party systems, and repressive practices which infringe on political rights and civil freedoms (Cheeseman and Klaas, 2018; Bleck and van de Walle, 2019. On the other hand, after several hundred competitive elections over the last thirty years, the holding of elections has become the 'default option of politics' (Bleck and van de Walle, 2019, 6), and elections have caused changes to African politics as citizens have become voters with expectations and hopes of better lives (Bratton and Logan, 2006). Bleck and van de Walle (2019, 20–22) argue that elections are political moments of 'heightened citizenship' and can have both positive as well as negative implications. They might promote exclusionary and demagogic politics as much as they can also promote responsiveness on the part of the government. Generally, the turn to regular competitive elections has implied 'an unprecedented explosion in political participation' (ibid, 22), which is (as stressed by Prichard, 2015) an important precondition of revenue bargaining.

Elections, even if not free and fair, have caused African governments to promise and sometimes deliver public goods (Stasavage, 2005). However, taxation is rarely central in election campaigning. Bleck and van de Walle (2019) report that public services often appear as topics in election campaigns; however, they do not mention any debate about the financing of these services or indeed any issues related to tax (Bleck and van de Walle, 2019, chapter 6). To the best of our knowledge, there have been just a few recent examples of tax-related issues being raised during elections (see e.g. Rakner, 2017). In Tanzania and Uganda, the unpopular poll taxes were abolished in connection with national elections (Fjeldstad and Therkildsen, 2008; Kjær and Therkildsen, 2013). Elections could offer new windows of opportunity for revenue bargaining and reciprocity.

During the period when elections have become institutionalized, civil society activism has been strengthened too. This could provide a mechanism for citizen engagement with the state around revenue bargaining, both during and between elections. Though some observers of African politics point to shrinking civic space in some countries in very recent years (Smidt, 2018; HRW, 2019; Musila, 2019),[1] civil society organizations (CSOs) are in many countries in a stronger position vis-à-vis the state than they were prior to the 1990s. There have been improvements in civil rights and political liberties, even if there are still restrictions (i.e. on liberties). Lindberg (2006) showed that repeated multi-party elections, even if not free and fair, did serve to expand civil liberties, which has meant more room for citizens to raise their voices, also between elections. Tripp (2017) observes that, in spite of restrictions in the 2000s and 2010s, CSOs continue to operate but have shifted their orientation. According to Tripp, CSOs have found new ways to claim autonomy and new types of movements have surfaced, such as stronger women's organizations and LGBTQ movements.

Focusing on civil society activism around taxation, several international CSOs—such as Oxfam, ActionAid, and Tax Justice Network Africa—have invested in putting taxation on the political agenda by supporting capacity-building and promoting fiscal education and tax justice. These civil society organizations play a pivotal role in tax debates with analyses of existing tax policies and support for protests over unpopular taxes (Sharp, Sweet, and Rocha Menocal, 2019). Interest groups such as trade unions and business

[1] See also the Africa report of the CIVICUS monitor assessing the conditions for civil society: https://findings2021.monitor.civicus.org/africa.html.

associations also find space to negotiate with governments, although with varying success. Bräutigam et al. (2002) found that the business sector in Mauritius was able to build a strong coalition with government to promote economic growth, whereas such coalitions failed to establish themselves in Zambia and Zimbabwe. Whitfield et al. (2015) also present several cases of successful industrial policies characterized by mutual interests between organized industry sector actors and the ruling elite. CSOs and interest groups play a role in most of the cases of revenue bargaining explored in this book.

The political progress on the African continent in terms of increased political competition and civil society participation gives reason to revisit older insights on state–society relations. The politicization of taxation following two decades of expansion of domestic revenue mobilization is likely to have an effect on these relations. We have not seen signs of exchange-based fiscal social contracts, and therefore we should look below the macro level. However, to do so we need a framework that theorizes processes of revenue bargaining at the micro level while remaining cognisant of political power structures.

1.5 Towards a theoretical framework of revenue bargaining in Africa

The literatures on taxation and on state–society relations give plenty of reasons to look closer at the politics of revenue bargaining in Africa. However, so far, the fiscal contract literature has not developed a conceptual and theoretical foundation for doing so. Therefore, we build a theoretical framework that draws on the fiscal contract theory and combine it with an important body of research within the study of state–society relations in Africa, namely the political settlement literature. In combining these approaches, we add a systematic view of politics to the fiscal contract theory while integrating a nuanced revenue dimension to the political settlement literature. Since both literatures have primarily focused on the macro level, a major contribution of this book is our endeavour to improve the conceptualization of the key theoretical concepts of these approaches and to operationalize them to facilitate micro-level analyses of revenue bargaining. In the following, we briefly discuss these contributions to the two literatures. Thereafter, we elaborate on our comparative design that sets the stage for the empirical case studies presented in Chapters 3–12. Our theoretical framework is developed in detail in Chapter 2.

The fiscal contract literature has long focused largely on the macro level and on the expectations of the potential governance dividends of taxation. With the recognition that this stylized relationship is difficult to find in contemporary state-building, there have been important efforts to nuance and condition the expectations by highlighting important contextual factors (Fjeldstad, 2001; Kjær, 2009; Prichard, 2015; Bodea and Lebas, 2016; Broms, 2017; Meagher, 2018; Prichard and van den Boogaard, 2017; Bak, 2019). A few studies focus on the preconditions and processes of revenue bargaining (Prichard, 2015; van den Boogaard et al., 2021); others focus on links between the contributions and influence of specific groups of revenue providers (Timmons, 2005; Castañeda, 2017; Fairfield, 2019); and still others emphasize that power structures condition some taxpayers' capacity to bargain over revenue (Prichard and van den Boogaard, 2017; Fairfield, 2017; Meagher, 2018). To the best of our knowledge, none has studied systematically and comparatively cases of micro-level revenue bargaining between specific groups of revenue providers and the state. Consequently, we know little about the political dynamics of revenue bargaining in Africa.

This book contributes to the fiscal contract literature by theorizing the political, organizational, and economic importance of individual or groups of revenue providers and by applying this theoretical framework in analyses of the processes and outcomes of revenue bargaining. To provide a systematic analysis of the politics of revenue bargaining, we draw on the political settlement approach to theorize and observe the relative bargaining power of revenue providers vis-à-vis ruling elites (or representatives thereof) (elaborated in Chapter 2). Across this book's empirical chapters, the authors apply the concept of relative bargaining power in analyses of instances of revenue bargaining in order to explain the conditions under which revenue bargaining leads negotiating parties to enter into micro-level fiscal contracts, and to understand what such fiscal contracts look like.

The point of departure for the political settlement approach is that an understanding of the basic socio-economic power structures in a society is instrumental for the analysis of how political economy factors affect the formulation and implementation of policies as well as their institutional and social outcomes. The approach insists on going beyond formal institutional categories such as regime type and instead focusing on the power relations that underpin political institutions (Khan, 2005; 2017). A political settlement is defined not as a pact or agreement, but as 'the combination of the structure of power and institutions at the level of a society that is mutually "compatible" and also "sustainable" in terms of economic and political viability'

(Khan, 2017, 20). This definition directs our attention to powerful organizations and actors. If political institutions do not align with the most powerful actors' interests, they are not sustainable. To understand this potential misalignment, the political settlement approach disaggregates state and societal actors and applies the concept of holding power. Holding power refers to 'the capability of an individual or group to engage and "hold out" in conflicts' (Khan, 2010, 6). Holding power is based on income and wealth as well as historically rooted capacities of different groups to organize (Khan, 2010, 1). An organization with holding power can be a group of business elites, a strong religious community, an ethnic or regional group, or a chief and his followers. Ruling elites would need the support of the most powerful organizations and actors in order to maintain the coalition that holds them in power. The political settlement approach with its focus on organizational power has proven effective in explaining, for example, variations in industrial policies across sectors (Whitfield et al., 2015), regional differences in the allocation of education spending (Abdulai and Hickey, 2016), differences in petroleum governance (Hickey et al., 2015), and various countries' paths of learning reforms in education with a focus on why it is easier to enrol pupils than achieve learning outcomes (Hickey and Hossain, 2019).

While holding power has been the starting point of many of these studies, there has arguably been less focus on the sources of such power. Moreover, even if the financing of the political settlements is an important dimension of power (Behuria, Buur, and Gray, 2017, 513), the power that actors can hold as potential revenue providers has received little attention. In this book, we contribute to the political settlement literature by elaborating and emphasizing the revenue dimension of societal actors' holding power. At the micro level, we theorize individual and groups of revenue providers' holding power in relation to state actors, the impact on their relative bargaining positions, and how this shapes the processes and outcomes of revenue bargaining.

We combine and adapt the fiscal contract and the political settlement theories to study revenue bargaining at the micro level. The theoretical framework (see Chapter 2) allows us to explore in depth the triggers of bargaining processes and how these processes unfold, including how and where state actors and revenue providers interact, the strategies they apply, how their relative bargaining positions change, and if and when they reach an agreement (whether a fiscal contract or not). The theoretical framework is applied in the ten empirical chapters' case studies of revenue bargaining across our five case countries. Together, we contend that these case studies of state–society negotiations around revenue provision represent a microcosmos of macro-level state–society relations, and hence illustrate the nature and dynamics not only of revenue bargaining but also of state–society reciprocity in Africa.

1.6 Setting the stage: The political economy of the case countries

This book studies the politics of revenue bargaining in five African countries: Mozambique, Senegal, Tanzania, Togo, and Uganda. As a group, these countries reflect the region south of the Sahara desertquite well. They are all characterized by a mix of capitalist production and subsistence agriculture, and they can all be categorized as hybrid regimes where formal democratic institutions coexist with authoritarian features such as the concentration of executive power and infringement of political rights and civil freedoms, to varying degrees. The study of the countries in this group enables us to provide nuanced answers to this book's research question while also providing a comparative foundation that allows us to make claims generalizable to most relatively stable low- and lower middle-income African countries.

In this section, we present data on the economic and political structures of our case countries and, in more detail, the characteristics of their political settlements. This presentation sets the stage for a brief discussion of the macro-level conditions of revenue bargaining in the countries.

1.6.1 Macro-level economic and political conditions for revenue bargaining

The fiscal conditions of our case countries, along with those of the average African country, have changed on two dimensions over the last decades: the level of total tax revenue has increased, while revenue from external grants has decreased. This can be seen in Figures 1.2 and 1.3.

Figure 1.2 shows the development in total tax revenue over the last four decades. In the 1980s and the beginning of the 1990s, tax revenues in our case countries were below average (south of the Sahara) and generally fluctuated, in Uganda and Mozambique as a result of conflicts, and in Togo, Tanzania, and Senegal due to political instability. Since the 1990s, however, there has been a clear trend of a steady increase in tax revenues. Today, the countries are at their highest level of tax revenue as share of GDP since the late 1980s. Note that this is during a time where the economies have grown, implying that the increase of tax revenue in absolute terms is significant. The large jumps in

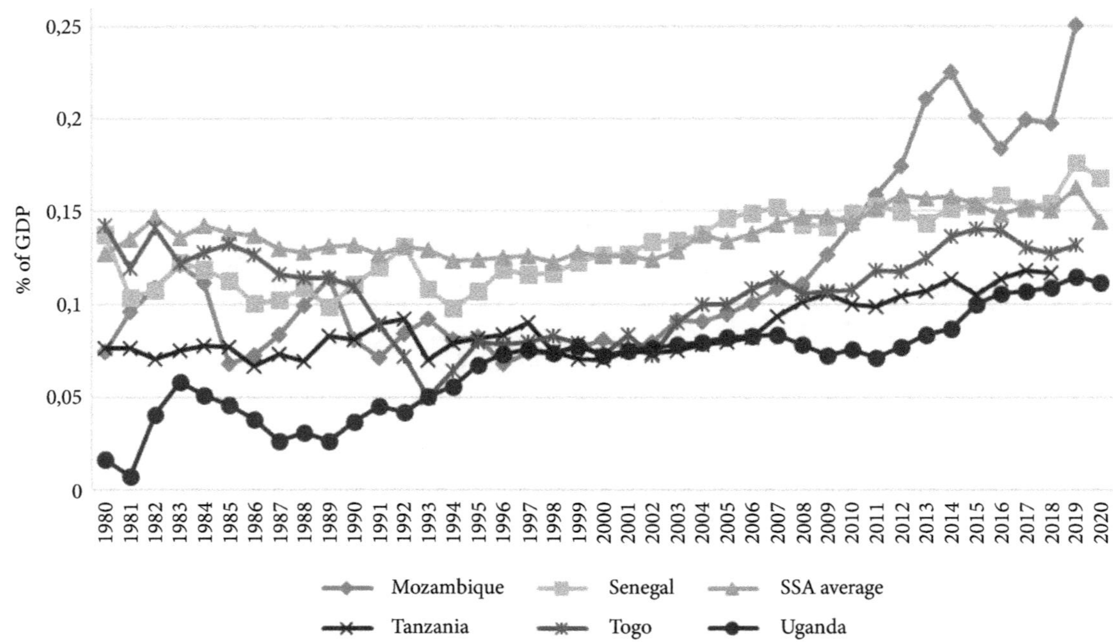

Figure 1.2 Total tax revenue as a percentage of GDP, 1980–2020.

Source: 'UNU-WIDER Government Revenue Dataset'. Version 2021. https://doi.org/10.35188/UNU-WIDER/GRD-2021.

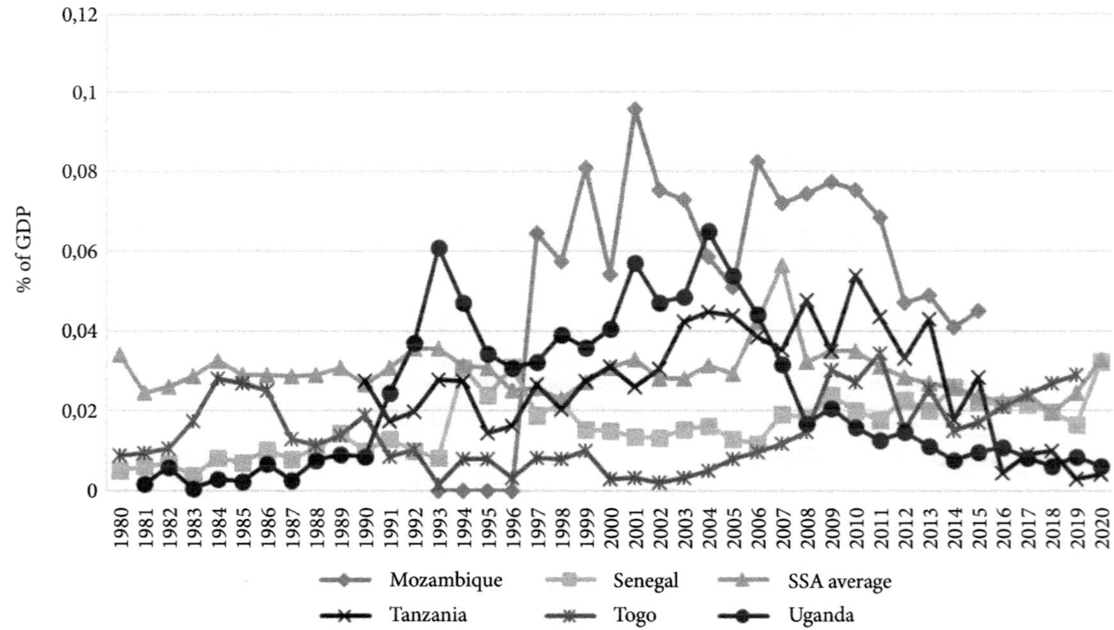

Figure 1.3 Grants, percentage of GDP, 1980–2020.

Source: 'UNU-WIDER Government Revenue Dataset'. Version 2021. https://doi.org/10.35188/UNU-WIDER/GRD-2021.

Mozambique's tax revenue in 2013, 2017, and 2019 are largely explained by large one-off winnings from capital gains taxation of asset sales in the extractive industry (IMF, 2016, 20; 2020, 14). Most recently, the fall in revenue between 2019 and 2020 in the countries where data are available indicates a clear impact of the COVID-19 pandemic on the economies (Fjeldstad and Therkildsen, 2020).

The other essential change is that the countries have become less aid dependent. This is shown in Figure 1.3. Throughout the period displayed in the graph, the level of grants, measured as share per GDP, is highly volatile, but since the change of the millennium the tendency, with some variation, is relatively clear: the countries are generally less aid dependent and are thus in need of expanding domestic revenue. Following the fiscal contract theory, these two significant changes (rising domestic revenues and declining aid dependence) would lead to the expectation of a fiscal impetus to revenue bargaining.

Upon examination, the economic structures of the five case countries appear typical of low- or lower-middle-income countries (see Table 1.1). The five countries' GDPs per capita range from USD 587 (Mozambique) to USD 1,585 (Senegal), which are all below the average in sub-Saharan Africa of USD 1,656. They also score below average on the Human Development Index, and the proportion of the population living below the USD 1.90 poverty line ranges from 38.5% to 63.7%, with only Senegal below the sub-Saharan Africa average. None of the countries benefit from large, stable flows of extractive natural resource rents.

The economies in all five countries are still dominated by agriculture. While the sector only accounts for about one quarter or less of overall economic output, agriculture provides livelihoods for the large majority of the countries' populations. Agriculture thus constitutes between 30 (Senegal) and 72% (Uganda) of total employment. Agricultural productivity, as shown by cereal yields in kilogrammes per hectare, is low, between 835 kg and 2 tonnes, on average almost half of the average yields for South Asia (Abraham and Pingali, 2020, 186). Subsistence agricultural production is widespread and informal commercial sectors are large.

From a political settlement perspective, this suggests that the level of capitalist development is limited, and therefore that a capitalist class of any significant size or influence will be limited. Consequently, the political settlements in our case countries are mainly clientelist rather than capitalist, a feature which characterizes all poor countries (Khan, 2010). This also means that few organized societal groups are able to create wealth outside access to rent opportunities nurtured through their relationships with political elites (Khan, 2010, 54–55; Hickey and Hossain, 2019, 26).

Ultimately, the lack of economic transformation, together with the consequent absence of a capitalist class, implies that substantial structural barriers to expanding the tax base remain in all our five case countries. This has implications for the politics of revenue bargaining and taxation. Under the conditions of a small tax base, the national budget is similarly constrained. This makes it difficult to secure political stability through the reallocation of domestic revenue to powerful groups (Khan, 2010). Instead, distribution of resources and access to rents must happen off budget and through clientelist or other informal networks. In clientelist settlements like our case countries, building a stable ruling coalition requires that elites balance and accommodate powerful factions, and this is likely to manifest in whether and how revenue bargaining emerges. Furthermore, the holding power of the individual and groups of revenue providers vis-à-vis the ruling elite will be significant for the kind of outcomes that result from such bargaining.

Table 1.2 presents the scores of our case countries on a number of political features that have been found to condition where and how we expect revenue bargaining to occur (Moore, 2004; Prichard, 2015; van den Boogaard et al., 2021). All five countries have institutionalized regular elections, which provide one possible political channel through which societal actors can engage state actors over tax policies. The quality of the elections and the openness of the political space do vary between the countries. Senegal stands out among the cases as the most democratic with the highest level of political rights, civil liberties, government effectiveness, and political stability, but a look beyond these indicators leaves little doubt that Senegal still falls within the category of a hybrid regime with strong executive power, politicization of the judiciary, and instances of violent repression, together with strong clientelist networks permeating democratic institutions (Dumont and Kanté, 2019; Kohnert and Marfaing, 2019; Kelly, 2020). At the other end of the scale, Uganda should undoubtedly be considered an electoral autocracy, but there is still meaningful political competition, and political rights and civil liberties are not considerably worse affected than in Tanzania.

1.6.2 The political settlements of our case countries

The political indicators only tell part of the story. To understand the political space for revenue bargaining and specifically the contextual conditions of bargaining power of different revenue providers vis-à-vis the ruling elites, we

Table 1.1 Economic indicators

	Senegal	**Mozambique**	**Togo**	**Tanzania**	**Uganda**	**SSA** (sub-Saharan Africa) **average**[g]
GDP per capita[a]	1,381.6	598.8	630.8	1,071.4	894.5	1,656.1
HDI[b]	0.512	0.456	0.515	0.529	0.544	0.547
Poverty head count under USD 1.90 (share of population)[c]	38.5 % (2011)	63.7 % (2014)	51.1 % (2015)	49.4 % (2017)	41.3 % (2016)	42.3 % (2014)
Employment in agriculture (share of total employment)[d]	30.1%	70.2%	32.4%	65.1%	72.1%	52.9%
Cereal yield (kg per hectare)[e]	1301.9	835.1	1145.6	1568.3	2049.5	1445.2
Natural resource income (share of GDP)[f]	0.016 %	0.04 %*	0.014 %**	0.015 %*	0.007 %	0.029 %

[a] Year: 2019 (constant 2015 USD), from World Bank national accounts data, and OECD National Accounts data files.
[b] Year: 2019, index from 0–1, from Human Development Report Office, 2020.
[c] Respective years in parentheses, from World Bank, Development Research Group. Data are based on primary household survey data obtained from government statistical agencies and World Bank country departments.
[d] Year: 2019, from International Labour Organization, ILOSTAT database. Data retrieved on 29 January 29 2021.
[e] Year: 2018, from Food and Agriculture Organization, electronic files and website.
[f] Year: 2015–2020 (average of period), from UNU-WIDER Government Revenue Dataset. Version 2021. https://doi.org/10.35188/UNU-WIDER/GRD-2021. Indicator: Non-tax Revenue. Average of non-tax revenue between 2015 and 2020 is made by own calculation. *Missing data from 2020. **Missing data from 2019–2020.
[g] WDI's definition of sub-Saharan Africa (excluding high income).

Table 1.2 Political indicators

	Senegal	Mozambique	Togo	Tanzania	Uganda
Electoral democracy[a]	0.75	0.37	0.42	0.41	0.31
Political rights[b]	29	14	15	12	11
Civil liberties[b]	39	29	27	22	23
Government effectiveness[c]	0.01	−0.72	−0.69	−0.77	−0.58
Political stability[c]	−0.02	−1.16	−0.92	−0.41	−0.69
Nature of Political Settlement[d]	Strong dominant	Weak dominant	Strong dominant	Vulnerable authoritarian	Competitive clientelist

Source:
[a] Year: 2021, index 0–1, from Nazifa Alizada, Rowan Cole, Lisa Gastaldi, Sandra Grahn, Sebastian Hellmeier, Palina Kolvani, Jean Lachapelle, Anna Lührmann, Seraphine F. Maerz, Shreeya Pillai, and Staffan I. Lindberg. 2021. Autocratization Turns Viral. Democracy Report 2021. University of Gothenburg: V-Dem Institute.
[b] Year: 2022, index 0–100, from Freedom House Score. Countries and Territories. 2022. https://freedomhouse.org/countries/freedom-world/scores.
[c] Year: 2020, index from −2.5 to +2.5, from World Government Indicators http://info.worldbank.org/governance/wgi/Home/Reports.
[d] Year 2018, Categorization from the ESID data, except for Togo (lacking in ESID), which is based on secondary sources.

need to take as our point of departure the case countries' political settlements (see also bottom of Table 1.2).

In the following, we briefly present the political settlement typology and use it both to introduce the typical features of our case countries' political settlements, and to outline where they differ. Each chapter considers (implicitly or explicitly) how individual or specific groups of revenue providers involved in instances of revenue bargaining are positioned in relation to the ruling coalition and the ruling elites.

We follow the original political settlement typology as introduced by Khan (2010, 55). This typology has been discussed and further elaborated by others (e.g. Whitfield et al., 2015; Hickey and Kelsall, 2020; Schulz and Kelsall, 2021), work which we draw on in what follows when categorizing our case countries.[2] Khan's typological categorization follows two steps. The first is to distinguish between capitalist and clientelist settlements. As discussed, all our case countries fall into the latter of these two categories: Clientelist

[2] Particularly, we draw on the Political Settlements (PolSett) dataset (Schulz and Kelsall, 2021), developed by the Effective States and Inclusive Development (ESID) programme based in Manchester, which categorizes countries in terms of their political settlement based on expert surveys and their openly available detailed descriptions. The original Khan typology has subsequently been subject to much discussion, but for our purposes here (to characterize different settlement and therefore to emphasize the diversity of the countries in which case studies are carried out), it suffices.

settlements are characterized by the fact that 'significant holding power is based on sources outside the incomes generated by formal institutions' (Khan, 2010, 53). While formal institutions such as property rights or regular elections will be in place, they are rarely enforced, because they are at odds with the interests of powerful groups. When this is the case, there is a mismatch between formal institutions and how politics work informally.

The second step in Khan's typology is to categorize different types of clientelist settlement. To this end, Khan (2010, 64–65) distinguishes between the horizontal and the vertical distribution of power. The horizontal distribution of power refers to 'the power of excluded factions, relative to the ruling coalition'. Some ruling elites can create a broad-based coalition which includes many powerful factions, while others cannot. In the latter case, if excluded factions are strong, the ruling coalition is more vulnerable. The vertical distribution of power distinguishes between higher- and lower-level factions within the ruling coalition. Lower-level factions are the ones who mobilize support in local constituencies, and their source of holding power depends largely on how much support they can mobilize for the ruling coalition. The stronger the lower-level factions, the more the ruling elite will have to attend to their interests in order to keep them within the ruling coalition.

Between the vertical and horizontal power dimensions, there are four types of clientelist settlement: (1) Strong lower-level as well as strong excluded factions imply competitive clientelism, where competition between factions is strong. (2) Strong lower-level combined with weak excluded factions imply weak-dominant party coalitions, in which the dominant party is not threatened by excluded factions but where the strong lower-level factions have the power, for example, to block policy implementation or to achieve good access to rents. (3) Where both lower-level and excluded factions are weak, the coalition is strong-dominant, meets little resistance, and the ruling elite is fairly free to implement the policies it pleases. (4) Finally, when lower-level factions are weak and excluded factions are strong, the political settlement is characterized by a vulnerable authoritarian coalition, which enjoys some enforcement capacity but suffers from instability because it has to resort to repression of excluded factions.

Within this typology, **Uganda** can be categorized as competitive clientelist (Schulz and Kelsall, 2021). Primarily as a result of the colonial borders, the country has since independence been characterized by many different regional, religious, ethnic, and socio-economic cleavages. In the south there were relatively strong centralized kingdoms with a history of conflicts between them, and north of the river Nile there were smaller chiefdoms belonging to different ethnic groups (e.g. the Alur in West Nile closer to

Sudan and the Karamojong closer to Kenya) (Karugire, 1996; Reid, 2017, 118). These cleavages made for a fragmented political settlement, that is, a balance of power that had many competing groups and factions. In such a fragmented political settlement, it is always difficult to construct a stable ruling coalition with factions that provide reliable and lasting support for the ruling elite (Kjær, 2015; Whitfield et al., 2015). Several early post-independence leaders in Uganda struggled to create durable coalitions, but since the National Resistance Army (NRA) and its leader, Yoweri Museveni, won a guerrilla war in 1986, the coalition has been relatively durable even if its composition has changed character over the years, with fragmentation and increasing competition between factions. A key driver of the increased fragmentation was the introduction of multi-party elections in 2006 and the simultaneous lifting of presidential term limits. Elections and the introduction of NRM party primaries have served to increase the power of lower-level factions (Kjær and Katuusiihmeh, 2021). At the same time, power is more dispersed among the elites, and although there is a powerful circle around the president, the military seems more fragmented (Reuss and Titeca, 2017). During the latest elections, opposition candidates have been able to mobilize substantial support (Khisa, Vokes, and Wilkins, 2021). So, even if it is strongly authoritarian and with the exercise of power personalized around the president, the fragmentation and competition between factions gives Uganda the categorization of competitive clientelist. For revenue bargaining, Uganda's competitive clientelism means that elites will be incentivized to give in to demands from powerful factions to a higher extent than in a strong-dominant party settlement. Chapters 7 (by Kjær and Arinanye) and 8 (by Ngabirano) focus on revenue bargaining with, respectively, Uganda's agricultural sector and multinational companies in the petroleum sector. In Chapter 9, Khisa, Msami, and Therkildsen examine campaign financing and revenue bargaining in both Uganda and Tanzania.

Tanzania is categorized by the PolSett dataset as vulnerable authoritarian with rather strong excluded factions and weak lower-level factions (see Table 1.2). This labelling shows a significant change from the Julius Nyerere period when power was more concentrated with much fewer powerful excluded factions. For a long period after Nyerere's retirement, the coalition became more fragmented, especially during the Jakaya Kikwete years (Therkildsen and Bourgoin, 2012; Kelsall, 2018). However, this changed when the CCM party had to elect a new chairman in 2015. Factional competition within the party led to an internal party split, whereby the central figure Edward Lowassa broke away to the opposition party Chadema taking with him both financial and political power (Kelsall, 2018, 18). The new party chairman John Magufuli understood the need to control excluded factions and centralize power in the party. In vulnerable authoritarian settlements, the expectation is that the government should be able to enforce some policies and, for example, could expand their tax effort without having to compromise for less in specific instances of revenue bargaining. However, several chapters in this book provide grounds for questioning whether this is the case for the politics of taxation. It should be noted that fieldwork for the chapter contributions was done under the now late Magufuli's presidency. After two years in power, it is evident that the ruling coalition has changed with the new president Samia Suluhu Hassan, allowing for more political opposition and rejuggling the coalition so as to exclude some of Magufuli's supporters. It is still early to assess the implications of this change. In Chapter 3, Edslev Jacobsen focuses on revenue bargaining in the urban informal sector in Dar es Salaam, while Chapters 5 (by Ulriksen, Katera, and Msami) and 6 (by Fjeldstad and Rakner) examine the negotiation processes around various tax reforms in Tanzania. Lastly, in Chapter 11, Ulriksen, Myamba, and George study bargaining between the Tanzanian government and international aid agencies around the financing of a cash transfer programme.

Senegal is categorized as strong-dominant with weak excluded factions, weak lower-level factions, and concentrated power in the leadership. There has been little change in the political ruling elite over the years despite Senegal's two political turnovers: in both cases, the new incumbents had served with the former regimes. Nevertheless, around elections marking the end of a president's two terms (in 2000 and in 2012), momentary fragmentation of the ruling coalition occurred, and political competition opened in the fight around succession. In 2000, political competition was in part facilitated by the fact that structural adjustment programmes and reduced domestic revenue constrained Abdou Diouf's abilities to maintain the ruling coalition through buying the support of, amongst others, important religious groups (Diop and Diouf, 1990; Koter, 2021). In 2012, Abdoulaye Wade's attempt at securing an unconstitutional third term was countered by a strong popular movement and a united opposition. Following both elections, the new incumbents succeeded in reconsolidating the ruling coalitions and ensuring stability in the political settlement by clientelist means (Mbow, 2008; Kelly, 2012; Dumont and Kanté, 2019). These bouts of more competitive clientelism and subsequent reconsolidation are important for understanding the revenue bargaining with revenue providers in the informal economy and their brokers as well as the evolution of informal sector taxation in Senegal, as discussed by Bak in Chapter 12.

Mozambique's political settlement is characterized as weak-dominant with strong lower-level factions but weak excluded factions. The current Mozambican coalition has its roots in the peace deals that ended the long-running civil war between the FRELIMO and the RENAMO resistance. The FRELIMO strategy was a mix of co-opting and dividing RENAMO factions, and this strategy has generally been deemed successful (Vines, 2018; Buur and Salimo, 2018). Under the Guebuza presidency (2005–2012), the coalition became strong-dominant, as Guebuza strengthened control over the party, relying on a powerful narrative of 'national unity' (Macuane, Buur, and Monjane, 2017). However, even if the regime is authoritarian and repressive, control of lower-level factions has weakened somewhat during the recent Nyusi leadership. One driver was the local elections in 2018, which served to strengthen the importance of these factions. In Chapter 4, von Schiller examines the implications of the relations between local and central governments for revenue bargaining in Mozambique.

Togo is not included in the ESID's PolSett dataset, but from our own analysis (Beach, 2018; Chapter 10), we categorize the political settlement in Togo as strong-dominant with weak excluded factions and rather weak lower-level factions. President Faure Gnassingbé has chosen a strategy of co-optation of the leaders of other political parties, and like his father before him, has often resorted to brutal oppression to ensure that electoral results lean in his favour. His father, Eyadéma Gnassingbé, came to power in a coup in 1967 and ruled as a dictator for 38 years. Eyadéma did face a national conference in 1991, which introduced space for political competition and opposition voices; however, he removed term limits shortly thereafter. Faure further manipulated the electoral system to favour his well-organized party, UNIR (l'Union pour la République). The party, dominated by his people the Kabiyé, holds the majority of seats in parliament despite representing a lower proportion of the population. There are four main ethnic groups in Togo: the Ewe (and Minas), the Kabiye, the Moba, and the Kotokoli and Tem. The Ewe people live along the more economically advantaged coast in the south and dominate in both the civil service and commercial sectors, while the president's clan dominates the military and law enforcement in Togo (Beach, 2018). In recent years, there has been increasing pressure for more democratic modes of governing, including the possibility of decentralizing and devolving some power. However, there has been no effective political opening so far. In Chapter 10, Beach describes two instances of revenue bargaining in rural and urban Togo.

The five case countries of this book have all seen an expansion in domestic revenue mobilization during the last two decades that, like elsewhere, has prompted many instances of revenue bargaining. Some of these are the focus of the case studies in this book. Our case countries are typical of lower-income countries in Africa, with economies largely not having undergone economic structural transformation, with a limited tax base, and with the ruling elites' continuous need to maintain their ruling coalitions through distribution of resources and access to rents. The case studies set in these five countries provide new knowledge on when and how revenue bargaining emerges, evolves, and leads to fiscal contracts in clientelist political settlements across different degrees of ruling coalition fragmentation. Together, our case countries provide a foundation for comparative and generalizable observations of the politics of revenue bargaining in Africa.

1.7 Conclusion

Domestic revenue mobilization has been increasing in Africa, and taxation has become more politicized since the turn of the millennium. However, there seem to be few signs of exchange-based fiscal social contracts emerging at the macro level, where citizens pay taxes in return for public service delivery and accountability. Nevertheless, recent developments in terms of increased political competition and civil society participation offer grounds for revisiting older insights about the potential role of taxation in state–society relations. Perhaps we have been looking in the wrong places for the political effects of taxation.

Revenue bargaining, that is, negotiations related to revenue provision, arguably happens on the micro level between, on the one side, individual or groups of revenue providers and, on the other side, state actors or ruling elites. However, systematic and comparative research on micro-level revenue bargaining in Africa remains limited. This book attends to this gap and seeks to deepen our knowledge and understanding of the dynamics and politics of revenue bargaining in Africa.

In doing so, this book contributes to two key literatures in the studies of African politics: the fiscal contract literature and the political settlement literature. In combining these approaches, we add a systematic view of politics to the fiscal contract theory while integrating a nuanced revenue dimension to the political settlement theory. Furthermore, a major contribution of this book is to operationalize these two primarily macro-level theories to facilitate micro-level analyses of revenue bargaining. The theoretical framework is elaborated in more detail in Chapter 2. The book then explores instances of revenue bargaining in five case countries spread across Southern, Eastern and Western Africa. Together, the case studies presented in Chapters 3–12 provide a strong empirical foundation for making comparative and generalizable observations of the politics of revenue bargaining in Africa. Chapter 13 presents these concluding observations.

References

Abdulai, A.-G., and S. Hickey. 2016. 'The Politics of Development under Competitive Clientelism: Insights from Ghana's Education Sector'. *African Affairs* 115(458): pp. 44–72.

Abraham, M., and P. Pingali. 2020. 'Transforming Smallholder Agriculture to Achieve the SDGs'. In *The Role of Smallholder Farms in Food and Nutrition Security*, edited by S. Gomez y Paloma et al. Cham: Springer. https://doi.org/10.1007/978-3-030-42148-9_9

Africanews. 2017. 'Ethiopia Forced to Withdraw Tax Hike That Resulted in Protests'. 24 July. https://www.africanews.com/2017/07/24/ethiopia-forced-to-withdraw-tax-hike-that-resulted-in-protests/ (accessed 23 August 2022).

Albers, T. and M. Suesse. 2022. 'State Capacity across the Twentieth Century: Evidence from Taxation'. In *The Wealth and Poverty of African States: Economic Growth, Living Standards and Taxation since the Late Nineteenth Century*, edited by M. Jerven. Cambridge: Cambridge University Press. https://doi.org/10.1017/9781108341080.005: pp. 105–131.

Azarya, V. 1988. 'Reordering State–Society Relations: Incorporation and Disengagement'. In *The Precarious Balance: State and Society in Africa*, edited by D. Rothchild and N. Chazan. Boulder, CO: Westview Press.

Bak, A. K. 2019. *When the Fiscal Social Contract Is Not About Tax: Understanding the Limited Role of Taxation in Social Accountability in Senegal.* Aarhus: Politica.

Bak, A. K., M. Jeppesen, and A. M. Kjær. 2021. 'Fiscal States in Sub-Saharan Africa. Conceptualization and Empirical Trends'. *WP 2021-182.* Helsinki: UNU WiDER Working Paper Series. UNU-WIDER: Working Paper: Fiscal states in sub-Saharan Africa: conceptualization and empirical trends

Baskaran, T. 2014. 'Taxation and Democratization'. *World Development* 56: pp. 287–301. https://doi.org/10.1016/j.worlddev.2013.11.011.

Baskaran, T., and A. Bigsten. 2013. 'Fiscal Capacity and the Quality of Government in Sub-Saharan Africa'. *World Development* 45: pp. 92–107. https://doi.org/10.1016/j.worlddev.2012.09.018.

Bates, R. (1981). *Markets and States in Tropical Africa: The Political Basis of Agricultural Policies*. Berkeley, CA: University of California Press.

BBC. 2022. E-levy Ghana: Ghanaians Hit Streets of Accra to Protest against Electronic Transactions Tax Wey Govment Wan Introduce. 10 February. https://www.bbc.com/pidgin/media-60329635 (accessed 23 August 2022).

Beach, R. 2018. *The Hunt for Revenues in a Poor State*. Aarhus: Politica.

Behuria, P., L. Buur, and H. Gray. 2017. 'Studying Political Settlements in Africa'. *African Affairs* 116(464): pp. 508–525.

Bleck, J., and N. van de Walle. 2019. *Electoral Politics in Africa since 1990: Continuity and Change*. Cambridge: Cambridge University Press.

Bodea, C., and A. LeBas. 2016. 'The Origins of Voluntary Compliance: Attitudes toward Taxation in Urban Nigeria'. *British Journal of Political Science* 46(1): pp. 215–238. https://doi.org/10.1017/S000712341400026X.

Boone, Catherine. 1992. *Merchant Capital and the Roots of State Power in Senegal, 1930–1985*. Cambridge: Cambridge University Press.

Bratton, M., and G. Hyden, eds. 1992. *Governance and Politics in Africa*. Boulder, CO: Rienner.

Bratton, M., and C. Logan. 2006. Voters but not yet Citizens: The Weak Demand for Political Accountability in Africa's Unclaimed Democracies. *Afrobarometer Working Papers 63*. Cape Town: Afrobarometer.

Bratton, M., and N. Van de Walle. 1997. *Democratic Experiments in Africa: Regime Transitions in a Comparative Perspective*. Cambridge: Cambridge University Press.

Bräutigam, D. A. 2002. 'Building Leviathan: Revenue, State Capacity and Governance'. *IDS Bulletin* 33(3): pp. 1–17.

Bräutigam D. A. 2008. 'Introduction: Taxation and State-building in Developing Countries'. In *Taxation and State Building in Developing Countries: Capacity and Consent*, edited by D.A. Bräutigam, O.-H Fjeldstad, and M. Moore. Cambridge: Cambridge University Press: pp. 1–33.

Brautigam, D.A., O.-H Fjeldstad, and M. Moore, eds. 2008. *Taxation and State Building in Developing Countries: Capacity and Consent*. Cambridge: Cambridge University Press.

Bräutigam, D. A., L. Rakner, and S. Taylor. 2002. 'Business Associations and Growth Coalitions in Sub-Saharan Africa'. *The Journal of Modern African Studies* 40(4): pp. 519–547.

Broms, R. 2015. 'Putting Up or Shutting Up: On the Individual-Level Relationship between Taxpaying and Political Interest in a Developmental Context'. *The Journal of Development Studies* 51(1): pp. 93–109. https://doi.org/10.1080/00220388.2014.957276.

Broms, R. 2017. 'Colonial Revenue Extraction and Modern Day Government Quality in the British Empire'. *World Development* 90: pp. 269–280. https://doi.org/10.1016/j.worlddev.2016.10.003.

Buur, L., and P. Salimo. 2018. 'The Political Economy of Social Protection in Mozambique'. *ESID Working Paper No. 103.* Manchester.

Castañeda, N. 2017. 'Business Coordination and Tax Politics'. *Political Studies* 65(1): pp. 122–143.

Cheeseman, N., and B. Klaas. 2018. *How to Rig an Election.* New Haven, CT: Yale University Press.

Cogneau, D., Y. Dupraz, J. Knebelmann, and S. Mesplé-Somps. 2021. Taxation in Africa from Colonial Times to Present Evidence from former French colonies 1900–2018, *Working Paper No. 2021–62.* Paris: Paris School of Economics.

Dahir, Abdi Latif. 2017. Ethiopia's troubled Oromia region has been hit with anti-tax protests. 20 July 2017. Quartz Africa. URL: https://qz.com/africa/1032961/ethiopias-oromo-people-are-protesting-new-taxes-in-the-oromia-region (accessed 23 August 2022).

Diop, M. C., and M. Diouf. 1990. *Le Sénégal sous Abdou Diouf.* Paris: Karthala.

Dom, R. 2018. 'Taxation and Accountability in Sub-Saharan Africa: New Evidence for a Governance Dividend'. *ODI Working paper 544.* London: ODI.

Doumbia, D., and M. Lykke Lauridsen. 2019. 'Closing the SDG Financing Gap: Trends and Data. IFC. International Finance Corporation. Note 73.

Dumont, G.-F., and S. Kanté. 2019. *La géopolitique du Sénégal De Senghor à l'élection de Macky Sall.* Paris: L'Harmattan.

The East African. 2021. 'Tanzania Reduces Mobile Money Levy by 30 percent'. 2 September. URL: https://www.theeastafrican.co.ke/tea/business/tanzania-reduces-mobile-money-levy-3535616 (accessed 23 August 2022).

Ekeh, P. P. 1975. 'Colonialism and the Two Publics in Africa: A Theoretical Statement'. *Comparative Studies in Society and History* 17: pp. 91–112.

Eubank, N. 2012. 'Taxation, Political Accountability and Foreign Aid: Lessons from Somaliland'. *Journal of Development Studies* 48(4): pp. 465–480.

Fairfield, T. 2017. Business Power and Protest: Argentina's Agricultural Producers Protest in Comparative Context. *Studies in Comparative International Development* 46(4): pp. 424–453. https://doi.org/10.1007/s12116-011-9094-z.

Fairfield, T. 2019. Taxing Latin America's Economic Elites. In *The Political Economy of Taxation in Latin America*, edited by G. Flores-Macías. Cambridge: Cambridge University Press. https://doi.org/10.1017/9781108655934.007: pp. 172–192.

Fjeldstad, O.-H. 2001. 'Taxation, Coercion and Donors: Local Government Tax Enforcement in Tanzania'. *The Journal of Modern African Studies* 39(2): pp. 289–306.

Fjeldstad, O.-H., and O. Therkildsen 2008. 'Mass Taxation and State–Society Relations in East Africa'. In *Taxation and State Building in Developing Countries: Capacity and Consent*, edited by D. A Bräutigam, O.-H. Fjeldstad, and M. Moore. Cambridge: Cambridge University Press. 114–135.

Fjeldstad, O.-H., and O. Therkildsen. 2020. 'Implications of the COVID-19 pandemic for revenue generation in poor African countries'. *DIIS Working Paper, 2020: 13.*

Gatt, L., and O. Owen. 2018. 'Direct Taxation and State–Society Relations in Lagos, Nigeria'. *Development and Change* 49(5): pp. 1195–1222.

Genschel, P., and L. Seelkopf, eds. 2022. *Global Taxation: How Modern Taxes Conquered the World*. Oxford: Oxford University Press.

Goodfellow, T., and O. Owen. 2018. 'Taxation, Property Rights and the Social Contract in Lagos'. *ICTD Working Paper 73*. Brighton: International Centre for Tax and Development.

Guimaraes, A. S., F. Duca, and T. Ndlovu. 2018. *Taxation and State–Society Relations in Sub-Saharan Africa*. Friedrich Ebert Stiftung. PARI report.

Guyer, J. 1992. 'Representation Without Taxation: An Essay on Democracy in Rural Nigeria'. *African Studies Review* 35(1): pp. 41–79. https://doi.org/10.2307/524445.

Harbeson, J. W., D. Rothchild, and N. Chazan, eds. 1994. *Civil Society and the State in Africa*. Boulder, CO: Lynne Rienner Publishers.

Hickey, S., A-G. Abdulai, A. Izama, and G. Mohan. 2015. 'The Politics of Governing Oil Effectively: A Comparative Study of Two New Oil-rich States in Africa'. *ESID Working Paper No. 54*. Manchester: University of Manchester.

Hickey, S. and N. Hossain. 2019. *The Politics of Education in Developing Countries: From Schooling to Learning*. Oxford: Oxford University Press.

Hickey, S., and T. Kelsall (2020). 'What Is Political Settlement Analysis?' ESID blog, September 14. https://www.effective-states.org/what-is-political-settlements-analysis/ (accessed 1 August 2022).

HRW. 2019. Human Rights Watch. 'East Africa: Civic Space Shrinking'. January. https://www.hrw.org/news/2019/01/17/east-africa-civic-space-shrinking (accessed July 2022).

Hyden, G. 1980. *Beyond Ujamaa in Tanzania: Underdevelopment and an Uncaptured Peasantry*. London: Heinemann.

Hyden, G. 1983. *No Shortcuts to Progress: African Development Management in Perspective*. London: Publisher.

Hyden, G. 1992. 'Governance and the Study of Politics'. In *Governance and Politics in Africa*, edited by M. Bratton and G. Hyden. Boulder, CO: Rienner: pp. 3–26.

IMF. 2016. *Republic of Mozambique*. IMF Country Report No. 16/9. Washington D.C.: IMF.

IMF. 2018. *Regional Economic Outlook, April 2018, Sub-Saharan Africa. Domestic Revenue Mobilization and Private Investment.* Washington D.C.: IMF.

IMF. 2020. *Republic of Mozambique.* IMF Country Report No. 20/141. Washington D.C.: IMF.

Jerven, M. 2022. *The Wealth and Poverty of African States: Economic Growth, Living Standards and Taxation since the Late Nineteenth Century.* Cambridge: Cambridge University Press. https://doi.org/10.1017/9781108341080.

Jibao, S. S., and W. Prichard. 2015. 'The Political Economy of Property Tax in Africa: Explaining Reform Outcomes in Sierra Leone'. *African Affairs* 114(456): pp. 404–431. https://doi.org/10.1093/afraf/adv022.

Karugire, S. 1996. *Roots of Instability in Uganda.* Kampala: Fountain Publishers.

Kelly, C. L. 2012. 'Senegal: What Will Turnover Bring?' *Journal of Democracy* 23(3): pp. 121–131. https://doi.org/10.1353/jod.2012.0048.

Kelly, C. L. 2020. *Party Proliferation and Political Contestation in Africa: Senegal in Comparative Perspective.* Cham: Palgrave.

Kelsall, T. 2018. 'Thinking and Working with Political Settlements: The Case of Tanzania'. *ODI Working Paper 541.* London: Overseas Development Institute.

Khan, M. H. 2005. 'Markets, States and Democracy: Patron–Client Networks and the Case for Democracy in Developing Countries'. *Democratization* 12(5): pp. 704–724. https://doi.org/10.1080/13510340500322157.

Khan, M. H. 2010. 'Political Settlements and the Governance of Growth-Enhancing Institutions'. *SOAS Working Paper.* London: SOAS.

Khan, M. H. 2017. 'Political Settlements and the Analysis of Institutions'. *African Affairs* Virtual issue, p. 20, https://doi.org/10.1093/afraf/adx044.

Khisa, M., R. Vokes, and S. Wilkins. 2021. 'Contextualizing the Bobi Wine Factor in Uganda's 2021 Elections', *African Affairs* 120(481): pp. 629–643.

Kjær, A. M. 2009. 'Sources of Local Government Extractive Capacity: The Role of Trust and Pre-Colonial Legacy in the Case of Uganda'. *Public Administration and Development* 29(3): pp. 228–238. https://doi.org/10.1002/pad.532.

Kjær, A. M. 2015. 'Political Settlements and Productive Sector Policies: Understanding Sector Differences in Uganda'. *World Development* 68: pp. 230–241. https://doi.org/10.1016/j.worlddev.2014.12.004.

Kjaer, A. M., and M. Katusiihmeh. 2021. 'Nomination Violence in Uganda's National Resistance Movement'. *African Affairs* 120(479): 177–198.

Kjær, A. M., and O. Therkildsen. 2013. 'Elections and Landmark Policies in Uganda and Tanzania'. *Democratization* 20(4): pp. 592–614.

Kohnert, D., and L. Marfaing. 2019. 'Senegal: Presidential Elections 2019: The Shining Example of Democratic Transition Immersed in Muddy Power-Politics'. *SSRN Electronic Journal*, 92739. https://doi.org/10.2139/ssrn.3350710.

Koter, D. 2021. 'Religion and Electoral Competition in Senegal'. In *The Oxford Handbook of Politics in Muslim Societies*, edited by M. Cammett and P. Jones. New York: Oxford University Press.

Lemarchand, R. 1989. 'African Peasantries, Reciprocity and the Market: The Economy of Affection Reconsidered'. *Cahiers d'Études Africaines* 29(113): pp. 33–67.

Levi, M. 1988. *Of Rule and Revenue*. Berkeley, CA: University of California Press.

Lindberg, S. 2006. *Democracy and Elections in Africa*. Baltimore, MD: The Johns Hopkins University Press.

Lucas, B. 2017. *Impacts of Tax Capacity on Development Outcomes*. K4D Helpdesk Report. Brighton: Institute of Development Studies.

Macuane, J. J., L. Buur, and C. M. Monjane. 2017. 'Power, Conflict and Natural Resources: The Mozambican Crisis Revisited'. *African Affairs* 117(468): pp. 415–438.

Mbow, P. 2008. 'Senegal: The Return of Personalism'. *Journal of Democracy* 19(1): pp. 156–169.

Meagher, K. 2018. 'Taxing Times: Taxation, Divided Societies and the Informal Economy in Northern Nigeria'. *The Journal of Development Studies* 54(1): pp. 1–17. https://doi.org/10.1080/00220388.2016.1262026.

Migdal, J. S. 1988. *Strong Societies and Weak States: State–Society Relations and State Capabilities in the Third World*. Princeton, NJ: Princeton University Press.

Miriri, D. 2018. Kenya's President Signs Finance Bill with Contested New Taxes into Law. Nairobi: Reuters. URL: https://www.reuters.com/article/kenya-economy-taxes-idINKCN1M10O5 (accessed 29 April 2022).

Moore, M. 2004. 'Revenues, State Formation, and the Quality of Governance in Developing Countries'. *International Political Science Review* 25(3): pp. 297–319. https://doi.org/10.1177/0192512104043018.

Moore, M. 2007. *How Does Taxation Affect the Quality of Governance?* IDS working paper 280. Brighton: Institute for Developing Studies.

Moore, M. 2015. 'Tax and the Governance Dividend'. In *Perspectives on Politics, Production and Public Administration in Africa*, edited by A. M. Kjær, L. Engberg-Pedersen, and L. Buur, 159–172. Copenhagen: DIIS, Danish Institute for International Studies.

Moore. M. 2021. 'Glimpses of Fiscal States in Sub-Saharan Africa'. *WIDER Working Paper 2021/151*. Helsinki: UNU-WIDER. https://doi.org/10.35188/UNU-WIDER/2021/091-7.

Moore, M., W. Prichard, and O.-H. Fjeldstad. 2018. *Taxing Africa: Coercion, Reform, and Development*. London: Zed Books.

Musila, G. 2019. *Freedoms under Threat: The Spread of Anti-NGO Measures in Africa*. New York: Freedom House Special Report.

OECD. 2021. *Africa: The Rising Debt Burden Highlights the Need for Further Progress in Domestic Revenue Mobilisation.* Paris: OECD. URL: https://www.oecd.org/tax/tax-policy/africa-the-rising-debt-burden-highlights-the-need-for-further-progress-in-domestic-revenue-mobilisation.htm (accessed 15 August 2022).

Okunoye, B. 2019. 'In Africa, a New Tactic to Suppress Online Speech: Taxing Social Media'. Retrieved on 17 November from https://www.cfr.org/blog/africa-new-tactic-suppress-online-speech-taxing-social-media.

Paler, L. 2013. 'Keeping the Public Purse: An Experiment in Windfalls, Taxes, and the Incentives to Restrain Government'. *American Political Science Review* 107(04): pp. 706–725. https://doi.org/10.1017/S0003055413000415.

Prichard, W. 2015. *Taxation, Responsiveness and Accountability in Sub-Saharan Africa.* Cambridge: Cambridge University Press. https://doi.org/10.1017/CBO9781316275511.

Prichard, W. 2019. 'Tax Politics and the Social Contract in Africa'. *Oxford Research Encyclopedia of Politics.* https://doi.org/10.1093/acrefore/9780190228637.013.853.

Prichard, W., and V. van den Boogaard. 2017. Norms, Power and the Socially Embedded Realities of Market Taxation in Northern Ghana. *African Studies Review* 60(1): pp. 171–194.

Rakner, L. 2017. 'Tax Bargains in Unlikely Places: The Politics of Zambian Mining Taxes'. *The Extractive Industries and Society* 4(3): pp. 525–538.

Rakner, L., and S. Gloppen. 2003. 'Tax Reform and Democratic Accountability in Sub-Saharan Africa'. In *Beyond Structural Adjustment. The Institutional Context of African Development*, edited by N. Van De Walle, N. Ball, and V. Ramachandran, 77–100. New York: Palgrave Macmillan. https://doi.org/10.1057/9781403981288_3.

Reid, R. J. 2017. *A History of Modern Uganda.* Cambridge: Cambridge University Press.

Reuss, A., and K. Titeca. 2017. 'When Revolutionaries Grow Old: The Museveni Babies and the Slow Death of the Liberation'. *Third World Quarterly* 38(10): pp. 2347–2366.

Reuters. 2018. 'Uganda Police Use Teargas to Disperse Protest against Social Media Taxes'. 11 July. https://www.reuters.com/article/us-uganda-socialmedia-protests/uganda-police-use-teargas-to-disperse-protest-against-social-media-taxes-idUSKBN1K121S.

Ross, M. L. 2004. 'Does Taxation Lead to Representation?' *British Journal of Political Science* 34(2): pp. 229–249. https://doi.org/10.1017/S0007123404000031.

Rothchild, D., and N. Chazan, eds. 1988. *The Precarious Balance: State and Society in Africa.* Boulder, CO: Westview.

Schneider, A. 2020. 'Democratic Deepening and State Capacity: Taxation in Brazil and India'. In *The Politics of Domestic Resource Mobilization for Social Development*, edited by K. Hujo. Cham: Palgrave Macmillan: pp. 173–206

Schulz, N., and K. Kelsall. 2021. 'The Political Settlements Dataset: An Introduction with Illustrative Applications'. *ESID Working Paper No. 165*. Dataset available at: The political settlements dataset: An introduction with illustrative applications – ESID (effective-states.org) (accessed 28 August 2023).

Sharp, S., S. Sweet, and A. Rocha Menocal. 2019. *Civil Society Engagement in Tax Reform*. London: ODI Report.

Sjursen, I. H. 2018. *Essays on Behavioural Development Economics*. PhD thesis, Department of Economics, Norwegian School of Economics.

Smidt, H. 2018. 'Shrinking Civic Space in Africa: When Governments Crack Down on Civil Society'. *GIGA Focus Africa*. No 4.

Smith, G. 2021. *Where Credit Is Due: How Africa's Debt Can Be a Benefit, Not a Burden*. London: Hurst and Company.

Stasavage, D. 2005. 'Democracy and Education Spending in Africa'. *American Journal of Political Science* 49(2): pp. 343–358.

Therkildsen, O., and F. Bourgouin. 2012. 'Continuity and Change in Tanzania's Ruling Coalition: Legacies, Crises and Weak Productive Capacity'. *DIIS Working Paper, 2012: 6*. Copenhagen: Danish Institute of International Studies.

Tilly, C. 1992. *Coercion, Capital, and European States. AD 990-1992*. Cambridge: Blackwell Publishers.

Timmons, J. F. 2005. The Fiscal Contract: States, Taxes, and Public Services. *World Politics*, 57(4), 530–567. http://www.jstor.org/stable/40060117

Tripp, A. M. 2017. 'In Pursuit of Autonomy: Civil Society and the State in Africa'. In *Africa in World Politics*, edited by J. W. Harbeson and D. Rothchild. New York: Routledge.: pp. 89–110.

UN. 2021. Committee of Experts on International Cooperation in Tax Matters. October.

UNU-WIDER. 2021. UNU-WIDER Government Revenue Dataset. Helsinki: UNU-WIDER Available at: https://www.wider.unu.edu/project/government-revenue-dataset.

van den Boogaard, V., W. Prichard, R. Beach, and F. Mohiuddin. 2021. 'Enabling Tax Bargaining: Supporting More Meaningful Tax Transparency and Taxpayer Engagement in Ghana and Sierra Leone'. *Development Policy Review*. https://doi.org/10.1111/dpr.12563.

Vines, A. 2018. 'Elite Bargains and Political Deals Project: Mozambique Case Study. Stabilization Unit. UK.

Whitfield, L., O. Therkildsen, L. Buur, and A. M. Kjær. 2015. *The Politics of African Industrial Policy: A Comparative Perspective.* Cambridge: Cambridge University Press.

Winckler Andersen, O., and O. Therkildsen. 2019. Can the SDGs in Low-income Countries Be Financed? And Should We Care? *DIIS Woking Papers, 2019, no 2.* Copenhagen: Danish Institute for International Studies.

2

Unpacking revenue bargaining

Triggers, processes, and outcomes

Marianne S. Ulriksen, Ane Karoline Bak, and Anne Mette Kjær

2.1 Introduction

In the introductory chapter, we offered an overview of the fiscal contract literature and argued that there is a need for more knowledge about the extent to which increased revenue mobilization leads to revenue bargaining and potentials for state–society reciprocity. In particular, we need to study systematically the micro-level politics of revenue bargaining, and to this end, we need to theorize and study the fiscal and political importance that revenue provides. This chapter therefore develops a theoretical framework (see also Figure 1.1 in Chapter 1) to help us answer our research question, namely how and under what conditions revenue bargaining emerges, evolves, and leads to fiscal contracts.

We begin by defining the main theoretical concept of revenue bargaining and distinguish it from that of fiscal contracts. Second, integrating fiscal contract theory and the political settlement approach, we disaggregate the concept of bargaining power, add the dimension of revenue providers' fiscal importance, and theorize how it influences their relative bargaining position vis-à-vis ruling elites. Thereafter, we discuss how revenue providers, given their relative bargaining position, can influence policy and when revenue providers and ruling elites are able to reach agreements in the form of fiscal contracts. Finally, we discuss potential triggers of revenue bargaining, that is, the events or actors that kick-start revenue bargaining. The theoretical framework that we develop here is applied in this volume's empirical Chapters 3–12 that analyse micro-level instances of revenue bargaining in our five case countries: Uganda, Tanzania, Togo, Mozambique, and Senegal (discussed in Chapter 1). We end this chapter with a brief discussion of the methodology applied across the contributions in this volume, followed by an introduction to each of the empirical chapters.

Marianne S. Ulriksen, Ane Karoline Bak, and Anne Mette Kjær, *Unpacking revenue bargaining*. In: *The Politics of Revenue Bargaining in Africa*. Edited by: Anne Mette Kjær, Marianne S. Ulriksen, and Ane Karoline Bak, Oxford University Press.
 DOI: 10.1093/oso/9780192868787.003.0002

2.2 The concepts of revenue bargaining and fiscal contract

In this book, we define *revenue bargaining* as implicit or explicit negotiations related to revenue provision between individual or groups of revenue providers and ruling elites (or representatives hereof). This definition differs from that of former literature in two ways. First, it delimits bargaining to the process of negotiation and distinguishes it from the potential outcome. In the fiscal contract literature, the process of revenue bargaining has often been implied and hence conflated with the outcome in the form of a contract (Bak 2019, 53). Earlier definitions have thus described revenue bargaining as 'the *exchange* of revenues (for the state) for institutionalized influence over public policy (for citizens)' (Moore, 2008, 36, emphasis added). We stress that revenue bargaining happens, in principle, prior to the exchange or, as we focus on, an agreement related to revenue provision. With our definition, we avoid the semantic and possibly analytical conflation of revenue bargain*ing* (processes) with *bargains* (the potential outcomes, e.g. in the form of fiscal contracts). Second, we use the term *revenue* rather than *tax bargaining* (as employed, e.g., by Prichard, 2015 and van den Boogaard et al., 2021) because it, per definition, includes other sorts of income sources that are not strictly taxes, such as various sorts of levies, fees, royalties, or development aid. As Wilson Prichard (2019, 7) has argued, 'a narrow focus in legally defined taxes will exclude large parts of how governance and services are actually financed in Africa'.

As a research object, revenue bargaining can be difficult to observe. As Moore (2008, 37–38) suggests, bargaining includes:

> [a] wide range of types of (political) exchange, ranging from explicit haggling ('If you do this, I will do that') to indirect, strategic, anticipatory interaction ('Let us announce more public spending on health now, in the hope that Parliament will be ready to accept an increase in VAT rates next year').

Revenue bargaining can be direct and observable, such as when Ghanaians in 1999 protested against the 2.5% increase in the VAT rate and the government reacted by earmarking the won revenue the Ghana Education Fund (Prichard, 2015). In line with Moore's description, we emphasize that revenue bargaining will also—and perhaps more often—be indirect, with no observable negotiation involving two parties with distinct interests. This was the case with the abolition of informal sector personal taxes in Uganda and Tanzania around election time (Kjær and Therkildsen, 2013). Here, the governments abolished taxes because they were unpopular, and given that opposition candidates campaigned against them, the rulers would not risk losing rural votes by insisting the taxes remain. The ruling elites thus anticipated a loss of votes to the opposition, and the policy of abolishing the tax was based more on a perception than on a direct bargain with taxpayers.

Hence, revenue bargaining could happen anywhere and anytime; as protests in the streets over new taxes, as op-eds in newspapers pushing for new taxes, at campaign meetings, during closed conversations in MPs' offices, as a part of legislative reform process, and at the market floor between vendors and tax collectors. The instances of revenue bargaining analysed in this book span the spectrum and allow us to make comparative observations about when and where revenue bargaining is likely to take place and how these conditions shape the outcomes.

Across the chapters of this book, revenue bargaining includes a range of stakeholders. A revenue provider is any actor who contributes funds to the public budget including individual taxpayers, sector groups, local elites, multinational companies, and even international donors. On the state side, we see the involvement of heads of state, members of the government, and politicians elected for national or local offices, as well as bureaucrats. Some of these may be members of the ruling elite, that is, individuals who hold formal or informal positions of political power, and others who may not. For example, a cabinet minister can hold a formal position but might not be a member of the ruling elite given lack of political influence. On the other hand, a person may be a close adviser to the president but without any formal position of power.

Our definition of revenue bargaining is broad in the sense that negotiation simply must 'relate to revenue provision'. Thereby, we recognize that revenue bargaining may not only concern positive exchanges of taxation for a return but may also result in revenue *foregone* (Moore, 2015). This includes situations that can be difficult to categorize as cases of revenue bargaining because there might not be a tax in place or a tax could have been abolished, such as in Kampala, Uganda where *boda bodas*, the motorbike taxis, have been exempted because they constitute an important support group for the ruling elite (Goodfellow, 2015). Judith Tendler (2002) called this type of arrangement 'the devil's deal'—you vote for me and I will not tax you—while Holland (2016) terms intentional non-enforcement of laws for the sake of maximizing votes 'forbearance'. Other powerful groups may be able to avoid paying tax by influencing members of the government to get exemptions. Such exemptions have perceivable consequences for policy and fiscal outcomes. For example, the granting of tax exemptions reduces the overall tax take and hence impedes the provision of public services. The influence of powerful groups may also result in the ruling elite prioritizing the provision of club goods, for example power supply for a specific industry rather than, say, countrywide rural electrification programmes. Thus, specific instances of revenue bargaining can result in micro-level contracts that are counterproductive to the macro-level achievement of accountability and broad-based development.

To deepen the understanding of when revenue bargaining leads to micro-level fiscal contracts, the two must be conceptually and empirically distinguishable. Where revenue bargaining denotes the *processes* of implicit or explicit negotiations, fiscal contracts are the potential *outcomes* of these processes; they occur in cases where the involved parties are able to reach an agreement or compromise.

In the literature on taxation and governance, the fiscal contract has most often been associated with a loose conception of a 'healthy', broad-based exchange relationship between state and society in which taxes are exchanged for public goods and political accountability (Moore, 2004; 2008; Martin and Prasad, 2014). Since the analytical interest of this book is revenue bargaining at the micro level, including its potential outcomes, we need a fiscal contract understanding on the same analytical level. Levi (1988) and Timmons (2005) represent a strand of the fiscal contract literature that describes micro-level fiscal relations between state and revenue providers. They both argue that governments strike different bargains with different groups of actors. Specifically, Levi (1988, 12) suggests that in a country, several (fiscal) contracts can exist in parallel, comprising the different deals a ruler enters into with different groups of societal actors in order to stay in power. Such micro-level fiscal contracts denote direct exchanges between a (group of) revenue provider(s) and the ruling elite, and it allows us to capture the immediate outcomes of micro-level instances of revenue bargaining. Specifically, we define micro-level fiscal contracts as *explicit or implicit agreements between ruling elites (or representatives hereof) and either individual or a group of revenue providers related to revenue provision.* Four points of elaborations are in order.

First, the micro-level fiscal contract does not have to be a balanced compromise in absolute terms that materializes in an equal exchange (Hyden, 1992). The agreement can manifest itself as much in mutual recognition and commitment as in material terms (Hyden, 1992; see also Levi and Sacks, 2009). Second, the contribution by revenue providers can take many forms. The contribution can be *formal*, public (most often tax) payments, supporting the ruling elite via the national budget, or *informal*, private payments to ruling elites, for example in the form of campaign financing rather than through state coffers. Third, the ruling elite side of the contract could include *positive* actions, such as goods or service provision, or *negative* actions including non-decisions, forbearance, and 'devil's deal' (Tendler, 2002; Holland, 2016; Piracha and Moore, 2016). In other words, positive or negative does not refer to a value judgement but rather to positively delivering a public service or negatively refraining from taxing and/or delivering. Here, our understanding of the fiscal contract differs from both Levi (1988) and Timmons (2005), who only consider exchanges of revenue for benefits or political influence. Fourth, the contract does not have to be in line with the initial proposal. Theoretically, the implication could be larger as well as smaller revenue mobilization by the government. Given the economic and political contexts (as theorized in detail below), agreements are, however, more likely to involve a compromise of a lower tax burden for the revenue provider and therefore less revenue mobilization by the government. Whether formal or informal contributions, positive or negative actions, or an agreement of lower tax payments, the agreements constitute contractual relations between ruling elites and revenue providers with implications for the shape of the tax system, fiscal outcomes, and for state–society reciprocity.

While a case study approach does enable one to get closer to the often difficult-to-observe attributes of an explicit or implicit agreement, mutual recognition, and commitment, it is not an easy task. We suggest several observable implications of micro-level fiscal contracts. One is an exchange. Evidence of an exchange related to revenue provision, whether positive or negative, can be taken at least as an indication of a micro-level fiscal contract. Another approach is to identify when revenue bargaining ends and inquire why it ended and what happened after it did so. Further, a fiscal contract can be implied from contract parties' expressions of expectations of and commitment to each other.

Whereas fiscal contracts are always preceded by revenue bargaining, revenue bargaining does not always end in agreement and a fiscal contract. They might end in non-exchanges. To illustrate different non-contractual outcomes, we can draw on recent efforts to levy a tax on social media across the African continent. In Benin, the government's proposal to tax certain types of social media prompted widespread mobilization of social media users, both online under the hashtag *#TaxePasMesMo* ('Don't Tax My MegaBytes') and taking to the streets (Okunoye, 2019). In response, the President withdrew the tax. In Uganda, the social media tax was also met with protests; however, here the government ignored the opposition and went ahead with the taxes without committing to a return. Both cases constitute instances of revenue bargaining that did not lead to fiscal contracts, though in two different ways. In the Beninese case, the tax was withdrawn and thus no exchange established. The Ugandan case is, at face value, a case of coercive taxation without an exchange. However, in reaction, many Ugandans decided to quit the targeted internet services (or use VPNs). To the extent that this is seen as tax resistance, one could argue that the revenue bargaining is ongoing.

Ultimately, whether a micro-level fiscal contract is present or not is an empirical question, and this book's empirical chapters provide illustrations of the many kinds of fiscal contracts to which revenue bargaining might lead. Analysing under which conditions micro-level fiscal contracts emerge is an instrumental means to determining the implications of the politicization of taxation.

2.3 The politics of bargaining

Having distinguished between the concepts of revenue bargaining and fiscal contracts, we also need to be able to see how power relations affect the bargaining processes. Political settlement theory offers a tool to grasp the relative bargaining power of revenue actors. A political settlement refers to the distribution of power among groups and institutions in a society based on which the ruling elites create coalitions of different key political factions (Khan, 2010; Whitfield et al., 2015). Ruling coalitions are maintained, and the ruling elites' hold on power secured, by giving powerful groups or factions in society access to rents such as government contracts, land rights, or tax exemptions (North et al., 2013; Kjær, 2015; Bak and Therkildsen, 2022). The *holding power* of these groups or individuals refers to their ability to engage in and survive conflicts and, by implication, to impose their interests on other groups or the state.

In the following, we first discuss the power of the ruling elite and revenue providers, respectively. Subsequently, as actual bargaining power must be understood as a relational concept whereby the two parties engage in negotiations, we further elaborate on the relative bargaining positions of the ruling elite and revenue providers. The model of bargaining positions emphasizes that negotiating parties go into the bargaining process from a certain position within the political settlement. From the outset, the groups have certain resources and holding power that may put them on either a better, a weaker, or an equal footing with respect to those on the other side of the bargaining table. Initial bargaining positions, even if they change along the way, may thus matter for the fiscal contract outcomes.

2.3.1 The bargaining power of ruling elites

Literature on African politics tends to view ruling elites as rather autonomous policymakers because, as they often deal with weak political opposition parties and civil society organizations, they are rarely constrained in making policy decisions (van de Walle, 2001). However, rulers do not act in isolation; they are responsive to the groups with strong holding power, whose support they need in order to remain in power (Khan, 2010; North et al., 2013). The power of the ruling elite depends on the political, economic, and administrative resources in the ruling elite's possession (Levi, 1988, 19), which again are derived from the political settlement.

Ruling elites are *politically* resourceful if factions opposing them are not strong—and if lower-level factions supporting the ruling elite are weak, merely complying and supporting rather than acting as veto-players from within (see Khan, 2010; Whitfield et al., 2015). On the other hand, ruling elites are less powerful when such factions *are* strong and therefore need to be accommodated. Hence, decisions to increase revenue can be politically costly if taxes target important constituents. A political settlement perspective shows that given the need to maintain legitimacy and support, rulers may not be able to maximize revenue, as is often assumed. This follows Levi's (1988, 10) argument that rulers' ability to maximize revenue is constrained by their need for supportive constituents. Further, as Fjeldstad and Therkildsen (2020, 39) point out, while macro-level agreements around some level of redistribution from rich to poor through taxation is rare in West and East Africa, some kind of redistribution does occur as rulers distribute resources in exchange for political loyalty to maintain stable ruling coalitions.

With regard to *economic* resources, the availability of non-tax revenue such as aid or natural resource revenues can change the autonomy of the ruling elite, simply because they depend less on domestic taxpayers and can afford to disregard their interests. Although, as regards aid, ruling elites instead become dependent on aid agencies (Ulriksen 2013). Aid dependency weakens the bargaining power of the ruling elites vis-à-vis donors whereas the availability of incomes from extractives would strengthen bargaining power towards taxpayers and donors alike (ibid.). Related to economic resources are also the costs of bargaining, including the costs of acquiring information, of the actual bargaining, and of subsequently implementing the policy resulting from the bargain (Levi, 1988, 27). Such costs will also influence ruling elites' bargaining power.

Finally, the *administrative* resources of the ruling elite matter too. Well-educated and adequately paid public employees are more likely to have the analytical capacity, information, and knowledge needed to be in a strong bargaining position vis-à-vis the taxpayers. In poor countries, states usually do not have strong capacity. However, although low-income countries often have weak state capacity, pockets of effectiveness in the state bureaucracy can be built with political support (Evans, 1995). A common definition of pockets of effectiveness is that they are organizations that are reasonably effective in carrying out their functions despite operating in an environment in which most agencies are ineffective and subject to serious corruption, patronage, etc. (Leonard, 2010, 91; Roll, 2014, 1). Administrative resources are largely a function of the political incentives that ruling elites have to strengthen certain agencies in an environment in which good governance across the board is not possible (Grindle, 2004; Khan, 2012). Moreover, agencies such as revenue authorities might also generate their own organizational interests that may not align with those of the political elites. For example, if politicians abolish taxes (as in the 'devil's deal'), this can run counter to the revenue authority's interest in meeting their set revenue targets. Therefore, at times, increased administrative resources may not strengthen the ruling elite's bargaining power.

2.3.2 The bargaining power of revenue providers

Neither the political settlement approach nor the fiscal contract theory has systematically theorized the bargaining power of revenue providers vis-à-vis ruling elites or the sources hereof. Specifically, with focus on macro-level fiscal social contracts in the literature (as discussed in Chapter 1), there has been a tendency to treat taxpayers as one entity.

The seminal contribution of Jeffrey Timmons (2005) succeeded in taking the theory a step further by disaggregating taxpayers into groups. He suggested that governments are likely to motivate compliance to the groups they are most dependent on for tax contributions through compensating policies that most directly address taxpayers' interests. Distinguishing between groups of taxpayers and seeing them as powerful given their (potential) financial contributions has also been studied in Africa, where an important observation is that powerful groups may be able to strike deals to be exempted from paying tax (Tendler, 2002; Moore, 2015). For example, in produce markets in northern Ghana, the daily fees that are supposed to be levied on all sellers are sometimes not collected from the larger traders (Prichard and van den Boogaard, 2017).

We follow this line of research and disaggregate the taxpayers into individual and groups of revenue providers. Drawing on the political settlement approach and the concept of holding power—that is, the ability to impose one's interests on other groups or the state—we theorize and distinguish between different sources of bargaining power of revenue providers vis-à-vis the ruling elite. According to Khan (2010, 63), holding power is partly based on income and wealth but also on the historically rooted capacities of different groups to organize. In the political settlement literature, the latter has been used to explain variations in policy outcomes across countries, and within countries across sectors. Though financing is important for understanding political settlements (Behuria et al., 2017, 513), the bargaining power that actors hold based on their potential revenue contributions has been overlooked. We argue that to understand the politics of revenue bargaining, it is necessary to add a fiscal dimension to the concept of bargaining power.

Accordingly, we theorize two dimensions of revenue provider bargaining power. One dimension is related to *fiscal importance*: revenue providers are individuals, groups, or organizations who provide finances that enable the ruling elite to maintain its position of power and the state to function. Thus, revenue providers hold some bargaining power in a strictly fiscal sense by way of contributing to the national budget, enabling broader public goods provision. This is in line with how Timmons (2005) operationalizes taxpayers' fiscal importance. Revenue providers can also hold bargaining power by providing direct, often informal, sometimes covert, payments to the ruling elite that can be used strategically to buy support and legitimacy. Formal contributions are made to government coffers and/or towards public goods such as tax payments or aid to government-run programmes. These are important for the ruling elite to sustain general public provisions for the population. Informal contributions can be smaller, but are strategically important as such funds can be used directly to maintain power and legitimacy, for example for political campaigning or to buy individual or club goods (e.g. tax-exempt payments) in return for political support.

The second dimension of bargaining power refers mainly to the revenue provider's *organizational importance*, that is, the ability to mobilize political support through organizational capacity, knowledge, and networks vital for the ruling elite's ability to maintain the ruling coalition (Khan, 2010; Whitfield et al., 2015). Organizational importance implies that revenue providers are important to the ruling coalition because they have an ability to grant political legitimacy to the ruling elite. For instance, groups can be supportive of government policies in parliament (MPs), they can use coercive measures against opponents (members of the army), or they can portray the ruling elite in a positive light (journalists and news reporters). Further, religious or traditional leaders can help maintain stability and/or mobilize voters, and citizens can, on occasion, challenge the ruling elite's position in power through their ability to vote. Importantly, the organizational importance of revenue providers relies on whether the ruling elite *perceives* them to be of importance for its political survival.

Additionally, collective action may be a source of bargaining power. Trade unions may organize and push for policy influence through strong mobilization and collective action. Such mobilization matters for the maintenance of the ruling coalition only to the extent that the ruling elite finds that the unions can provide essential financial and political support, or conversely can potentially threaten stability and the elite's legitimacy. Although we argue that collective action can be distinct from fiscal and non-economic power, the ability to mobilize does tend to enhance revenue providers' ability to bargain with the ruling elite. For instance, scattered and unorganized farmers are not likely to promote their interests as effectively as an organized urban sector (Bates, 1981). Individual negotiations with the government may be more desirable from the perspective of each individual industrialist, but the interests of the industry as such are likely to be better promoted through an organization.

2.3.3 Relative bargaining positions

So far, we have discussed the bargaining power of the ruling elite and that of (actual or potential) revenue providers. We have argued that the ruling elite has political, economic, and administrative resources at its disposal, while the bargaining power of revenue providers can be analysed along two dimensions: their fiscal and their organizational importance within the overall political settlement.

As we focus on the ruling elite's engagement with revenue providers, we suggest that it is useful to consider what the relative bargaining *positions* of the revenue providers vis-à-vis the ruling elite would look like at the beginning of the bargaining process. Do they stand in a strong or weak position relative to the ruling elite, or might the two parties have relatively equal bargaining power? The initial bargaining positions of the revenue providers may matter for their ability to negotiate as well as for the strategies they pursue.

Therefore, determining these at the outset of analysis will help to understand and perhaps to explain why a process of revenue bargaining unfolds as it does. Subsequently, revenue providers' bargaining power and, with it, their relative bargaining positions may change during negotiations. This is discussed in detail shortly.

We illustrate the relative bargaining positions of revenue providers and the ruling elite in Table 2.1 based on the two dimensions of bargaining power of revenue providers. In scenario 1, the revenue providers (individually or as a group) provide large or strategic (actual or potential) funds and are also of such organizational importance to the ruling elite that they stand in a very strong bargaining position. An example here could be the exemption on import duties for cars for public servants in Tanzania. Despite the Tanzanian government's step to remove many exemptions in the taxation system, the benefits for public servants have not been touched—arguably because the large group of public officials is an important political constituency for the ruling elite (Msami et al., 2022).

The mirror image of scenario 1 is scenario 4 where revenue providers are of little organizational importance and provide only small/unimportant contributions. An example could be the income taxation on formal sector workers. Typically, they do not constitute essential political support as the urban middle class is small and often votes against the ruling elite anyway, and economically, they typically do not contribute to the ruling coalition or make up a large part of the total collected domestic revenue. They are, therefore, taxed relatively hard but do not receive much in the form of a return, and as they are not organized in one group, they are unlikely to enter into revenue bargaining. Another example could be small

Table 2.1 The relative bargaining positions of the ruling elite and revenue providers

Organizational importance / **Fiscal importance**	(Potential or actual) revenue provider is organizationally powerful in relation to the ruling coalition	(Potential or actual) revenue provider is not organizationally powerful to the ruling coalition
(Potential or actual) contribution to the budget is large or strategically important to the ruling elite	1. (Actual or potential) revenue provider has strong bargaining position vis-à-vis the ruling elite	2. (Actual or potential) revenue provider has weak to medium bargaining power vis-à-vis the ruling elite
(Potential or actual) contribution to the budget is small or strategically unimportant to the ruling elite	3. (Actual or potential) revenue provider has a medium to weak bargaining position vis-à-vis the ruling elite	4. (Actual or potential) revenue provider has a weak bargaining position vis-à-vis the ruling elite

or medium-sized foreign companies that may be relatively easy to tax and not of political significance.

Scenarios 2 and 3 illustrate situations where the ruling elite and revenue providers may have relatively equal bargaining power. In scenario 2, the revenue providers (can) contribute large or strategically important funds but are of little organizational importance to the ruling elite. An example here could be the removal of VAT exemptions for the tourism sector in Tanzania, which is one of the largest contributors to the country's economy but is of limited political relevance to the ruling elite (Chapter 5 in this volume). In scenario 3, the relationship is the reverse: revenue providers are of high organizational importance but of low fiscal importance. For example, in Uganda, south-western dairy farmers constitute an important lower-level faction of the ruling coalition. They thus have considerable organizational power but are of less fiscal importance to the ruling elite (Kjær, 2015).

Table 2.1 presents ideal-type scenarios, and obviously there are no straightforward categorizations in reality. There can, for example, be overlaps between the ruling elites and revenue providers because politicians are often also businesspersons (Tangri and Mwenda, 2013; 2019). Influential cabinet members or individuals who are close to the inner circle around the president own companies for which they receive favourable conditions. Under such circumstances, it is not possible to distinguish between the ruling elite and revenue providers. Nevertheless, the typology is useful in reminding us that any bargaining process will start with the parties holding certain resources and power that affect the nature of the negotiations, whether they occur at all, and what the eventual outcome will be if they do.

Having outlined the initial bargaining positions, we emphasize that these can change in the bargaining process. Bargaining power and positions change as actors enter into new alliances, apply different strategies, or draw on different kinds of resources to promote their interests in the revenue bargaining. One example is how the bargaining power of rural poll taxpayers in relation to the ruling elite was strengthened due to the institutionalization of elections in Uganda and Tanzania, which led to the abolition of poll taxes in both countries (Fjeldstad and Therkildsen, 2008). In Uganda, the so-called graduated tax (GT) was in effect until 2005, when it was abolished prior to the 2006 parliamentary and presidential elections. The GT was the only countrywide effort to tax the informal sector broadly (Kjær, 2009). Even if the GT was set at a very low rate, it offered a significant source of income for local governments but did not contribute as such to the government budget. Furthermore, subsistence farmers were not organizationally important, and therefore, initially, the relative bargaining position of the ruling elite was strong (scenario 4 in Table 2.1). Then, in the political context of competitive elections, rural voters came to be seen as more significant to the ruling elite, who could not ignore claims by the opposition that the GT was unpopular and unfair. This strengthening of rural voters happened with the introduction of the first elections under the 1995 constitution and was subsequently strengthened in the 2006 elections, Uganda's first multi-party elections. The importance of GT payers as voters thus increased (moving to scenario 3), illustrating how the group of otherwise small taxpayers gained political leverage vis-à-vis the ruling elite given their significance as voters.

Relative bargaining power may also change during a bargaining process as a result of the various strategies revenue actors apply. If revenue providers manage to act collectively and enter strategic alliances with other organizations, they build up their organizational power and may have a better chance of influencing the ruling elites. Alternatively, if they find a way to access the president or someone in his inner circle personally, they may be able to enhance their bargaining position. Generally, it matters in which arena the revenue providers choose to promote their interests. Typically, articles in the news media are not as influential as direct access to the president. The strategies applied and the arenas accessed will reflect the relative resources of revenue actors. Many of the empirical chapters in this volume explore the changing strategies, alliances, and resources of parties to the bargaining process. In the concluding chapter, we summarize these findings, emphasize comparative observations, and draw up cross-case patterns related to the political dynamics of revenue bargaining in Africa.

2.4 Triggers

Finally, we should address what may trigger a revenue-bargaining process (see also Figure 1.1 in Chapter 1). The fiscal contract literature has, so far, mainly focused on why states in Africa seek to expand taxation (as also discussed in Chapter 1) and, in turn, under which conditions changed tax efforts lead to revenue bargaining (e.g. Prichard, 2015; van den Boogaard et al., 2021). There is little systematic research on the immediate triggers of micro-level revenue-bargaining processes beyond government initiatives to reform tax policies. The empirical chapters in this book show that revenue bargaining can be set off by many different kinds of triggers including actions, events, and changes in circumstances.

The focus on expansion of domestic revenue mobilization as a trigger of state–society interactions originates in the European state-building experiences. Non-democratic rulers introduced new taxes in order to mobilize resources to win wars, and in return, they needed to provide openings for political representation (Schumpeter, 1991; Tilly, 1992). Negotiations over revenue in African countries operate in a post-colonial political context characterized by the absence of inter-state war, hybrid institutions, and economies in which the majority remains employed in low-technology subsistence agriculture (Jackson and Rosberg, 1982; van de Walle, 2001; Moore, 2004; Bräutigam, 2008; North et al., 2013). Thus, revenue pressure and the drive to collect revenue in Africa come from many factors other than inter-state war. One such factor is rulers' need to maintain political stability in a situation of what Doner et al. (2005) call 'systematic vulnerability'. Systemic vulnerability is present under a combination of resource scarcity, perceived threats to the ruling elite, and the need for resources to maintain political stability. While systemic vulnerability is more expedient in a situation characterized by external security threats, vulnerabilities can also arise from a fiscal crisis, a decline in foreign aid, or a shortage of opportunities to take up loans.

Many African elites have experienced rising political costs of staying in power. Most African countries have institutionalized, regular, and relatively free and fair elections (Bleck and van de Walle, 2018). Elections offer an impetus to collect revenue to win votes through public service provision (Stasavage, 2005). Running election campaigns is also costly, so incumbent ruling elites may want to raise revenue for their campaign purposes, although the converse scenario is also plausible, namely that elections lead to declining revenue as exemptions may be granted in return for support (Bak and Therkildsen, 2022). Elections may also offer the opportunity for a tax to be politicized, as happened with the informal sector taxes in Uganda and Tanzania (Kjær and Therkildsen, 2013). Finally, and less directly connected to elections, threats from, and needs to offer side payments to, important groups (within or outside the ruling coalition) could instigate a sense of vulnerability and hence motivate the ruling elite to search for revenue (Donor et al., 2005; Whitfield et al., 2015).

Summing up, ruling elites in Africa do experience revenue pressure, which is an important driver in governments' move to increase resource mobilization. However, given that most African states are economically vulnerable, their fiscal need is constant, though it may be latent. Therefore, it alone cannot explain the emergence of revenue bargaining. To broaden our knowledge hereof, we need to look for the immediate factors that trigger revenue bargaining.

Such factors could include *actions* by state actors including government officials, local politicians, and tax administration employees, such as an announcement or an adoption of a new tax. But not all attempts to increase taxation leads to revenue bargaining. Therefore, some empirical chapters explore the conditions under which this is more likely to happen. Triggers could also be *events* such as elections or a *change in circumstances* that render an already implemented tax the sudden focal point of revenue bargaining. The tax administration may begin to enforce a tax policy hitherto left unimplemented. Citizens may receive new information about the taxes they pay or learn about a corruption scandal, prompting a resistance towards paying taxes. Similarly, the entry of civil society organizations promoting human rights and tax awareness could trigger a bargaining process. These are just a few of the broad variety of triggers and conditions under which revenue bargaining emerges that are explored in this book's empirical chapters.

2.5 The book's methodological approach and introduction to chapters

The theoretical framework presented and discussed in this chapter has as its point of departure the political settlement and fiscal contract literatures, and is based on a synthesis of the two. However, the purpose has not been to build a comprehensive theory of the politics of revenue bargaining to be tested in the book's case countries. Instead, we take an iterative approach to our inquiries. We have conceptualized key notions and theorized to the extent possible a priori. The theory, the concepts, and the theoretical framework were then continuously revisited and discussed in light of emerging findings at workshops of the Political Settlement and Revenue Bargains in Africa Project, and at conferences, including a designated European Consortium for Political Research joint session in Cyprus, where contributors were present. Within this collaboratively developed framework, the book's chapters take an explorative approach to uncover new empirical knowledge of the politics and dynamics of revenue bargaining, which in turn allows us to deepen our understanding hereof and to build a micro-level theoretical foundation of the fiscal contract theory.

To develop a comprehensive understanding of the politics of revenue bargaining at the micro level, we argue that it is imperative to study a large variation of cases. The book includes both cases where revenue bargaining does unfold and cases where revenue bargaining could have been expected but did not occur. Different chapters focus on different aspects of revenue bargaining in their case studies; these include whether and when revenue providers mobilize, whether they are able to get state actors to negotiate, how the bargaining evolves, or what the outcome is. One example is studying how differences in bargaining power between different groups of revenue providers influence the outcome of their revenue bargaining with state actors. This is done in Chapter 7 where the bargaining power of agricultural sector actors in Uganda differs depending on their position in relation to the ruling coalition and whether they are able to join forces with other organizations. Another example focuses on instances of collective action prompted by tax-related grievances and whether these actually lead to revenue bargaining, as in Chapter 3 where informal women traders in Dar es Salaam, Tanzania, even when organized felt unable to influence whether they were taxed or if they received a return. A third example is whether and how the presence of third parties influences the processes and outcomes of different cases of revenue bargaining which is the focus of Chapter 10 in which local chiefs in Togo play a large role in the bargaining processes between revenue officials and taxpayers. Most of the cases have been selected based on an understanding of the contextual conditions of the revenue-bargaining instances, which in turn helps us to understand and explain variations in the processes and outcomes.

All the book's contributions build on extensive field research, including interviews with concerned revenue providers, relevant state actors, and experts. Some draw as well on participant observation data (Chapters 3 and 10), original survey data (Chapters 4 and 9), or data from primary and secondary sources such as news articles, reports, and legal texts (Chapters 5, 6, 7, 8, 11, and 12). Based on extensive empirical knowledge of the cases combined with original collected data, the authors present the cases of revenue bargaining in qualitative narratives of different forms. This is an instrumental means of uncovering the dynamics of revenue bargaining, how positions and relations of power may change, and whether and under what conditions instances of revenue bargaining lead to some sort of agreement in the form of a (micro-level) fiscal contract.

Employing the explorative approach has meant that some case studies are so-called negative cases of fiscal contracts where revenue bargaining occurs but does not lead to an agreement between revenue providers and the ruling elite. To mention one, revenue bargaining between the Tanzanian government and international aid agencies does not lead to an agreement around payment of the social protection programme (Chapter 11). Such a negative case is helpful, methodologically, to rule out spurious causes, and empirically it appears to serve as initial engagements, which in some cases shape or directly lead to future revenue bargaining and build reciprocity.

We now briefly introduce the empirical Chapters 3–12 of this book.

In Chapter 3, Ane Edslev Jacobsen draws on extensive field research among informal women traders in Dar es Salaam, Tanzania. Edslev Jacobsen finds that even if these women are taxed and do experience tax-related grievances, they very often do not act collectively because of their already marginalized position. Only with the aid of an NGO are they able to organize and initiate a dialogue with local government actors.

In Chapter 4, Armin von Schiller examines what may lead to revenue bargaining between Mozambican municipalities and their citizens, based on original interview data. He finds that revenue pressure plays a large role and that opposition municipalities face stronger revenue pressure than others because of the unpredictability of central transfers. This incentivizes them to bargain with citizens over revenue in consensual rather than conflictual ways.

In Chapter 5, Marianne S. Ulriksen, Jamal Msami, and Lucas Katera examine four different instances of revenue bargaining in Tanzania, based on in-depth interviews with key actors. In their analysis, they focus on the different arenas of bargaining and the strategies employed by the negotiating parties. They find that revenue providers can succeed in getting the government to concede to lower tax payments, particularly when bargaining is moved to arenas that enable the building of structured, repeated, and trusted relationships.

In Chapter 6, Lise Rakner and Odd-Helge Fjeldstad examine the 2014 VAT Act reform in Tanzania and the role of lobbying in the bargaining process, based on document analysis and original interviews with involved parties. They find, among other things, that by creating alliances, business associations and other lobby groups worked purposefully and managed to shape the VAT act in accordance with their own interests.

In Chapter 7, Anne Mette Kjær and Clayton Arinanye present findings on seven instances of bargaining concerning Uganda's agricultural sector. Based on extensive field observations, interviews, and policy documents, they show that agricultural sector actors succeed more when they protest against taxes than when they try to lobby for improved service delivery. In the former case, it is easier for them to ally with other actors and easier for the ruling elite to give concessions.

In Chapter 8, Dan Ngabirano examines revenue bargaining in the judicial arena in his study of how the Ugandan government took a multinational oil company to court. The government won and the corporation was made liable to pay a large sum of capital gains tax. Based on an analysis of legal documents combined with interviews, Ngabirano's chapter shows that revenue providers who we know to be economically important for the ruling elites have a weak bargaining position because they are not politically important.

In Chapter 9, Moses Khisa, Jamal Msami, and Ole Therkildsen examine the connection between campaign financing and tax exemptions in Uganda and Tanzania through original survey data and interviews. They argue that campaign finance gives donors of such finance more bargaining power than tax paying does.

In Chapter 10, Rachel Beach examines two instances of revenue bargaining in Togo based on extensive fieldwork and participatory observation within the Togolese revenue authority. She finds that a third party's intervention can bolster as well as invert the bargaining power and position of the revenue authorities in important ways.

In Chapter 11, Marianne S. Ulriksen, Flora Myamba, and Constantine George explore the revenue-bargaining process between the international aid agencies—the current revenue providers of Tanzania's cash transfer programme—and the Tanzanian government. They pay particular attention to the preferences of negotiating parties and how the parties seek to maximize their own interests in the negotiations, and they find that even if the international aid agencies provide substantial revenue, the agencies are unable to fully impose their preferred interests on the Tanzanian government.

In Chapter 12, the book's final empirical chapter, Ane Karoline Bak offers a historical analysis of revenue bargaining between the Senegalese ruling elites and the informal commercial sector. Bak finds that the evolution in taxation of the sector can be explained in part by the relative bargaining positions that shift over time depending on the composition of the ruling coalition and the changing bargaining power of the revenue providers and, in particular, of their broker UNACOIS.

The chapters all draw on the theoretical framework developed and outlined in this chapter to examine instances of revenue bargaining. Though the book's chapters focus on different parts of the revenue-bargaining processes, they do overlap in multiple ways, allowing comparative and cross-case, cross-sector, and cross-country observations to be made. When relevant and possible, cross-chapter comparisons are referenced in the respective chapters. Not least given the shared theoretical framework, we are able to draw out with confidence some broadly generalizable patterns in the conclusion (Chapter 13). Beyond that, the concluding chapter discusses comprehensively the collective answers that the chapters provide to our research question of how and under what conditions revenue bargaining emerges, evolves, and leads to fiscal contracts.

2.6 Conclusion

Over the past two decades, domestic revenue mobilization has been expanding and taxation has become politicized across Africa. Concurrently, a literature studying the political outcomes of taxation has blossomed, but found few signs of the expected exchange-based fiscal social contracts between state and society. Despite the proliferation of fiscal contract research, the dynamics and politics of revenue bargaining remain undertheorized. As discussed in Chapter 1, we therefore need to develop a theoretical framework that helps us move from the macro to the micro level and allows us to embed the analysis of revenue bargaining within the economic and political power structures. It has been the purpose of this chapter to present a theoretical framework that allows us to study the politics of revenue bargaining through case studies of micro-level instances hereof.

This theoretical framework is based on the existing fiscal contract theory and the political settlement approach and provides two major contributions. First, the framework contributes to the fiscal contract literature by defining and unpacking the concept of revenue bargaining and, importantly, distinguishing it from its potential outcome: micro-level fiscal contracts. This allows us to separate processes from outcomes, and analyse the conditions that shape each of them as well as their relationship. Second, the framework facilitates bringing politics into the analysis of revenue bargaining. We theorize that both revenue providers' organizational importance and their fiscal importance for ruling elites determine the strength of their bargaining positions. We include a heuristic device to identify bargaining parties' initial bargaining position as a point of departure for exploring how and under what conditions revenue providers are able to promote their demands in negotiations related to revenue provision.

Equipped with this theoretical framework, the empirical chapters that follow take an explorative approach to understanding processes of revenue bargaining. Besides examining the role of power, the empirical chapters also go beyond the common studies of revenue bargaining by paying attention to the actual immediate triggers besides the fairly static revenue pressure, as well as leaving the imaginary bargaining table behind and going to where instances of revenue bargaining actually take place.

References

Bak, A. K. 2019. *When the Fiscal Social Contract Is Not about Tax: Understanding the Limited Role of Taxation in Social Accountability in Senegal.* PhD dissertation, Department of Political Science, Aarhus University. Aarhus: Politica.

Bak, A. K., and O. Therkildsen. 2022. 'Democratisation in Tanzania: No Elections without Tax Exemptions'. *Journal of Eastern African Studies* 16(1): pp. 47–67.

Bates, R. 1981. *Markets and States in Tropical Africa: The Political Basis of Agricultural Policies.* Berkeley: University of California Press.

Behuria, P., L. Buur, and H. Gray. 2017. 'Studying Political Settlements in Africa'. *African Affairs* 116(464): pp. 508–525.

Bleck, J., and N. van de Walle. 2018. *Electoral Politics in Africa: Continuity in Change.* New York: Cambridge University Press.

Bräutigam, D. 2008. 'Introduction: Taxation and State-Building in Developing Countries'. In *Taxation and State-Building in Developing Countries*, edited by D. Bräutigam, O.-H. Fjeldstad, and M. Moore, pp. 1–33. Cambridge: Cambridge University Press.

Doner, R., B. Ritchie, and D. Slater. 2005. 'Systematic Vulnerability and the Origins of Developmental States: Northeast and Southeast Asia in Comparative Perspective'. *International Organization* 59(2): pp. 327–361

Evans, P. 1995. *Embedded Autonomy: States and Industrial Transformation.* Princeton, NJ: Princeton University Press.

Fjeldstad, O.-H., and O. Therkildsen. 2008. 'Mass Taxation and State–Society Relations in East Africa'. In *Taxation and State-Building in Developing Countries*, edited by D. Bräutigam, O.-H. Fjeldstad, and M. Moore, pp. 114–135. Cambridge: Cambridge University Press.

Fjeldstad, O.-H., and O. Therkildsen. 2020. *Implications of the Covid-19 Pandemic for Revenue Generation in Poor African Countries.* DIIS Working Paper 2020: 13. Copenhagen: DIIS, Danish Institute for International Studies.

Goodfellow, T. 2015. 'Taming the "Rogue" Sector: Studying State Effectiveness in Africa through Informal Transport Politics'. *Comparative Politics* 47(2): pp. 127–147.

Grindle, M. S. 2004. 'Good Enough Governance: Poverty Reduction and Reform in Developing Countries'. *Governance: An International Journal of Policy, Administration and Institutions* 17(4): pp. 525–548.

Holland, A. 2016. 'Forbearance'. *American Political Science Review* 110(2): pp. 232–246.

Hyden, G. 1992. 'Governance and the Study of Politics'. In *Governance and Politics in Africa*, edited by M. Bratton and G. Hyden, pp. 3–26. Boulder, CO: Rienner.

Jackson, R. H., and C. G. Rosberg. 1982. *Personal Rule in Black Africa: Prince, Autocrat, Prophet, Tyrant.* Berkeley, CA: University of California Press.

Khan, M. H. 2010. *Political Settlements and the Governance of Growth-Enhancing Institutions.* London: SOAS Working Paper.

Khan, M. H. 2012. 'Governance and Growth: History, Ideology, and Methods of Proof'. In *Good Growth and Governance in Africa*, edited by Akbar Noman, Kwesi Botchwey, Howard Stein, and Joseph E. Stiglitz, pp. 51–79. Oxford: Oxford University Press.

Kjær, A. M. 2009. 'Sources of Local Government Extractive Capacity: The Role of Trust and Pre-Colonial Legacy in the Case of Uganda'. *Public Administration and Development* 29(3): pp. 228–238. https://doi.org/10.1002/pad.532.

Kjær, A. M. 2015. 'Political Settlements and Productive Sector Policies: Understanding Sector Differences in Uganda'. *World Development* 68: pp. 230–241. https://doi.org/10.1016/j.worlddev.2014.12.004.

Kjær, A. M., and O. Therkildsen. 2013. 'Elections and Landmark Policies in Uganda and Tanzania'. *Democratization* 20(4): pp. 592–614.

Leonard, D. K. 2010. 'Pockets of Effective Agencies in Weak Governance States: Where Are They Likely and Why Does It Matter?' *Public Administration and Development* 30(2): pp. 91–101.

Levi, M. 1988. *Of Rule and Revenue.* Berkeley, CA: University of California Press.

Levi, M., and A. Sacks. 2009. 'Legitimating Beliefs: Sources and Indicators'. *Regulation and Governance* 3(4): pp. 311–333. https://doi.org/10.1111/j.1748-5991.2009.01066.x.

Martin, I. W., and M. Prasad. 2014. 'Taxes and Fiscal Sociology'. *Annual Review of Sociology* 40(1): pp. 331–345. https://doi.org/10.1146/annurev-soc-071913-043229.

Moore, M. 2004. 'Revenues, State Formation, and the Quality of Governance in Developing Countries'. *International Political Science Review* 25(3): pp. 297–319. https://doi.org/10.1177/0192512104043018.

Moore, M. 2008. 'Between Coercion and Contract: Competing Narratives on Taxation and Governance'. In *Taxation and State-Building in Developing Countries: Capacity and Consent*, edited by D. Bräutigam, O.-H. Fjeldstad, and M. Moore, pp. 34–63. Cambridge: Cambridge University Press.

Moore, M. 2015. 'Tax and the Governance Dividend'. In *Perspectives on Politics, Production and Public Administration in Africa*, edited by A. M. Kjær, L. Engberg-Pedersen, and L. Buur, pp. 159–172. Copenhagen: Danish Institute for International Studies.

Msami, J., L. Katera, and M. Ulriksen. 2022. *Bargaining Strategies in Recent Tax Reforms in Tanzania.* Working paper 16-03-AU. Aarhus: Department of Political Science, Aarhus University.

North, D. C, J. J. Wallis, S. B. Webb, and B. R. Weingast. 2013. *In the Shadow of Violence: Politics, Economics, and the Problems of Development*. Cambridge: Cambridge University Press.

Okunoye, B. 2019. 'In Africa, a New Tactic to Suppress Online Speech: Taxing Social Media'. *Net Politics* blog. 10 January. https://www.cfr.org/blog/africa-new-tactic-suppress-online-speech-taxing-social-media.

Piracha, M., and M. Moore. 2016. 'Revenue-Maximising or Revenue-Sacrificing Government? Property Tax in Pakistan'. *The Journal of Development Studies* 57(2): pp. 209–225.

Prichard, W. 2015. *Taxation, Responsiveness and Accountability in Sub-Saharan Africa*. Cambridge: Cambridge University Press.

Prichard, W. 2019. 'Tax Politics and the Social Contract in Africa'. *Oxford Research Encyclopedia of Politics*. https://doi.org/10.1093/acrefore/9780190228637.013.853.

Prichard, W., and V. van den Boogaard. 2017. 'Norms, Power and the Socially Embedded Realities of Market Taxation in Northern Ghana'. *African Studies Review* 60(1): pp. 171–194. https://doi.org/10.1017/asr.2017.3.

Roll, M., ed. 2014. *The Politics of Public Sector Performance: Pockets of Effectiveness in Developing Countries*. London: Routledge.

Schumpeter, J. A. 1991. 'The Crisis of the Tax State'. In *Joseph A. Schumpeter: The Economics and Sociology of Capitalism*, edited by R. Swedberg, pp. 99–140. Princeton, NJ: Princeton University Press. https://doi.org/10.2307/j.ctv173f01t.5.

Stasavage, D. 2005. 'Democracy and Education Spending in Africa'. *American Journal of Political Science* 49(2): pp. 343–358.

Tangri, R., and A. M. Mwenda. 2013. *The Politics of Elite Corruption in Africa*. New York: Routledge.

Tangri, R., and A. M. Mwenda. 2019. 'Change and Continuity in the Politics of Government–Business Relations in Museveni's Uganda'. *Journal of Eastern African Studies* 13(4): pp. 678–697. https://doi.org/10.1080/17531055.2019.1655879.

Tendler, J. 2002. 'Small Firms, the Informal Sector, and the Devil's Deal'. *IDS Bulletin* 33(3): pp. 1–15. https://doi.org/10.1111/j.1759-5436.2002.tb00035.x.

Tilly, C. 1992. *Coercion, Capital and European States, AD 990–1992*. Oxford: Blackwell.

Timmons, J. F. 2005. 'The Fiscal Contract: States, Taxes and Public Services'. *World Politics* 57(4): pp. 530–567.

Ulriksen, M. S. 2013. 'The Politics of Social Protection Expenditure and Financing in Southern Africa'. *Development Southern Africa* 30(1): pp. 39–53.

van de Walle, N. 2001. *African Economies and the Politics of Permanent Crisis, 1979–1999*. Cambridge: Cambridge University Press.

van den Boogaard, V., W. Prichard, R. Beach, and F. Mohiuddin. 2021. 'Enabling Tax Bargaining: Supporting More Meaningful Tax Transparency and Taxpayer Engagement in Ghana and Sierra Leone'. *Development Policy Review* 40(1): p. e12543. https://doi.org/10.1111/dpr.12563.

Whitfield, L., O. Therkildsen, L. Buur, and A. M. Kjær. 2015. *The Politics of African Industrial Policy*. Cambridge: Cambridge University Press.

3

We pay, we act?

Conditions for collective action among informal women traders in urban Tanzania

Ane Edslev Jacobsen

3.1 Introduction

Since 2000, there has been a growing informalization, urbanization, and feminization of the national economies in many developing countries (Chant and Pedwell, 2008; Johnston-Anumonwo and Doane, 2011; Joshi et al., 2014; International Labour Office, 2014). Elucidating how these developments shape not only taxation as a practice but also revenue bargaining and state–society relations is key to our continued understanding of political economy. Correspondingly, this chapter investigates when and why revenue bargaining emerges—and when it does not—in the informal, gendered context of urban Tanzania. Focusing on the initial phase of a revenue-bargaining process, the chapter studies whether taxation spurs collective action among urban, informal women market traders—a group of small-scale, intersectionally disadvantaged revenue providers—in Dar es Salaam.

Based on fiscal contract theory, taxation may cause grievances among revenue providers, which in turn can prompt them to engage in collective action to make reciprocal demands on the government (Prichard, 2015, 254). However, this initial, micro-level phase of the bargaining process linking taxation to collective action is somewhat undertheorized (see Chapters 1 and 2 of this volume; Meagher, 2018). Therefore, this chapter first investigates what role taxation plays in revenue providers' *motivation* to engage in collective action at the micro level. Specifically, I investigate whether two tax-related economic grievances—economic hardship and lack of reciprocity—can motivate collective action. Second, the chapter elaborates on and theorizes what constitutes revenue provider *capacity* for collective action and what influences the capacity to act. Here, I investigate variations in and sources of relational and

Ane Edslev Jacobsen, *We pay, we act?*. In: *The Politics of Revenue Bargaining in Africa*. Edited by: Anne Mette Kjær, Marianne S. Ulriksen, and Ane Karoline Bak, Oxford University Press. © Oxford University Press (2024).
DOI: 10.1093/oso/9780192868787.003.0003

organizational capacity among the women traders—one of the least powerful population groups, tending to have low levels of capacity for collective action (Chen et al., 2002; Clark, 2010; Lindell, 2010a; Meagher, 2010b; Brown et al., 2010; Gallien and van den Boogaard, 2020).

Integrating revenue provider motivation and capacity into the revenue-bargaining framework contributes to our understanding of what happens at the micro level early in the process, before revenue bargaining has materialized, and thus explores mechanisms and conditions under which revenue bargaining emerges.

3.2 Taxation and collective action in an informal, gendered context

This chapter adopts a broad definition of *taxation* to capture all revenue provider payments that contribute to the financing of local and central governance (van den Boogaard et al., 2019). Formal taxation includes formally labelled taxes as well as user fees to the central or local government, and informal taxation encompasses payments outside of formal laws to state or non-state actors contributing to financing public goods or broader state or non-state governance functions (van den Boogaard et al., 2019, 266). Even in the informal economy, people are charged with numerous formal and informal payments, by both state and non-state actors (Prud'homme, 1992; Meagher, 2009; Lindell, 2010a; Olken and Singhal, 2011; Joshi et al., 2014). That is also the case for people in Dar es Salaam who work in informal market trading; that is, non-criminal commercial activity dependent on access to somewhat established public (or privately owned) premises of markets (Lyons et al., 2009, 5; Brown et al., 2010; Vanek et al., 2015). Market traders in urban Tanzania pay different forms of levies (*ushuru*) to the local government, and some even pay presumptive tax (colloquially referred to as *kodi ya mapato*) to the central government. As such, they are subjected to formal taxation. Moreover, research shows that people in urban Tanzania are also subjected to informal taxation by police, local street leaders, or influential businesspeople (IMED, 2016). As such, informal market traders in Dar es Salaam are indeed revenue providers.

There has been a long-standing focus on the link between broad-based taxation and revenue bargaining, fiscal contracts, government accountability, and state building (Chapter 1; Moore, 2004; Timmons, 2005; Bräutigam, 2008; Prichard, 2015). A core argument is that revenue providers, when taxed, may engage in collective action to pressure power holders to

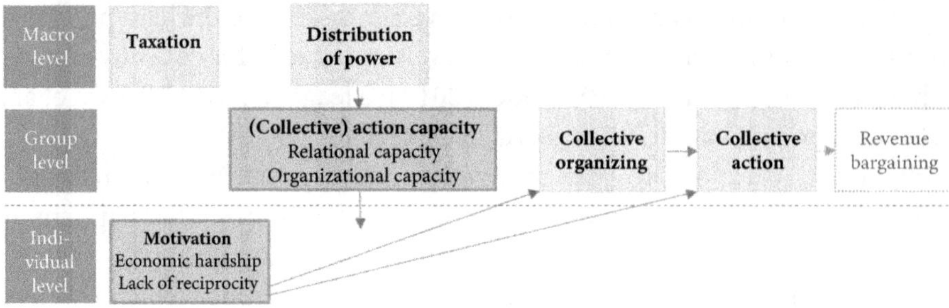

Figure 3.1 The role of motivation and capacity in the links between taxation and collective action.

reciprocate by providing them with public goods or influence over public policy. With that, revenue bargaining—and institutional change—may emerge (Prichard, 2015, 254). Expanding on the micro-level mechanisms underlying this proposition, this chapter argues that taxation can motivate revenue providers' collective organizing and action through economic grievances at the individual level, and that the societal distribution of power influences revenue providers' relational and organizational capacity to translate these grievances into collective engagement at the group level. Focusing on a structurally marginalized revenue provider group, I argue that collective organizing can be an important precondition to collective action. Figure 3.1 illustrates the theoretical model.

3.2.1 Does taxation serve as a motivational factor at the micro level?

Taxation can trigger collective action among revenue providers through two kinds of tax-related economic grievances: economic hardship and lack of reciprocity (Knoke, 1990). First, revenue providers can experience taxation as loss of earned income and, therefore, as a contributing factor to economic hardship (Martin, 2013). As such, taxation can aggravate revenue providers' economic grievances. This may be particularly true for informal women workers, who—as self-employed operators with low turnovers working in the extremely competitive, unequal, and uncertain environment of the informal economy—already struggle with economic hardship (Lindell, 2010a; WIEGO, 2014). If taxation is experienced as a contributor to economic hardship and grievance, it may motivate revenue providers to engage in collective action to improve their economic conditions.

Second, taxation can motivate collective action if revenue providers are unsatisfied with what they get in return for their taxes. Assuming that revenue providers want something in return for their taxes, non-satisfactory returns will likely be perceived as an unfair lack of reciprocity (Levi, 1988; Martin, 2013; Broms, 2015; Prichard, 2015). Such grievance can trigger discontent with taxation and the taxing actors, including the state, and make revenue providers less tolerant of non-accountable state behaviour (Knoke, 1990; Fjeldstad and Semboja, 2001; Kayuza, 2006). Accordingly, if the traders experience a lack of reciprocity or unsatisfactory return for their payments, it may motivate them to engage in collective action, demanding lower taxes, better public services, greater representation, or influence over public policy in return (Knoke, 1990; Prichard, 2015).

3.2.2 Can disadvantaged revenue providers translate motivation into action?

It is well established that revenue providers' capacity for collective action conditions whether taxation triggers collective action and, ultimately, whether revenue bargaining emerges (Joshi and Ayee, 2008; Prichard and van den Boogaard, 2017; Meagher, 2018). Capacity is understood from a power perspective implying that people's capacity to act is embedded in their social positions in the societal and local power structure—that is, in the distribution of power related to gender and to economic, social, and political status (Giddens, 1984; Sewell, 1992; Fujii, 2008; Lindell, 2010b).

The informal economy is a space of unequal distribution of power, and women working in the informal economy tend to be marginalized along multiple axes of power: economically, socially, and politically (Chen et al., 2002; Meagher, 2010b; Clark, 2010; Lindell, 2010a). Economically, women tend to be overrepresented in the low-skill, low-income economic activities with little prospect of advancement (Meagher, 2010a), particularly in informal trading (Chen and Snodgrass, 2001; Roever, 2014). Moreover, patriarchal gender norms allocate a disproportionate share of unpaid care to women (Joshi, 2017), which creates severe time and participatory constraints for them. Socially, women often face a hostile working environment because the public sphere is traditionally seen as the men's sphere (Jagero and Kushoka, 2011) and gender-based harassment is widespread (Capraro, 2017). On a political level, these power-related gendered constraints often limit informal women workers' ability to translate tax-related grievances into a collective political voice (Brown et al., 2010; Gallien and van den Boogaard, 2020).

At a structural level, they are not important clienteles to the ruling elites, who in turn have very little incentive to bargain over revenue with the women. Against this backdrop, exploring whether and how women traders are able to overcome these power-related barriers to collective action is thus imperative for understanding whether they can take part in any future fiscal contracts.

In spite of the structural constraints on informal women workers' collective action, there are multiple empirical examples hereof (Chen et al., 2007; Lindell, 2010a) indicating that at the micro level, the capacity to act and local pockets of collective engagement can emerge. In the face of limited economic resources, it is the women's *organizational* and *relational capacity* that is likely to condition whether they manage to translate their tax-related grievances into collective action.

Organizational capacity refers to a set of organizational capabilities, including vocational know-how, and human resources with knowledge of mobilization, advocacy, organizational development, access to information, and potential channels of influence. It is thus a political resource and source of bargaining power. This type of capacity can help the traders overcome the time and economic barriers and potentially the political barriers to collective action. Surely, there are women traders who, due to the multiple constraints mentioned above, have very limited organizational capacity, and this likely hinders their collective engagement even though they may have grievances. Such women have little or no holding power and, therefore, a weak relative bargaining position vis-à-vis ruling elites, which makes revenue bargaining unlikely. However, surely, there are also women traders who enjoy higher organizational capacity based on previous training, collective engagement, or their social network. This will enable them to engage in collective action in a time and cost-efficient way.

Relational capacity is a social resource that can help the traders overcome the psychological, social, and gendered barriers to collective action. It refers to the extent of social capital and collective identity among the women traders. Social capital—that is, social networks based on norms, reciprocity, and trust—provides the traders with a sense of community (Putnam et al., 1994; Brown et al., 2010, 33; Ganz, 2010). For the individual trader, this sense of belonging can have an empowering effect, and at a group level, this sense of community is conducive to cultivating a collective identity among the women—this 'shared sense of "one-ness" or "we-ness" anchored in real or imagined shared attributes and experiences' (Snow and Soule, 2010, 125; see also Polletta and Jasper, 2001). Importantly, trust-based networks and we-ness do not emerge just because people share living or working conditions; both must be cultivated and sustained. Therefore, relational capacity is likely to vary across markets. In markets where no efforts have been made to cultivate social capital and collective identity, the women's relational capacity will be limited and their collective engagement minimal. Conversely, in markets where conscious efforts have been made to strengthen the women's social networks, a greater relational capacity among the women will foster their collective action and make revenue bargaining more likely.

Recalling the theoretical model in Figure 3.1, revenue provider motivation and capacity play an important role in whether taxation triggers collective action. *Collective action* is defined as any form of united action taken by a group with a common objective and with the intention to pressure authorities to accede to its demands (Olson, 1965; Bonner, 2009). Such action can range from one-time protests by loose, localized networks to large-scale advocacy efforts by formal organizations. As market revenue collection is mainly governed by local governments in Dar es Salaam, traders who engage in collective action over taxation issues will mostly target these local authorities.

As collective action can be a high-risk activity, especially in the absence of legal protection and social security as is the case in the informal economy (Kabeer et al., 2013), collective organizing may be a necessary first step towards—or even a precondition for—collective action. *Collective organizing* is defined as a process in which people come together to formulate common group interests and goals, mobilize like-minded individuals, and undertake actions that advance the group's agendas—without the aim to pressure authorities to accede to their demands (Lindell, 2010a). Collective organizing can provide the traders with a collective platform—a sense of community and security, and the reassurance of 'being in the right'—all of which may be essential for a structurally marginalized revenue provider group, such as informal women traders, to overcome the multiple barriers to collective action.

In short, the theoretical expectations are that taxation can motivate disadvantaged revenue providers' collective engagement through economic grievances linked to economic hardship and an experienced lack of reciprocity. Situated in disadvantaged positions in the social, economic, and political power structures, it is the revenue providers' organizational and relational capacity that can enable them to translate these grievances into collective organizing and, ultimately, collective action.

3.3 Methodology

This comparative case study has been conducted in Tanzania's largest city, Dar es Salaam, a rapidly growing city with a sizeable informal economy and a large share of informal women workers. By limiting the focus to Dar es Salaam, multiple macro-level historical, social, political, cultural, and economic factors are held constant. At the same time, the study is carried out in seven markets across three municipalities in Dar es Salaam to exploit the variations in taxation and capacity for collective action. Across the municipalities, taxation of market traders varies because the local government in each municipality has the mandate to formulate regulations on market taxation within the municipality. Capacity for collective action varies across the different markets because of the markets' diverse social composition and organizational landscape.

The researched market sites are Mtambani, Magomeni, and Tandale (Kinondoni Municipality); Ilala, Kisutu, and Mchikichini (Ilala Municipality); and Ferry (Kigamboni Municipality). The study is based on interviews and participant observations with 22 women market traders in Dar es Salaam in March–April 2018. Four focus group discussions (FGDs) of four people each and seven in-depth interviews (IDs) were conducted. The interviewees differ in age, educational level, family status, commodity traded, and work history. The participant observations were conducted at a VICOBA (village community bank) group meeting in Ilala and an inauguration event for a VICOBA group in Mchikichini (O1–O2). Cases in which the women reported to collectively having taken united action with the aim of pressuring authorities to accede to their demands are denoted cases of collective action. Cases in which the women have joined or founded an organized group without the intent to influence authorities are denoted cases of collective organizing. Cases in which neither of the above was identified are denoted negative cases.

3.4 Findings

3.4.1 Patterns of collective action and collective organizing

Table 3.1 provides an overview of the identified cross-market patterns in collective action and collective organizing. Of the 22 interviewed women, 12 women had never engaged in collective action or collective organizing (marked by '–' in Table 3.1). Of these 12 women, 11 worked in markets in Kinondoni Municipality, and one worked in Ilala market. The remaining

10 interviewed women were all engaged in collective organizing. Spread across five markets, these women reported engaging in different market-based organized groups. A woman in Tandale participated in a market-based *upatu* group (informal self-lending group) (ID1). In Mchikichini market, two women were members of VICOBA groups (self-loaning groups), and one of these was also a member of cooperative society for kiosk traders in the market (ID2–ID3, O1). Two women in Mchikichini market were members of the National Women Traders Association (NWTA), which, at the time of research, was in the process of registering as a formal organization (NWTA1).[1] In Ilala market, a woman was a member of both a VICOBA group and the NWTA (ID7, NWTA2, O2). In Kisutu market, four women were members of a VICOBA group and a market-based women's association accessible for all women in the market (FGD4). Lastly, in Ferry market, two women were VICOBA group members and also participated in a women's platform, a women-empowerment group in the market and surrounding neighbourhood initiated by the municipal development department (ID4–ID5).

Table 3.1 Patterns of collective organizing and collective action

Municipality	Market	Collective organizing	Collective action	Data source
Kinondoni	*Mtambani*	–	–	FGD1
	Magomeni	–	–	FGD2
	Tandale	–	–	FGD3
		Upatu	–	ID1
Ilala	*Mchikichini*	VICOBA	–	ID3
		VICOBA	Inauguration event	ID2, O2,
		NWTA*	–	NWTA1
		Kiosk cooperative society		ID3
	Ilala	–	–	ID6
		VICOBA	Electricity fee protest	O1, ID7
		NWTA	–	NWTA2
	Kisutu	VICOBA	–	FGD4
		Women's association	–	
Kigamboni	*Ferry*	VICOBA	–	ID4–ID5
		Women's platform	–	

Note: *NWTA is an abbreviation for the National Women Traders Association. FGD stands for focus group discussion, ID is in-depth interview, and O is observation.

[1] As of 2022, the National Women Traders Association is formally registered as an association.

Only two cases of collective action (related to taxation) were identified. The first case of collective action, the electricity fee protest, refers to an event in Ilala market in the beginning of 2018 when the electricity supply was unstable, with the traders sometimes experiencing hour-long power cuts. At this time, the market leadership, headed by a municipal representative, decided to raise the weekly electricity fee in Ilala market by TZS 500 (Tanzanian shillings) for all stall traders. At first, most of the traders accepted this because they expected it to be accompanied by electricity improvements. However, as power cuts kept occurring, the traders became discontented with the lack of improvement and demanded the fee be lowered to the previous level. Therefore, several of the VICOBA groups in Ilala market jointly protested to the market leadership. After a few weeks, the market leadership agreed to lower the electricity fee. A woman that had headed the protest reported that, in her opinion, it was the united front by the VICOBA groups that had forced the market leadership to accede to the traders' demands (ID7, O1). Interestingly, this case illustrates how collective organizing (VICOBA groups) can metamorphose into a vehicle for collective action directed towards municipal authorities.

The second collective action case, the inauguration event, was a one-time event held by a VICOBA group in Mchikichini market (Ilala Municipality). The women wanted to showcase the potential of VICOBA groups for women's empowerment and to draw the local authorities' attention to the challenging economic conditions and gender-related issues experienced by women traders in Mchikichini. For this purpose, the women had managed to invite the District Commissioner of Ilala Municipality and other prominent local government actors. The women held speeches and sang about their concerns to persuade the local government to prioritize women's economic empowerment and to provide better security for women in the market. By the end of event, the women had asked the local government to provide financial support to the VICOBA group to alleviate their economic hardship (O1). Later, a VICOBA member stated that the main sources of their economic hardship were a lack of access to loans and capital, high prices charged by middlemen (*madalali*), low incomes, and high levies charged by the municipality (ID2).

3.4.2 Understanding the patterns

Most of the collective organizing and the two collective action cases are in the markets in Ilala Municipality and in Ferry market in Kigamboni Municipality, whereas the negative cases are mainly located in the markets of

Kinondoni Municipality. In the following, I use the women's experiences of taxation and level of capacity for collective action to explore whether taxation motivated collective action and whether differences in capacity can explain the collective engagement patterns identified above.

3.4.2.1 Motivation: Does taxation trigger collective action and collective organizing, and if so, how?

As argued earlier, taxation can motivate revenue providers' collective engagement if they experience that paying taxes contributes to their *economic hardship*. Table 3.2 shows the market traders' self-reported formal payments that they make to conduct business. Some traders pay on a weekly basis, while others pay every day.

The most noticeable difference is between the vegetable traders in markets in Kinondoni Municipality, who reported paying TZS 1,400–2,900 weekly, and the vegetable traders in Ferry market in Kigamboni Municipality, whose weekly payments amount to TZS 7,000 (FGD1–FGD3, ID4–ID5). In 2018, TZS 1,400 corresponded to about USD 0.6, and now TZS 7,000 is about USD 3. While this may seem a small amount—and a small difference between the highest and lowest payment—it is worth noting that most of the women were small-scale traders reporting to have very low incomes, which meant that even small levy changes were felt. However, since most of the women

Table 3.2 Market traders' self-reported weekly formal payments (Tanzanian shillings (TZS))

Municipality	Market	Self-reported formal payments (weekly)	Patterns of collective organizing (1) and collective action (2)
Kinondoni	*Mtambani*	1,400	–
	Magomeni	2,900–5,000	–
	Tandale	1,750–3,000	1: Upatu group
Ilala	*Mchikichini*	4,200–4,600	1: VICOBA groups, NWTA, Kiosk coop. society 2: Inauguration event
	Ilala	4,900	1: VICOBA, NWTA 2: Electricity fee protest
	Kisutu	4,500	1: VICOBA, women's association
Kigamboni	*Ferry*	7,000	1: VICOBA, women's platform

Note: Data from interviews FGD1–FGD4 and ID1–ID7.

reported not to hold accounts of purchases, sales, or levies paid, it has not been possible to establish exactly how much these weekly payments ate away from the traders' income. This also meant that it was difficult to establish whether the higher formal taxation in Ferry market put a greater economic pressure on the Ferry traders compared to the traders in the other markets.

Women in all markets expressed being under severe economic pressure, and across the cases of collective organizing and action, economic hardship seemed to motivate collective engagement with the prospect of easing the economic pressure (FGD4, ID2–5, O1–O2), among other things. Illustratively, a VICOBA member in Ferry said the following about why she joined the group:

> . . . because you can save up little by little. If you have 2 million TZS [Tanzanian shillings] in shares, you can borrow up to 6 million, and then you are in a position to bring about development. I have been able to take my children to school, I have built a house, and I have bought a land while in VICOBA. (ID4)

In Kisutu market, informal taxation appeared to be a challenge, and some women reported this to be their main reason for joining a VICOBA group. Here, in addition to paying stall rent to Ilala municipal authorities, the women were unlawfully charged between TZS 30,000and 50,000 a month in stall rent by other traders who had previously occupied the stalls. The women said they had complained to the market leadership, but only individually as it had not occurred to them to use the VICOBA group or the women's association to voice their complaints (FGD4). As such, this is an example of taxation issues triggering collective organizing but not collective action. Generally, the women said that this economic hardship could, in part, be ascribed to taxation because they had to pay the formal levies even on days where they did not make any sales. However, taxation seemed to be one of many factors rather than the paramount triggering factor for their collective engagement.

Another way taxation could motivate revenue providers' collective engagement is if they experience a *lack of reciprocity* or unsatisfactory return for their payments. To examine whether this motivation is present, it is first important to understand what the women would expect in return for their tax payment. The women themselves explained that they pay the aforementioned levies to be allowed to conduct business in the market and to cover a range of market services. The women reported that the levies were paid to the local authorities or the market leadership and that the levies were collected by municipal officials, market leadership, or appointed traders. Results differed as to whether

Table 3.3 Market traders' accounts of what their weekly payments are supposed to fund

Municipality	Market	Garbage collection	Cleaning	Security	Electricity	Stall rent	Market infrastructure and repair work
Kinondoni	*Mtambani*	X		X			
	Magomeni	X	X			X	X
	Tandale	X	X	X			X
Ilala	*Mchikichini*	X	X	X			
	Ilala	X			X		
	Kisutu			X		X	
Kigamboni	*Ferry*	X	X	X			

the traders were aware that the rates and purpose of the formal levies figure in municipal bylaws. Table 3.3 shows the traders' accounts of what the weekly payments were supposed to fund.

According to the traders, the formal levies are supposed to fund different types of market services as well as stall rent (FDG1–FDG4, ID1–ID5). Interestingly, results differed quite a bit regarding whether the women were satisfied with the return they got from their payments and whether they experienced a lack of reciprocity on the part of the local government (and sometimes the market leadership). In Mtambani and Ferry markets, the interviewed women were quite satisfied with their returns (ID4–ID5, FDG1). In the other markets, the women expressed significant discontent with the service provision. In Tandale market, the traders said that the payments they made for 'market infrastructure' were supposed to fund a functioning drainage system. However, during the interviews, the women would point to the open sewers with stagnant water and waste surrounding us and say that the local authorities were clearly not upholding their end of the agreement (FDG3). A similar problem was articulated by the women in Magomeni market (FDG2).

Whether this experience of a lack of reciprocity motivated the women's collective engagement varied across the markets. In Magomeni and Tandale markets, the dissatisfaction with the service provision did not trigger any kind of collective engagement; here, only one woman reported to be in an *upatu* group to deal with her economic challenges. Conversely, in other markets, the lack of reciprocity triggered discontent and collective engagement. The electricity fee protest in Ilala market is one such case. Here, the traders were discontented that the increase in electricity fees was not accompanied by electricity improvements, and this made them protest to the market leadership headed by a municipal representative (ID7, O2). The inauguration party in Mchikichini market is another case. Here, the women's complaints to the local government were based on dissatisfaction with the poor state of security for women traders in the market now that they actually paid for security (O2). In the cases of collective organizing, the issues of dire economic conditions and lack of service delivery (in particular, security) contributed to the women's decisions to form and join groups. In these cases, the women said they felt like they had to rely on themselves—and their own organized groups—to handle these challenges (along with the social and gender-related challenges). Arguably, this implicitly speaks to a lack of reciprocity. Most of these traders connected the issues of poor service delivery, substandard market infrastructure, and the experience of having to rely on themselves for tackling these challenges to the issue of a lack of reciprocity on the part of the local government. However, as evidenced, it was only in a few cases that these organized groups metamorphosed into vehicles of collective action to complain to the local authorities about this experienced lack of reciprocity.

Summing up, taxation can motivate collective engagement among revenue providers through the two economic grievances. However, even though almost all the traders said they experienced these grievances, there was quite a variation in the collective engagement: over half of the traders did not participate in any form of collective engagement, and I only identified two cases of actual collective action around taxation. Thus, tax-related grievances do not seem sufficient to *trigger* collective organizing and, particularly, collective action.

3.4.2.2 Capacity: Preconditions for the link between taxation and collective action?

As argued earlier, women traders' collective level of organizational and relational capacity is likely to condition whether they manage to overcome power-related barriers to collective action. In the following, I show how variations in organizational and relational capabilities help explain the negative and positive cases of collective engagement across markets.

3.4.2.2.1 Organizational capacity

First, in the markets where no collective engagement was identified, the organizational capabilities of the women were indeed very limited. For example, in Magomeni market, the women apparently viewed collective organizing as a potential way to address their economic hardship and voice their discontent with their conditions, but they also expressed a lack of knowledge of how to do it in practice. One woman simply put it: 'We do not how to deal with that [collective engagement]' (FGD2). Another woman added: 'The one way, we know, is the way you see us: coming from home to the market here and home again . . . we end up discussing our challenges as normal conversation, but nothing will change [because] us women in this market, we do not have that understanding' (FGD2). As such, the women experienced having a fundamental lack of know-how in organizational development. Moreover, the women expressed having a limited understanding of their rights and a lack of access to information and channels of advocacy. In Magomeni, a woman said: 'Things like groups are not here, and there is no one who can speak for us. There should be a person who could enlighten us, telling us that we as women need to fight for our rights by choosing one person who will speak on our behalf' (FGD2). This quote also offers another interesting insight: the woman talks of an 'us' and 'we as women' illustrating that womanhood, even in spaces without collective engagement, may invoke a sense of community, thus making womanhood a potentially fruitful identity around which to mobilize. I return to the potential of the collective identity of womanhood later.

The women participating in collective engagement had a greater organizational capacity; as such, organizational capacity and engagement seem to reinforce each other. However, from the women's accounts it was evident that their organizational capabilities to some extent had preceded and enabled the emergence of their collective engagement. In Ferry market, for example, one woman had previously participated in vocational and organizational training facilitated by the NGO CARE International. When she started her business in the market, she used her acquired organizational capabilities to mobilize other women traders in Ferry market into forming a VICOBA group to alleviate economic hardship: 'I learnt [with CARE] till I understood about leadership, and now I have the ability to teach other people, and teach them so that they can teach other people' (ID4). Another trader in Ferry indicated that the woman trained by CARE was a decisive human organizational resource: 'Yes, that woman [ID5] was one of the people who influenced me to join [VICOBA]. She gave me information, and we decided that we should work to be like women we always [see] in the news; we should fight to have our own group' (ID4).

In Ilala, Mchikichini, and Kisutu markets, it was the training by a local civil society organization (CSO) called Equality for Growth (EfG) that sparked their organizational capacity. The women in these markets explained that EfG—a CSO established in 2008 with the aim to empower informal women workers in Tanzania—started hosting seminars for the women traders focusing on legal and human rights, advocacy, and building capacity for collective engagement. Later, EfG assisted the women in establishing VICOBA groups, and in 2018, the women traders—primarily centred in the markets of Ilala Municipality—took steps to establish the National Women Traders Association (NWTA) (ID2–ID3, FGD4, ID7, O1–O2, NWTA). The NWTA was registered as an NGO in 2021; has engaged in its first advocacy efforts on behalf of women market traders; and is currently formulating a constitution, building up the internal organization, and accessing funding (Interviews with EfG and the chairperson of NWTA, March–April 2022).

In relation to overcoming barriers to collective engagement, it was evident that most of these women's views on the costs of collective engagement changed as their organizational capacity grew. Previously, they had viewed collective engagement as yet another time-consuming and costly activity, but with the organizational training, most of them said they had learned how to organize in ways that were cost and time efficient (e.g. holding meetings in the market on a regular basis at a time in between peak business hours). As attested by the cases of collective action, some of the women eventually started using their groups as channels of influence to municipal and market authorities. This attests to the fact that organizational capacity—at least over time—can help revenue providers overcome political barriers to collective action and thus become a political resource that the revenue providers can use to their advantage (O1–O2, ID4). It also substantiates that for disadvantaged revenue provider groups there is a certain sequencing in the collective engagement: collective organizing can be a necessary step to overcome, over time, the political barriers of collective action.

3.4.2.2.2 Relational capacity

Starting with Tandale and Magomeni markets where collective engagement was almost non-existent, the women's accounts attested to quite a limited relational capacity. Several women described that there was a lack of social trust in the markets. In Magomeni market, one woman said: 'That relationship of trust, to be honest, is not there. Here, we just know each other, but whenever you encounter a challenge, you will have to deal with it yourself' (FGD2). Interestingly, a woman in Ilala market who did not participate in any form of collective engagement voiced a similar experience: 'Most people here have groups in the streets where they live, because here, they do not trust each other very much' (ID6). Other accounts spoke to a lack of reciprocity. In Tandale market, a woman who had previously been in an *upatu* (self-lending) group said that she had stopped participating because 'people will cheat you . . . they become brutal, because they only receive, but when it's their time to pay, they won't pay' (FDG3). In these contexts marked by a lack of trust and reciprocity, I did not observe a strong sense of community or sense of 'we-ness'. Rather, the social relations seemed to be dominated by an 'every person for herself' notion. Illustratively, when I asked if the traders generally helped each other, one woman responded: 'No! It's like this: If I'm experiencing challenges myself, how can I support someone else who has challenges?' (FGD3). This lack of relational capacity was decisive for the women's lack of collective engagement. In Magomeni market, a woman said it well: 'In this market, there is a lot of selfishness, so it is a bit hard to organize' (FGD2).

Conversely, women participating in collective engagement in Mchikichini, Ilala, Kisutu, and Ferry markets displayed a much greater social capital and often a strong collective identity. Interestingly, the women's relational capacity was not just a product of their collective engagement. Rather, it was evident that their collective engagement was most often preceded and enabled by the women's close, trust-based, and reciprocal social relationships. A woman in Ferry market recounted that it was her friendship with another woman trader in the market that made her want to form a VICOBA group, explaining that they were 'like a family' and helped each other with capital and family-related activities (such as funerals and weddings) (ID5). A woman in Mchikichini market similarly said: 'I was reluctant to join, because I did not get enough information about it. But after I came here, I met other women and they advised me to join VICOBA, so the fear went away, and I became confident and joined' (ID2). Friendships between women traders thus arguably help the women overcome psychological barriers to collective engagement. For the positive cases of collective action, high relational capacity clearly preceded the actual action, as both acts happened under the auspices of well-functioning VICOBA groups.

3.4.2.2.3 The collective identity of womanhood: A strong source of community

Across the markets, it becomes clear that a strong source of community, and the most prevailing and unifying collective identity, was related to the notion of *womanhood*—that is, the perceived commonalities related to being women. The interviews offered several insights into why this was the case. In general, it seems that this notion of womanhood is shaped by patriarchal gender norms and power hierarchies. First, the women's perceived commonality stemmed from their experience that they, as women, had family responsibilities. A woman in Ferry market explained it like this: 'Look, women, like me, we have huge responsibilities . . . . We women should come forward because we have families to take care of' (ID5). Second, the notion of womanhood stemmed from generally being subjected to (and having to navigate) patriarchal gender expectations, which strained the women's participation and influence. In Ilala market, one woman said that if there were both men and women in the room, only the men would discuss and make decisions because men are expected to be discussing and women are expected to not interfere (ID7). Another woman said that she felt more comfortable speaking up when there were women only because experienced men would often discredit the women's perspectives (O2). Third, the sense of community also stemmed from the women's urgent need for physical and psychological security and a safe space free from gender-based harassment, violence, and a lack of respect for women's rights—issues that were widespread across the markets (ID–ID3, O2, FGD4). A woman in Mchikichini market said:

> Here, there has been a lot of harassment and humiliation, and there has been male dominion in the past years. Women used to consider it to be normal to be touched on their body parts.... I used to be timid, thinking that because I am a woman, I can't ask for my rights. If someone did me wrong, I wouldn't speak out, because the place you could report it: it was to the same men [who did me wrong]. (ID3)

Another woman, in Tandale market, said: 'In Tanzania, once a man divorces you, you become of no value . . . women are discriminated [against] a lot in the marketplaces; humiliated, abused, and denied of the right to leadership' (ID1). These often difficult experiences led the women to feel a strong sense of commonality and community with other women. Lastly, a decisive source of community and 'we-ness' among the women was their perception that women, in general, possessed distinctive qualities. Illustratively, an Ilala market trader said: 'You know, women will listen more.... Women are more compassionate' (ID6).

When asked why the women had chosen to participate in collective engagement with other women—and not men—the women would repeatedly return to the commonalities of women. As evident throughout this section, the women would often use phrases such as 'us women', 'we women are the ones . . .', 'as women, we . . .', and 'we women are like a family'. This illustrates the prevalence and potential of the womanhood collective identity among informal women market traders—rather than collective identities related to other social identities such as revenue provider, worker, or self-employed. Combined, these feelings of community, trust, reciprocity, and the collective we-ness among the women appear to help them decisively in overcoming the significant social, psychological, and gendered barriers to collective action present in the Dar es Salaam market contexts.

If womanhood is such a strong source of community, why was it much less pronounced in the markets where no collective engagement was identified? A primary reason seems to be that a collective identity is socially constructed—it must be cultivated. The mere fact that people, women, share the same living conditions does not seem to be sufficient to trigger this unifying notion of womanhood. For the cases of collective organizing, it appears that a trigger of collective identity and social capital can be a human resource within the market or the arrival of an external actor—such as a CSO—who can facilitate the cultivation of social trust, reciprocity, and a sense of community among the women market traders.

3.5 Conclusion

This chapter has delved into the micro-level links between taxation and collective action among urban, informal women market traders in Dar es Salaam—an intersectionally disadvantaged group faced with multiple power-related barriers to collective action (Chen et al., 2002; Clark, 2010; Lindell, 2010a; Meagher, 2010b). Investigating the role of revenue provider motivation and capacity, the chapter contributes to understanding when and how taxation triggers collective action in an informal, gendered context—that is, a context where the revenue providers have limited resources and holding power vis-à-vis the state (see Chapter 2; Meagher, 2018).

The chapter offers several important insights. First, the findings demonstrate that tax-related grievances can serve as triggers for collective organizing and collective action, as shown in previous research (Levi, 1988; Knoke, 1990; Fjeldstad and Semboja, 2001; Prichard, 2015). While taxation might only be one of many components, it appears that the traders generally experience taxation as a contributing factor to their economic hardship, and economic hardship in turn seems to motivate the traders to engage in collective organizing—mainly with the goal of improving their economic conditions. Moreover, most of the traders expressed being discontented with the market infrastructure and service delivery, both of which the traders expected would be covered by the payments they made to the local authorities. For the women experiencing this as a lack of reciprocity on the part of local government, this was clearly a motivational factor for engaging in collective action. As such, taxation does seem to create economic grievances, which in turn motivates both collective organizing and, in fewer cases, collective action.

Second, the study shows that even in the face of severe barriers to collective action, relational and organizational capacity can foster the women traders' ability to translate their grievances into collective engagement. Organizational capacity, which is a political resource, in particular helps the women overcome time constraints and economic barriers to collective engagement. Over time, high organizational capacity may enable the women to overcome political barriers to collective action and to start using organized groups as channels of influence to local authorities. Relational capacity, which is a social resource, is important for this intersectionally disadvantaged group to overcome psychological, social, and gendered barriers to collective action. In this particular case, the traders' social capital and collective identity are based to a significant degree on the notion of 'womanhood'; as such, the shared experience of being women appears to provide a strong sense of community that provides an identificational foundation for the women's collective engagement. If cultivated, this shared sense of womanhood can be a significant social resource for the women—a group whose economic and political resources tend to be limited on a structural level. Relatedly, the variations in the women's collective engagement across markets indicate that even within a bounded local context and a single revenue provider group, capacity appears to vary. This emphasizes the importance of paying attention to micro-level differences if we want to know more about when taxation triggers collective action. Moreover, corresponding with recent research (Sharp et al., 2019; van den Boogaard et al., 2022), the findings suggest that external civil society organizations, such as the women's organization Equality for Growth, have the potential to act as *enablers* of collective engagement; *translators* of inaccessible rules and information; and *trainers* of legal, social, and economic empowerment among traditionally revenue provider groups.

Lastly, the findings indicate that for this revenue provider group, there may be a degree of sequencing between collective organizing and collective action. Collective *organizing* can provide a platform for strengthening their social relations, vocational practices, access to capital, awareness of rights, and belief that they are entitled to get something in return for the taxes they pay. Over time, it appears that even small-scale collective organizing can become a vehicle for collective *action*, where the women voice social accountability demands to the local power-holders. Ultimately, collective organizing can provide women market traders with social, economic, and political resources, which increases their bargaining power. Compared to non-organized women market traders, this puts them in a stronger bargaining position vis-à-vis the local government, to engage in revenue bargaining and perhaps eventually assert themselves and their demands in contractual fiscal relations.

These findings suggest that further theorization and exploration of taxpayer motivation and capacity for collective action is needed. A better understanding of when and why taxation motivates revenue providers to engage in collective action is necessary for answering when and how revenue bargaining emerges, evolves, and leads to fiscal contracts.

References

Bonner, C. 2009. *Collective Action for Informal Workers (ICCC6)*, no. 6, Organising in the Informal Economy: Resource Books for Organiser. Cambridge, MA: WIEGO.

Bräutigam, D. A. 2008. 'Introduction: Taxation and State-Building in Developing Countries'. In *Taxation and State-Building in Developing Countries*, edited by D. Bräutigam, O.-H. Fjeldstad, and M. Moore, pp. 1–33. Cambridge: Cambridge University Press. https://doi.org/10.1017/CBO9780511490897.001.

Broms, R. 2015. 'Putting Up or Shutting Up: On the Individual-Level Relationship between Taxpaying and Political Interest in a Developmental Context'. *The Journal of Development Studies* 51(1): pp. 93–109.

Brown, A., M. Lyons, and I. Dankoco. 2010. 'Street Traders and the Emerging Spaces for Urban Voice and Citizenship in African Cities'. *Urban Studies* 47(3): pp. 666–683. https://doi.org/10.1177/0042098009351187.

Capraro, C. 2017. *Rights and Realities: A Briefing on Women and the Economy*. London: Womankind Worldwide. https://www.womankind.org.uk/wp-content/uploads/2020/08/Rights-and-Realities_A-briefing-on-women-and-the-economy.pdf.

Chant, S., and C. Pedwell. 2008. *Women, Gender and the Informal Economy: An Assessment of ILO Research and Suggested Ways Forward*. Geneva: International Labour Office. http://www.ilo.org/gender/Informationresources/WCMS_091605/lang--en/index.htm.

Chen, M., R. Jhabvala, R. Kanbur, and C. Richards. 2007. *Membership-Based Organizations of the Poor*, 1st edn. London: Routledge. https://doi.org/10.4324/9780203934074.

Chen, M. A., R. Jhabvala, and F. Lund. 2002. *Supporting Workers in the Informal Economy: A Policy Framework*. Geneva: International Labour Office. http://www.ilo.org/employment/Whatwedo/Publications/WCMS_122055/lang—en/index.htm.

Chen, M. A., and D. Snodgrass. 2001. *Managing Resources, Activities, and Risk in Urban India: The Impact of SEWA Bank*. Washington, DC: Assessing the Impact of

Microenterprise Services (AIMS), 216. https://www.wiego.org/sites/default/files/publications/files/Chen-Snodgrass-AIMS-Study-of-SEWA-Bank.pdf.

Clark, G. 2010. 'Gender Fictions and Gender Tensions Involving "Traditional" Asante Market Women'. *African Studies Quarterly* 11(2/3): p. 43.

Fjeldstad, O.-H., and J. Semboja. 2001. 'Why People Pay Taxes: The Case of the Development Levy in Tanzania'. *World Development* 29(12): pp. 2059–2074.

Fujii, L. A. 2008. 'The Power of Local Ties: Popular Participation in the Rwandan Genocide'. *Security Studies* 17(3): pp. 568–597. https://doi.org/10.1080/09636410802319578.

Gallien, M., and V. van den Boogaard. 2020. *Unpacking Formalisation: The Need for a New Research Agenda on Taxation and the Informal Economy*. ICTD—International Centre for Tax Development, 21 April. https://www.ictd.ac/blog/unpacking-formalisation-need-new-research-agenda-taxation-informal-economy/.

Ganz, M. 2010. Leading Change: Leadership, Organization, and Social Movements. *Handbook of Leadership Theory and Practice* 19: pp. 1–10.

Giddens, A. 1984. *The Constitution of Society: Outline of the Theory of Structuration*. Berkeley, CA: University of California Press.

IMED (Institute of Management and Entrepreneurship Development) (2016). *A Study on the Informal Sector with a View to Formalisation*. Paper presented to the BEST-Dialogue.

International Labour Office. 2014. *Transitioning from the Informal to the Formal Economy*. International Labour Conference, 103rd Session. Geneva: International Labour Office. https://www.ilo.org/wcmsp5/groups/public/---ed_norm/---relconf/documents/meetingdocument/wcms_218128.pdf.

Jagero, N., and I. Kushoka. 2011. 'Challenges Facing Women Micro Entrepreneurs in Dar es Salaam, Tanzania'. *International Journal of Human Resource Studies* 1(2): pp. 1–9. https://doi.org/10.5296/ijhrs.v1i2.1023.

Johnston-Anumonwo, I., and D. L. Doane. 2011. 'Globalization, Economic Crisis and Africa's Informal Economy Women Workers'. *Singapore Journal of Tropical Geography* 32(1): pp. 8–21.

Joshi, A. 2017. *Tax and Gender in Developing Countries: What are the Issues?* ICTD. https://www.ictd.ac/publication/ictd-sumbrief6/.

Joshi, A., and J. Ayee. 2008. 'Associational Taxation: A Pathway into the Informal Sector?' In *Taxation and State-Building in Developing Countries*, edited by D. Bräutigam, O.-H. Fjeldstad, and M. Moore, pp. 183–211. Cambridge: Cambridge University Press. https://doi.org/10.1017/CBO9780511490897.008.

Joshi, A., W. Prichard, and C. Heady. 2014. 'Taxing the Informal Economy: The Current State of Knowledge and Agendas for Future Research'. *The Journal of Development Studies* 50(10): pp. 1325–1347.

Kabeer, N., R. M. Sudarshan, and K. Milward, eds. 2013. *Organizing Women Workers in the Informal Economy: Beyond the Weapons of the Weak*. London: Zed Books.

Kayuza, H. M. 2006. *Real Property Taxation in Tanzania: An Investigation on Implementation and Taxpayer Perceptions*. Stockholm: Building and Real Estate Economics, Royal Institute of Technology (KTH).

Knoke, D. 1990. *Organizing for Collective Action: The Political Economies of Associations*. New York: Aldine de Gruyter.

Levi, M. 1988. *Of Rule and Revenue*, vol. 13. Berkeley, CA: University of California Press. https://www.jstor.org/stable/10.1525/j.ctt1pngtk.

Lindell, I. 2010a. *Africa's Informal Workers: Collective Agency, Alliances and Transnational Organizing in Urban Africa*. London: Zed Books.

Lindell, I. 2010b. 'Informality and Collective Organising: Identities, Alliances and Transnational Activism in Africa'. *Third World Quarterly* 31(2): pp. 207–222. https://doi.org/10.1080/01436591003711959.

Lyons, M., A. Brown, and C. Msoka. 2009. *Multiple Reform Agendas and the African Street: What Makes Tanzania's Micro-Traders Illegal?* IDEAR Working Paper 2009/4. London: South Bank University. http://www.lsbu.ac.uk/__data/assets/pdf_file/0007/9556/what-makes-tanzanias-microtraders-illegal-refugee-studies-research-working-paper.pdf.

Martin, L. 2013. 'Taxation and Accountability: Experimental Evidence for Taxation's Effect on Citizen Behavior'. *Workshop on African Political Economy*, Washington, DC. http://cega.berkeley.edu/assets/cega_events/55/Martin_WGAPE-WB.pdf.

Meagher, K. 2009. *Culture, Agency and Power: Theoretical Reflections on Informal Economic Networks and Political Process*. DIIS Working Paper 2009/27. Copenhagen: Danish Institute for International Studies (DIIS).

Meagher, K. 2010a. 'The Empowerment Trap: Gender, Poverty and the Informal Economy in Sub-Saharan Africa'. In *The International Handbook of Gender and Poverty*, edited by S. Chant, pp. 472–477. Cheltenham, UK: Edward Elgar Publishing. https://www.elgaronline.com/view/edcoll/9781848443341/9781848443341.00088.xml.

Meagher, K. 2010b. 'The Politics of Vulnerability: Exit, Voice and Capture in Three Nigerian Informal Manufacturing Clusters'. In *Africa's Informal Workers: Collective Agency, Alliances and Transnational Organizing in Urban Africa*, edited by I. Lindell, pp. 46–64. London: Zed Books.

Meagher, K. 2018. 'Taxing Times: Taxation, Divided Societies and the Informal Economy in Northern Nigeria'. *The Journal of Development Studies* 54(1): pp. 1–17.

Moore, M. 2004. 'Revenues, State Formation, and the Quality of Governance in Developing Countries'. *International Political Science Review* 25(3): pp. 297–319.

Olken, B. A., and M. Singhal. 2011. 'Informal Taxation'. *American Economic Journal: Applied Economics* 3(4): pp. 1–28.

Olson, M. 1965. *The Logic of Collective Action: Public Goods and the Theory of Groups*. Cambridge, MA: Harvard University Press.

Polletta, F., and J. M. Jasper. 2001. 'Collective Identity and Social Movements'. *Annual Review of Sociology* 27(1): pp. 283–305. https://doi.org/10.1146/annurev.soc.27.1.283.

Prichard, W. 2015. *Taxation, Responsiveness and Accountability in Sub-Saharan Africa: The Dynamics of Tax Bargaining*. Cambridge: Cambridge University Press. https://doi.org/10.1017/CBO9781316275511.

Prichard, W., and V. van den Boogaard. 2017. 'Norms, Power, and the Socially Embedded Realities of Market Taxation in Northern Ghana'. *African Studies Review* 60(1): pp. 171–194.

Prud'homme, R. 1992. 'Informal Local Taxation in Developing Countries'. *Environment and Planning C: Government and Policy* 10(1): pp. 1–17. https://doi.org/10.1068/c100001.

Putnam, R. D., R. Leonardi, and R. Y. Nanetti. 1994. *Making Democracy Work: Civic Traditions in Modern Italy*. Princeton, NJ: Princeton University Press. https://press.princeton.edu/books/paperback/9780691037387/making-democracy-work.

Roever, S. 2014. *Informal Economy Monitoring Study Sector Report: Street Vendors*. Cambridge, MA: WIEGO.

Sewell, W. H. 1992. 'A Theory of Structure: Duality, Agency, and Transformation'. *American Journal of Sociology* 98(1): pp. 1–29.

Sharp, S., S. Sweet, and A. R. Menocal. 2019. *Civil Society Engagement in Tax Reform*. London: Overseas Development Institute. https://cdn.odi.org/media/documents/12926.pdf.

Snow, D. A., and S. A. Soule. 2010. *A Primer on Social Movements*. New York: W.W. Norton.

Timmons, J. F. 2005. 'The Fiscal Contract: States, Taxes, and Public Services'. *World Politics* 57(4): pp. 530–567.

van den Boogaard, V., W. Prichard, R. Beach, and F. Mohiuddin. 2022. 'Enabling Tax Bargaining: Supporting More Meaningful Tax Transparency and Taxpayer Engagement in Ghana and Sierra Leone'. *Development Policy Review* 40(1): pp. 1–22. https://doi.org/10.1111/dpr.12563.

van den Boogaard, V., W. Prichard, and S. Jibao. 2019. 'Informal Taxation in Sierra Leone: Magnitudes, Perceptions and Implications'. *African Affairs* 118(471): pp. 259–284.

Vanek, J., M. A. Chen, and G. Raveendran. 2015. *A Guide to Obtaining Data on Types of Informal Workers in Official Statistics*. Cambridge, MA: WIEGO.

WIEGO. 2014. *The Urban Informal Workforce: Street Vendors*. Cambridge, MA: WIEGO.

4

Triggers and strategies of revenue bargaining

Evidence from Mozambican municipalities

Armin von Schiller

> There is only one hope. If more people believe in what we are doing, they'll start paying tax. That will be our budget. Then we can start to rebuild.
>
> **Araujo, Mayor of Quelimane, in a BBC interview in 2013[1]**

4.1 Introduction

Revenue bargaining implies an explicit or implicit negotiation between a government and revenue providers (see Chapters 1 and 2 in this volume). When considering revenue bargaining and fiscal contracts, there is a natural tendency to focus on national governments as they control most of the public revenue. However, revenue bargaining also happens at the international as well as subnational levels, and, in order to better understand revenue bargaining, it seems that the subnational level is a particularly promising avenue of investigation. Most citizens feel that national and international bargaining processes are reserved for more powerful actors.[2] Their own power and influence will tend to be perceived as higher at the subnational level. In addition, incentives to engage in revenue bargaining might also be stronger at this level because, beyond expected influence, the links between revenue and public services are stronger and more visible here.

Based on this idea, this chapter explores drivers of revenue bargaining based on a comparative analysis of Mozambican municipalities. The focus is

[1] Johnson (2013).
[2] See discussion on dimensions of bargaining power in Chapter 2.

Armin von Schiller, *Triggers and strategies of revenue bargaining*. In: *The Politics of Revenue Bargaining in Africa*.
Edited by: Anne Mette Kjær, Marianne S. Ulriksen, and Ane Karoline Bak, Oxford University Press.
 DOI: 10.1093/oso/9780192868787.003.0004

on the role of factors connected to the concept of political settlements, which has received little attention so far in understanding the tax performance of subnational units (Kjær, 2009; Jibao and Prichard, 2015). Mozambique is a particularly appealing case for this explorative analysis as it is a highly polarized political environment combined with some level of political and fiscal decentralization. As a consequence, a disputed decentralization process over recent decades has led to the creation of 53 municipalities, with some remarkable autonomy in decision-making around taxation coupled with locally elected municipal governments.

In particular, the chapter aims to improve the understanding of two aspects: what triggers municipalities to reach out to citizens and initiate revenue-bargaining processes, and what strategies do they employ, including explanations of the differences in intensity and use. In addition, it assesses the degree to which these activities appear to be successful and actually influence the content of the municipal fiscal contract as the expected final outcome of revenue bargaining (see Chapter 2).

To answer these questions, data was collected from 101 semi-structured interviews conducted in Mozambique with representatives of municipal and national-level government. At the municipal level, interviewees included members of the municipal government, the municipal assembly, local administration, and civil society organizations (CSOs). At the national level, academic experts, representatives of different ministries involved in the decentralization process, and international donors were interviewed. The sample of municipalities included 11 out of the 53 municipalities in Mozambique, including diverse municipalities in terms of size, province, and intra-municipal level of political competition as well as political alignment with the national government.

The results indicate that two factors trigger the predisposition of municipalities to reach out to citizens and initiate revenue-bargaining processes: perceived revenue pressure and political competition (see Chapter 2). Prichard (2015) extensively discusses the relevance of the level of revenue pressure facing governments on their predisposition to bargain. In essence, a government facing stronger revenue pressure is more likely to be open to compromise with taxpayers in order to access revenue. In this analysis, revenue pressure increases for the municipalities as a result of the uncertainty regarding the timeliness and size of intergovernmental transfers. This effect is particularly strong in municipalities governed by parties not in power at the national level. Hence, the results suggest that the potential politicization of the transfer system is a main determinant of revenue pressure.[3] Political

[3] Evidence on politicization of the transfer system can, for instance, be found in Banful (2011) and Brollo and Nannicini (2012).

competition triggers revenue bargaining by increasing the pressure on local governments to show themselves as performing well. Although this factor is identified as relevant in all municipalities, it appears to be particularly strong in municipalities governed by opposition parties.

In terms of strategies, the interview material indicates that among representatives of local governments and administrations, the narrative around a more cooperative approach with citizens is present everywhere but is somehow stronger in municipalities characterized by political competition. This positive perspective towards revenue bargaining does not, however, seem to result in concrete measures. Conversations with representatives of CSOs do not, on the whole, confirm the alleged efforts. When comparing perceptions in municipalities with a lower and higher degree of political competition, the differences are also minimal. Similarly, while self-reported initiatives around revenue bargaining by the municipalities differ between low- and high-competition environments, these seem not to be particularly successful and do not result in substantial variation in the revenue bargaining taking place at the local level. Also, in many cases, it seems that initiatives were driven externally and, in particular, by donors, which may explain the lack of identifiable success.

Overall, this chapter contributes to the growing effort to understand the politics of revenue bargaining by focusing on identifying factors shaping the predisposition of local governments to bargain. The analysis also indicates limitations on measures in this area and the necessity of thinking carefully about preconditions if revenue bargaining is to work. Following from this, the results also carry relevant policy implications. Enhancing revenue mobilization and promoting revenue bargaining is high on the agenda of international donors. This is also based on the assumption—only partly backed up in the literature—that revenue bargaining can have a substantial governance 'dividend' by affecting politicians' responsiveness and citizens' engagement in public affairs, ultimately leading to more accountable government institutions (see Chapter 1; Fjeldstad, 2014; Moore et al., 2018, chapter 8). The results presented in this chapter call for caution and for thinking carefully about preconditions for revenue bargaining to emerge and for it to represent a meaningful process, able to bring the aforementioned desirable outcomes. In particular, the analysis shows how—where CSOs are too weak to coordinate and represent revenue providers—the outlook for the success of any initiatives around revenue bargaining is slim, even if we assume the political authorities instigated them with good intentions. This is connected to the accepted premise that lack of capacity for collective action undermines the potential for bargaining (Prichard, 2015).

The chapter proceeds as follows. Section 4.2 describes the political context and the decentralized system in Mozambique in order to understand the context in which municipalities operate. Section 4.3 provides details on the methodological approach, before the results are presented in Section 4.4. Section 4.5 concludes.

4.2 Fiscal and political decentralization system in Mozambique

Mozambique has been in an ongoing process of decentralization since the peace accords of 1992. In fact, political and fiscal decentralization represented a crucial part of the peace negotiations (Ames et al., 2010, 103; Maschietto, 2016). However, the decentralization process, especially in its fiscal and political dimension, turned out to be less ambitious than initially envisioned. It took until 1997 to establish autonomous municipal governments in Mozambique (Weimer, 2012, 4). The main reason was political in nature. The Resistência Nacional Moçambicana (RENAMO, Mozambican National Resistance) received unexpected electoral support in the northern and central rural areas at the first multi-party elections in 1994. The potential loss of power in the event of decentralization led the Frente de Libertação de Moçambique (FRELIMO, Mozambican Liberation Front) to contest the planned ambitious decentralization model, which was then reformulated in a new compromise with RENAMO (Forquilha, 2016, 130; Maschietto, 2016, 109).

As a result, a dual-structured system of local governance was introduced by law number 9/96, and in Mozambique, two types of decentralization coexist: devolution and deconcentration (Buur, 2009, 99; Maschietto, 2016, 105). Municipalities (*autarquias locais*) represent the devolution aspect of the system. They have autonomous political power and control a remarkable number of revenue instruments. At the other end of the spectrum, provinces, districts, and localities represent the deconcentrated part of the system. At the time this research was undertaken, deconcentrated units lacked autonomous political power, were directly accountable to the central state, and controlled only a limited number of revenue instruments.[4]

[4] This was changed by a constitutional reform in 2018 (after the time of this research), by which assemblies at all levels are now directly elected and subsequently elect the head of the subnational executive out of their members. How or whether this new change in political decentralization will be matched in fiscal terms is unclear and is the subject of debate at the time of writing.

Table 4.1 Year of establishment and types of municipalities

Year of creation	Municipality	Type of municipality
1997	Maputo	A
	Matola, Beira, Nampula	B
	Xai-Xai, Inhambane, Chimoio, Tete, Quelimane, Lichinga, Nacala, Ilha de Moçambique, Pemba	C
	Chokwe, Chibuto, Maxixe, Manica, Dondo, Mocuba, Gurue, Angoche, Montepuez, Cuamba	D
	Manhiça, Mandlakazi, Vilankulo, Catandica, Marromeu, Moatize, Milange, Monapo, Metangula, Mocimboa da Praia	*Vilas*
2008	Namaacha, Macia, Massinga, Gorongoza, Gondola, Ulongue, Ribaue, Alto Molocue, Moeda, Marupa	*Vilas*
2013	Boane, Praia do Bilene, Quissico, Sussundenga, Nhamatanda, Nhamayabue, Maganja da Costa, Malema, Chiure, Mandimba	*Vilas*

Source: Law no. 10/97 (República de Moçambique, 1997); Law no. 11/2013 (República de Moçambique, 2013); MAEFP, (2016)

Given the focus of this chapter on the effect of factors connected to political settlement on shaping revenue bargaining at the local level, the empirical analysis is centred on Mozambican municipalities, as, in comparison to deconcentrated units, they control substantial tax handles and have some degree of freedom in setting up their strategies and priorities. As shown in Table 4.1, 53 municipalities have been established since then in three waves (1997, 2008, and 2013).[5]

The Ministério da Administração Estatal e Função Pública (MAEFP, Ministry of State Administration and Public Function) divides all municipalities into the following five categories based on a series of vaguely defined socio-economic and political indicators: type A, the capital city Maputo; type B, the largest provincial capitals besides Maputo; type C, the capitals of all other provinces as well as two other cities; type D, cities that are particularly relevant to the local development of broader regions; and *vilas*, towns that do not qualify for category D (MAEFP, 2016, 28). According to the MAEFP, around one third of the Mozambican population lives in municipalities. Moreover,

[5] These 53 municipalities include all of the country's 23 cities and 30 out of 68 towns (MAEFP, 2016). In theory, the establishment of new municipalities should be based on technical arguments following the official policy, pursued since 1997, of *gradualismo* (Buur, 2009). However, the decision about where to create new municipalities has been identified to be largely driven by political reasons and FRELIMO's incentive to favour its own strongholds and avoid potential loss of political power (Forquilha, 2016).

60% of Mozambique's GDP and 85% of its fiscal revenues are generated in municipalities (MAEFP, 2016, 26),

Law number 1/2008 (Art. 17; República de Moçambique, 2008b) and decree number 63/2008 (República de Moçambique, 2008a) define the fiscal competencies of the municipalities at the time this study was undertaken. The most prominent taxes are the municipal poll tax (Imposto Pessoal Autárquico—IPA), the municipal property tax (Imposto Predial Autárquico—IPRA), the municipal property transaction tax (Imposto Autárquico de SISA—IASISA), and the municipal vehicle tax (Imposto Autárquico sobre Veículos—IAV). It is important to highlight that discretionary revenue policy is limited. A significantly larger degree of discretion can be exercised in the realm of non-tax revenue—meaning fees, service charges, fines, and short-term loans—than when it comes to taxes, for which, in most cases, general principles are determined according to national law (World Bank, 2014, 109).

As is the case in many African countries (see Moore et al., 2018, 159), although municipalities have several instruments with which to generate their own revenue, they are highly dependent on intergovernmental transfers. On average, transfers represent well above 65% of revenue. In reality, this number is probably much higher as available information tends to come from bigger cities with more capable administration and higher revenue potential. In this sense, the weight of transfers is especially high when it comes to municipalities of type D, with a level around 90% (Ilal and Weimer, 2017; Weimer and Carrilho, 2017, 88).

Data quality and availability are poor in Mozambique, but aggregating the evidence from individual case studies suggests that municipal revenue potential is highly underexploited (Chimunuane et al., 2010b; 2010a; Boex, 2011; Nguenha et al., 2012; 2017; Weimer, 2012; Bunk et al., 2017; Weimer and Carrilho, 2017).

Politically, Mozambique is a highly polarized country. Its political settlement can be considered to have gradually shifted over recent decades towards more exclusion and centralization of power and resources. At the same time, competition between factions within the ruling coalition has increased, as well as among the opposition, which is far from united.[6] At the national level, FRELIMO has been in power since 1994. At the municipal level, however, opposition parties have been able to win some municipal elections, held in

[6] See extensive analysis of the historical development of the political settlement in Mozambique in Macuane et al. (2018).

1998, 2003, 2008, 2013, and 2018 (MAEFP, 2016, 7).[7] Since 2009, the Movimento Democrático de Moçambique (MDM), which evolved from within RENAMO, has been challenging the country's bipartisan political system.[8] In the municipal elections of 2013, which RENAMO boycotted, MDM won the majority of votes in four municipalities located in the north and the centre of Mozambique (Beira, Quelimane, Nampula, and Gurué), whereas FRELIMO won the remaining 49 municipalities. In 2018, RENAMO participated again in the local elections. MDM suffered a remarkable loss of votes and only kept control of its stronghold Beira. RENAMO won in eight municipalities, including in big influential cities such as Nampula, Quelimane, and Nacala.[9] FRELIMO still dominates in the vast majority of municipalities. Its power base was confirmed again in the 2019 presidential election in which it reached a support of around 73% of the electorate, although irregularities were denounced.[10]

Overall, this section has offered some background to the polarization of the political system in Mozambique as well as the fiscal architecture within which the municipalities operate. It also highlights that local revenue potential remains highly underused. Together, these features indicate the relevance of exploring what leads municipalities to pursue local revenue mobilization in general and revenue bargaining with their citizens in particular.

4.3 Methodological approach

The nature of this study is explorative. The main goal is to understand better what factors trigger local governments to engage in revenue bargaining with citizens and how they do it. To answer these questions, 101 semi-structured in-depth interviews were conducted with a range of stakeholders. The list of interviewees includes municipal government officials, municipal administrators, staff from national ministries and agencies, civil society actors, international donors, and academic experts. The interviews were conducted in Maputo (with national experts) and in 11 municipalities between February and May 2017.[11]

[7] At the national level, the first democratic presidential and parliamentary elections took place in 1994 and are held regularly every five years (Bertelsmann Stiftung, 2016, 7). In all presidential and parliamentary elections, FRELIMO gained the majority of the votes.

[8] For further details concerning the emergence of the MDM party, see Maihack and Plagemann (2010).

[9] Comissão Nacional de Eleições (2018).

[10] For instance, by the European Union Election Observation Mission (2019).

[11] Interviews were conducted by all members of the project 'The Political Economy of Local Taxation in Mozambique', listed in the acknowledgments.

Table 4.2 Municipalities selected as cases for the comparative analysis

Municipality	Province	Type of municipality	Political leadership at the local level (as of 2017)
Matola	Maputo	B	Aligned
Inhambane	Inhambane	C	Aligned
Maxixe	Inhambane	D	Aligned
Beira	Sofala	B	Non-aligned
Dondo	Sofala	D	Aligned
Quelimane	Zambézia	C	Non-aligned
Nacala	Nampula	C	Aligned
Monapo	Nampula	*Vila*	Aligned
Pemba	Cabo Delgado	C	Aligned
Xai-Xai	Gaza	C	Aligned
Vilankulo	Inhambane	*Vila*	Aligned

Note: Aligned equals ruled by FRELIMO; non-aligned equals ruled by MDM.

The municipalities were selected based on the diverse cases selection strategy (George and Bennett, 2005, 83). Hence, in order to assure maximum variation in the variables of interest, the sample includes municipalities from different provinces, characterized by different levels of administrative capacity, political competition, and political alignment (See Table 4.2).[12] Administrative capacity is proxied by the type of municipality, with cities of type B being considered to have the highest capacity, while type D municipalities and so-called *vilas* have the lowest (see the previous section for information on legal basis for the different types of cities). Municipalities are considered aligned if the municipality is governed by the same party in power at the national level (FRELIMO).[13] Political competition is measured by the margin of victory in the municipal elections to identify strongholds versus more competitive political environments.

In 2019, local elections took place in Mozambique. As this was after the data collection, these election results could not be considered; however, the two municipalities labelled as 'non-aligned' in this study remained as such after the 2019 elections.[14] Also, the level of political competition and the distribution of political power remained similar in all other

[12] It is also important to underline that practical issues, including accessibility, security concerns, and data availability before the interview phase, also affected the case selection. We particularly rely on data provided by GIZ (2017).

[13] At the time of data collection, four out of a total of 53 municipalities were governed by opposition parties. Two of them (Beira and Quelimane) are represented in the sample.

[14] In Quelimane, RENAMO won with 59% of the vote, while in Beira, MDM won again with 48% of the vote (Comissão Nacional de Eleições, 2018).

municipalities included in the sample. Particularly noteworthy was that in Nacala, RENAMO regained power by a small margin and that in the disputed municipalities of Monapo and Matola, FRELIMO won but with a very narrow margin. This further reinforces the idea that these were particularly competitive environments at the time of this data collection.

In all municipalities, interviews were held with the same set of actors.[15] In terms of politicians, the mayor and (sometimes or) the councillor for finance were contacted. The municipal assembly, including members from different political parties, was also approached. In the administration, the head of finances or revenue and a member of the broader revenue team were interviewed. In most cases, support from the donor organization was helpful when making contact with the interviewees. A less standardized approach was used to contact CSOs. In most cases, the initial contact was through donors or research partners in Mozambique. The semi-structured interviews were run based on guidelines developed for specific types of actors.[16] Topics addressed included perceptions about the funding situation of the municipality, challenges in exploiting revenue potential and the degree to which revenue is an issue of public debate, and information on activities to reach out to citizens and explain to them how revenue systems work and how money is spent, as well as the degree to which political considerations affect the interaction between local governments and citizens regarding revenue matters. All interviewees were asked for their consent and assured confidentiality. Normally, two researchers from the team participated in the interview. In the vast majority of the cases, a translator was involved.

4.4 Identified triggers and strategies of revenue bargaining

4.4.1 Triggers to pursue local tax collection: Perceived revenue pressure and political competition

The analysis of the interview material strongly indicates that there are two major triggers that explain the predisposition of municipal governments to engage in revenue bargaining: the unreliability of the fiscal transfer system and political competition.

[15] You can find an overview of the interview partners by municipality and type of actor in the Appendix (Tables 4.A1 and 4.A2).

[16] Guidelines can be provided upon request.

4.4.1.1 Perceived revenue pressure

With regard to revenue pressure, the main problem is the uncertainty related to the timeliness and predictability of transfer payments. Not receiving the payments on time makes it hard for municipalities to deal with the implementation of their policies. Furthermore, the punctuality of payments affects the municipalities' ability to act according to their financial plans. Fear of this makes them more attentive to the potential of raising own revenue as this is seen as the way out of dependence on transfers from central government. Furthermore, it opens up more financial space for financing activities that the municipal government values as being relevant. While aligned municipalities can rely more on the government and might have an incentive to lower the burden on citizens in order not to antagonize them, in non-aligned municipalities, the necessity of gaining financial independence overshadows the risk of antagonizing citizens.

A large number of interviews revealed that although timeliness is an issue in general, non-aligned municipalities in particular face this challenge with regard to both discretionary and non-discretionary transfers. Since 2015, Mozambique's overall economic and financial situation has worsened, with the consequence that delays of transfers generally affect all municipalities. However, opposition municipal governments had experienced these uncertainties for years prior to the start of the crisis (e.g. I6, donor employee; I77, member of Quelimane municipal assembly).

According to the interviews, the delay differs in terms of length among municipalities and for both discretionary and non-discretionary transfers. For example, an interviewee indicated that transfers of the Fundo de Estradas of 2015 and 2016 for the non-aligned municipality of Beira had not been fully disbursed by the time the interview took place in March 2017 (I59, member of Beira municipal government). Furthermore, transfers were paid at the end of the year instead of regular payments every three months (I56, public administrator in Beira). Besides Beira, representatives of the municipal assembly and public administrator in Quelimane, the other non-aligned municipality in the sample, claimed to be facing delays of transfers such as the Fundo de Compensação Autárquica (FCA), the Fundo de Investimento de Iniciativa Autárquica (FIIA), and especially the Fundo de Estradas (I73, I75, and I77).[17] This tone was consistent among the interviews in non-aligned municipalities with very diverse actors and was often linked to the appreciation and importance of own revenue mobilization. In aligned municipalities, the delay was

[17] Some voices from donor employees supported this point (e.g. prominently I1).

not perceived as a particularly salient issue, although some claimed to have experienced it.

Several interviewees expressed explicitly that, with regard to transfers, the non-aligned municipalities were treated differently for political reasons. The following quote by a member of the municipal assembly of Quelimane illustrates this point:

> Delays have been the case even before the economic crisis. This has political reasons. Where an opposition party rules, transfers are not channelled the same way as compared to municipalities ruled by the party in power at the national level. (I77, member of Quelimane municipal assembly).

> Also a donor employee stated very clearly that: if you are in opposition, then they will delay the disbursements (...) so that you cannot implement your programme. They do it. It is a *common sense* issue. (I32, donor employee).

The degree to which the perception of unequal treatment between aligned and non-aligned municipalities is true is difficult to assess. In fact, available numbers do not provide strong evidence that transfers have been politically biased. Based on a comparison of transfer data within individual types of municipalities, provided in Ilal and Weimer (2017), the claim of an unequal distribution of non-discretionary transfers cannot be confirmed. It is relevant to underline, however, that potentially biased treatment with regard to punctuality of payment, a key aspect for municipalities, cannot be assessed because comprehensive data are missing. Also, data on other measures that the government can use to support municipalities—such as on material donations, capacity building for municipal employees, technical support through national-level experts, and funds for specific purposes—are not available. In fact, it is precisely on these aspects for which we lack data that the accounts presented in aligned and non-aligned municipalities differ most substantially and about which non-aligned municipalities complain most vehemently.

While interviewees from all groups in aligned municipalities explicitly mention that they receive support from the central government in different areas, in non-aligned municipalities interviewees indicate that they receive little support from the central government. Furthermore, non-aligned municipalities claim that the central government is not responsive to their requests and does not provide comprehensive reasons when refusing requests, a point that was confirmed by politicians, public administrators, and CSOs in Quelimane and Beira (I55, I56, I58, I60, I62, I74, and I77). Overall, it is true that the system can be labelled as opaque. Furthermore, beyond transfers as such, public administrators and politicians in non-aligned municipalities also perceive that the central government tries to direct donor activities and investments away from them to aligned municipalities (I55, I56, and I62).

Beyond the factual question of whether there is unequal treatment or not, the interviews show that non-aligned municipalities perceive themselves as being treated unfairly and that in instances of increasing resource scarcity, they believe that they will suffer proportionally greater cuts in budgets. This creates uncertainty and fear that trigger activities related to revenue bargaining as a way of generating own resources.

4.4.1.2 Political competition

The interview material also points to another trigger for municipalities to reach out to citizens and engage in processes of revenue bargaining, namely political competition. Non-aligned municipalities tend to emerge where political competition is higher. While in FRELIMO strongholds electoral victories are very clear, with the winning party achieving more than 80% of the vote, victories in opposition party strongholds are less clear. Given that the municipal level of government is the only one at which opposition parties have control of executive power, governments of non-aligned municipalities have a particularly strong incentive to present themselves as a good and high-performing political alternative.[18] For that reason, it becomes a central necessity to generate revenue to finance the implementation of their own political initiatives and excel in their responsibilities towards their citizens. Most of the transfers cannot be used on a discretionary basis (Ilal and Weimer, 2017). Hence, own-generated revenue is not just another source of revenue, but one that the government has the freedom to spend as its wants. This flexibility in using own-generated revenue has also been identified elsewhere as a major incentive for local politicians (see e.g. Kjær and Therkildsen, 2013).

A large number of interviews indicated that, rather than political alignment, it is political competition at the municipal level that drives higher performance in general and more efforts to collect revenue in particular.[19] In seven of the selected 11 municipalities, respondents argued that high political competition would result in improved service delivery and/or increased efforts to perform well in terms of revenue mobilization.[20] The following statement illustrates the impact of increased political competition:

[18] This result resonates with the results of, for instance, Lambright (2014), Jibao and Prichard (2015), and Cheeseman and de Gramont (2017).

[19] For instance, this point was raised by members of the municipal government, the municipal assembly, public administrators, and CSOs in both aligned and non-aligned municipalities (I18, I21, I22, I25, I30, I49, I51, I57, I59, I60, I61, I67, I71, I77, I97, and I100).

[20] Some interviewees occasionally referred to 'opposition-governed' municipalities when asked about the impact of political competition on revenue mobilization (e.g. a member of Xai Xai municipal assembly

> 'I think decentralization is important for all parties because they can feel that they can gain more at the national level if they win the cities. . . . So they will just fight seriously this time [at the upcoming 2018 elections] . . . . And I think it will help to increase the management there' (I97, member of Pemba local government).

In fact, municipalities governed by FRELIMO but characterized by a high level of competition, such as in Matola and Nacala, are perceived by a large number of interviewees, alongside non-aligned municipalities like Beira and Quelimane, to be particularly active in trying to improve service delivery, own-revenue collection, and citizen–local government relationships more generally.

For instance, one representative of a donor agency stated in an interview when referring to Beira[21] that 'the good example of Beira is the political competition first of all. You have to deliver, you have to make sure your party is different, is providing services to citizens. . . . Because if he [the PCM] doesn't do that, he may lose potentially' (I1, donor employee).

From the insider perspective, a member of Beira local assembly responded when asked about the reasons for a relatively high willingness to pay taxes among Beira's citizens that: 'They [the citizens] see the difference in the realization of projects here in Beira' (I62).

In Matola, a municipality governed by FRELIMO but only by a small and contested number of votes, a member of a local assembly responded when asked about the potential impact of political competition on revenue mobilization that

> 'yes, it [political competition] has an impact. Before, there was almost no opposition. But in this legislature there is actually a real opposition . . . almost 50:50. This has a big influence on how decisions are taken and we do everything to show that we are from the opposition.' (I21, member of Matola municipal assembly).

Overall, the evidence indicates that excelling as a high performer and having funds to realize defined own projects is a major incentive for municipal governments to exploit their revenue potential. The causal links seem to be more connected to political competition than alignment, although this is difficult

and a public administrator in Beira; I30 and I57). Thus, in these cases, it is difficult to disentangle the effects of political competition and alignment.

[21] Overall, the case of Beira has repeatedly been labelled as best practice for responsive service delivery and successful revenue mobilization (e.g. by donor employees in I1 and I4). In many cases, this has been explicitly attributed to the high level of political competition. See, for instance, interviews with members of the municipal government and assembly of Beira itself (I59 and I60), but also with donor employees (I1) as well as members of the municipal assembly and CSOs in other, even non-aligned municipalities like Maxixe and Xai Xai (I30 and I51).

to disentangle in the highly polarized political context of Mozambique. Theoretically, non-alignment can be expected to reinforce the incentive connected to political competition more generally as it makes performance relevant not only to re-election at the municipal level but also for politics at the national level. However, political competition seems to have its own effect through two mechanisms: first, by increasing pressure for the incumbent to deliver in order to be re-elected; and second, by increasing the available tools and power for the opposition to control local government activities.[22]

4.4.2 Municipal strategies to approach taxpayers and initiate revenue-bargaining processes

This section focuses on the strategies used to engage in revenue bargaining and the degree to which these are sufficient to start meaningful and inclusive processes. Based on the interviews, this section shows that approaching citizens is widely perceived as a relevant issue in almost all municipalities. However, an analysis of the nature of the measures indicates that they tend to be unidirectional and are, in many cases, driven by external actors rather than the municipalities themselves. Furthermore, citizen engagement is limited and insufficiently supported by third parties, such as CSOs, which makes it impossible for any effort (even if well-meant) aimed at creating broad-based, inclusive bargaining processes to be successful.

In general, representatives in almost all municipalities expressed that it was important to reach out to citizens to inform about and discuss revenue issues; this included administrative and political representatives from the municipal government and the municipal assembly. The rationale behind approaching citizens is well summarized in the following statement: 'Sensitizing [the citizens] is key to increasing compliance with municipal rules' (I61, member of Beira municipal assembly). Still, it cannot be taken for granted that there is a genuine interest in revenue bargaining, understood as a process in which two or more parties engage with each other. In many cases, the discourse in the municipalities indicated that the measures are seen as the provision of unidirectional information to citizens that is not necessarily intended to be followed up with any exchange or dialogue.

In terms of available tools to engage with citizens, a remarkable array of outreach measures was identified. This includes formats specifically designed

[22] This result resonates with the results and ideas presented in, for instance, Faguet (2014).

to present and highlight the relevance and use of collected revenue. Often-found measures include participatory budgeting and planning, field meetings of the municipal assembly and municipal government with citizens in the neighbourhoods, information campaigns via the media, and by working with CSOs. The number of activities was higher in non-aligned municipalities with more proactive outreach activities, and discussions with citizens were more elaborate and consistent.

In the majority of cases, civil society actors—key actors supporting citizens in engaging with governments—had heard about the efforts and activities listed above, although the number of activities tended to be perceived as being significantly lower than the ones claimed by municipal politicians and administrators. Furthermore, CSOs reported that many of the outreach activities appear to reach only a few people. Closely connected to this point, alongside representatives of CSOs, experts interviewed at the national level also often mentioned that there were a lot of selection and self-selection biases in municipal outreach activities. Thus, due to the polarized political climate, tools such as consultative councils, meetings of community leaders, and open meetings with politicians only attracted people already affiliated with or at least close to the political parties in power, limiting the value of these tools for broad-based, inclusive revenue-bargaining processes.[23]

In addition, some interviewees — for instance prominently a public administrator and a member of the municipal assembly in Quelimane, a city that has been particularly active in the area of public awareness campaigns — claimed that due to the complexity of political processes, only well-educated citizens could engage meaningfully in outreach activities (I74 and I77). In this regard, the material shows mixed evidence on the perceptions about citizens' awareness and knowledge regarding the division of competences between the municipality and other administrative levels, a prerequisite for meaningful engagement in revenue bargaining. In general, experts at the national level and CSOs tended to be more pessimistic in regard to this than local actors did.[24] Most interviewees, however, agreed that the awareness of the municipality as an actor with separate responsibilities from those of the national government is increasing over time and is stronger in municipalities that exist for a longer time period.[25] This might imply

[23] This has been strongly suggested in interviews with members of CSOs but also admitted by members of municipal assemblies, municipal governments, and public administrators in aligned and non-aligned municipalities (e.g. I16, I58, I59, I77, I98, and I100).

[24] For instance, interview partners in I1, I8, I32, I80, I87, and I88 claim strongly that citizens are unable to differentiate competencies.

[25] Please note that the case studies included only municipalities founded in the first wave: 1997. Hence, this statement is based on interviews with experts at the national level and insights provided by persons

better preconditions for bargaining in the future. In terms of ownership and sustainability, it is questionable whether municipal governments were, in most cases, the main initiators of information and outreach activities. Rather than the municipalities themselves, it seems that third parties—donors and national-level institutions—play a crucial role in facilitating and initiating measures.[26] Examples of this include the successful coordination of civil society through local committees such as SAMcoms in Pemba (I101, CSO representative in Pemba), the introduction of a social audit in Inhambane (I43) with the help of MASC (Fundação Mecanismo de Apoio à Sociedade Civil—the Foundation Support Mechanism for Civil Society), and an information campaign about the municipal poll tax (IPA) launched in Maxixe that was conceptualized by national ministries (I53, member of Maxixe municipal assembly). In the case of participatory budgeting in Nampula and Quelimane, this reliance on donors resulted in the cancellation of the whole programme once the municipality was supposed to use its own funds instead of donor money to implement outreach measures (I8, donor employee).

The effectiveness of the measures is also doubtful. Although interviewees in all municipalities stated that outreach activities should continue, and considered them valuable, most interviewees indicate that the activities did not have any clear measurable impact on the tax culture and level of engagement of citizens. Only very few were confident in attributing a positive effect to these initiatives and could name concrete examples of successes (e.g. I47, I55, and I67; public administrators and members of the municipal assemblies in Maxixe, Beira, and Dondo).

The limited success of the measures highlights a precondition of revenue bargaining that is commonly ignored. The municipal government might be open to bargaining, but if revenue providers lack a minimum organizational power, they will not only have a weak bargaining position (see Chapter 2), but they will also be unable to engage in revenue-bargaining processes in a meaningful manner.

As such, there is only very little anecdotal evidence of a systematic organization of interests among citizens to discuss revenue matters at the municipal level. CSOs are perceived to exert only very limited influence on municipal policymaking, particularly in the revenue area, even when supported

in the municipalities when explicitly asked whether they consider that municipal identities are evolving over the years, as well the knowledge of citizens about the division of responsibilities between levels of government.

[26] In particular, this point was made strongly in interviews with donor employees (I2 and I8) and CSOs (I43, I58, and I79) as well as members of municipal assemblies (I60, I75, and I82) in aligned and non-aligned municipalities.

by donors. Reasons cited are mostly connected to lack of organizational strength and thematic expertise. In fact, supporting doubts about honesty in the alleged openness to engage in revenue bargaining by some municipalities, some interviewees described cases where municipalities were unwilling to cooperate with them as soon as CSOs started to engage more intensively in public finance topics.[27]

All in all, municipalities implement many outreach activities that could serve as an invitation to start the process of revenue bargaining. However, the effectiveness in terms of providing platforms for inclusive revenue bargaining seems to be questionable. Beyond that, even where municipalities might be honestly willing to engage in such processes, it seems that the preconditions are not in place for meaningful revenue bargaining to emerge since CSOs as third parties coordinating and aggregating citizen's demands, wishes, and arguments lack the organizational capacity to fulfil these roles.

4.5 Conclusion

This chapter has explored factors that trigger revenue bargaining between municipal governments and citizens. Furthermore, it has analysed the strategies they use to approach citizens. In this regard, the greatest contribution of this chapter is in going beyond revenue collection and performance towards understanding what leads municipalities to engage in revenue bargaining. This is an essential step to developing a more nuanced understanding of factors that explain differences in predisposition for revenue bargaining across municipalities as well as preconditions required for meaningful revenue bargaining to take place.

The results indicate that political competition and perceived unreliability of the transfer system strongly incentivize municipalities to engage in revenue bargaining. The interview material also shows that the narrative about the relevance of revenue bargaining is present in almost all municipalities. Concrete initiatives are more often named in municipalities characterized by high political competition, although they exist in all. However, these efforts are perceived by civil society to be significantly lower, regardless of whether the municipality is aligned with the central government or not.

[27] Donor employees raised this issue repeatedly (in particular, I2 and I8). Also, CSOs themselves claimed this in both aligned and non-aligned municipalities (e.g. I43, I58, and I79).

These results underline that the openness of government will be insufficient to trigger meaningful revenue bargaining. Openness is a necessary, but certainly not a sufficient condition. Bargaining implies the engagement of two sides. Hence, either the individual revenue providers or at least the CSOs—as the third party coordinating the voices of the revenue providers—must be sufficiently organized to purposively interact with the local governments. Currently, in Mozambique, the civil society at the municipal level is too weak to fulfil this role. As a result, even if we assume that municipal governments are honestly open to starting revenue-bargaining processes, which is doubtful as donors seem the strongest drivers of these initiatives, the scope for revenue bargaining to emerge and have major impacts on the micro-level fiscal contract is small.

More tentatively, a question that derives from the results and would deserve further scrutiny is the potential paradox that the efforts of national governments to manipulate transfer systems to disadvantage municipalities governed by opposition parties might, under certain circumstances, have the opposite effect than the one expected. In this line, the additional fiscal pressure might trigger a strengthening of the micro-level fiscal contracts between these local governments and their citizens and, thereby, put these very same municipal governments in a better political position in the mid and long term as well as, more generally, increase the political salience of these municipalities. Wang (2017) describes how China depoliticized its public finance to disincentivize the activity of local politically active social groups. The analysis in this chapter would suggest that in a somewhat reverse logic, putting revenue pressure on the municipalities controlled by the political opposition might encourage the interaction between society and local government, improving their relationship and potentially leading national government to face problems of legitimacy. From a revenue-bargaining perspective, it is important to note that the potentially associated political polarization might subvert any possibility for broad-based fiscal contracts between central government and the broader society at the national level, creating the paradox that a stronger fiscal contract at the local level weakens the national one.

The results presented in this chapter also have relevant policy implications. In particular, they send a clear warning. Scholars and international donors have proposed revenue collection to have a governance dividend for state building and government–citizen relationships (Chapter 1; see also Moore, 2015; Prichard, 2015). The analysis shows that even if governments are willing to actively approach and engage with citizens, the desired outcomes will only take place if the counterpart, the citizens, are able to meaningfully engage in the bargaining process. This implies that donors need to approach this issue from a more holistic perspective. Revenue collection based on more inclusive revenue bargaining demands more than increasing the technical and administrative capacity of governments and more than pushing government to formally offer the channels. Strengthening civil society in this field, institutionally and in terms of technical capacity around fiscal issues, is at least equally relevant.

4.6 Appendix

Table 4.A1 Overview of interview partners by municipality

Beira	9
Dondo	9
Inhambane	7
Matola	7
Maxixe	8
Monapo	8
Nacala	6
Pemba	7
Quelimane	9
Vilankulo	4
Xai-Xai	10

Note: 17 interviews were held with individuals working at the national level.

Table 4.A2 Overview of interview partners by type of actor

Local administration	26
Municipal assembly	27
Municipal government	14
CSO (incl. community leaders)	16
Donors	12
National experts (incl. academics and official of ministries)	6

Acknowledgements

This chapter presents part of the results of the project 'The Political Economy of Local Taxation in Mozambique', implemented within the context of the 52nd Postgraduate Training Programme of the German Institute of Development and

Sustainability (IDOS)—formerly Deutsches Institut für Entwicklungspolitik/ German Development Institute (DIE). The research was funded by the Ministry for Economic Cooperation and Development (BMZ). Members of the research team included, beyond the author, Saida Bunk, Salvador Forquilha, Dominique Klawonn, Jonathan Krull, Alina Sennewald, Conrad Steinhilber, and Juliane von Boeselager. Their fundamental contribution to this analysis is gratefully acknowledged. The author and project members also wish to thank the partners: Instituto de Estudos Sociais e Económicos (IESE), Project Programa de Boa Governação Financeira (German Development Cooperation in Mozambique), and Associação Nacional dos Municípios de Moçambique (ANAMM). Without their support, this research would not have been possible.

Special thanks go to Katharina Hübner, Amandio Jaquete, Eduardo Nguenha, Bernhard Weimer, Michael Sambo, Bernardino António, Stefan Leiderer, Christian von Haldenwang, and Julia Leininger for their helpful ideas, comments, and support. The project team is also grateful for the indispensable support of a large team of translators, as well as all the administrative support provided by the different partner institutions in Germany and Mozambique. Finally, I want to thank Anne Mette Kjaer, Marianne Ulriksen, Ane Karoline Bak, Odd Helge Fjeldstad, and all other participants of the ECPR Joint Sessions Workshop 'The Politics of Revenue Bargaining' for their feedback on previous versions of this chapter.

References

Ames, B., E. Connerley, D. M. do Rosario, E. Nguenha, and L. Francisco. 2010. *Comparative Assessment of Decentralization in Africa: Mozambique In-Country Assessment Report.* Vermont: ARD, Inc. http://pdf.usaid.gov/pdf_docs/PNADX220.pdf.

Banful, A. B. 2011 'Do Formula-Based Intergovernmental Transfer Mechanisms Eliminate Politically Motivated Targeting? Evidence from Ghana'. *Journal of Development Economics* 96(2): pp. 380–390.

Bertelsmann Stiftung. 2016. *BTI 2016—Mozambique Country Report.* Gütersloh: Bertelsmann Stiftung. https://bti-project.org/fileadmin/api/content/en/downloads/reports/country_report_2016_MOZ.pdf.

Boex, J. 2011. *An Analysis of Municipal Revenue Potential in Mozambique: Summary Report.* Washington, DC: World Bank.

Brollo, F., and T. Nannicini. 2012. 'Tying Your Enemy's Hands in Close Races: The Politics of Federal Transfers in Brazil'. *American Political Science Review* 106(4): pp. 742–761.

Bunk, S., S. Forquilha, D. Klawonn, J. Krull, A. Sennewald, C. Steinhilber, and A. von Schiller. 2017. *Socio-Political and Administrative Determinants of Municipal Revenue Performance: Insights from Mozambique.* Briefing Paper No. 14/2017. Bonn: Deutsches Institut für Entwicklungspolitik.

Buur, L. 2009. 'The Politics of Gradualismo: Popular Participation and Decentralised Governance in Mozambique'. In *Rethinking Popular Representation*, edited by O. Törnquist, N. Webster, and K. Stokke, pp. 99–118. New York: Palgrave Studies in Governance, Security, and Development.

Cheeseman, N., and D. de Gramont. 2017. 'Managing a Mega-City: Learning the Lessons from Lagos'. *Oxford Review of Economic Policy* 33(3): pp. 457–477.

Chimunuane, O., M. Hassam, S. Hindkjaer, and B. Weimer. 2010a. *Estudo sobre Potencial Tributário no Município da Vila de Vilankulo.* Ministério para a Coordenação da Acção Ambiental (MICOA) in cooperation with the World Bank.

Chimunuane, O., M. Hassam, and B. Weimer. 2010b. *Estudo sobre Potencial Tributário no Municipio da Vila de Marromeu.* Ministério para a Coordenação da Acção Ambiental (MICOA) in cooperation with the World Bank.

Comissão Nacional de Eleições. 2018. 'Edital'. http://www.open.ac.uk/technology/mozambique/sites/www.open.ac.uk.technology.mozambique/files/files/Resultados%20e%20mandatos%202018.pdf.

European Union Election Observation Mission. 2019. *Republic of Mozambique. Final Report: General and Provincial Assembly Elections.* Election Observation Mission. https://www.eeas.europa.eu/sites/default/files/eueom_moz2019_final_report_en.pdf.

Faguet, J.-P. 2014. 'Decentralization and Governance'. *World Development* 53(C): pp. 2–13.

Fjeldstad, O. H. 2014. 'Tax and Development: Donor Support to Strengthen Tax Systems in Developing Countries'. *Public Administration and Development* 34(3): pp. 182–193.

Forquilha, S. 2016. 'Municipalização em Moçambique: Lógicas e Dinâmicas Políticas'. In *Desafios para Moçambique 2016*, edited by L. D. Brito, C. N. Castel-Branco, S. Chichava, S. Forquilha, and A. Francisco, pp. 129–150. Maputo: Instituto de Estudos Sociais e Económicos IESE.

George, A. L., and A. Bennett, 2005. *Case Studies and Theory Development in the Social Sciences.* Cambridge, MA: MIT Press.

GIZ. 2017. *Base de dados sobre as finanças municipais em Moçambique: 2009–2015* [Data file and code book]. Data collection commissioned by GIZ in cooperation with MEF and implemented by MAP Consultoria. Maputo: Deutsche Gesellschaft für Internationale Zusammenarbeit GIZ–Programa Boa Governação Financeira.

Ilal, A., and B. Weimer. 2017. *O Sistema de Transferências Fiscais Intergovernamentais (STFI) em Moçambique: Uma Análise Fiscal e Institucional. Relatório Final.* Maputo: Ministério de Economia e Finaças/GIZ.

Jibao, S. S. and W. Prichard. 2015. 'The Political Economy of Property Tax in Africa: Explaining Reform Outcomes in Sierra Leone'. *African Affairs* 114(456): pp. 404–431.

Johnson, L. 2013. 'Quelimane: One Square Mile of Mozambique'. 2 April. https://www.bbc.com/news/world-radio-and-tv-21831810.

Kjær, A. M. 2009. 'Sources of Local Government Extractive Capacity: The Role of Trust and Pre-Colonial Legacy in the Case of Uganda'. *Public Administration and Development: The International Journal of Management Research and Practice* 29(3): pp. 228–238.

Kjær, A. M., and O. Therkildsen. 2013. 'Elections and Landmark Policies in Tanzania and Uganda'. *Democratization* 20(4): pp. 592–614.

Lambright, G. M. S. 2014. 'Opposition Politics and Urban Service Delivery in Kampala, Uganda'. *Development Policy Review* 32(1): pp. 39–60.

Macuane, J. J., L. Buur, and C. M. Monjane. 2018. 'Power, Conflict and Natural Resources: The Mozambican Crisis Revisited'. *African Affairs* 117(468): pp. 415–438.

MAEFP (Ministério da Administração Estatal e Função Pública). 2016. *Breve Avaliação da Situação Actual dos Municípios em Moçambique*. Maputo: Ministério da Administração Estatal e Função Pública.

Maihack, H., and J. Plagemann. 2010. 'Eine Dritte Politische Kraft in Mosambik?' *GIGA Focus Afrika* 8. Hamburg: GIGA. https://pure.giga-hamburg.de/ws/files/24543752/gf_afrika_1008.pdf.

Maschietto, R. H. 2016. 'Decentralisation and Local Governance in Mozambique: The Challenges of Promoting Bottom-Up Dynamics from the Top Down'. *Conflict, Security & Development* 16(2): pp. 103–123.

Moore, M. 2015. 'Tax and the Governance Dividend'. In *Perspectives on Politics, Production and Public Administration in Africa*, edited by A. M. Kjær, L. Engberg-Pedersen, and L. Buur, pp. 159–174. Copenhagen: Danish Institute of International Studies.

Moore, M., W. Prichard, and O. Fjeldstad, eds. 2018. 'Small Taxes and Large Burdens: Informal and Subnational Revenues'. In *Taxing Africa: Coercion, Reform and Development*, pp. 147–178. London: Zed Books.

Nguenha, E., O. Muianga, and A. António, A. 2017. *Empenho e Potencial Tributários dos Municípios em Moçambique: Estudo de casos de Nampula e Quelimane.* Maputo: Associação Nacional dos Municípios de Moçambique (ANAMM).

Nguenha, E., U. Raich, and B. Weimer. 2012. 'Subnational Finances: Performance and Sustainability of Mozambican Municipalities'. In *Moçambique: Descentralizar o Centralismo: Economia Politica, Recursos, Resultados*, edited by B. Weimer. pp. 197–215. Maputo: Instituto de Estudos Socias e Económicos (IESE).

Prichard, W. 2015. *Taxation, Responsiveness and Accountability in Sub-Saharan Africa.* Cambridge: Cambridge University Press.

República de Moçambique. 1997. *Lei no. 10/1997 of 31 May 1997.* Maputo: Boletim da República.

República de Moçambique. 2008a. *Decreto 63/2008.* Maputo: Boletim da República.

República de Moçambique. 2008b. *Lei no. 1/2008 of 16 January 2008.* Maputo: Boletim da República.

República de Moçambique. 2013. Lei no. 11/2013 of 3 June 2013. Maputo: Boletim da República.

Wang, Y. 2017. 'Why Tax Policy Is Not Politics in China: Public Finance and China's Changing State–Society Relations'. *Politics and Policy* 45(3): pp. 194–223.

Weimer, B. 2012. *Municipal Tax Base in Mozambique: High Potential—Low Degree of Utilisation.* Discussion Paper No. 1/2012. Bonn: Deutsches Institut für Entwicklungspolitik.

Weimer, B., and J. Carrilho. 2017. *Political Economy of Decentralisation in Mozambique: Dynamics, Outcomes, Challenges.* Maputo: Institute for Social and Economic Studies (IESE).

World Bank. 2014. *Mozambique Public Expenditure Review: Addressing the Challenges of Today, Seizing the Opportunities of Tomorrow.* http://documents.worldbank.org/curated/en/677921468275102771/Mozambique-Public-expenditure-review-addressing-the-challenges-of-today-seizing-the-opportunities-of-tomorrow.

5

Tax reforms in Tanzania

Where and how are compromises negotiated?

Marianne S. Ulriksen, Lucas Katera, and Jamal Msami

5.1 Introduction

The then Tanzanian Finance Minister, Dr Phillip Mpango, caused uproar in Parliament when he proposed, during the presentation of the 2016/2017 budget, 'the amendment of the Income Tax Act, Cap 332, with a view to removing income tax exemptions on MPs' gratuity in order to promote equity and fairness in taxation'.[1] The Members of Parliament from both sides of the floor 'were not ready to accept the idea'.[2] And they were not the only ones to get upset that June of 2016. The government proposed a range of tax reforms targeting a wide variety of taxpayers, thereby setting in motion protests and attempts to revert the reform proposals. Hence, the spate of tax reforms was a unique opportunity to study the subsequent revenue bargaining between government and different revenue providers, allowing us to explore questions such as how and where are revenue providers engaging with the government around tax reforms, does the government at times compromise on its initial proposal, and what are the micro-level fiscal contract outcomes?

We selected four cases where we, based on the theoretical framework in Chapter 2, assumed that revenue providers and government would engage in negotiations over tax reform (see Msami et al., 2022). The cases are: the MPs who saw taxes introduced on their retirement benefits; the security forces whose duty-free shops were abolished; the tourism sector, which ceased to benefit from VAT exemptions on services offered; and the transport sector, where VAT was imposed on auxiliary services. Because the theoretical framework in Chapter 2 does not theorize where and how the bargaining processes

[1] See Tanzania's *The Citizen* newspaper: https://www.thecitizen.co.tz/tanzania/news/national/mps-gang-up-against-taxation-of-their-send-off-package-2558092 (accessed 16 June 2022).

[2] Ibid.

Marianne S. Ulriksen, Lucas Katera, and Jamal Msami, *Tax reforms in Tanzania.* In: *The Politics of Revenue Bargaining in Africa.* Edited by: Anne Mette Kjær, Marianne S. Ulriksen, and Ane Karoline Bak, Oxford University Press.
 DOI: 10.1093/oso/9780192868787.003.0005

actually unfold, we explore *how* targeted revenue providers and government[3] engage in negotiations; that is, what *strategies* are used to convince/win over the other party. Furthermore, we contribute to the taxation literature by studying the role of institutional settings—what we term *arenas*—in facilitating bargaining. We identify three arenas where revenue providers and government actors engage in bargaining: public, bureaucratic, and political. Findings from our fieldwork (see Msami et al., 2022 for the full in-depth analysis) suggest that the public arena comprises few institutionalized spaces for dialogue, which makes engagements between revenue providers and government conflictual and compromise unlikely. Instead, in the bureaucratic and political arenas, where more formal and informal institutions allow for structured, repeated, and trusted relationships to develop, the revenue providers are more likely to push the government to compromise on the initial tax proposal. Hence, fiscal outcomes of revenue bargaining may be less than originally anticipated in policy proposals, although tax reforms also trigger better organization of revenue providers and the building of relationships between state and societal actors.

5.2 Arenas and strategies of revenue bargaining

The (re-)introduction of tax by government can cause initial protests and reactions from revenue providers (see Chapter 1). However, as Moore (2007, 16) argues, 'any realistic understanding [of the tax bargaining] processes requires that we go beyond the initial reaction to taxation of each type of actor and take into account the ways in which they then interact, whether conflictingly, cooperatively, or in more complex ways'. The nature of these interactions is informed by institutions, which the taxation literature notes as crucial in forming revenue bargaining. Levi (1988) argues that institutions can facilitate bargaining by reducing transaction costs and enabling less confrontational forms of bargaining. Prichard (2015), in his seminal contribution on contextual factors shaping tax bargaining, highlights how institutions shape the feasibility of tax bargaining by allowing taxpayers to engage with government in constructive ways. Essentially, institutions—such as effective parliamentary processes, forums of engagement, and informal relations based on trust and bargaining—are *spaces for dialogue* where compromises

[3] Although we consistently refer to the 'government' in this chapter, we understand the government within the political settlement approach to consist of the inner circles around the president, that is, the ruling elite.

can be reached. Conversely, if there are 'few spaces for dialogue . . . tax bargaining is likely to be comparatively confrontational' (Prichard, 2015, 75).

The cited contributions all emphasize how institutions can facilitate less confrontational interactions between revenue providers and government, and hence it is hardly surprising that taxation scholars and practitioners explore 'how taxpayer engagement may be strengthened by supporting safe, secure and sincere forums of engagement' (van den Boogard et al., 2022, p. 10). However, even if forums of engagement could be strengthened, there are already spaces for dialogue within which revenue-bargaining processes are ongoing as our four cases exemplify. Consequently, we need a better theoretical conceptualization of the different institutional settings that facilitate bargaining between actors.

To complement the taxation literature, we therefore draw on contributions from the pluralist tradition[4] and the organizational management field. Within the pluralist tradition, a growing body of literature focuses on interest groups' access to and influence over public policy with specific attention to institutional *arenas* and choice of strategies, although primarily in western liberal democracies (Beyers, 2004; Binderkrantz, 2005; Kriesi, Tresch, and Jochum, 2007; Binderkrantz, Christiansen, and Pedersen, 2015; Binderkrantz, Pedersen, and Beyers, 2017; Halpin and Fraussen, 2017; Crow, Albright, and Koebele, 2019; De Bruycker, 2019). The organizational management literature looks not at tax policy per se but rather at organizational responses to institutional pressures of various kinds, with focus on the settings for and strategies of negotiations (Oliver, 1991; Levy and Egan, 2003; Demil and Bensedrine, 2005; Hargrave and van de Ven, 2006; Aaltonen and Sivonen, 2009). As should become clear in the following, these contributions help us distinguish between different types of institutional settings and the variety of strategies used in influencing policy reforms, which in turn inform our analysis of revenue-bargaining processes in Tanzania.

To influence policy decisions, interest groups—in our case revenue providers[5]—need to gain access to key political institutional settings. Binderkrantz et al. (2017) speak of a political arena including the parliament, the administration, and the media. Although they are all defined as being within a political arena, Binderkrantz and colleagues acknowledge in other work (2015, 100) that there are important distinctions: the bureaucracy is a

[4] Going back to scholars like Arthur F. Bentley, *The Process of Government* (1908), and Roald A. Dahl, *Who Governs* (1961), the tradition explores how policymaking involves a plurality of actors and groups in society.

[5] Revenue providers may not be organizations but can be individuals such as MPs. However, in most cases, revenue providers are, or organize themselves into, organizational structures.

'predominant[ly] insider arena, where political decisions are prepared and implemented', the parliament is an arena that is 'more open' and important for 'decision making', whereas the media 'is the most public arena'. These arenas vary from publicly visible arenas (the media) to less visible arenas (the bureaucracy), with corresponding different sets of strategies (ibid.). From the perspective of the political settlement approach, the concept of arena is useful as it implies a set of institutions that *facilitate* bargaining while also emphasizing that actors in the arenas have different positions of power. The relative bargaining power of actors, also termed *holding power*, is shaped by actors' economic, organizational, or other resources (see Chapter 2).

The less visible, closed arenas require 'access' (Beyers, 2004) or 'direct' (Binderkrantz, 2005) strategies whereby interest groups engage policy- and decision-makers in institutionalized and regular forums with opportunities for sharing information, providing expert input, and lobbying to affect policy formulation and revision. While gaining access is not the same as influence (Binderkrantz, Pedersen, and Beyers, 2017; Halpin and Fraussen, 2017), the ability to influence policy is greatly improved when interest organizations are at the 'negotiating table' (Demil and Bensedrine, 2005) and have 'relative bases of power' vis-à-vis the decision-makers (Hargrave and van de Ven, 2006, 880). Hence, if interest organizations can access the less visible arenas and have the necessary resources, they may be able to pursue strategies leading to government concessions. In the organizational management literature, it is termed a *compromising strategy*, which entails '[n]egotiating with the stakeholders, listening to their claims . . . offering possibilities and arenas for dialogue, [and] making reconciliations and offering compensation' (Oliver, 1991; Aaltonen and Sivonen, 2009).

The visible and public arena requires instead 'voice' (Beyers, 2004) or 'indirect' (Binderkrantz, 2005) strategies where influence on policy is sought in more indirect ways such as by gaining the attention and interest of policy- and decision-makers through the media. The media is not a forum of engagement where one can go into detailed scrutiny and dialogue about technicalities and feasibilities of policies. Instead, the media can serve as a 'megaphone for advocacy groups' (De Bruycker, 2019, 105), where groups can reach an audience beyond their core constituency to signal broad sympathy that may affect the views of policy- and decision-makers. The media can therefore advocate for a cause and may be a platform to share information. However, media presence can backfire if the coverage is negative. There is, furthermore, some indication that media attention is insufficient to influence policy (De Bruycker, 2019). If it is difficult to gain access to the closed arenas, the public arena can be an avenue to stage protests to attract attention, although this strategy can also cause or expand conflict and thereby increase the costs of seeking policy influence (Beyers, 2004; Crow et al., 2019). Additional insights from the literature are that interest groups use multiple strategies, and that access to one arena can spill over to another arena (Kriesi et al., 2007; Binderkrantz et al., 2015).

These theoretical insights of negotiations and policy influence across distinct arenas and following a variety of strategies can be transferred to our context with a few amendments. We need to be cognisant that Tanzania, during the fifth government (2015 – 2021), was characterized as a poor electoral autocracy with weak institutions, limited political competition, and restricted civil freedoms. Consequently, the parliament as an arena may not be as open as suggested by the pluralist tradition, the bureaucracy may not have the same institutional capacities as assumed in the organizational management literature, and use of the media may be viewed more as a strategy to increase conflict than as a space for open and free exchange of opinions. Following this, we suggest distinguishing between three arenas for revenue bargaining: a political arena (i.e. cabinet, parliament, party committees), a bureaucratic arena (i.e. ministries, government agencies), and a public arena (i.e. media, rallies). The first two are considered closed arenas that are difficult to access but with better opportunities for productive bargaining, whereas the latter arena is open but has fewer opportunities for revenue providers to influence policy change.[6]

This distinction follows the taxation literature that emphasizes the importance of having arenas that provide spaces for dialogue and where bargaining is structured, manageable, and 'mutually beneficial' (Moore, 2004, 300). If there are fewer spaces for actual—trustful—dialogue, the engagement is likely to be more conflictual, and it will be harder to reach a compromise (Prichard, 2015; van den Boogard et al., 2022). The former scenario is likely to materialize if revenue providers gain access to the political and bureaucratic arenas, which are relatively closed but also more regulated and institutionalized forums for exchange and information sharing. In such contexts, the stakeholders can present their arguments, have dialogue, offer (overt or covert) compensation, build relationships, and together develop mutually beneficial solutions. Hence, there is a potential to create an environment for structured and amicable negotiations, even if disagreements remain, and revenue providers may be able to convince the government to change the initial policy proposal.

[6] One could also expect an arena based on personalized relationships to the president. We have left this out of the analysis, as it is difficult to study and to discern any clear findings.

Conversely, in the public arenas, where stakeholders engage at open meetings/rallies and/or through the media, there are few facilitating institutions, and we therefore expect that the engagement will be more conflictual, based on strategies of protesting, stating demands, and blaming the other party. With no structures for dialogue, there is little room for fruitful engagement in building relationships and sharing information. However, if the parties recognize the need to reach an agreement, there may be attempts to offer dialogue by moving the bargaining in the direction of a mutually trusted institutional set-up, most likely in the political and/or bureaucratic arenas. If bargaining remains in the public arena, strategies continue to be conflictual, and the other party is openly blamed and criticized, bargaining may stall.

Furthermore, the ability of the revenue provider to act collectively will affect the extent to which they can put sufficient pressure on government to change the original policy proposal. If the revenue provider, as a collective, is not organized enough to speak with one voice, the government is met with an array of different voices, carrying different demands, often in a public domain as each voice is struggling to be heard. This increases the risk that the government will back off or only negotiate with the part of the group with preferences close to itself. This may be an incentive for the revenue provider—facing the threat of a costly policy—to become organized in order to engage better with the government (Demil and Bensedrine, 2005). The revenue-bargaining process is therefore highly dynamic, and the government's push for tax reform may drive revenue providers to build organizational capacity and create negotiating relationships where there were none before.

To sum up, we expect stakeholders to employ strategies that range from amicable, low-key, and closed-door negotiations in the political and bureaucratic arenas to conflictual, ostentatious, and open bargains in the public arena. In the latter case, revenue bargaining is unlikely to lead to compromise. Thus, if revenue providers want the government to give concessions, they are best placed to pursue bargaining in the bureaucratic and political arenas where there are more institutionalized spaces for dialogue. In cases of compromise, we consider this outcome to be a micro-level fiscal contract defined as an agreement between the government and revenue providers related to revenue provision (see Table 2.1, Chapter 2).

5.3 Incidences of revenue bargaining

In the following, we present the analysis of four micro-incidences of revenue bargaining in Tanzania, focusing on the institutional settings of bargaining (*arenas*) and the strategies applied by the negotiating parties.[7] The four cases were selected among different potential revenue providers that the Tanzanian government targeted in 2016 when a range of tax reforms were introduced. Each case study explores the different arenas in which interactions between the government and the revenue provider take place and investigates the strategies pursued by the stakeholders. All case studies cover the period from shortly before the tax reforms were announced in mid 2016 through to the end of 2017. The cases are informed by about thirty specifically targeted interviews with both revenue providers and government officials during 2017 and 2018. These primary data are supplemented by news information, government reports, other documents provided by stakeholders, as well as the authors' in-depth knowledge of Tanzania.

In accordance with the theoretical framework established in Chapter 2, the selected cases are scenarios where the government and revenue providers are assumed to have relatively equal bargaining power. The revenue provider (be it an individual, a group of individuals, or a company) would have strong resources due to either its economic strength (fiscal importance) or its political position (organizational importance), but not both. Two cases—the transport and tourism sectors—represent revenue providers that have relatively limited ability to support the ruling elite's position of power (organizational importance) but are major contributors to the Tanzanian economy (fiscal importance). The other two cases—MPs and the security forces—represent revenue providers of high political importance to the ruling elite (organizational importance) but with limited fiscal importance.

Table 5.1 summarizes the four cases. The tourism and transport sectors are characterized by a mix of international and domestic companies of varying sizes, and both sectors are of relatively limited political importance to the ruling elite. Although some actors in the two sectors have close contacts to the ruling elite (see for instance Rizzo, 2017), the two sectors as a whole cover a diversity of small and big companies with occasionally conflicting interests. Both sectors are of considerable fiscal importance to the ruling coalition as they are central for domestic production and employment and therefore have high revenue potential. Whereas the sectors have relatively low political weight, their fiscal importance thus ensures them a relatively strong bargaining position vis-à-vis the government. The two sectors vary on an important aspect, which we expected to matter for the strategies that stakeholders choose: the nature of collective action. Whereas the tourism

[7] For the full in-depth empirical analyses, including elaborate references to material and interviews, see Msami et al. (2022).

Table 5.1 Revenue-bargaining cases

Revenue provider	Type of tax reform	Organizational importance	Fiscal importance	Collective action
Tourism sector	Removal of VAT exemption on tourist services	LOW: Mix of international and domestic companies, with limited political connections	HIGH: The largest single contributor to the economy. Income from VAT likely to be substantial	HIGH: Relatively well organized and mobilized with a main umbrella organization
Transport sector	VAT on auxiliary services at Dar es Salaam Port	LOW: Mix of international and domestic companies, with limited political connections	HIGH: Backbone of the economy. Revenue potential substantial	LOW: Organized in small associations that each pursue diverging interests
Members of Parliament	Tax on gratuity payment	HIGH: The majority part of the inner circle or the broader ruling coalition	LOW (but of symbolic significance)	LOW(-ish): Small group of resourceful individuals, opposing political positions
Security forces	Abolishment of duty-free shops	HIGH: Military part of ruling coalition	LOW: Small tax base	HIGH: Clearly defined, resourceful, and hierarchical collective

sector is well organized under the umbrella of the TCT (Tourism Confederation of Tanzania), the transport sector has traditionally been organized in sometimes competing subsectors. Hence, the former is able to speak with 'one voice', whereas the latter is not.

Our two cases of revenue providers that are of political importance to the ruling elite are the MPs and the security forces, which were also targeted by the tax reforms in 2016. These taxes were not expected to raise substantial revenue relative to many other revenue sources, implying the limited fiscal importance to the ruling elite. Although MPs and the security forces are central to supporting the ruling coalition (of high organizational importance), they are organized differently as collectives. MPs meet in the same physical space, are easily mobilized, and have the means to create noise and put pressure on the cabinet. However, given that the Tanzanian Parliament is strongly divided between ruling party and opposition party members, it is unlikely that they can find a common voice and organize as one coherent collective. The security forces, on the other hand, comprise a large organization with centrally placed, high-level officials who may be in, or close to, the inner political circles. Additionally, as the force is—by its very nature—a hierarchical and secretive organization, it is expected to be well organized and have a powerful leadership (Therkildsen and Bourgouin, 2012). Thus, from a collective action perspective, the security force can speak from one common preference position.

In sum, the four cases shared the experience of being targeted by the government in the 2016 tax reforms. The tourism and transport sectors faced the introduction of VAT payments, MPs' gratuity payment was taxed, and the security forces' perk of duty-free shops was abolished. The stark surprise of being targeted for tax payments triggered immediate reactions from the revenue providers (except the security forces) and set in motion a bargaining process.

5.3.1 The tourism sector

Before the 2016 tax reform proposal, the main arenas in which discussions took place between the government and the tourism sector were the political and bureaucratic arenas during the national budget processes and through the parliamentary standing committee responsible for tourism. The tourism sector, represented by the Tanzania Private Sector Foundation (TPSF) and TCT (Tourism Confederation of Tanzania), was able to lobby for a continuous VAT exemption to the sector.

It was therefore a surprise when the Minister of Finance announced the introduction of VAT during the budget session of 2016/17 in June 2016. After the budget session where the VAT was introduced, the main arena of engagement was in the parliamentary standing committee on tourism. During the meetings between the TCT and the TPSF on one hand and the standing committee of the Parliament on the other, the tourism sector stakeholders sought to revoke the decision. In the lobbying process, the members of the TPSF met formally with the standing committee and informally with some members pushing their case. Despite efforts by the TCT and other tourism stakeholders, under the umbrella of the TPSF, the government went ahead with its decision.

After the introduction of VAT and the endorsement by Parliament, the main forum of exchange moved to the public arena, and the bargaining became antagonistic. The tourism sector used the media to make their case and drum up popular support (*The Citizen*, 2016a). It claimed that it was not unwilling to pay taxes but argued that the introduction of VAT would have an adverse effect on its competitiveness. The government used the media to tarnish the tourism sector's reputation by saying that they did not want to pay taxes (*Daily News*, 2016). The debate in the media became heated, and parts of the tourism sector acknowledged that constantly attacking the Ministry of Tourism in the newspapers was not constructive. The President closed the debate by saying that the VAT would stay, even if it affected the number of tourists visiting Tanzania negatively (*The Citizen*, 2016b).

Later in 2016, TCT continued to push the government to reconsider reversing the decision. This time, the TCT wrote to the Minister of Tourism to ask for a meeting to discuss the case and reach a mutual understanding. While the government accepted this meeting, it never took place. However, the tourism sector continued to reach out and sought to establish dialogue with the budget committees and other stakeholders like Tanzania Revenue Authorities (TRA) by travelling from Dar es Salaam to the capital, Dodoma. In the first half of 2017, the TCT was invited to make a presentation to the Parliament on the private-sector perspective of the tourism industry. During the seminar, the budget parliamentary committees learnt more about the tourism industry and how a retainment of the VAT would affect the sector. Persons we interviewed in the sector (see Msami et al., 2022) explained how the presentation of material and evidence-based advocacy opened dialogue at the formal meeting as well as more informal conversations with parliamentarians wanting to know more. These kinds of dialogues in which different stakeholders in the sector engaged with the government were instrumental in the considerations to remove some of the taxes in the sector from the financial year 2017/18.

Table 5.2 provides a schematic summary of the case of revenue bargaining between the tourist sector and the government in Tanzania. Initially, the relationships between the government and the organizations representing the tourism sector were amicable and took place in formal institutions such as the budget and parliamentary committees. However, the government's announcement to introduce VAT surprised the sector, and bargaining moved to the public arena and turned more conflictual. Despite pressure through media stories, the government did not change its mind. Over the following months, the tourist sector re-engaged with government officials in the political arena, which allowed them to present their case and plea for a reconsideration of how the VAT was implemented. The government did not waive the VAT but offered a compromise by specifying that tax authorities would not impose VAT on licences and fees, which they had done since the VAT was introduced. Hence, the bargaining ended with a micro-level fiscal contract, although the revenue outcome was lower than initially anticipated, as the government waived some VAT payments by the sector.

Table 5.2 Summary of the tourism sector case

Sequence	Arenas	Strategies	Policy outcome
Before announcement June 2016	Political arena: voice in budget and parliamentary committees	Dialogue and negotiation	⇒ Agreement to postpone introduction of VAT
Between announcement and approval by Parliament	Political arena	Lobby parliamentarians	⇒ Government unwilling to change policy
After approval by Parliament; second half of 2016	Public arena: use of media	Non-compromising strategies: tactics of blame and criticism in the media by both parties	
		However, also some compromising strategies: e.g. writing to minister asking for dialogue (although meetings did not materialize)	⇒ Government unwilling to change policy
Late 2016 and first half of 2017	Political arena re-established somewhat:	Compromise and influence:	
	Meetings with ministries / budget committee ⇒ (re-)engagement in forums of exchange	Strategies by tourist sector: – engage with different stakeholders in Dodoma (build relationships) – share information on importance of and impact on the sector – question legality of VAT implementation	
		Strategies by ruling elite: – listen and offer dialogue (budget committee) – bring in other government stakeholders	⇒ Clarification: no VAT on licences and fees

5.3.2 The transport sector

The transport sector covers the provision of passenger or freight transport, whether scheduled or not, by rail, pipeline, road, water, or air and associated activities such as cargo handling, storage, etc. Given the various subsectors, organizations, and companies that comprise it, the sector as a whole is not always well organized.[8] As in the tourism sector, the government introduced tax reforms that affected the transport sector.[9] In addition to the sector's non-participation in the decision, the timing and the expected hasty implementation of the reforms caught members by surprise. The rapid pace with which the government moved from the proposal phase to incorporating reforms in the 2016/17 finance bill denied the sector time and space to mobilize a coalition against the tax reforms. In addition to reducing the volume of imports and transited cargo, the reforms precipitated a price war among transporters as the transited cargo sector struggled to remain operational. Increased licence fees forced the closure of many small and medium-scale transporters. Thus, while the industry continued to portray a collective and cohesive external front, there were internal disagreements.

Upon learning of the reforms on 1 July 2016, one of the sector's representatives, the Tanzania Association of Transporters (TAT), convened a series of meetings with members, clients, and affiliates—including the freight forwarders' association (TAFFA) and the truck owners' association (TATOA)—to establish the scale of likely impact, a common position, and a strategy for engaging the state to address their concerns. Of primary concern was the maximum time an importer had to clear their goods without incurring additional port and handling charges (wharfage and storage) that would incrementally have an impact on the amount of VAT incurred. At the meetings, members agreed to advance two major positions: request a moratorium on new charges and petition for an increase in maximum allowable time to clear goods from the revised 14 days to at least 90 days.

The establishment of a sectoral common position on the reforms provided the TAT with a mandate to find a compromise with the authorities. However, a supporting coalition had to be established discreetly rather than through open channels, as senior ministry officials were wary of being seen as overtly siding with the private sector in its agitation against the government. TAT was forced to rely on informal approaches to present its initial case, which involved direct but discreet personal appeals by one of its members to the

[8] For an interesting account of the limitation of collective action in the transport sector, see Rizzo (2017).

[9] For details on the tax reforms see Msami et al. (2022).

minister and his permanent secretary. It was also indicated in interviewees that these meetings involved exchange of money for support. Thus, the TAT was forced to co-opt the ministry, which then guided it in how to engage with the powerful budget and transport parliamentary standing committees. The TAT also claimed that it had to furnish payments to prominent members of these committees (as well as a few prominent opposition MPs) in exchange for their support.

Collectively, the purchase of support allowed the TAT to establish a powerful coalition of actors capable of heaping and sustaining pressure on the treasury. One of the coalition's first acts was large-scale awareness-building of the adverse effects of the reforms on the transport sector. This was done in collaboration with the TAFFA and the TPSF. Awareness-building occurred through media briefings, interviews on national print and digital media, as well as audio and television—with multiple appearances by the TAT's top officials. Through its members and networks, the TAT succeeded in influencing the national media to publicize its cause adequately. A key element in its media strategy was that ordinary Tanzanians would lose their jobs due to loss of business and decline in import volumes. The TAT's message was simple: the reforms were hurting national livelihood and pride. This did strike a chord with the authorities as they moved to reassure the public and neighbouring landlocked countries of the viability of the port of Dar es Salaam.

In March 2017, the TAT, along with other members of the TPSF, was invited by the Treasury to present their case at a series of pre-budgetary meetings involving parliamentary committees and the government in Dodoma. At the meetings, only the TAT and the tourism lobby were given substantial time to present their cases, mainly because they—through their media engagements in the public arena—were at the forefront in complaining about the introduction of VAT, which would reduce their competitiveness and affect the national economy due to loss of jobs and revenues. It appears that the return to the political and bureaucratic arenas in which the TAT could present details on the implications of the VAT to the sector caused the government to waive VAT charges on ancillary services, and the 2017/18 Finance Act passed in July 2017 confirmed the revisions of the reforms sought by the TAT.

Summing up (see Table 5.3), the introduction of VAT and other tax charges came as a surprise to the transport sector. Initially, the sector was poorly organized and lacked a unified voice in its interactions with the government, but the tax reform prompted the sector to organize and find a common position through the TAT. The sector was able to gain increased access to the political arena by buying support in the bureaucratic arena and via a successful

Table 5.3 Summary of the transport sector case

Sequence/ timeline	Arenas	Strategies	Policy outcome
At announcement (July 2016)	Introduction of tax a surprise ⇒ no access to political arena		
Right after announcement (July–Sept 2016)	Gaining access to bureaucratic arena	Sector establishes internal collaboration and buys access to side-lined ministry	
Sept 2016–Mar 2017	Public arena	Awareness-building in the media	
Nov 2016–June 2017	Increased access to political arena (invited by treasury)	Direct negotiation in discreet meetings	⇒ waiving VAT charges on ancillary services

public campaign in the news media. Thus, a micro-level fiscal contract was reached, although the government would receive less revenue than initially anticipated.

5.3.3 The members of parliament

The ruling party, CCM (Chama Cha Mapinduzi—'Party of the Revolution'), has since the inception of multi-party elections in 1995 accounted for 71–93% (currently about 93%) of MPs. The opposition, comprising four political parties, has largely presented itself as a unified block to counter its minority position. In June 2016, as part of the government's push to reform the tax system, the government proposed to waive tax exemptions on MPs' gratuities, meaning that MPs would pay 30% in tax of their gratuity payment at the end of their five-year term. This case study documents the revenue bargaining following the tax proposal, which led to a compromise: waivers of exemptions on gratuity payments would be a 5% levy (rather than 30% tax), and it would take effect in 2020 after the end of the current parliamentary term.

Stakeholders involved in gratuity tax reforms were adamant that the bargaining outcome represented a poor compromise, with major concessions given by the government. Apparently, the motive behind attempts to tax MPs stemmed from the ruling party's loss of parliamentary seats, increasing costs of elections, and the need to weaken the financial base of opposition MPs. However, due to multi-party representation, the government had to disguise these attempts at weakening parliamentary democracy by imposing the tax on the ruling party's own MPs. This caused cross-party mobilization against the tax, with MPs on both sides of the political divide adopting creative strategies to agitate against reforms.

The MPs realized that they could not easily find strong popular support due to past public opposition to hikes in MPs' salaries and gratuity payments, first in 2009 and then in 2014. Consequently, MPs sought to influence public opinion more discreetly in two principal ways: CCM MPs emphasized that their gratuities and allowances provided out-of-pocket assistance to their constituents, whereas opposition MPs publicly endorsed the reforms and challenged the government to extend them to the exempted gratuities of other political elites, notably the President and the Prime Minister.[10] While the former strategy sought to highlight the productive uses of gratuities and the burden facing individual MPs, the latter challenged the reach and legitimacy of the reforms. These measures backfired, however, as the president revealed his earnings and indicated his willingness to be taxed. Riding on a wave of favourable public opinion, the president appealed for public support for reforms by highlighting the discrepancies in earnings between MPs and ordinary Tanzanians, urging MPs to live by their political promises of serving ordinary Tanzanians by acquiescing to the proposed reforms.

Not be deterred, MPs enlisted the support of the powerful religious and civil society community, keenly aware of the mobilization powers of mainly religious bodies, owing to their contribution to social services as well as the strong religious values of the Tanzanian society. The head of the powerful parliamentary budget committee offered concessions to religious groups by suggesting a revision of proposed tax rates to the groups in return for their support in fighting the gratuity tax reforms. Facing the prospect of an undesired alliance between MPs and civil society, the government swiftly moved to placate religious groups by proposing a maintenance of exemptions for the religious and civil society community.

This left MPs in a difficult position, unable to mobilize support from any legitimate external constituency. Facing a lack of options, MPs threatened to wield a collective veto by rejecting the 2016/17 finance bill. The president Magufuli retaliated by threatening the use of constitutional powers to bypass Parliament and/or dissolve it and call a general election. Within CCM, senior figures were wary of the financial and political consequences of fresh elections and appealed to the council of elders, consisting of past party chairmen and secretary generals, who helped convey a message to the president for a

[10] https://en.igihe.com/news/tanzania-leaders-gratuity-for-income-tax; https://www.ippmedia.com/sw/makala/wabunge-ccm-walivyogeuka-mbogo-kodi-ya-kiinua-mgongo.

negotiated compromise. This was reached with a downward revision of the tax rate from 30 to 5%, rescindment of intended tax reforms on allowances, and postponement of application of taxes until 2020.

In sum (see also Table 5.4), MPs were not able to speak with one voice, even though the majority was against the tax reform. Engaging with the political leadership in the public arena, both CCM and opposition MPs were confrontational but used different arguments to appeal to the public. However, the strategy of using media stories backfired when the President proved unwilling to make any concessions. Moreover, an attempted alliance with civil society organizations proved unsuccessful. In the end, it was in the political arena that the revenue providers were able to reach a compromise with the government. The MPs collectively threatened to veto the budget, thereby—as with the transport sector—revealing the importance of mobilizing collective action. Nevertheless, it appears that informal institutions and relations within the CCM party's inner circles were decisive in enabling MPs to push the president to soften his initial stand. Once again, as with

Table 5.4 Summary of the MP case

Sequence	Arena	Strategies	Policy outcome
Initial proposal (2016)	Public arena	Use of media - CCM MPs emphasize their out-of-pocket assistance to constituencies - Opposition MPs challenge for reform to be extended to others in the ruling elite President retaliates in media to get public support	⇒ No change
Latter half of 2016	Public/political arena	MPs seek alliance with civil society, i.e. religious groups (possibly due to strategic political positions/knowledge) Government makes separate agreements with religious groups	⇒ No change (but for civil society maintenance of exemptions)
First half of 2017	Political arena	Overt: threat to reject finance bill Covert: Key CCM members seek to convince President to give concessions	⇒ Government gives concessions, although policy remains (5% instead of 30%, and by 2020)

the tourism and transport sectors, a micro-level fiscal contract was reached, although the government compromised its initial stand.

5.3.4 The security forces

The army, police, and prison forces comprise a large share of civil servants in Tanzania, and the forces are strong politically because their devotion to national service and national security is considered very important (URT, 2016). The security forces had been benefitting from duty-free shops operating at the Tanzania Peoples' Defence Force, Police and Prisons' barracks and selling a range of products, both durables and non-durables, at prices that excluded both VAT and excise duty. Legally, only members of the Tanzania Peoples' Defence Force, Police Force, and the Prison Service had access to the shops, but misuse was widespread, causing loss of government revenue. In addition, it is claimed that senior officials sold goods from the duty-free facilities in other shops at cheap prices in unfair competition with other traders paying VAT. This behaviour created difficult business environments for those complying with the tax laws.

There were persistent public complaints about the misuse of duty-free shops, and the business community criticized the unfair competition.[11] Concurrently, in its preparation of the 2016/17 budget, which was characterized by VAT reforms in many sectors, the government saw an opportunity to reform the tax exemptions of duty-free shops and announced removal of the exemptions for the financial year 2016/17. Compensation was introduced in the form of an additional salary payment, a flat rate of TZS 100,000/month to all soldiers regardless of rank. This amount was expected to cover the costs of taxes that army members now had to pay in the shops. According to the Minister of Finance and Planning during the budget speech of 2016/17, the government considered this the best targeting mechanism while also avoiding misuse.

It is difficult to fully detect what happened, but it is probable that this case involved a *pre-emptive* concession by the government to counter possible opposition to the tax. Arguably, there was also informal bargaining between government and top-level officials in the security forces, who may have been more interested in a solution benefiting the forces broadly. At least, it is interesting to note that lower-level members of the security forces were positive about the new compensation scheme, whereas mid-range senior officials

[11] https://www.thecitizen.co.tz/tanzania/news/national/no-more-tax-exemptions-for-military-shops--2557650

Table 5.5 Summary of the security forces case

Sequence	Arena	Strategies	Policy outcome
Before proposal	Public arena	Public outcry and complaints by business sectors provide legitimacy of reform of duty-free shops	
	Political arena	Although hard to observe directly, government gives pre-emptive concession, either in agreement with top army officials or on its own	⇒ pre-emptive concession
Announcement of proposal	Public arena	Tax reform of disputed army barracks announced	⇒ tax reform, but compensatory scheme introduced at the same time

were more critical (Msami et al., 2022). Perhaps this is not surprising, as a flat payment would be proportionally more lucrative at lower salary levels.

To sum up (see also Table 5.5), the general move by the government to reform the tax system as well as public concerns about the misuse of duty-free shops urged the government to remove tax exemptions. However, the security forces are clearly of such political importance that the government pre-empted any upsets by introducing a compensatory scheme despite the financial implications for tax mobilization. While senior officials decried the changes as they had been benefitting disproportionately from the exemptions, their influence did not counter possible agreements made between top-level officials and the government or the general support for the new scheme among low-level members in the security forces. In addition, the public arena was not a place for engagement between revenue provider and government as they had other arenas for dialogue. Instead, public debates gave the government's tax reforms some legitimacy as it made the government appear proactive in dealing with a widely recognized problem. Again, the final compromise was most likely settled in the political arena, although we cannot prove this due to the secretive relations between the army and the government: either the government came up with a compensation scheme itself, or it was agreed in consultation with top-level officials.

5.4 Case comparison and conclusion

In this chapter, we contribute to the understanding of how and when revenue bargaining leads to direct government concessions, and we have an

Table 5.6 Arenas, strategies, and likelihood of government concession

Arenas	Strategies	Possibility for government concession
Public arenas, e.g. media, civil society	- Appeal to public opinion - Seek public legitimacy - Seek alliance with civil society organizations	Bargain open and often conflictual ⇒ unlikely that government bends but can lead to access to other arenas if case has public legitimacy and appeal
Bureaucratic arenas, e.g. line ministries	- Create alliance with ministry/ department through common interest and/or by paying for access	Can indirectly lead to policy change as revenue provider gains useful knowledge and points of access to present and argue their case
Political arenas, e.g. committees, task forces, Parliament, internally in parties	- Present case in meetings - Negotiate directly with decision-makers - Build relationships over time	If revenue providers want the government to give concessions, best achieved by gaining access to the political arena

illustrating case of pre-emptive concessions (that of the security forces). Both outcomes of revenue bargaining are under-studied in the taxation literature (Prichard, 2015). It is worth noting that we did not select our cases on the outcome (i.e. concession by the government) as these were not known to us when we started our study (immediately following the introduction of taxes in 2016). Furthermore, we explored the micro-level interactions of revenue providers and government in the search for likely strategies pursued by the parties, which again depended on the arena in which bargaining takes place (see Table 5.6).

Public arenas provide for open engagement where legitimacy and alliances with the public are sought in order to pressure the other party. However, as there are fewer spaces for dialogue—institutionalized relations based on trust—the engagement, and any bargaining, will often remain conflictual, and it is unlikely that the government will compromise (e.g. in the cases of the MPs and the tourism sector). However, at times the media is useful for public sensitization and building of popular support (as in the transport sector case), and through such media strategy revenue providers can (re)gain access to the bureaucratic and political arenas.

In closed institutional settings in the political and bureaucratic arenas, revenue providers can benefit from access to key committees and other formal forums. Here, direct negotiations, knowledge sharing, and relationship building seem to be good strategies for revenue providers opposing tax policy changes, particularly if they are organized to speak with one voice. Hence, the government's push for tax reform may drive revenue providers to build organizational capacity[12] and create negotiating relationships where there were none before. In addition to gaining access to formal forums, the informal relations that the negotiating parties establish with one another are critical; at times, this exchange includes discreet even corrupt—engagements, such as buying access to the political arena, whereas at times, informal relations merely imply a continued and open dialogue about the proposed policy reforms.

In all our cases, the micro-level fiscal contracts constitute compromises that limited the government's revenue compared to the original policy proposals. However, even powerful groups, such as the MPs, did not get exemptions, which is otherwise found to be a common outcome of revenue bargaining in Africa (see Chapter 13). Nor are the contracts examples of 'exchange' where revenue providers get something in return for paying tax, which is the expectation in the traditional taxation literature (see Chapter 1). Instead, the revenue providers' achievement in the bargaining was a lower level of tax than originally proposed. So, the government and the revenue providers reached a compromise, which constitutes a micro-level fiscal contract as defined in this book: 'an explicit or implicit agreement between ruling elites and revenue providers related to revenue provision' (Chapter 1). However, the processes of reaching these compromises have wider implications. The cases constitute examples of continued engagements between revenue providers and government actors where reciprocal relations are building as the parties become responsive to each other and engage in repeated negotiations based on understandings of mutual obligations. The case studies also show that even if ruling elites still hold power partly based on clientelistic networks, formal institutions such as the parliamentary committees are arenas where policies are negotiated, debated, and made. The late President Magafuli centralized decision-making during his period in power (2015–2021) and was known as a no-nonsense leader (Cheeseman et al., 2021; Paget, 2021); but even he could not push through the proposed tax reforms in their original form as revenue providers mobilized, organized, and bargained for a compromise.

[12] See also Chapter 6 on how business associations created alliances to better influence the 2014 VAT Act in Tanzania.

References

Aaltonen, K., and R. Sivonen. 2009. 'Response Strategies to Stakeholder Pressures in Global Projects'. *International Journal of Project Management* 27(2): pp. 131–141. https://doi.org/10.1016/j.ijproman.2008.09.007.

Bentley, A. F. 1908. *The Process of Government*. Cambridge, MA: Harvard University Press.

Beyers, J. 2004. 'Voice and Access: Political Practices of European Interest Associations'. *European Union Politics* 5(2): pp. 211–240. https://doi.org/10.1177/1465116504042442.

Binderkrantz, A. 2005. 'Interest Group Strategies: Navigating between Privileged Access and Strategies of Pressure'. *Political Studies* 53(4): pp. 694–715. https://doi.org/10.1111/j.1467-9248.2005.00552.x.

Binderkrantz, A. S., P. M. Christiansen, and H. H. Pedersen. 2015. 'Interest Group Access to the Bureaucracy, Parliament, and the Media: Interest Group Access'. *Governance* 2 (1): pp. 95–112. https://doi.org/10.1111/gove.12089.

Binderkrantz, A., H. H. Pedersen, and J. Beyers. 2017. 'What Is Access? A Discussion of the Definition and Measurement of Interest Group Access'. *European Political Science* 16(3): pp. 306–321. https://doi.org/10.1057/eps.2016.17.

De Bruycker, I. 2019. 'Blessing or Curse for Advocacy? How News Media Attention Helps Advocacy Groups to Achieve Their Policy Goals'. *Political Communication* 36(1): pp. 103–126. https://doi.org/10.1080/10584609.2018.1493007.

Cheeseman, N., H. Matfess, and A. Amani. 2021. 'Tanzania: The Roots of Repression'. *Journal of Democracy* 32(2): pp. 77–89.

Crow, D. A., E. A. Albright, and E. A. Koebele. 2019. 'Stakeholder Participation and Strategy in Rulemaking: A Comparative Analysis'. *State Politics & Policy Quarterly* 19(2): pp. 208–235. https://doi.org/10.1177/1532440018821655.

Dahl, R. A. 1961. *Who Governs?* New Haven, CT: Yale University Press.

Daily News. 2016. 'Government Adamant On VAT for Tourism Services'. 13 July. Available at: https://allafrica.com/stories/201607130035.html (accessed: 4 April 2018).

Demil, B., and J. Bensedrine. 2005. 'Processes of Legitimization and Pressure toward Regulation: Corporate Conformity and Strategic Behavior'. *International Studies of Management & Organization* 35(2): pp. 56–77. https://doi.org/10.1080/00208825.2005.11043728.

Halpin, D. R., and B. Fraussen. 2017. 'Conceptualising the Policy Engagement of Interest Groups: Involvement, Access and Prominence'. *European Journal of Political Research* 56(3): pp. 723–732. https://doi.org/10.1111/1475-6765.12194.

Hargrave, T. J., and A. H. van de Ven. 2006. 'A Collective Action Model of Institutional Innovation'. *Academy of Management Review* 31(4): pp. 864–888. https://doi.org/10.5465/AMR.2006.22527458.

Kriesi, H., A. Tresch, and M. Jochum. 2007. 'Going Public in the European Union: Action Repertoires of Western European Collective Political Actors'. *Comparative Political Studies* 40(1): pp. 48–73. https://doi.org/10.1177/0010414005285753.

Levi, M. 1988. *Of Rule and Revenue*. Berkeley, CA: University of California Press.

Levy, D. L., and D. Egan. 2003. 'A Neo-Gramscian Approach to Corporate Political Strategy: Conflict and Accommodation in the Climate Change Negotiations'. *Journal of Management Studies* 40(4): pp. 803–829. https://doi.org/10.1111/1467-6486.00361.

Moore, M. 2004. 'Revenues, State Formation, and the Quality of Governance in Developing Countries'. *International Political Science Review* 25(3): pp. 297–319.

Moore, M. 2007. 'How Does Taxation Affect the Quality of Governance?' *IDS Working Paper 280*. Brighton: Institute for Developing Studies.

Msami, J., L. Katera, and M. Ulriksen. 2022. *Bargaining Strategies in Recent Tax Reforms in Tanzania*. Working paper 16-03-AU. Aarhus: Department of Political Science, Aarhus University.

Oliver, C. 1991. 'Strategic Responses to Institutional Processes'. *Academy of Management Review* 16(1): pp. 145–179. https://doi.org/10.5465/AMR.1991.4279002.

Paget, D. 2021. 'Tanzania: The Authoritarian Landslide'. *Journal of Democracy* 32(2): pp. 61–76.

Prichard, W. 2015. *Taxation, Responsiveness and Accountability in Sub-Saharan Africa: The Dynamics of Tax Bargaining*. Cambridge: Cambridge University Press.

Rizzo, M. 2017. *Taken for a Ride: Grounding Neoliberalism, Precarious Labour, and Public Transport in an African Metropolis*. Oxford: Oxford University Press.

The Citizen. 2016a. 'Tourism "to lose Sh2tr" as VAT bites'. 9 July. Available at: https://www.thecitizen.co.tz/News/Tourism—to-lose-Sh2tr—as-VAT-bites/1840340-3287054-qrwemo/index.html (accessed: 4 April 2018).

The Citizen. 2016b. 'Magufuli closes debate on VAT'. 19. July. Available at: https://www.thecitizen.co.tz/tanzania/news/national/magufuli-closes-debate-on-vat-2561696 (accessed: 30 September 2017).

Therkildsen, O., and F. Bourgouin. 2012. 'Continuity and change in Tanzania's ruling coalition: Legacies, rises and weak productive capacity'. *Working Paper No. 6*. Copenhagen: Danish Institute of Development Studies.

URT, United Republic of Tanzania. 2016. *National Five Year Development Plan 2016/17–2020/21: Nurturing Industrialization for Economic Transformation and Human Development*. Dar es Salaam: Ministry of Finance and Planning.

van den Boogard, V., W. Prichard, R. Beach, and F. Mohiuddin. 2022. 'Enabling tax bargaining: Supporting more meaningful tax transparency and taxpayer engagement in Ghana and Sierra Leone'. *Development Policy Review* 40: e12563.

6

Lobbying in tax policymaking

The case of VAT reform in Tanzania

Odd-Helge Fjeldstad and Lise Rakner

6.1 Introduction

Tax reforms in developing countries have long been considered the exclusive domain of the International Monetary Fund (IMF), external experts, and the countries' ministries of finance (Tait, 1990; Bird, 1991; 2013; Goode, 1993; Barbone et al., 1999; World Bank, 2000; Bird and Zolt, 2003; Mahon, 2004; Fjeldstad and Moore, 2008). However, recent studies have found that tax policy debates are opening up to a wider range of political actors, including business and professional associations, civil society organizations, and individual companies (Moore, 2013; Prichard, 2015; Moore et al., 2018). Although the involvement varies across countries and issues, interest groups seem to be increasingly engaged in tax reform processes, in particular in relation to tax exemptions (Van Parys and James, 2009; Fairfield, 2010; Schiller, 2016; Castañeda, 2017; Bak and Therkildsen, 2022).[1] While some scholars argue that bribery is the preferred way to influence policy decisions in developing countries (Lambsdorff, 2002; Harstad and Svensson, 2011), an emerging literature suggests that lobbyism and interest group mediation are more prevalent in revenue bargaining than previously assumed (Yadav, 2008; Campos, 2009; Weymouth, 2012; Moore, 2013; Lumi, 2014; Nownes, 2017). Yet there is little empirical evidence, especially in Africa, on what specific interests are involved in revenue bargaining, how bargaining processes are set in motion and evolve, how they are organized, what activities are involved, at what level of government the lobbying is directed, and the outcomes of lobbyism on tax reform (see Chapters 1 and 2). This may have important policy

[1] In Chapter 7, Kjær and Arinanye conduct a detailed analysis of how interest groups in the agricultural sector in Uganda successfully lobbied for reduced taxes and exemptions.

Odd-Helge Fjeldstad and Lise Rakner, *Lobbying in tax policymaking*. In: *The Politics of Revenue Bargaining in Africa*. Edited by: Anne Mette Kjær, Marianne S. Ulriksen, and Ane Karoline Bak, Oxford University Press.
 DOI: 10.1093/oso/9780192868787.003.0006

implications, as the nature of the different bargaining positions may affect the political–economic outcomes of micro-level fiscal contracts.

This chapter aims to advance the literature on revenue bargaining in a developing-country context through an analysis of the role that lobbyism by various interest groups plays in shaping tax policies. We use the process behind a recent value-added tax (VAT) reform in Tanzania as our case. VAT was introduced in Tanzania in 1998, with support from the IMF. The VAT Act of 1997 allowed for few exemptions and the zero-rating of only a limited range of products (United Republic of Tanzania, 1997). It was expected that the new tax would broaden the revenue base, leading to increased tax revenue without distorting investment decisions. Over time, however, successive legislative amendments created more exemptions and increased the number of goods and services that were zero-rated. Some of these amendments were framed as incentives for investors, while others reflected private deals between individual business owners and ministers. As a result, VAT administration became more complex, opportunities for abuse and avoidance multiplied, and VAT collections decreased sharply (Krelove et al., 2012, 9). To address these challenges, the government, supported by the IMF, established a technical reform team that produced a new 'model' VAT bill. The new bill was tabled at the National Assembly in May 2014, along with an explanation of the reasons for reform.[2] The new bill allowed only a few exemptions and zero-ratings (mostly food, agricultural implements, and other necessities), and removed the discretionary power of the Minister of Finance to grant and modify tax exemptions. New exemptions were hence to be created or modified only through legislation.

This could have been the end of the VAT reform story. But in contrast to 1997, the private sector quickly mobilized to oppose the new bill, with individual businesspeople pushing for their own special interests.[3] More significantly, the lobbying of Parliament and the Ministry of Finance was coordinated by business associations, especially the Tanzania Private Sector Foundation (TPSF). They employed the services of tax consultants from

[2] The Value Added Tax (VAT) Bill 2014 is a Special Bill Supplement No. 3 of 12 May 2014. It was gazetted in the *Gazette of the United Republic of Tanzania* 20(95), dated 16 May 2014 (United Republic of Tanzania, 2014a). It is a bill for the Act that established the legal framework for the administration and management of VAT. The Valued Added Tax Act 2014, Act Supplement no. 10, was gazetted in the *Gazette of the United Republic of Tanzania* 51(95), dated 19 December 2014 (United Republic of Tanzania, 2014b).

[3] The private sector was poorly coordinated and organized in 1997. Private-sector representatives in the Task Force on Tax Reform acted not on behalf of business associations but for their own companies. TPSF was founded in November 1998, but it took years to build the organization. To the extent that the Big Four worked on taxation in the 1990s, it was mainly as accountants and auditors of companies.

the Big Four global accounting and professional services firms,[4] as well as a former deputy commissioner general of the Tanzania Revenue Authority. Individual businesspeople also lobbied for their specific interests. In addition, public-sector agencies, the Ministry of Agriculture, and the ministry responsible for tourism mobilized against the bill. The lobbyists argued that the abolition of exemptions would make the country unattractive for investors and leave Tanzanian companies uncompetitive in domestic and regional markets.

Working together in a concerted fashion, business associations and other lobby groups succeeded. Even though the governing party, the CCM, holds a majority vote in Parliament (Bunge) and the bill had been drafted by a technical team appointed by the government, the VAT Act that the President signed in January 2015 reintroduced many exemptions that had been abolished in the draft bill and restored to the Minister of Finance some discretionary power to grant further exemptions. A member of the VAT technical team in the Ministry of Finance described the new act as 'old wine in a new bottle'.[5]

Analysing the process leading up to the new VAT Act 2014, our study makes three contributions. First, it shows that tax lobbying in Tanzania has become better organized and coordinated through the larger business associations, sometimes under the umbrella of the Tanzania Private Sector Foundation. Their capacity for collective action has been strengthened and contributed to shaping the ability of business groups to make demands of the government (Prichard, 2015). In the context of the VAT Act 2014, well-organized associations were able to mobilize more powerfully for their demands, partly by engaging professional tax consultants and lobbyists to promote their position to parliamentarians and senior government officials. The enhanced role of the international accounting and consultancy firms in revenue bargaining in Tanzania is a reflection of the importance of lobbying and the substantial resources spent on influencing policymakers and legislators. Professional tax advisors with in-depth knowledge of the tax legislation target their lobbying towards influential stakeholders, including parliamentarians and public agencies who would be affected by the proposed legislation.

[4] The Big Four are the world's four largest international professional services networks, offering audit, tax, consulting, advisory, actuarial, corporate finance, and legal services. Ordered by size they are PricewaterhouseCoopers (PwC), Deloitte, Ernst & Young (EY), and KPMG. In 2012, they had a combined turnover of USD112 billion, with 2,800 offices and over 700,000 employees worldwide. All four companies have businesses in over 150 countries (based on information published in the official global websites of the firms PwC, Deloitte, EY, and KPMG).

[5] Interview, Dar es Salaam, 11 March 2015.

Second, the study adds important nuances to our understanding of legislative performance in single- and dominant-party regimes. Descriptions of African legislatures in the popular press and academic works often depict these institutions as uniformly weak and inconsequential for political and policy outcomes. However, recent scholarly work challenges this view (Opalo, 2019; Collord, 2019). This research underlines how in dominant party regimes, parliamentary institutions play a significant role, as parliament has become an important bargaining arena between powerful political elites and the executive; see Chapter 2 of this volume). Tanzania is considered one of the most institutionalized dominant one-party regimes in Africa (Nyirabu, 2002; Morse, 2014; Collord, 2019). As it is an institutionalized, dominant-party state, it could be assumed that once government is united, there is very little room for lobbying Parliament. Arguably, as a unitary actor, we would expect reforms approved by the executive to be approved by Parliament with relative ease, in contrast to less institutionalized political systems characterized by political alternations and deinstitutionalized party systems (Rakner and Svåsand. 2013; Opalo, 2019). However, in connection with the VAT reform, we find that the government was not able to instruct individual members of parliament who proved receptive when confronted by an increasingly professional group of lobbyists. In Tanzania, during the past decade, political elites have sought to entrench their bargaining power through legislative reforms, creating the institutional resources needed to better extract benefits from the executive. The bargaining process behind the 2014 VAT Act is illustrative of the complexities of implementing tax reforms in contexts of multiple interests (see also Chapter 5 on revenue-bargaining processes in Tanzania that include a multiplicity of actors and strategies).

Third, our study challenges the argument that bribery is the preferred way to influence policy decisions in developing countries whereas lobbyism is more common in rich countries (Harstad and Svensson, 2011). Our study shows that this is an oversimplification that does not reflect how policy influencing actually takes place in poor, weakly regulated countries. Lobbyism might be more prevalent than previously assumed in the literature (Fjeldstad and Johnsøn, 2017). When interest groups grow in influence, companies and business associations may develop a preference for lobbyism over corruption. Our analysis of the implementation of the VAT reform in Tanzania shows that there are numerous entry points for lobbying. Having escalated in the period after 2000, elite bargaining around policy reform in Tanzania now involves private-sector financiers who contest for parliamentary seats, fund MPs' campaigns, and lobby in an ad hoc, issue-based manner (Collord, 2019, 219).

The analysis draws on findings from research carried out in Tanzania during the period 2014–2016. We analyse the development of the VAT Act, from the process started in December 2012, to the presentation of the draft bill in Parliament in May 2014, through to its final vote in Parliament in November 2014, and its final signing by the Executive in December 2014. Our main sources of data are: (i) careful reading of the VAT bill (draft May 2014), the amended bill (November 2014), and the VAT Act (December 2014); (ii) interviews with representatives of the business community, individual business people, partners of the Big Four international accountancy and advisory companies, domestic tax practitioners, IMF representatives, staff of the Ministry of Finance and the Tanzania Revenue Authority (TRA), and sector interests; and (iii) reports and newspaper articles collected for the period December 2012–June 2016. Our findings resonate with other case studies in this book, and, as such, contribute to substantiating and elaborating the theoretical framework.

The remainder of the chapter is divided into five sections. In the next section, the VAT reform is presented. The third section explores the conditions that triggered the VAT-reform initiative and provided entry points for revenue bargaining. The lobbying process and its organization are examined in the fourth section. The fifth section discusses the outcome of the revenue bargaining as reflected in the new VAT Act. A concluding section completes the chapter's analysis.

6.2 The case: Background for the VAT reform

VAT was implemented in Tanzania in July 1998, advised by and with technical assistance from the IMF.[6] The VAT was expected to broaden the tax base, leading to substantial increase in tax revenue without distorting investment decisions. With few exemptions and zero-ratings, the original VAT Act of 1997 was perceived by the IMF and international tax advisors as a 'best practice model' for VAT design in a developing-country context. Subsequent developments, however, deviated from the that model.[7] When the new act was introduced in 1998, it was estimated that VAT would generate revenues equivalent to 6% of GDP. However, the VAT regime was gradually undermined by exemptions, and revenues never exceeded 4.5% of GDP.

[6] As early as 1991, introduction of VAT was proposed by a Tax Commission appointed by the government (United Republic of Tanzania, 1991, chapter 12). However, before 1997 little progress was made in this area.

[7] Interview with senior officer, Research and Policy Department, TRA HQ (member of the VAT Technical Team), Dar es Salaam, 11 March 2015.

Over time, amendments of the Act incorporated an expanding number of exemptions and zero-ratings of goods and services and of persons entitled to receive exempt supplies. Some of these exonerations were promoted by the Tanzania Investment Centre (TIC) in order to attract investments. Generous tax incentives granted to multinational companies, especially in agriculture and extractive sectors such as mining, led domestic enterprises to lobby for tax exemptions to adjust for the perceived unfairness of the tax regime.[8] The VAT Act provided discretion and hence a space for domestic companies to request for exemptions. The Minister of Finance had power to grant exemptions and could channel requests for exemptions through the Task Force on Tax Reform (composed of representatives from the public and private sectors), a process that made it relatively easy to add exemptions.[9] Other ministries and government agencies were also involved in tax policymaking. Fragmented policymaking and bureaucratic competition made it easy for interest groups and individuals to lobby for their interests.[10] According to Ali Mufuruki, a leading business owner in the country, a 'tax-incentives industry developed to advise clients on how to legally access incentives'.[11] The Big Four became a big part of this industry.

The numerous exemptions and zero-rated goods and services complicated the underlying VAT structure, caused complexity in the tax system, and added to widespread leakages through the many opportunities for abuse and avoidance. This also had adverse effects on revenue generation. By 2012, Tanzania ranked among the countries with lowest VAT productivity among the Southern African Development Community (SADC) and East African Community (EAC) countries. An IMF aide-mémoire from 2012 describes the Tanzanian VAT regime as follows: 'The ever-expanding list of preferences has deteriorated VAT tax base. Tax exemptions of inputs add to tax cascading and numerous tax relieves seriously undermine VAT revenue productivity' (Krelove et al., 2012, 46). By 2012, senior managers in the Ministry of Finance and the (Tanzania Revenue Authority) TRA recognized that the VAT regime needed reform.[12] The Minister consulted the IMF, an IMF mission was put

[8] By the end of 2014, 80 per cent of the strategic investors granted tax exemptions by the Tanzania Investment Centre were domestic companies. Interview with Director of Investment Facilitation, TIC, Dar es Salaam, 17 November 2014.

[9] Interview with two senior officers, Research and Policy Department, TRA-HQ, Dar es Salaam, 11 March 2015.

[10] Interview with IMF representative, Dar es Salaam, 25 August 2014.

[11] Interview, Dar es Salaam, 10 November 2014. The late Ali Mufuruki was a co-founder and chairman of the CEO Roundtable of Tanzania, a policy-dialogue forum that brings together more than a hundred CEOs of leading companies in Tanzania.

[12] Interviews with members of the VAT Technical Team from the Ministry of Finance and the TRA, Dar es Salaam, 11 March 2015.

in motion, and external VAT consultants were engaged. A technical reform team composed of staff from the Ministry of Finance, the Tanzania Revenue Authority, and the Office of the Attorney General was established. According to the IMF, the original VAT regime in Tanzania from 1997 was almost 'textbook', but some structural features affected its intentions negatively over time and contributed to the low tax-to-GDP ratio. Two problems were noted: (i) poorly structured refunds (paid late, leaving businesses cash strapped, legitimizing the 'cry for exemptions'),[13] and (ii) the stated aim of providing incentives for foreign capital (FDI). Amendments of the VAT Act of 1997 introduced many exemptions and zero-ratings for intermediate inputs to various industries and sectors, originally intended in part to work around tax refund problems, in part to enhance investment and protect the local market, and in part to reduce the tax burden on consumers and some sectors, especially agriculture (Krelove et al., 2012).

6.3 The VAT-reform initiative and conditions that triggered revenue bargaining

While revenue concerns played a major role in the initiation of the VAT-reform process, the reform was also triggered by pressure from various stakeholders demanding more tax fairness. The excessive VAT exemptions were routinely lamented by civil society groups, Members of Parliament, as well as the Controller and Auditor General (CAG), who in his various reports pointed to the increasing and escalating exemptions (IMF, 2008; Uwazi, 2010; TRA, 2011; Ndunguru, 2012; CAG, 2013; IFC, 2013).[14] The extensive discretionary power of the Minister of Finance to grant exemptions was also noted as a major problem by all parties. Based on recommendations from the IMF, pressure from the international donor community as well as increasing pressure from the main opposition party Chadema, the Parliament's Public Accounts Committee (PAC) in 2012 directed the Controller and Auditor General to conduct a special audit of the exemptions to ascertain whether the waivers were beneficial to the country.

In 2013, the government decided to develop a new VAT Act and established a technical reform team to lead this work. The team was composed

[13] In Tanzania, like in many other many African countries, it may take several months, and sometimes up to a year, to process refund claims (Carter, 2013).

[14] In an interview in *The East African* (8 February 2014), Mr Rakesh Rajani, director of the civil society organization Twaweza East Africa, questioned the government's commitment to review the exemptions, saying the job should take less than six months to accomplish, but that the government had been dragging its feet.

of staff from the Ministry of Finance, the Tanzania Revenue Authority, and the Office of the Attorney general, with support from an external VAT expert recruited by the IMF. During 2013 and 2014, a new VAT bill was drafted. According to the IMF resident representative in Tanzania, the original draft was very ambitious, almost aiming to be a 'perfect VAT Act with very limited number of exemptions'.[15] The new bill included a few exemptions and zero-ratings (food and basic necessities), but all special reliefs for named bodies were abolished (URT, 2014a). The draft bill removed the discretionary power of the Minister of Finance to grant and modify tax exemptions (ibid., 88). The bill stipulated that exemptions be approved by Parliament and that new exemptions should be created or modified by Parliament only. The draft VAT Bill was sent to Parliament from the Ministry of Finance in May 2014.

The work leading up to the draft bill was run by the technical reform team supported by the IMF. According to a member of the technical team, the multi-stakeholder Task Force on Tax Reform 'was not consulted since it was seen as being part of the problem'.[16] The first version of the bill was drafted by a technical expert engaged by the IMF. Thereafter, the Tanzanian VAT Technical Team made some 'improvements of the draft act during first half of 2014 to make it better fit the Tanzanian context'.[17] The IMF's resident representative confirmed that the Tanzanian team did not take on board all recommendations from the IMF, claiming they would not work in the Tanzania context.[18] In this process, the technical team also had consultations with some Cabinet members.

According to members of the technical team, an early draft of the VAT bill was sent to the Confederation of Tanzania Industries (CTI), the Oil and Gas Association of Tanzania (OGAT), the Tanzania Petroleum Development Corporation (TPDC), the Tanzania Private Sector Foundation (TPSF), and the Big Four. However, according to the TPSF, no consultations took place prior to the bill being presented to Parliament in May 2014.[19] Conceding this point, the IMF representative referred to the drafting of a bill as a rather closed process, where technical assistance and outside forces are somewhat limited in their inputs: 'By Tanzanian standards there were some consultations, but consultations could have been made better, more widely, and

[15] Interview, Dar es Salaam, 27 October 2015.
[16] Interview, Dar es Salaam, 11 March 2015.
[17] Interview with members of the technical team, Dar es Salaam, 11 March 2015.
[18] Interview, Dar es Salaam, 27 October 2015.
[19] Interviews with Ali Mufuriki (CEO Roundtable Tanzania), 10. November 2014; Lathifa Sykes (CEO Hotel Association of Tanzania), 19 March 2015; and Edward Furaha (Research and Policy Manager, TPSF), 27 October 2015.

involved more interest groups for example from the private sector'.[20] He further reflected that: 'IMF had expected that the Cabinet would approve the May 2014 Bill and agree on the Bill before it was sent to the Bunge. This did not happen. The line ministries—especially tourism and agriculture—were not aware that the exemptions for their sectors had been removed and reacted when they saw the bill'.[21]

It is not surprising that different stakeholders hold different views when describing a consultation process that happened some time back, a process with which at least one party (the private sector) was unhappy. However, based on evidence acquired through interviews with key stakeholders, it is evident that the process of drafting the 2014 VAT bill was neither participatory nor consultative. Key stakeholders in the private sector were not properly consulted, and some Cabinet members and ministries, especially Tourism and Agriculture, had not been provided with adequate information about the short-term consequences of the proposed changes of the VAT Act. The fact that the Parliament's Budget Committee sent the draft bill back to the Cabinet for a redrafting adds credence to the argument that stakeholder consultations were limited in the first stage of drafting the VAT bill.

The above analysis illustrates that revenue bargaining can be triggered by reforms drafted by technocratic government staff (or external actors) tasked with how to increase revenue. The case further illustrates that such 'technocratic reforms' have distinct limits, as stakeholders who have not been consulted in the initial stages of a reform may seek to influence the design of the reform before it is finally tabled as an act.

6.4 Political settlement and arenas of revenue bargaining

The political settlement in Tanzania is rooted in a strong institutionalized party dominating the parliament upheld and legitimized through its ties to the country's business elites (Ishiyama and Quinn, 2006; Babeiya, 2011; Gray, 2018).[22] The ruling party the Chama Cha Mapinduzi (CCM)[23] has governed Tanzania since independence with remarkable stability (Phillips, 2010; Coulson, 2013; Lofchie, 2014). Whereas legal reforms have officially

[20] Interview, Dar es Salaam, 27 October 2015.

[21] Interview with IMF representative, Dar es Salaam, 27 October 2015.

[22] The CCM's majority position does not include Zanzibar, where the opposition is strong. The main opposition party in mainland Tanzania, Chadema, has succeeded in winning a number of subnational elections since 2010 in several of the major cities, including Dar es Salaam and Arusha.

[23] Chama Cha Mapinduzi means 'Party of the Revolution' in English.

detached the party from the state, most state institutions are still informally linked behaviourally to the ruling party. The lack of separation between the state and the party (Makulilo, 2008) makes the CCM a *state-party* or a *party-state*. The party remains the 'party of choice' for anyone seeking a political career (Therkildsen and Bourgouin, 2012). As noted by one Tanzanian describing the CCM's likelihood of winning the 2005 elections, 'CCM has its roots everywhere.... It has taken up all the earth. There is no room for other parties to grow' (Phillips, 2010, 109). Signalling the ruling party's control over commercial business, Babeiya (2011, 95) argued that: 'The use of threats also continues to guarantee CCM much support from the business community as businesspersons fear repression if they do not support the incumbent party'.

With economic liberalization, the CCM's ability to retain centralized control over wealth accumulation began to unravel due to a combination of economic decline, growing informalization, corruption, and, ultimately, economic liberalization (Kiondo, 1994; Mmuya, 1998; Babeiya, 2011). As argued by Collord (2019), Tanzania's changing economy saw CCM leaders adopt a new pattern of politicized accumulation, one characterized by ad hoc connections between an expanded private-sector elite and various factional networks within the CCM itself. Business owners of Asian origin won two out of four by-elections between 1992 and 1995, an unprecedented occurrence in Tanzania (ibid., 118). Despite the CCM's dominant position and executive dominance, Babeiya (2011, 97) argues that individual MPs' influence relies heavily on private resources in their election campaigns, and their individual resources are shaping voting behaviour: 'The power of the purse is currently one of the tickets to pass the nomination and election test in both party and intra-party competitions'. Corresponding to the earlier discussion of government capture, arguably this culture of private wealth shaping electoral outcomes, businesspeople are venturing into political careers, suggesting a strong link between business and politics (see Chapter 9 of this volume).

The political settlement outlined above could be expected to have yielded a different outcome of the VAT revenue-bargaining process. In a state where one party dominates, holding a majority of the parliamentary seats, we would not expect a law endorsed by the government to be altered by lobbying or treatment in Parliament. However, because individual MPs rely heavily on resources and business support to finance their electoral campaigns, the VAT bill was susceptible to changes during the vote in Parliament. During the bargaining process, the draft bill was substantially reshaped. For instance, many items that are referred to as 'VATable' in the May 2014 Bill are exempted in the VAT Act passed in Parliament in November 2014. While central actors in government, particularly in the Ministry of Finance and the Tanzania Revenue

Authority, and in the parliamentary opposition, NGOs, the media, and some donors had argued for a simplified VAT Act with a drastically reduced exempt list, Tanzania ended up almost in 'status quo'.

Interviews with both members of the technical drafting team and representatives from the private sector established that the draft bill of May 2014 was met with protests from the private sector.[24] The private sector argued that the drastic removal of exemptions would imply severe challenges for the business environment in Tanzania. For the private sector, the key issue was fiscal predictability. They argued, for instance, that the tourism sector needed more time to adjust. The Parliament Budget Committee demanded more consultations due to what it to be considered weaknesses and shortfalls in the draft bill. Public hearings on the VAT bill starting in August 2014 led to extensive lobbying, especially for exemptions, and amendments of the bill. The debate that took place in the Cabinet as the bill was returned suggests that the Cabinet had not fully grasped the implications of the removal of exemptions for the private sector and some line ministries. The Cabinet was not united. Some ministries, in particular those of Agriculture and of Natural Resources and Tourism, were much in favour of tax exemptions for enterprises in their respective sectors. The Minister responsible for tourism personally lobbied for exemptions in Parliament.

Members of the main business associations, the IMF, the TRA, and the Ministry of Finance all confirmed in interviews that lobbying gathered momentum after the drafted bill was presented to Parliament in May 2014. However, initial attempts to ensure that the new VAT Act avoided the problems of exemptions and loopholes associated with the previous act did not succeed. IMF initially suggested that Parliament should be involved in developing the new act, in order to reduce exemptions and sensitize MPs on the costs of exemptions. However, as Parliament only became involved late in the process when the bill was presented for a vote, the opportunity to build a common understanding in Parliament on the costs of exemptions was lost. This again left Parliament open for lobbying during the period after the draft bill was presented to the legislature. As a result, paradoxically, considering that the debate about the new VAT Act started with opposition MPs publicly shaming the VAT exemptions inherent in the amended VAT Act of 1997, Parliament did not emerge as a constituency favouring reducing exemptions.

The claim that MPs were being lobbied individually by representatives of the private sector was confirmed by the private sector. As Edward Furaha

[24] Interviews with representatives from TPSF, 12 November 2014 and 27 October 2015; managers from TRA, 14 November 2014 and 11 March 2015; and officials from the Ministry of Finance, 11 March 2015.

of the TPSF said at the time, 'Individual members who do not know issues are normally made to understand issues in the process of lobbying'.[25] A typical strategy would be to start with general issues that touch everyone (such as VAT imposed on funeral services) and use these as evidence of the impacts of the draft bill of May 2014 if implemented. The direct lobbying of MPs was also confirmed by public-sector representatives. According to a senior TRA manager: 'MPs listen to too many lobby groups . . . . Allocation of responsibility is problematic . . . . MPs are swayed by the Big Four and TPSF. . . .... Clearly, government should have done their own explanation, as politicians were misled by lobbyists.'[26] While tax practitioners from KMPG claimed that KMPG had not been involved in the lobbying of MPs, they nevertheless conceded that extensive lobbying of individual MPs had taken place and that 'the exemptions are all back and the draft VAT bill has gone through a complete overhaul'.[27]

The VAT law changed considerably between its submission to Parliament for debate in May 2014 and the final vote in November. Lobbying against the VAT bill was coordinated by TPSF towards members of the Budget Committee. They also had meetings with the Ministry of Finance, presenting the private sector's position. Much of this lobbying was done by tax experts from PwC engaged by the TPSF. According to Lathifa Sikes, representative of the Hotels Association of Tanzania (HAT), PwC and the TPSF were present in Dodoma to lobby MPs.[28] She argued, however, that they did not pay bribes to MPs: 'We went to Dodoma and argued our case'. This observation is important and suggests that it is too simplistic to expect that businesses will prefer to bribe rather than lobby if both strategies can achieve the same goal. While it is difficult to substantiate that lobbying took precedence over bribery, the rise of large, reasonably well-organized business associations, combined with stricter perceived enforcement of international legislation and conventions against corruption, lead us to tentatively conclude that lobbying was considered a preferred strategy by the Tanzanian business sector. Arguably, 'revenue bargaining' took a number of forms. The debate around the VAT Act witnessed little direct bribery. Instead, bargaining was done through several channels, including individual lobbying where companies acted in their individual capacity, by individual business associations such as the HAT, and by coordinated efforts by the TPSF.

[25] Interview, Dar es Salaam, 27 October 2015.
[26] Interview with senior manager in TRA, 14 November 2014.
[27] Interview, Dar es Salaam, 18 March 2015.
[28] Interview, Dar es Salaam, 19 March 2015.

The Parliament's handling of the VAT Act of 2014 illustrates the ambivalent role the national assembly played in safeguarding elite interests. Following the 2010 election, both Parliament and government took steps towards fiscal reforms. The then Speaker of the National Assembly, Anne Makinda, convened a special parliamentary committee, referred to simply as the Speaker's Committee, and tasked it with recommending changes to Tanzania's tax regime, including reducing the number of exemptions. The government's VAT bill (2014) was largely in line with recommendations made by the Parliament's own Speaker's Committee. Yet Parliament proceeded to amend the VAT bill, rolling back many of the key changes. Many exemptions abolished through the bill were reinstated; there was no clarity on what should happen to exemptions granted by the Tanzania Investment Centre (TIC); and the discretionary powers of the Minister of Finance were reduced but not removed. According to Collord (2019, 219), this legislative activity appeared to follow a 'parliamentary business cycle', shaped by MPs' changing incentives ahead of expensive re-election campaigns.

6.5 Outcome of the revenue bargaining

Chapters 1 and 2 of this volume outline how the fiscal contract literature emphasizes the circumstances under which taxation may lead to reciprocal positive exchanges of revenue and public goods and/or accountability. However, in the case of bargaining around the VAT act in Tanzania, the outcome of revenue bargaining is more succinctly depicted as an agreement regarding tax *exemptions*. In January 2015, the President signed the new VAT Act, and it took effect in July 2015. According to Rished Bade, then Commissioner General of the TRA, the VAT Act that was presented to and debated in Parliament in November 2014 was more 'realistic' than the draft bill of May 2014. Due to the many vested interests who were likely to resist major changes to the tax system, particularly changes related to exemptions, the original (May) draft VAT bill was not realistic: 'It was unrealistic to go from one extreme to the next'.[29] This position is supported by the IMF's resident representative, arguing that 'the Cabinet had not grasped the implications of the removal of exemptions in the May 2014 Bill for the private sector and some sectors under some line ministries, especially tourism and agriculture. It would have been better if the Cabinet had represented a united front'.[30]

[29] Interview, TRA HQ, Dar es Salaam (11 March 2015).
[30] Interview, Dar es Salaam, 27 October 2015.

The VAT bill of May 2014 suggested removing the discretionary power of the Minister of Finance to grant and modify tax exemptions. This would imply that any future changes in existing exemptions had to be approved by Parliament, and new exemptions could be created or modified only through legislation. This provision was altered in the new Act, which now states that the Minister of Finance can grant exemptions in cases of 'emergencies and calamities' (URT, 2014b, para. 6(2)).

Although the new act removed the special relief schedule and the list of exempted items was reduced, some of the exemptions that were removed in the draft bill were reinstated in the new act (e.g. the exemption for tourism services). Further, any tax incentives already granted to investors under the Economic Processing Zones Act and the Special Investment Processes Zones Act continued to apply. Since the VAT Act is silent on incentives granted under the Tanzania Investment Act, it is not clear whether these incentives will continue to be granted. The discretionary power of the Minister of Finance to grant exemptions was reduced but not entirely removed in the new act. The Minister may grant exemptions for government imports of goods and services intended for relief of natural calamities or disasters.

Interviewed business representatives argued that tax incentives were not of major importance for their investment decisions.[31] They viewed improvements in the investment and business climate as a better way for Tanzania to boost growth and, thus, increase government revenue. To do so, they argued, the government should improve efficiency and transparency in the public administration to reduce corruption. Rather than increasing tax exemptions, businesspeople argued in favour of a simple and predictable tax regime. What, then, explains the extensive lobbying for exemptions? The short answer is that tax incentives reduce business costs, and incentives granted to other companies and/or sectors in a non-transparent way are perceived to be unfair. When 'everyone else' is granted tax exemptions, one's own competitiveness depends on exemptions. Further, tax lobbying in Tanzania has become better organized and coordinated through the larger business associations, sometimes under the umbrella of the Tanzania Private Sector Foundation. The TPSF represents both domestic and multinational companies. Although lobbying by individual businesspeople still features, larger, organized associations are able to mobilize more powerfully for their demands, partly by engaging professional tax consultants and lobbyists to

[31] Interview with Ali Mufuruki, then chairman of the CEO Roundtable of Tanzania, a policy dialogue forum that brings together more than 100 CEOs of leading companies in Tanzania, Dar es Salaam, 10 November 2014.

promote their position to parliamentarians and senior government officials. The enhanced role of the Big Four in Tanzania is a reflection of the importance of lobbying and the substantial resources spent on influencing policymakers and legislators.

Professional tax advisors target their lobbying on influential stakeholders including parliamentarians and public agencies affected by the proposed legislation. For instance, the agriculture sector has benefited from a vast array of VAT and customs duty exemptions. The lobbyists could easily mobilize the Ministry of Agriculture against any attempt to remove these exemptions. The same applies to the tourism sector. Removal of tax exemptions for elected officials would also easily mobilize parliamentarians against such a move, even if this would simply imply that public leaders receive the same tax treatment as the electorate.

Interest groups in Tanzania managed partly to reshape the VAT reform. A member of the technical VAT team in the Ministry of Finance said that 'The new act is completely diluted'.[32] This statement reflects a disappointment that the new act did not go as far as anticipated in removing exemptions. One may argue, however, that the VAT Act of 2014 is a move in the right direction. As they have to be publicly debated, it will be harder to make new tax exemptions; the Minister's discretionary options have become more restricted. Still, given the recent history of tax lobbying in Tanzania, we may expect that pressure will soon emerge to amend the Act to bring back more exemptions and zero-ratings.

6.6 Conclusion

This chapter has highlighted how revenue-bargaining processes shape tax policies and tax legislation. Tracing the various stages behind the 2014 VAT Act in Tanzania, weighing the various interests, lobbyists, and political actors, we have documented a tax reform outcome that changed significantly from the draft stage to the final gazette stage. The analysis of the process behind the Act illustrates how a political settlement characterized by an institutionalized dominant party state, legitimized by major business interests, was vulnerable to lobbying from interest groups and international consulting firms acting on behalf of business interests.

It is a paradox that, after 2014's reforms, which aimed to address the poor performance of taxes, the VAT system in Tanzania remains riddled with

[32] Interview, Dar es Salaam, 11 March 2015.

exemptions and zero rates on imported and domestic goods and services. These exemptions have been actively defended and expanded through lobbying by the beneficiaries. Tanzania's tax-to-GDP ratio is well below the average of low- and lower-middle-income countries, and lower than the average for the countries in the East African Community (UNECA, 2019). The country's poor revenue performance is, according to the IMF, mainly driven by the low VAT collection (IMF, 2016). Thus, Tanzania is categorized as a 'low tax effort' country with respect to VAT, defined as a country collecting 'two-thirds or less of the revenue that [it] can be expected to raise in view of [its] institutional and economic circumstances' (Cnossen, 2015, 1078).

The lobbying process against the draft VAT Bill of May 2014 may be considered a case of coordinated lobbying by private business associations influencing and greatly shaping a set of uncoordinated policy positions by different government bodies. Accounting for this suboptimal equilibrium—that initially neither major private-sector interests nor the government wanted—we have shown how lobbying is shaped by political institutions. The tax literature has not adequately addressed this critical dimension of revenue bargaining in tax reform processes. Our analysis suggests that lobbyism in poorly regulated developing countries may be much more important than previously assumed in both the academic and policy-oriented literature. Our analysis further underscores the need for better understanding of how the rules of the 'lobby' game are affected by uneven power relations between interest groups.

The process behind the VAT reform in Tanzania offers a vivid illustration of one kind of intensified public engagement in tax matters. This in turn suggests one potential road to more significant reform outcomes; the empowerment of a broader range of voices in tax debates to motivate and support political leaders willing to drive progress. A key area of concern is the extent to which revenue-bargaining outcomes benefitting only a few companies and wealthy people may affect the compliance behaviour of a larger segment of taxpayers, and ultimately the ability of governments to generate income and distribute it fairly. In some ways, the case of the VAT reform is yet another example of powerful interests securing special treatment. However, the political process was very different from the process of introducing VAT in 1998. This time, the decision was made not quietly behind closed doors but in a highly public and contested process. This exemplifies the increasingly active participation of business associations in tax policy debates in Africa. The revenue bargaining around the VAT Act in Tanzania suggests that in addition to individual lobbying, the business community acted as a unitary entity as members of the umbrella organization TPSF. In order for this new trend to yield broader public benefits, the enhanced and coordinated business activism must be accompanied by transparency and broader public debates in order to yield engagement by ordinary African taxpayers in the politics of taxation.

Acknowledgements

We would like to thank Ane Karoline Bak, Anne Mette Kjær, Prosper Ngowi, and Ole Therkildsen for valuable comments on earlier versions of this chapter. Helpful comments were also received from participants at the African Studies Association's panel on 'Revenue-bargaining dynamics in sub-Saharan Africa', Chicago, 17 November 2017, and the ECPR Joint session on 'Politics of revenue bargaining', Nicosia, 11–14 April 2018. Points of view and possible errors are entirely our responsibility. The chapter was prepared with financial support from the Research Council of Norway (grant no. 287105).

References

Babeiya, E. 2011. 'Electoral Corruption and the Politics of Election Financing in Tanzania'. *Journal of Politics and Law* 4(2): pp. 91–103.

Bak, A. K., and O. Therkildsen. 2022. 'Democratisation in Tanzania: No Elections Without Tax Exemptions'. *Journal of Eastern African Studies* 16(1): pp. 47–67.

Barbone, L., A. Das-Gupta, D. L. Wulf, and A. Hansson. 1999. 'Reforming Tax Systems: The World Bank Record in the 1990s'. *World Bank Policy Research Working Paper 2237*. Washington, DC: World Bank.

Bird, R. M. 1991. *Tax Policy and Economic Development*. Baltimore and London: Johns Hopkins University Press.

Bird, R. M. 2013. 'Foreign Advice and Tax Policy in Developing Countries', *International Center for Public Policy Working Paper 13-07* (4). Atlanta, GA: Georgia State University, Andrew Young School of Policy Studies.

Bird, R. M., and E. M. Zolt. 2003. '*Introduction to Tax Policy Design and Development*'. *Paper prepared for Course on Practical Issues of Tax Policy in Developing Countries*. Washington, DC: World Bank.

Campos, N. F. 2009. 'In Pursuit of Policy Influence: Can Lobbying Be a Legitimate Alternative to Corruption in Developing Countries?' *U4 Anti-Corruption Resource Centre Brief 2009(1)*. http://www.u4.no/publications/in-pursuit-of-policy-influence-can-lobbying-be-a-legitimate-alternative-to-corruption-in-developing-countries/.

Carter, A. (ed.). 2013. *Key Issues and Debates in VAT, SME Taxation and the Tax Treatment of the Financial Sector*. Paris: International Tax Dialogue. http://bit.ly/1CNopZb.

Castañeda, N. 2017. 'Business Coordination and Tax Politics'. *Political Studies* 65(1): pp. 122–143.

Cnossen, S. 2015. 'Mobilizing VAT Revenues in African Countries'. *International Tax and Public Finance* 22(6): pp. 1077–1108.

Collord, M. 2019. *The Political Economy of Institutions in Africa: Comparing Authoritarian Parties and Parliaments in Tanzania and Uganda*. PhD dissertation, Department of Politics and International Relations, University of Oxford, Oxford.

Controller and Auditor General. 2013. *Annual General Report of the Controller and Auditor General*. Dar es Salaam: National Audit Office.

Coulson, A. 2013. *Tanzania: A Political Economy*. 2nd edition. Oxford: Oxford University Press.

Fairfield, T. 2010. 'Business Power and Tax Reform: Taxing Income and Profits in Chile and Argentina'. *Latin American Politics and Society* 52(2): pp. 37–71.

Fjeldstad, O.-H., and J. Johnsøn. 2017. 'Governance Challenges in Tanzania's Natural Gas Sector: Unregulated Lobbyism and Uncoordinated Policy'. In *Corruption, Natural Resources and Development: From Resource Curse to Political Ecology*, edited by A. Williams and P. le Billon, pp. 44–57. Cheltenham, UK: Edward Elgar Publishing.

Fjeldstad, O.-H. and M. Moore. 2008. 'Tax Reform and State Building in a Globalized World'. In *Taxation and State Building in Developing Countries: Capacity and Consent*, edited by D. Braütigam, O.-H. Fjeldstad, and M. Moore, pp. 235–260. Cambridge: Cambridge University Press.

Goode, R. 1993. 'Tax Advice to Developing Countries: An Historical Survey'. *World Development* 21(1): pp. 37–54.

Gray, H. 2018. *Turbulence and Order in Economic Development: Institutions and Economic Transformation in Tanzania and Vietnam*. Oxford: Oxford University Press.

Harstad, B., and J. Svensson. 2011. 'Bribes, Lobbying, and Development'. *American Political Science Review* 105: pp. 46–63.

IFC (International Finance Corporation). 2013. *Measuring the Revenue Cost of Tax Incentives in the East African Community (EAC) Member States*. Preliminary version (April). Washington, DC: World Bank Group.

IMF. 2008. *Kenya, Uganda and United Republic of Tanzania: Selected Issues, 1 December*. Washington, DC. http://www.imf.org/external/pubs/ft/scr/2008/cr08353.pdf

IMF. 2016. *United Republic of Tanzania: Selected Issues, 30 June*. Washington, DC. https://www.imf.org/external/pubs/ft/scr/2016/cr16254.pdf.

Ishiyama, J., and J. J. Quinn. 2006. 'African Phoenix? Explaining the Electoral Performance of the Formerly Dominant Parties in Africa'. *Party Politics* 12(3): pp. 317–340.

Kiondo, A. S. Z. 1994. 'Economic Power and Electoral Politics in Tanzania'. In *Liberalization and Politics: The 1990 Election in Tanzania*, edited by Rwekaza S. Mukandala, and Haroub Othman, pp. 66–89. Dar es Salaam: Dar es Salaam University Press.

Krelove, R., A. Swistak, and A. Watson. 2012. 'Tanzania: Mining and Gas Fiscal Regimes and VAT reform'. *Aide-Mémoire*, Fiscal Affairs Department. Washington, DC: International Monetary Fund.

Lambsdorff, J. G. 2002. 'Corruption and Rent-Seeking'. *Public Choice* 113(1–2): pp. 97–125.

Lofchie, M. F. 2014. *The Political Economy of Tanzania: Decline and Recovery*. Philadelphia: University of Pennsylvania Press.

Lumi, O. 2014. 'Comparative Insight into the Status of the Lobbying Regulation Debate in Estonia'. *Journal of Public Affairs* 15: pp. 300–310.

Mahon, J. E. 2004. 'Causes of Tax Reform in Latin America, 1977–95'. *Latin American Research Review* 39(1): pp. 3–30.

Makulilo, A. B. 2008. *Tanzania: A de Facto One Party State?* Saarbrücken: VDM Verlag.

Mmuya, M. 1998. *Tanzania: Political Reform in Eclipse: Crisis and Cleavage in Political Parties*. Dar es Salam: Friedrich Ebert Stiftung.

Moore, M. 2013. 'The Changing Politics of Tax Policy Reform in Developing Countries'. *PREM Notes No. 12* (February). Washington, DC: World Bank. https://documents1.worldbank.org/curated/pt/488221523258263828/pdf/125051-BRI-Tax-Policy-Reform-GPSM-2-PUBLIC.pdf.

Moore, M, W. Prichard, and O-H. Fjeldstad. 2018. *Taxing Africa: Coercion, Reform and Development*. London: ZED Books Ltd.

Morse, Y L. 2014. 'Party Matters: The Institutional Origins of Tanzania's Competitive Hegemony'. *Democratization* 21(4): pp. 655–677.

Ndunguru, A. 2012. 'Tax Incentives and Exemptions in Tanzania: Challenges for Tax Policy and Revenue Administration'. Paper presented at the ICTD Annual Conference 2012, 12–13 December, Cape Town.

Nownes, A. 2017. 'Lobbying: The Preconditions of an Anti-Corruption Promise'. *U4 Issue No. 8* (June). Bergen: Chr. Michelsen Institute.

Nyirabu, M. 2002. 'The Multiparty Reform Process in Tanzania: The Dominance of the Ruling Party'. *The African Journal of Political Science* 7(2): pp. 99–112.

Opalo, K. O. 2019. *Legislative Development in Africa: Politics and Postcolonial Legacies*. Cambridge: Cambridge University Press.

Phillips, K. D. 2010. 'Pater Rules Best: Political Kinship and Party Politics in Tanzania's Presidential Elections'. *PoLAR: Political and Legal Anthropology Review* 33(1): pp. 109–132.

Prichard, W. 2015. *Taxation, Responsiveness and Accountability in Sub-Saharan Africa*. Cambridge: Cambridge University Press.

Rakner, L., and L. Svåsand. 2013. 'Competition and Participation, But No Democracy: The Politics of Elections in Africa's Feckless Regimes'. *Statsvetenskaplig Tidskrift* 115(4): pp. 365–384.

Schiller, A. von. 2016. 'Business Organisations, Party Systems and Tax Composition in Developing Countries: A Comparison between Colombia and Peru'. *Journal of Development Studies* 52(12): pp. 1722–1743.

Tait, A. 1990. 'IMF Advice on Fiscal Policy'. *Finance & Development* 27(1): pp. 33–36.

TRA (Tanzania Revenue Authority). 2011. 'Risk Assessment of Tax Exemptions, 2006/07– 2009/10'. *Report-RPD-001/2010/03* (March). Dar es Salaam: Tanzania Revenue Authority.

Therkildsen, O., and F. Bourgouin. 2012. 'Continuity and Change in Tanzania's Ruling Coalition: Legacies, Crises and Weak Productive Capacity'. *DIIS Working Paper 2012(6)*. Copenhagen: Danish Institute for International Studies.

UNECA (United Nations Economic Commission for Africa). 2019. *Fiscal Policy for Financing Sustainable Development in Africa*. Addis Ababa: UN Economic Commission for Africa. https://repository.uneca.org/bitstream/handle/10855/41804/b11928190.pdf?sequence=1&isAllowed=y.

URT (United Republic of Tanzania). 1991. *Report of the Presidential Commission of Enquiry into Public Revenues, Taxation and Expenditure*. Dar es Salaam: Government Printer.

URT. 1997. *The Valued Added Tax Act, 1997*. Act No. 24 of 1997. Dar es Salaam: Government Printer. http://parliament.go.tz/polis/uploads/bills/acts/1461160781-ActNo-24-1997.pdf.

URT. 2014a. *The Valued Added Tax Act, 2014*. Special Bill Supplement no. 3 to the Gazette of the United Republic of Tanzania no. 20 vol. 95, dated 16 May. Dodoma: Government Printer.

URT. 2014b. *The Valued Added Tax Act, 2014*. Act Supplement no. 10 to the Gazette of the United Republic of Tanzania no. 51 vol. 95, dated 19 December. Dodoma: Government Printer.

Uwazi. 2010. 'Tanzania's Tax Exemptions: Are They Too High and Making Us Too Dependent on Foreign Aid?' *Policy Brief TZ.12/2010E* (October).

Van Parys, S., and S. James. 2009. 'Why Tax Incentives May Be An Ineffective Tool to Encouraging Investment? The Role of Investment Climate'. Washington, DC:

International Monetary Fund and the World Bank Group. Available at http://ssrn.com/abstract=1568296.

Weymouth, S. 2012. 'Firm Lobbying and Influence in Developing Countries: A Multilevel Approach'. *Business and Politics* 14(4): pp. 1–26. https://doi.org/10.1515/bap-2012-0030

World Bank. 2000. 'Reforming Tax Systems: Lessons from the 1990s'. *PREM Notes No. 37*. Washington, DC: World Bank.

Yadav, V. 2008. 'Business Lobbies and Policymaking in Developing Countries: The Contrasting Cases of India and China'. *Journal of Public Affairs* 8: pp. 67–82.

7

Service provision or tax exemptions

Revenue bargaining in Uganda's agricultural sector

Anne Mette Kjær and Clayton Arinanye

7.1 Introduction

The state's provision of agricultural extension services, rural infrastructure, and other public goods important for agricultural productivity is limited in Uganda. Likewise, regulation of markets for agricultural inputs such as fertilizer and seeds has been inadequate (Wiggins, 2014; World Bank, 2018). Yet the needs for such services are evidently pertinent. Seventy per cent of the population live in rural areas, and an increasing number of people are experiencing the challenges of food insecurity, droughts, or mudslides (Kakumba, 2021). In addition, there is very little taxation of agriculture in Uganda. A recent contribution estimates that agricultural production makes up 22% of GDP but contributes less than 1% of total collected domestic revenues (Stewart-Wilson and Waiswa, 2021).

So, the agricultural sector is generally very lightly taxed, and at the same time public goods for the agricultural sector are underprovided. In fiscal contract terms, this is a very weak basis for any revenue bargaining and a weak starting point to demand better services. Yet we have witnessed several attempts to introduce taxes affecting the agricultural sector, which have been followed by intense bargaining processes. There has also been lobbying for improved agricultural service provision. However, while farmers' associations have often successfully lobbied for tax exemptions, they are rarely able to push the government to deliver public goods.

The purpose of this chapter is to examine why this is the case. More specifically, in line with the theoretical framework outlined in Chapter 2 of this volume, we explore whether different outcomes of revenue bargaining and bargaining for improved services can be explained by features of the bargaining process, such as the bargaining positions and the strategies applied.

Anne Mette Kjær and Clayton Arinanye, *Service provision or tax exemptions*. In: *The Politics of Revenue Bargaining in Africa*.
Edited by: Anne Mette Kjær, Marianne S. Ulriksen, and Ane Karoline Bak, Oxford University Press.
 DOI: 10.1093/oso/9780192868787.003.0007

We examine four cases in which associations representing the agricultural sector have lobbied for a reduction or exemption of tax, and dig deeper into the dynamics of these bargaining processes. We examine what triggered the negotiations, what the farmers' claims were, how the farmers' groups or agricultural sector actors put their case, and whether the eventual policy decision reflected the associations' interests. The chapter then proceeds to examine three mirror cases where farmers have raised issues *not* about tax but regarding service provision. Across the seven cases, we find that there was stronger mobilization against taxation than there was in advocating for better services. In addition, in a situation where the government is struggling to deliver public goods, a more viable strategy to be responsive to the demands of farmers' associations may be through tax exemptions. The agreements about tax exemptions may help farmers' groups remain supportive of the ruling elite but do not help them get access to better production inputs, markets, credit, or any of the other collective goods that could help improve agricultural productivity or indeed create a sense of quid pro quo between the state and farmers' representatives.

7.2 The representation of interests in African agriculture

That public policy largely disfavoured African peasants was recognized more than 40 years ago in the so-called urban bias literature (Bird, 1974; Lipton, 1977; Bates, 1981). Even if peasants constituted the major part of the population, and even if African economies would clearly benefit from increased food production and exports of cash crops, policies did not cater to the peasants' interests. Agricultural production was overtaxed through monopsony pricing, and services were underprovided (Bates, 1981, 87–95). While the effects of structural adjustment programmes on African agriculture are widely debated, they did remove a number of policy distortions against rural Africa, such as dismantling marketing boards and liberalizing prices (Anderson and Masters, 2009). Yet the effect on agricultural productivity remained negligible, mainly because service provision in African agriculture remained rudimentary (World Bank, 2018).

Important contributions in the literature emphasize that collective action among rural smallholders is generally still weak (Booth, 2012; Poulton, 2014). Nevertheless, there is reason to think that conditions in recent years have become more conducive to farmers coming together to advocate for better service delivery or to react to taxation. First, there has been renewed focus on agriculture in the new millennium. Given that agricultural productivity remained almost stagnant on the African continent compared to other regions, heads of government (in the Maputo agreement of 2003) pledged to increase public allocations for agriculture to 10% of their budgets. Leaders and donors realized that price liberalization had not sufficed to spur growth in agricultural production and that public investments in rural public goods were necessary. The debate began to revolve around how to invest in rural roads, research, agricultural advisory services, better regulation of input markets, whether subsidized fertilizer was a good idea, and how to support access to credit (World Bank, 2007; Wiggins, 2014). The increased attention paid to agricultural policy should be an opportunity for organizations representing farmers to hold leaders accountable for their pledges. Second, international investors have become more interested in agricultural land. The food price hikes occurring in the late 2000s, combined with the discovery of availability of arable land in Africa, have increased foreign investments in the continent's agricultural sectors (Wiggins, 2014), which again could give farmers' organizations incentives to raise issues of the lack of, for example, rural infrastructure.

Third, rural voters have become more important with the institutionalization of elections. Since the third wave of democratic transition swept through Africa in the 1990s, competitive elections, even if not always free or fair, have increased the importance of the rural vote (Kjær and Therkildsen, 2013; Poulton, 2014); The significance of rural factions for the ruling elites has increased due to their ability to mobilize the rural voters (Whitfield et al., 2015). We know from surveys that rural Africans express a need for such things as government provision of rural infrastructure and advice and assistance to reduce food insecurity (Gyimah-Boadi et al., 2017). Elections should give farmers' organizations a possibility to voice these needs (Poulton, 2014), and if MPs do not deliver to local constituencies, they can be voted out. Election campaigns often appeal to the rural electorate and promise better primary services (Poulton, 2014). Prior to the 2001 elections in Uganda, for instance, the National Resistance Movement (NRM) government led by President Museveni launched a 'Plan for Modernization of Agriculture' to reach the campaign pledge of 'Prosperity for All' (Joughin and Kjær, 2010). For these reasons, we could expect agricultural sector actors to be able to mobilize at least some bargaining power vis-à-vis the ruling elite and government agencies.

There is some recent evidence that farmers' groups have reacted to attempts to tax them. There have been cases of protests over specific taxes—such as sales taxes on agricultural inputs—that have occurred in several

African countries.[1] Stewart-Wilson and Waiswa (2021) describe how the Uganda Revenue Authority (URA) attempted to enforce a withholding tax on agricultural suppliers, but that this was fiercely resisted.

Might it be the case that farmers' associations mobilize more when the issue is around taxation than when it is about public goods? The literature outlined above shows that there is reason to look closer at how and when farmers' groups raise tax issues, what the results of these bargaining processes are, and whether there are corresponding cases when it comes to demanding service provision.

7.3 Methodology

In order to examine the claims of farmers' associations and how these claims are made in specific instances of bargaining, we adopt a multiple-case design. First, we examine four tax-related instances of bargaining. In the four cases, we identify what triggered the bargaining, how it evolved, and what the outcome was. Subsequently, we ask the same questions in three mirror cases of bargaining where the claims were not about tax but about public goods provision.

Uganda is a relevant country in which to study cases of bargaining in the agricultural sector for several reasons. There is a politically recognized need to attend to the sector. The President and government have made recent pledges to improve agricultural productivity. They have also gone some way in increasing budget allocations to agriculture (GoU, 2018). Farmers raise the same concerns when asked in surveys (Kakumba, 2021); hence, there should be good opportunities for farmers to raise their voice. Further, the cooperative movement has seen something of a revival in Uganda in recent years (Wedig and Wiegratz, 2017). In post-Independence years, cooperatives were subjected to marketing boards and centralized price controls, and many of them were mismanaged. Liberalization policies did away with many cooperatives in the 1990s, but in the new millennium, many new cooperative unions have seen the light of day, and the Uganda Cooperative Alliance (UCA) now has more than 16,000 registered cooperatives (UCA, 2016). In addition, a large number of farmers' groups are registered with the Uganda National Farmers Federation, who report having 15,092 groups and cooperatives in their register, of which more than 2,400 are in coffee (UNFFE data accessed in April 2018). Finally, even if Uganda cannot be characterized as a democracy,

[1] See e.g. Times of Zambia (2004); Marete (2020).

it has regular multi-party elections. The elections do not give voters any alternative options for president, but they are fiercely competitive as for the members of Parliament. Elections could, therefore, be expected to give farmers an opportunity to put pressure on their local MPs to deliver (Wilkins, 2016; Chapter 9 in this volume).

When deciding on which instances of revenue bargaining to study, we opted for an open and exploratory approach. First, we simply asked agricultural experts and the farmers' organizations themselves about instances in which they had made a deliberate, successful or failed, attempt to influence a policy decision affecting them, regardless of whether this concerned tax. Asking this way enabled us to see whether tax issues mattered to the sector actors at all. We then chose the issues that most actors brought up and traced how the bargaining processes had occurred by using a combination of picking new interview respondents through snowballing and by reading available media and parliamentary debates about them. We also asked farmers more broadly about their grievances and challenges, to identify issues that it seemed are not generally raised and therefore do not reach the political agenda.

In January 2018, we conducted 33 interviews, with specific focus on farmers' organizations and cooperatives. For the dairy sector cases, data collection from a previous research project (2008–2013) was used in addition to 2017/2018 interviews of dairy sector actors. For the rice and coffee cases, additional interviews were carried out later in 2018 and in 2019. In all, over 80 interviews inform the following case narratives.

In what follows, we present four cases of successful revenue bargaining (see Table 7.1). Subsequently, we present three mirror cases in which issues of improved service provision were brought up. Finally, we discuss the empirical and theoretical implications of our case studies.

7.4 Attempts to influence agricultural taxation

7.4.1 VAT on agricultural inputs (2014/15)

On 12 June 2014, the Minister of Finance, Planning, and Economic Development, Maria Kiwanuka, held her annual budget speech and, to the surprise of many sector actors, announced the annulment of a number of tax exemptions on agriculture. Importantly, she announced the termination of VAT exemptions on input supply for agriculture such as machinery, tools, seed, fertilizers, and pesticides, with effect from 1 July 2014 (CSBAG, 2014). The statement immediately led to vocal protests from a number of

Table 7.1 Cases of revenue bargaining over agricultural taxation

Case	Trigger	Strategy	Bargaining power and process	Outcome
18% VAT on agricultural inputs (2014/15)	A push from technocrats in the Ministry of Finance and triggered when announced in the budget speech.	Signature collection. Petition to Speaker of Parliament. Discussion at President's round table. Protests in the newspapers and media.	The CSBAG and the PSFU organized resistance on the part of a number of associations, including farmers' organizations. The alliances strengthened the bargaining power of the groups who would be negatively affected by the tax.	The President announces that the 18% VAT is not to be effectuated.
Waiver on tax arrears and of corporate income tax for SACCOs (2017)	A push from the URA to collect income tax arrears, and subsequently regular income tax from the SACCOs.	Various SACCOs created alliances and made collective protests. Direct access to the President. Signatures and petition to Speaker of Parliament.	Farmers' organizations weaker than, e.g. army and Parliament or teachers' SACCOs. Together, they formed a strong protest group, but no sign that farmers' organizations had bargaining power on their own.	Cabinet agrees on the President's suggestion to abolish any arrears. Parliament votes to introduce a 10-year waiver on CET for SACCOs.
Waiver on income tax on fresh milk (2016)	The URA begins to collect income tax at the trading centres where farmers sell their fresh milk.	The umbrella cooperatives union (UCCCU) protests vocally through the public media and direct access to the President.	Large dairy farmers have bargaining power not so much as potential revenue providers but because they make up important political factions of the ruling coalition.	President intervenes directly and demands the Ministry of Finance abandons the idea of the tax.
Waiver on CET on imported rice (2016–2018)	One investor with links to the President gets a reduced tariff.	Other rice millers protest vocally. Rice farmers' protests are weak.	Some millers are also allowed waivers, which silences them. The millers mobilize more bargaining power than the rice farmers do.	Failure to uphold the CET.

associations and triggered a subsequent process of bargaining (interview, Head of CSBAG, March 2019).[2]

The Civil Society Budget Advocacy Group (CSBAG) is an umbrella association for civil society organizations in Uganda and has over 60 member organizations. Its purpose is to influence government budget decisions. Its executive director participates in international donor meetings such as the Public Finance Management Committee.[3] Immediately after the Minister of Finance's statement, the CSBAG issued a press release announcing the collection of signatures. It also released a longer policy paper with arguments against the tax, such as how it could harm agricultural production (interview, CSBAG Executive Director, March 2019).

The Uganda National Farmers Federation (UNFFE) is an organization representing all farmers; its purpose is to organize the farmers and advocate for their interests. The UNFFE has had different sponsors, but all making short-term donations and with little budget support to run the office. This means that the UNFFE is not well resourced (interview, Secretary General, May 2019). When interviewed, the UNFFE Deputy CEO pointed to the organization's advocacy for waiving the VAT tax as a success and referred to the joint signature collection (interview, 8 January 2018). However, the UNFFE joined an already existing initiative, taken by the CSBAG, and therefore cannot be said to have had a decisive influence. The civil society petition with the more than one million signatures was presented to the Speaker of Parliament in September 2014.

An additional important actor was the Private Sector Foundation (PSFU). The PSFU represents all private-sector actors (including farmers' associations) and is funded partly through members and partly through donors such as the UK Department for International Development. When asked to mention cases of lobbying relevant to agricultural policy, the Director of Policy in the PSFU brought up the VAT and said the PSFU had taken the case to the Presidential Round Table, an exclusive circle of CEOs from different companies in Uganda meeting with the President annually (interview, January 2018). Finally, traders in inputs—such as the Uganda Seeds Trade Association or the Uganda National Agro-input Dealers Association—were brought up as important actors as they had presented their case to the Ministry of Finance. Many of these dealers are said to be well connected politically

[2] See also ChimpReports (2014) where it is reported how the President states that 'some people passed behind me and included those taxes in our budget'.

[3] The present author took part in one such meeting concerning donor support to the revenue authority. The CSBAG was, at the time, fieldwork funded mainly by the multi-donor Democratic Governance Facility and by the US Agency for International Development.

(interview with former advisor to the Ministry of Agriculture, Animal Industry and Fisheries, Kampala, 17 January 2018; Kjær and Joughin, 2018).

In all, the CSBAG, with its insights and mandate to watch the budget, initiated the protest against the VAT on agricultural inputs and was joined by the farmers' association. In addition, the PSFU and input traders' association vocally resisted the tax. When the President was informed about the measure and the protests, he called a meeting of the NRM parliamentary caucus (which has the majority in Parliament) to convene the Cabinet and discuss the new tax. At the meeting, the President reportedly said, 'It is very sad that some people passed behind me and included those taxes into our budget. This is counterproductive and I Museveni who has been championing the growth of rural income through agriculture across the country cannot again be the one to put those taxes' (ChimpReports, 2014). When the CSBAG brought the joint petition to the Speaker of Parliament, she supported it, saying she was a farmer herself, and in September 2014, Parliament then voted to abolish the VAT on inputs (Kashaka, 2014).

'Success has many parents, but failure is an orphan', as the proverb goes. Many actors were indeed behind the successful lobbying against the 18% VAT on agricultural inputs, and all argued for their own key role when interviewed. The alliances with many organizations clearly strengthened the relative bargaining power of the farmers' associations vis-à-vis the government. The outcome was an agreement in which a VAT on agricultural inputs was *not* introduced, against the will of the Ministry of Finance, Planning, and Economic Development technocrats, and in which the President therefore arguably gained some political capital in terms of support for being responsive to the organizations' demands, or at least in terms of making sure that they did not vocally resist him. In this book's terms, the outcome was a type of fiscal contract that was not about a return for a tax but rather about *not* taxing, thus reducing the revenue for which better services for agriculture could, in principle, be offered.

7.4.2 Waiver on corporate income tax for SACCOs (2014–2017)

In 2014, the URA began to collect income tax from Savings and Credit Cooperative Organizations (SACCOs), which led to protests and a bargaining process that went on with varying intensity for the next three years. It was sometimes dormant and then was revived several times between then and 2017. A brief background on the role of SACCOs is necessary.

It is well established that rural smallholders lack access to credit in Uganda (World Bank, 2018). Government and donors have, over the years, taken an abundance of initiatives to ameliorate this state of affairs, but none so far has been very successful. Previous government-subsidized credit programmes have a reputation of being 'political', in that schemes have favoured local party cadres to mobilize support (Joughin and Kjær, 2010; Makoba and Wakoko-Studstill, 2015).

In 1998, the Rural Financial Services Programme, supported by the International Fund for Agricultural Development, began to support rural SACCOs. However, after the 2006 'Prosperity for All' campaign pledge, the government increased its support for agricultural cooperatives and SACCOs in the Rural Financial Services Strategy. The number of rural-based SACCOs then increased, and today there are about 700 (Nannyonjo, 2013). During the election campaigns of 2006, the President toured the country with the promise that all citizens' incomes would increase to 20 million shillings annually. On these so-called poverty tours, the President either delivered cash or promised to support local development through SACCOs (Makoba and Wakoko-Studstill, 2015). Consequently, the SACCOs were used as a means through which to channel funds for electoral support and to prop up lower-level NRM factions.

In 2007, the Uganda Cooperatives Act introduced government-led SACCOs with government subsidizing the credit facility. The Act provides for a triangular model consisting of rural producer groups, area cooperative enterprises, and SACCOs, the latter providing subsidized finance for the producers while the cooperatives market the crops (Nannyonjo, 2013; Onyilo and Adong, 2019). Existing rural credit schemes supported by donors were transformed to fit the new government strategy. Since then, SACCOs have been increasingly associated only with government initiatives, and not with farmers' own savings and credit associations. It has become more and more evident that the SACCOs are a means to increase government control and sustain loyalty from important factions who are able to mobilize support and votes (Adea, 2015; Makoba and Wakoko-Studstill, 2015), and they are often referred to as 'political SACCOs'.

Before 2014, the SACCOs had not been aware that according to the Income Tax Act, they were obliged to pay income tax on profits, and they had, therefore, been building up arrears.[4] When the URA in 2014 began to enforce the tax more systematically, including collecting the arrears (interviews, several

[4] See the microcredit associations' coverage at https://www.uccfs.co.ug/index.php/in-media/news/3-saccos-to-start-paying-tax-on-their-profits.

primary societies, January 2018; interview, ED of microcredit organization AMFIU, March 2019), the SACCOs and cooperatives began to protest vocally.

The trigger for the revenue bargaining was thus that the revenue officials had begun to collect the tax across all SACCOs. The Uganda Cooperative Alliance (UCA) pursued a strategy of linking up with various other groups, including representatives of the Uganda People's Defence Forces (the army) which also has a number of SACCOs (interview, UCA Director, January 2018). Through these connections, the UCA managed to access the President and argue their case. However, other SACCOs also protested. In 2015, the Cabinet decided to waive income tax plus the arrears that the SACCOs had been accumulating. This was emphasized as a success by the UCA. The actual income tax came to the table in July 2015, on the International Cooperatives Day, when the President announced that income tax on SACCOs should be abolished (Ndushabandi, 2015). The fact that elections were approaching, with NRM primary elections in October 2015 and general elections in early 2016, arguably played a large role in the President being responsive to the demands.

In the 2017 Income Tax Amendment Bill, the Ministry of Finance had not removed the tax on SACCOs. A large number of actors then mobilized. In 2017, Parliament agreed on a proposal to introduce a 10-year waiver. In the 2018/19 financial year, the Ministry of Finance again proposed the tax on SACCOs. The UCA protested again. But a more important actor was the Uganda Cooperatives Savings and Credit Union, who initiated a collection of signatures among its members (*The Independent*, 2018a). Then, 212 SACCOs signed a petition to Parliament (ibid.). In 2018, when debated in Parliament, the parliamentary finance committee again insisted on maintaining the 10-year waiver on income taxation of SACCOs. The arguments were, among others, that it is important to promote a savings culture in Uganda and that they should be given sufficient time to establish themselves. During the debate, Speaker Kadaga emphasized that Parliament had already debated this tax in 2017 and that she was very surprised that the tax was back. MPs voted overwhelmingly against reintroducing the tax.[5] So, for the second time, the organizations succeeded in challenging the technocratic attempt to maintain the income tax.

This outcome obviously benefits the SACCOs, who are often 'political' in the sense that they have become supporters of the ruling elite. Finally,

[5] See also http://uca.co.ug/national-level-advocacy/ and https://www.parliament.go.ug/news/1503/parliament-blocks-taxation-saccos.

the protest's success cannot be ascribed to the farmers' associations alone. As with the case on VAT on agricultural inputs, a number of actors joined forces to avoid the tax. Since practically all professional groupings have a SACCO—including MPs, the army, the teachers' unions, and even the staff of the Uganda Revenue Authority—it was not hard to join forces. The MPs' SACCO representative was one of the many MPs who spoke up. The bargaining power of the UCA alone is rather limited, as other cases where the UCA has tried to influence policy indicate, for example failing when it tried to influence the Cooperative Societies Amendment Bill (2016) to acquire more autonomy from the Ministry. The UCA had drafted a 10-point petition in June 2016, commenting on parts of the proposed amendments to the bill and asking for a 'specialized institution to supervise and regulate the operation of cooperatives' instead of the existing department of cooperatives under the Ministry of Trade and Industry, which the UCA feels is understaffed and politically biased (UCA, 2016).

7.4.3 Tax on incomes from fresh milk sales (2016)

During the Amin years and the subsequent civil war in the early 1980s, milk production and trade plummeted, and when the NRM came to power in 1986, Uganda was relying mainly on imported milk powder. However, during the 1990s, milk production increased tremendously and Uganda became self-sufficient. From 160,000 litres per day in 1993, milk production increased to over 1.4 million litres in 2014 (MAAIF, 1993; Makoni et al., 2014). In the south-western region of Uganda, a cold chain is in place with a large number of milk-collection centres with milk coolers equipped with generators, and two large dairy plants processing milk for export (Kjær and Joughin, 2018).

The NRM ruling elite had actively supported the establishment of this cold chain with grants and loans from the Food and Agriculture Organization, the African Development Bank, and Danida (Kjær and Mwebaze, 2014; Kjær, 2015). The dairy cooperative societies began to flourish during the 1990s, also encouraged by the President, as milk production grew in the south-west. The cooperatives have often challenged the government on key decisions concerning the dairy sector, but overall they remain supportive of the NRM government (Kjær and Joughin, 2018; interviews with former and present UCCCU members, August 2015, January 2018).

Because of the growth in the milk sector and increased incomes of the south-western dairy farmers, the Ministry of Finance and the URA saw a good source of revenue here, and in early 2016, they proposed to levy tax on incomes from fresh milk sales. This would be collected by the URA at the collection centres. When the URA started collecting this tax, it triggered revenue bargaining. The UCCCU immediately protested, arguing that such a tax would discourage small dairy farmers from selling their milk to them (interviews, January 2018). The UCCCU used several strategies. They talked to the media, and there were several articles about the issue (e.g. *The Monitor*, 2016a). More importantly, the UCCCU members used their connections to meet the Minister for Agriculture as well as the President in person. When asked about these channels of influence, several respondents with knowledge of Ugandan dairy politics would say that many of the large south-western dairy farmers have a direct link and can access the President relatively easily. After a meeting with the dairy farmers at his own ranch in Kiruhura, at the centre of the southern milk shed (as it is called), the President told the Ministry of Finance to give up the idea of taxing the farmers (*The Monitor*, 2016b). Subsequently, the idea of taxing them was abandoned (interview, former UCCCU Manager, January 2018).

This success can best be explained by the direct access south-western farmers have to the President. The main milk shed in Uganda is situated in the region where the President has his own dairy farm. The dairy farmers have been able to draw on these political connections in several instances. The milk coolers, for example, are tax exempt and so are aluminium containers and cooling trucks. Finally, the protest against the attempt to get income tax at the cooperatives' collection centres happened around election time, which perhaps made it easier for the UCCCU to avoid getting taxed since introducing a tax unpopular with a large number of dairy farmers (there are an estimated 800,000) prior to elections would not have been desirable.

7.4.4 Waiver on CET on imported rice (2016)

In 2017 and 2018, there was intense bargaining about whether domestic rice production should continue to be protected by a common tariff of 75%. Such a tariff is in the domestic rice producers' best interest, but they were not able to successfully argue their case.

Rice production in Uganda has increased since the mid 2000s, but since rice statistics are uncertain, precise data as to the size of the increase are not available. There seems to be a consensus that the production of rice has more than doubled, from about 121,000 metric tonnes in 2004 to an estimated 250,000 metric tonnes in 2017 (Van Campenhout et al., 2016; Joughin, 2019). This is in large part attributable to a common external tariff (CET) on rice, which was put into effect by the East African Community (EAC), effective from 1 January 2005. The tariff has worked to ensure a minimum price for domestic rice, which is not yet competitive. Its effects on rice production thus consist of increased rice production but not of higher productivity. This is not least due to the lack of supportive policies. Yields are still considerably below those of China or Vietnam, and there is little systematic research or development of new technologies going on, along with very low extension of existing knowledge to small-scale farmers (Joughin, 2019).

The most recent agricultural census from 2008 estimated that there are about 400,000 rice farmers in Uganda. Of these, 80% are small farmers with less than two ha of land, and they are generally poorly organized. There are some rice cooperatives, and rice producers are also represented in the rice farmers' association established in 2017 and by larger umbrella organizations such as the UNFFE or the UCA (interviews, UNFFE and UCA, 2018; Joughin, 2019). Though the tariff was in the interest of Ugandan farmers, they were not the ones who organized and pushed for its effectuation. Rather, one Ugandan rice producer and miller, Tilda Ltd, was instrumental in pushing the Ugandan government to negotiate the CET under EAC negotiations in Arusha (interview with Ugandan rice miller, January 2018). Since Tilda (now Kibimba Ltd) has a large rice-producing estate and an extensive outgrower scheme, the company was interested in having the government protect domestic production.

Since production has started to increase, rice farmers and millers in 2015 formed a joint association to cater for the interests of the rice industry (Joughin, 2019). This association was named the Rice Millers Council of Uganda (RMCU). However, a series of events since then has made the farmers break away from the RMCU and form their own association, the Rice Association of Uganda (RAU). These events started in 2016 when a Yemeni-based miller in Uganda, Kingdom Rice, successfully lobbied the government to reduce the tariff by 27.5% through a special concession only to this company (RMCU, 2017; interview, Ugandan miller, January 2018). The argument for the waiver was that there was a lack of sufficient domestic rice supply. The waiver resulted in a situation in which untreated (brown) rice imports from Pakistan to Uganda increased, some of them apparently re-exported after having been through the mill. This then made the other millers protest. In the subsequent months, the situation remained unsolved. The State House and President wanted to support the Yemeni company, which had invested in a large mill, and therefore wanted to maintain the waiver, whereas apparently the Ministry of Finance was less happy with allowing special terms for one company. During this period, the unity of the RMCU collapsed as more millers began to import brown rice. In other words, the CET was not enforced.

In April 2018, a meeting was held with the President and the millers. The parties reached a compromise, and 11 named millers were allowed a significantly reduced import duty, thus effectually reducing the CET (Kibimba, 2018). This agreement made Tilda (now Kibimba) threaten to close all its rice production on the grounds that it would no longer be viable without the protection. The company did so in a letter to the Ministry of Finance, with copies of the letter sent to the President's Office, the URA, and other relevant government agencies, saying that with these lower import duties, the company would have to shut down. The rice farmers were also angered by the removal of the CET. They therefore broke away from the RMCU and formed their own RAU. The RAU has raised the issue in the media and through letters to the Ministry of Finance (*The Independent*, 2018b). In May 2018, they also petitioned the Speaker of Parliament. So far, this has been to no avail—although the government seems to be sending out mixed messages, with Ministry of Agriculture and Ministry of Finance being more favourable to reintroducing the duty, but with the State House wanting to support the large rice miller. The farmers' associations such as the UCA and the UNFFE have not been active in this case. When asked, a UNFFE representative indicated that it would not be worth trying to influence the outcome, since 'government is there', as he put it (interview, March 2019).

7.4.5 Summarizing the four cases

The four cases inform us on the triggers, processes, and outcomes of revenue bargaining, providing a basis for exploring whether they differ in the tax cases from those of public goods. The four tax cases were triggered by a change in tax administration; three when technocrats tried to increase tax collections by enforcing an existing tax or by introducing a new tax, which then triggered protests. The fourth case was also triggered by a change in tax administration, but in this case, it was an individual exemption to the import tariff on rice that made the other rice millers protest.

In two of the four tax cases, farmers' associations were able to create alliances with other civil society groups because the taxes affected a wider number of stakeholders than only farmers. The VAT on agricultural inputs would not only hit peasants but also input traders and various subsector groupings. The income tax on SACCOs targeted not just farmer cooperatives, but also other professional groups including medical doctors, the army, and teachers. By creating alliances, the protesters' bargaining power increased. The political significance of the collective protest was increased, and the potential loss of political support was too great for the President to ignore. Hence, the political importance meant more than the potential revenue from the taxes. In the third case on taxation of fresh milk sales, a group of dairy farmers who made up an important faction of the ruling coalition effectively fought the enforcement of the tax. In the fourth case, an individual foreign investor was influential in having the rice tariff waived. The processors protested and acquired the same waiver. Nevertheless, the rice farmers were unable to team up with other organizations or in other ways influence the decision, so they did not have any bargaining power.

The bargaining processes took place in several arenas, but common to all of the cases was that the protests succeeded when the politicians, and most often the President, intervened in the bargaining. In both of the first cases, the Ministry of Finance was attempting to stand firm against the protests, and the MPs and the President would subsequently step in to have the technocrats give it up.

The findings inform us that when it comes to taxes, farmers' associations are indeed able to mobilize bargaining power to influence decisions in order to prevent taxation of their sector. However, the cases indicate that this is most likely to happen if the subsector group is of political significance or if they are able to create alliances with other groups affected by the tax. In the VAT on inputs case, for example, the real actor was a donor-supported umbrella association for civil society groups, not the farmers' associations. In the rice tariff case, rice farmers had very little say. Rice farmers are not of political significance; they are scattered over a large area in northern and eastern Uganda and they have not been well represented by the Rice Millers Council. As a result, they get a bad deal in which, despite their protests, their produce is no longer as protected against imported rice.

The fact that the outcomes are generally successful in waiving taxes raises the question of whether farmers' associations are able to bargain for the delivery of agricultural services.

7.5 Attempts to lobby for agricultural public goods

During our research, we encountered a number of attempts to lobby for better service provision. Here, we briefly outline three. Together, they provide important mirror cases that deepen our understanding of revenue-bargaining characteristics that may be distinct in public goods cases as compared to tax cases.

In the first instance of bargaining that we explored, coffee sector actors tried to influence the government's coffee seedling distribution programme. An estimated 19% of export earnings come from coffee exports in Uganda (Nsibirwa, 2012). One of the main challenges for coffee production has been the coffee wilt disease (Baffes, 2006; Nsibirwa, 2012). The government has tried to address this through replanting schemes in which farmers are helped to get new coffee seedlings, free from coffee wilt. The latest scheme is a seedling distribution programme though the NRM government's Operation Wealth Creation (OWC). The OWC is a programme launched in connection with the 2011 elections to promote production and wealth under the charge of the Ugandan army. The programme has been widely criticized for creating a parallel structure to the Ministry of Agriculture, Animal Industry and Fisheries and local governments. It has its own offices in Kampala, and the programme has hired army soldiers to implement initiatives such as input distribution that would otherwise have been carried out by agricultural officers.

Prior to the OWC programme, there had been a growing market for good coffee seedlings. However, this market was destroyed by the programme (interview, Director of Coffee Academy, April 2019). The farmers' groups had tried to address the issue using various channels. They had contacted the Head of the OWC, who is the President's brother, directly, and they had raised the issue several times in the public media to no avail. Many interviewees posited that they might as well give it up since the government had strong interests in the programme and used it to appease otherwise disgruntled army factions.

In the second case, dairy farmers have tried to achieve better government regulation of animal drugs and acaricides in order to ameliorate a growing problem of tick resistance—with the growth of Uganda's dairy sector, this is a problem of rising concern especially for south-western dairy farmers. The issue is caused by a lack of regulation and monitoring of drug use, as well as a lack of guidance for the farmers, who experiment with different drugs and mixtures. The result is that farmers lose many of their dairy cattle, which obviously hurts milk production (Vudriko et al., 2016; Abdallah, 2019). The situation began deteriorating during 2010, and dairy farmers have made increasingly vocal complaints about drugs that do not work,[6] though it is difficult to identify an exact event or date when they began. Farmers have tried to bring forward their complaints to the MPs representing their

[6] When this author gave a talk on agricultural policies at a local south-western university in January 2018, a number of dairy farmers brought up issues of bad acaricides and drugs during the Q and A session.

constituencies and to the President (interviews, UCCCU chair of board, January 2018; Kashari primary society Mbarara, 22 January 2018). They have also been interviewed on many occasions for public media (see e.g. *The Monitor*, 2017).

The MPs from the affected areas, particularly in the south-west, have taken the complaints further and brought them up in parliamentary debates on agricultural strategies, where MPs have complained about a lack of facilitation of local government offices. In response, the designated Minister for Agriculture admitted that the ministry does not have adequate resources to address the issue (Hansard, 2019). Even the President, at a private function (wedding ceremony) in Kiruhura, blamed various local officials and veterinary doctors for not being able to address the problem (*Kampala Post*, 2018). The issue is complex and would not be fixable by one institution alone. Further, the most important local supporters of the regime are well off and able to find individual solutions, such as accessing drugs from outside the country (interviews, January 2018; Hansard, 2019). Thus, in this case, the group was not able to influence government policy, despite normally receiving support from the NRM government and enjoying strong bargaining power. The government has a strong interest in the sector, and one would assume that the regulation of acaricides should be feasible.

Finally, the third case was an attempt by farmers' associations to influence input distribution programmes to have them use existing cooperatives and farmers' groups rather than setting up a parallel structure. The Operation Wealth Creation (OWC) programme was not only about coffee seedlings, but in general it is a scheme through which the government hands out agricultural inputs. An advisory programme, the NAADS, which also distributed inputs, preceded it. Both programmes were attractive to farmers' originations. The UCA and the UNFFE tried to persuade the OWC and the NAADS to use their groups (farmers' groups and primary societies) when handing out inputs. Their argument was that the groups had more knowledge and better potential to make good use of the inputs. The organizations reached out to the heads of the respective programmes as well as communicating with the Ministry of Agriculture, but the programmes remained with their own parallel structure. As described, both programmes had a political function that overshadowed other concerns.

Compared to the cases of tax waivers, four distinct features stand out from our cases of lobbying for service provision. First, they did not have an easily identifiable trigger, for example in the form of a public announcement of a tax. They rather emerged from a widespread dissatisfaction with poor services that had gradually grown. Second, they involved policies that did not have an immediate effect on other groups. Therefore, the farmers could not create alliances with other civil society groups, and their bargaining power was not strengthened during the process. Third, the arenas used by the farmers were similar, including, for example, contacting the President (or his brother). Yet the bargaining outcomes differed. The ruling elites would express their sympathy for the farmers' cause, but they took no action. Finally, lobbying for improved services did not succeed. This was the case even where the farmers were an important support faction to the ruling elite such as the dairy sector. However, the resourceful dairy farmers were able to find private solutions to the problem, a fact indicated to us in several interviews.

7.6 Conclusion

By studying specific instances of bargaining around policy issues raised by groups of farmers or organizations representing farmers' interests, we have shown that the most successful cases of policy influence are those in which the farmers' organizations seek a tax exemption. Conversely, attempts at influencing non-tax agricultural policies were not successful. When farmers' groups tried to influence the government to improve service provision in the agricultural sector, they failed.

The seven detailed case studies show us that the instances of bargaining where farmers' associations tried to have a tax reduced or waived differ in important ways from the cases where farmers lobbied for public goods. Such differences contribute to explaining these different outcomes. First, the instances of revenue bargaining were mostly triggered by a specific attempt by government technocrats to increase tax collections by enforcing an existing tax or by introducing a new tax, and politicians often intervened in favour of the farmers. In the public goods cases, no such trigger was evident. Rather, discontent with the level of services had built up over a long time. A tax reform appears to be a more visible trigger and a tax more easily identifiable as a target against which to mobilize.—Rallying resistance against it is more straightforward and has more visible results than advocating for better service delivery. Hence, we see much stronger mobilization and more cross-associational alliances against taxes than we do for improved service delivery. It is easier for ruling elites to respond to demands for tax exemptions or reductions than to respond to demands for better service delivery; the former, basically, just involves the stroke of a pen, whereas the latter is much more demanding on state resources and capacity. The President could express sympathy but still have no easy way to respond to the demands.

The findings resonate with key observations of the political settlement approach. In clientelist settlements with small national budgets, the implementation of schemes to provide rural public goods requires more resources than are available. Instead, resources are mainly distributed through patron–client networks. The agricultural schemes are easily subject to politicization, which is arguably the reason why the NRM ruling elite wished to maintain control over input distribution programmes such as the NAADS and the OWC, including the coffee seedlings programme. In Uganda, with competition between political factions and with fierce electoral competition, maintaining political support from rural voters is carried out through a combination of divide-and-rule policies, whereby agricultural programmes are used to buy support from powerful factions and by waiving taxes to appeal to rural voters.

The obvious implication is that the most important policies for increasing agricultural productivity and improving rural livelihoods, such as rural infrastructure or access to credit, are not provided. Moreover, politically sensitive issues, such as the politicized seedlings programme, are never even brought to the negotiation table. Though the farmers' organizations would like to see changes, they do not like to interfere in what they term 'tricky' areas. An example is the issue of access to land. When interviewing farmers in different regions of the country, land issues, such as sudden evictions, emerged as a huge challenge for many farmers. However, farmers' associations had never brought up the issue with the government. This indicates, as confirmed by several interview respondents, that farmers' associations have been co-opted, or at least neutralized, by the ruling elite. The implications of these findings for the possibility of strengthening the fiscal contract between the majority of poor farmers and the state are not encouraging.

References

Abdallah, H. 2019. 'Uganda Dairy Sector Performing below Full Potential'. *The East African*. 19 June. https://www.theeastafrican.co.ke/tea/business/uganda-dairy-sector-performing-below-full-potential-1420518.

Adea, M. 2015. 'Here Is the Magic Bullet for SACCOs'. *The Daily Monitor*. 14 May.

Anderson, K., and W. A. Masters. 2009. *Distortions to Agricultural Incentives in Africa*. Washington, DC: World Bank.

Baffes, J. 2006. 'Restructuring Uganda's Coffee Industry: Why Going Back to Basics Matters'. *Development Policy Review* 24(4): pp. 413–436.

Bates, R. 1981. *Markets and States in Tropical Africa: The Political Basis of Agricultural Policies.* Berkely, CA: University of California Press.

Bird, R. 1974. 'Agricultural Taxation in Developing Countries: A Discussion of the Policy Issues in Designing an Effective System of Agricultural Taxation'. *Finance and Development* 11(3): pp. 35–43.

Booth, D. 2012. *Development as a Collective Action Problem: Addressing the Real Challenges of African Governance. Africa Power and Politics Programme*, London: ODI. https://odi.org/en/publications/development-as-a-collective-action-problem-addressing-the-real-challenges-of-african-governance/.

ChimpReports. 2014. 'Museveni Angry, New Agricultural Taxes to be Scrapped'. 8 July. https://chimpreports.com/22915-museveni-angry-new-agricultural-taxes-to-be-scrapped/.

CSBAG. 2014. '*Reject Proposal to Tax Agriculture Inputs in the Budget Financial Year 2014/15*'. Press Statement.

GoU. 2018. *Background to the Budget, Financial Year 2018/19.* Kampala: Ministry of Finance, Planning and Economic Development.

Gyimah-Boadi, E., M. Bratton, and J. Leininger. 2017. *Cooperation between G20 and African States: Delivering on African Citizens' Demands.* G20 Insights.

Hansard. 2019. *The Hansards, Minutes from the Parliamentary Debates on July 19, Kampala, Uganda.* Last accessed 3 August 2022. https://www.parliament.go.ug/documents/3649/hansards-2019-july

The Independent. 2018a. 'SACCOs Make Case for Tax Exemption'. 26 April. https://www.independent.co.ug/saccos-make-case-for-tax-exemption/.

The Independent. 2018b. 'Rice Farmers Cry Out over Competition from Cheap Imports'. 30 April. https://www.independent.co.ug/rice-farmers-cry-out-over-competition-from-cheap-imports/.

Joughin, J. 2019. *Political Economy of Uganda's Rice Sector.* Consultancy Report. Unpublished material, Palladium.

Joughin, J., and A. M. Kjær. 2010. 'The Politics of Agricultural Policy Reform: The Case of Uganda'. *Forum for Development Studies* 37(1): pp. 61–79. https://doi.org/10.1080/08039410903558277.

Kakumba, R. M. 2021. *Covid-19 Impact? Ugandans Grow More Discontent with Economic and Living Conditions.* Dispatch No. 436, Afrobarometer.

Kampala Post. 2018. 'Museveni Commends People in Kiruhura District for Transformation'. 1 April.

Kashaka, U. 2014. 'Parliament Set to Scrap Taxes on Agricultural Inputs'. *New Vision.* 16 September. https://www.newvision.co.ug/news/1309917/parliament-set-scrap-taxes-agricultural-inputs.

Kibimba. 2018. *Letter Exchange between the Rice Miller and Ministry*. Unpublished material.

Kjær, A. M. 2015. Political Settlements and Productive Sector Policies: Understanding Sector Differences in Uganda. *World Development* 68: pp. 230–241. https://doi.org/10.1016/j.worlddev.2014.12.004.

Kjær, A. M., and J. Joughin. 2018. *The Political Economy of Uganda's Dairy Sector*. Kampala: SNV.

Kjær, A. M., and T. Mwebaze. 2014. 'Growth and Performance of the Ugandan Dairy Sector: Elites, Conflict and Bargaining'. *International Journal of Agriculture Innovations and Research* 2(3): pp. 287–298.

Kjær, A. M., and O. Therkildsen. 2013. 'Elections and Landmark Policies in Uganda and Tanzania'. *Democratization* 40(4): pp. 592–614.

Lipton, M. 1977. *Why Poor People Stay Poor: Urban Bias in World Development*. Cambridge, MA: Harvard University Press.

MAAIF. 1993. *Dairy Master Plan, I–V*. Entebbe, Uganda: Ministry of Agriculture, Animal Industry and Fisheries.

Makoba, J., and F. Wakoko-Studstill. 2015. 'From Prosperity for All to Prosperity for Few: Political SACCOs and Their Impact on Rural Development in Uganda'. *Journal of Third World Studies* 32(2): pp. 99–122.

Makoni, N., R. Mwai, T. Redda, A. J. van der Zijp, and J. van der Lee. 2014. *White Gold: Opportunities for Dairy Sector Development Collaboration in East Africa*. Centre for Development Innovation, Wageningen UR: Wageningen.

Marete, G. 2020. 'Farmers Protest Tax on Sorghum, Millet, Cassava'. *Business Daily*. 04 June. https://www.businessdailyafrica.com/bd/news/counties/farmers-protest-tax-on-sorghum-millet-cassava-2291782.

The Monitor. 2016a. 'Dairy Farmers Protest Milk Tax'. 13 January, updated 6 January 2021. https://www.monitor.co.ug/uganda/magazines/farming/dairy-farmers-protest-milk-tax-1636876.

The Monitor. 2016b. 'Uganda: Museveni Rejects Milk Tax'. 9 May. https://allafrica.com/stories/201605090705.html.

The Monitor. 2017. 'Ticks Defy Spray Drugs, Costs Farmers Millions'. 30 June. https://www.monitor.co.ug/uganda/special-reports/ticks-defy-spray-drugs-cost-farmers-millions-1708348.

Nannyonjo, J. 2013. *Enabling Agricultural Cooperatives through Public Policy and the State: The Case of Uganda*. Geneva: United Nations Research Institute for Social Development (UNRISD).

Ndushabandi, C. 2015. 'Museveni Abolishes Tax on SACCOs'. *ChimpReports*. 6 July. https://chimpreports.com/museveni-abolishes-taxes-on-saccos/.

Nsibirwa, R. W. 2012. *Analytical Coffee Report.* Entebbe: Ministry of Agriculture, Animal Industry and Fisheries.

Onyilo, F., and A. Adong. 2019. 'Agricultural Cooperative Marketing and Credit Policy Reform in Uganda: An Opportunity for Poverty Reduction'. *African Journal of Food Agriculture, Nutrition and Development* 19(1): pp. 14156–14170.

Poulton, C. 2014. 'Democratization and the Political Incentives for Agricultural Policy in Africa'. *Development Policy Review* 32(s2): pp: s101–s122.

RMCU. 2017. *Rice Millers Council of Uganda.* Unpublished memo.

Stewart-Wilson, G., and R. Waiswa. 2021. *Taxing Agricultural Income in the Global South: Revisiting Uganda's National Debate.* Brighton: Institute of Development Studies. https://opendocs.ids.ac.uk/opendocs/handle/20.500.12413/16626.

Times of Zambia. 2004. 'Zambia: Znfu Protests over VAT'. 18 February. https://allafrica.com/stories/200402190152.html.

UCA. 2016. *Uganda Cooperative Alliance.* Official statement to the government. Unpublished material.

Van Campenhout, B., W. Walukano, and P. Van Asten. 2016. *Addressing Knowledge Gaps in Rice Growing in Eastern Uganda.* USSP Policy Note 20. Washington, DC: International Food Policy Research Institute (IFPRI). http://ebrary.ifpri.org/cdm/ref/collection/p15738coll2/id/130718.

Vudriko, P., J. Okwee-Acai, D. S. Tayebwa, et al. 2016. 'Emergence of Multi-acaricide Resistant *Rhipicephalus* Ticks and Its Implication on Chemical Tick Control in Uganda'. *Parasites & Vectors* 9(4). https://doi.org/10.1186/s13071-015-1278-3.

Wedig, K., and J. Wiegratz. 2017. 'Neoliberalism and the Revival of Agricultural Cooperatives: The Case of the Coffee Sector in Uganda'. *Journal of Agrarian Change* 18(2): pp. 348–369. https://doi.org/10.1111/joac.12221.

Whitfield, L., O. Therkildsen, L. Buur, and A. M. Kjær. 2015. *The Politics of African Industrial Policy: A Comparative Perspective.* Cambridge: Cambridge University Press.

Wiggins, S. 2014. 'Presidential Address. African Agricultural Development: Lessons and Challenges'. *Journal of Agricultural Economics* 65(3): pp. 529–556

Wilkins, S. 2016. 'Who Pays for the Pakalast? The NRMs Peripheral Patronage in Rural Uganda'. *Journal of Eastern African Studies* 10(4): pp. 619–638.

World Bank. 2007. *Agriculture for Development. World Development Report 2008.* Washington, DC: World Bank.

World Bank. 2018. *Closing the Potential–Performance Divide in Ugandan Agriculture.* Washington, DC: World Bank.

8
Maximizing tax and other revenues for strategic rents in Uganda's petroleum sector

Dan Ngabirano

> *Then you hear people say 'Museveni should go'. But go and leave oil money? They want me to go so they can come and spoil the money.*
> **Y. K. Museveni, President of the Republic of Uganda**[1]

8.1 Introduction

After close to a decade of petroleum exploration, Uganda struck commercial oil in 2006. In the aftermath of this development, the country proceeded to enact one of the most robust and comprehensive petroleum regulatory and taxation legislative frameworks in its history.[2] Whereas it is too early to tell whether this will enhance sector governance and guarantee the country and its citizens a fair share of oil revenues, the law has had its successes, especially with taxation and revenue maximization (Hickey and Izama, 2020). Consequently, Uganda has so far generated close to USD 1 billion mainly from taxation of capital gains on the sale and transfer of petroleum rights and assets by international oil companies (Bank of Uganda, 2017, 2021; Muhumuza, 2017). This is a remarkable achievement considering that the country is yet to embark on commercial oil production. However, the key question is whether the petroleum revenues realized courtesy of these recent legislative gains will benefit citizens and catapult Uganda into the league of successful

[1] *Daily Monitor* (2015).
[2] Petroleum (Exploration, Development and Production) Act 2013, Petroleum (Refining, Conversion, Transmission and Midstream Storage) Act, 2013 Income Tax Act cap 340 (as amended) and the Public Finance Management Act, 2015 (as amended)

Dan Ngabirano, *Maximizing tax and other revenues for strategic rents in Uganda's petroleum sector.* In: *The Politics of Revenue Bargaining in Africa.* Edited by: Anne Mette Kjær, Marianne S. Ulriksen, and Ane Karoline Bak, Oxford University Press.
 DOI: 10.1093/oso/9780192868787.003.0008

oil-producing countries in Africa, or will merely be utilized by the ruling elite to further their own political interests.

In attempting to answer this question, this chapter relies on the political settlement theory to inquire into the power and interests of the different categories of groups as may be gleaned from their involvement in three distinct petroleum-sector legislative processes. The political settlement refers to 'the distribution of power among groups and institutions in a society based on which the ruling elites create coalitions of different key political factions' (see Chapters 1 and 2). The theory is critical to understanding the power as well as the political and economic interests of the different categories of groups directly and indirectly involved in the formulation and passage of Uganda's petroleum regulation and taxation laws. This is in turn helpful to understand the revenue-bargaining power of each group in the context of the petroleum sector, and whether current legislation is intended to benefit the greater citizenry or just a few groups with power and influence. In this context, five categories of groups have been identified, comprising the ruling elite, members of the legislature, international oil companies, civil society groupings, and foreign donors. Revenue bargaining is herein used to refer to 'implicit or explicit negotiations related to revenue provision between revenue providers and ruling elites' (see Chapter 1).

The major finding of this inquiry is that while the process of formulation and passage of Uganda's sector regulation and taxation laws involved diverse political and business groups, it was dominated by the ruling elite, which consists of the President and members of the executive arm of government (Golooba-Mutebi and Hickey, 2013; Bukenya and Nakaiza, 2020). Consequently, the ruling elite used their power and influence to insist on passage and enforcement of robust legislation for regulation, licensing, and taxation of international oil companies. In doing this, the ruling elite was motivated by the prospect of maximizing revenue generation from the sector to further its own political interests. This has yielded critical revenue gains to the extent that the country has so far generated close to USD 1 billion from the petroleum sector. However, the revenues generated have largely been spent in ways that enable the ruling elite to gain political mileage, such as construction of expensive infrastructure projects, campaign financing, and strengthening of the military machinery—a core feature of the current regime's 36-year rule (Tangri and Mwenda, 2013; Kabumba et al., 2017). The ruling elite has also used the hard stance and successful taxation of international oil companies to make a nationalistic appeal. Stringent taxation of oil companies complements the ruling elite's current strategy to maintain a more favourable and less burdensome tax regime for its core political support base, which consists mainly of peasants, the informal sector, and influential businessmen (Goodfellow and Titeca, 2012; Private Sector Foundation Uganda, 2009; Kjaer et al., 2021). This, it is argued, signals that deals are struck between the ruling elite and the different categories of influential groups that it sets out to appease to the detriment of broader fiscal contracts with citizens by which public goods are delivered for the petroleum income. Overall, the actions of the ruling elite point to its determination to dominate the petroleum sector for the purpose of revenue maximization, which is critical for its political survival and hold on power.

The chapter aims to contribute to the revenue-bargaining literature in the context of Uganda's petroleum sector regulation and taxation legislation. Current literature on Uganda's oil sector is heavily focused on institutional and industry best assessments. A great deal of emphasis is also placed on sector governance and management of public expectations (Kiiza et al., 2011; Shepherd, 2013), environmental management and sustainability (Kasimbazi, 2012), human rights and freedoms in the context of oil (Wass and Musiime, 2013), and corporate governance standards in the sector (Kyepa, 2012). However, while it is possible for the final text of the law to meet, and even in some cases surpass, each of these standards, it is no guarantee that the gains from Uganda's petroleum sector will benefit the greater citizenry and not just the interests of a specific group with higher bargaining power—an aspect that is addressed in this chapter. Moreover, the limited literature is heavily focused on bargaining processes in the context of negotiation of resource contracts, as opposed to those employed in the formulation of petroleum legislation, which I explore in this chapter (Hickey and Izama, 2017). Parts of the literature that presently look at the role of certain influential groups in tax-revenue bargaining are very general and do not specifically focus on petroleum legislation in the way this chapter does (Kangave and Katusiimeh, 2015). More broadly, the influence of powerful political and business groups on the design and formulation (including quality) of petroleum legislation has not received much attention in the literature.

The chapter takes a qualitative approach, with references to relevant primary and secondary sources of literature. These include petroleum regulation and taxation laws, official government reports, official statistics, and scholarly and newspaper articles. Further reference is made to interviews conducted with key informants drawn from government, parliament, industry, civil society, and the public. The chapter is organized into four main sections. Section 8.1 is the introduction. Section 8.2 looks at the revenue-bargaining power of different actors in the negotiation of early resource agreements and the formulation and passage of the 2013 petroleum legislation. Section 8.3 focuses on revenue bargaining in the context of petroleum taxation legislation. It shows that after the discovery of commercial oil in 2006, the ruling elite has gained even more confidence to insist on robust taxation of the activities of international oil companies. Section 8.4 concludes.

8.2 Bargaining in the context of Uganda's petroleum sector regulation legislation

This section looks at revenue bargaining in the negotiation of initial resource agreements (these are critical components of the petroleum sector regulation framework) and in the formulation of sector regulation legislation. It is shown that initially, international oil companies enjoyed great leverage in the negotiation of petroleum contracts. However, this began to change following the confirmation of the existence of commercial petroleum in 2006. This development emboldened the ruling elite to engage in tough negotiations with the companies and strengthened their resolve to gain monopoly over sector regulation and control despite protests from civil society and donors.

8.2.1 Early production-sharing agreements and the 1985 petroleum law

Early production-sharing agreements (PSAs) between the government of Uganda and international oil companies were negotiated and signed under the framework of the 1985 petroleum law.[3] The law vested the power to negotiate and sign PSAs in the Minister of Energy.[4] Pursuant to this arrangement, the first PSA was signed with Petrofina Petroleum in 1991 (Directorate of Petroleum, 2013). The second PSA was concluded with Heritage Oil and Gas Ltd in 1997 and gave the company exploration rights over the entire Semiliki basin. In 2001, the government signed another PSA with Hardman Petroleum regarding the Lake Albert Basin. In the period between 2001 and 2005, the two companies (Heritage and Hardman) signed additional PSAs with the government of Uganda in relation to different exploration areas. In 2005 and 2007 respectively, there were two new entrants: Neptune Petroleum and Dominion Petroleum. In 2010, the UK-based Tullow Oil Company acquired all of Heritage Oil's assets in Uganda, and in 2012, the

[3] Long Title, Petroleum (Exploration and Development) Act, cap. 150, Laws of Uganda, 2000.
[4] Section 3 of the repealed Petroleum Act 1985.

company executed several additional PSAs with the government of Uganda. The PSAs define the contractual relationship between the parties as well as the benefits, duties, and obligations of both the government of Uganda and the international oil companies (these include payment of different forms of taxes, fees, and royalties). In this way, the signed PSAs constitute an integral part of Uganda's petroleum regulatory framework.

From a revenue-bargaining perspective, early PSAs largely favoured the business interests of international oil companies, for several reasons. First, the agreements were signed under the broad framework of the 1985 petroleum law, which focused on attracting foreign investment into the sector rather than on stringent regulation imposing difficult obligations on the companies. Second, the PSAs were signed with international oil companies at a time when Uganda did not have sufficient technical or financial capacity to undertake capital-intensive petroleum exploration and development projects by itself. Therefore, the country turned to international oil companies since they had both the capital and the technical capacity to undertake the projects. This gave the companies leverage in the negotiation of the PSAs and enabled them to secure a favourable deal from the government of Uganda. Third, the companies' long experience of negotiating similar agreements in other countries gave them an advantage over the relatively inexperienced technocrats from the government of Uganda. Ultimately, the deals Uganda struck in the early PSAs could have been better (Global Witness, 2014).

According to Platform, the PSA entered into between the government of Uganda and Heritage Oil and Gas Ltd in 2004 in respect to Block 3A gave the oil company better and more favourable terms compared to similar agreements the company entered into with other countries around the same time (Lay and Minio-Paluello, 2010). It is observed that Kurdistan, whose government was embroiled in a legitimacy crisis at the time, was able to secure a better deal from Heritage. Uganda received USD 300,000 in signature bonuses from Heritage Oil under its PSA, which was significantly lower than the USD 3.5 million paid to the Democratic Republic of Congo (DRC) for a comparable oil block in 2008. Moreover, the terms of the PSA with Heritage exposed Uganda to the risk of oil companies benefiting from unreasonable and fraudulent claims in the form of recovery costs. For example, Heritage Oil was reported to have inflated its costs by USD 586,511 in the period between September 2004 and October 2006. Since the details of the PSA and other agreements signed with the rest of the oil companies are secret and unavailable for public scrutiny, it is difficult to tell whether other mistakes with a bearing on revenues were made (Kagenda, 2009; Ssekika, 2017). It has been said that the hard cash that was expected to be paid up front distracted the government of Uganda from bargaining for a better signature bonus (Lay and Minio-Paluello, 2010). This suggests that the ruling elite's interest at the time was to secure as quickly as possible what Heritage was able to pay in cash.

It is difficult to reconcile this view with the track record and long-term strategy of Uganda's ruling elite regarding development and management of the oil sector. It has been observed elsewhere that from the time the NRM government came into power in 1986, it was careful not to rush into development of the oil resource until it had built sufficient capacity to manage the sector. Instead, it invested in building the capacity of institutions and their staff, mainly through training. The NRM also established a dedicated unit, the Department of Petroleum, for regulation of the sector in the Ministry of Energy and Mineral Development, where the staff trained abroad were eventually deployed. In light of this and NRM's subsequent behaviour, which is explored later in this chapter, the concessions made in the negotiations of early PSAs are not sufficiently explained by mere pursuit of early revenues (Hickey and Izama, 2017).

It is argued that the initial timid approach of the NRM government in the negotiation of PSAs, and more specifically the one signed with Heritage Oil, was attributable to inadequate state capacity and experience in the sector, which affected its bargaining power at the time. The international oil company leveraged its capital abilities, technical capacity, and vast experience to negotiate favourable terms. However, the balance of power between the government of Uganda and international oil companies changed with the discovery of commercial oil in 2006, to which I now turn.

8.2.2 Commercial oil discovery and the momentum for petroleum legislative reforms (2006–2013)

The discovery of commercial petroleum at a time when there was a global surge in commodity prices greatly altered the balance of revenue-bargaining power in the sector. More critically, it emboldened the ruling elite to push for a hard deal while negotiating subsequent PSAs, and to initiate revisions in the sector-regulation framework. In 2008, the Cabinet (an integral part of the ruling elite) passed a policy for regulation and management of the sector (Ministry of Energy and Mineral Development, 2008). By implication, the executive arm of government was required to urgently formulate and pass a law to facilitate the implementation of the policy objectives. This notwithstanding, it took more than five years for the law to be enacted. Even then, it took the intervention of Parliament, donors, and civil society for the law to be passed.[5] Parliament's intervention in the petroleum legislative process was sparked by allegations that some members of the ruling elite—that is, the Minister of Energy and other prominent personalities in cabinet—had received bribes from international oil companies (Biryabarema, 2010; Imaka, 2012a). In response to the allegations, Parliament took two major steps. First, it appointed an ad hoc committee to investigate the conduct of each accused minister. The implicated individuals were urged to step down pending the conclusion of investigations.

Most significantly, Parliament imposed a moratorium on all petroleum activities until a comprehensive law had been debated and passed as required by the National Oil and Gas Policy (Parliament, 2011). This was a rare move considering that it is normally the executive's role to introduce a draft bill to Parliament at its own timing. Parliament rarely initiates a law, and then it is usually through an individual private member's bill, which requires a certificate of financial implication from the executive. The collective action of Parliament and the decisiveness with which it acted in this case stamped its authority over the petroleum legislative process and built pressure on the executive to enact an appropriate law. The executive hastily formulated a draft bill of the petroleum law, which was debated and passed by Parliament in 2013.

The law as passed is fairly progressive and comprehensive. It makes provision for robust regulation of the sector, competitive licensing, and protection of property rights, and puts in place environmental and health and safety measures and controls (Oloka, 2019). From a revenue-bargaining perspective, the law and the regulations passed require international oil companies to pay different forms of taxes, royalties, bonuses, rents, and institutional fees. However, there are two challenges with the law as is. First, the mandate to negotiate and set specific fees paid by international oil companies has been left to the minister, a member of the ruling elite.[6] As the contents of PSAs (including fees payable) negotiated with various companies have not been disclosed, the ruling elite may use this gap to apply the realized revenues without accountability. The second challenge is that the law gives the minister overwhelming discretion in the award of licences to international oil companies.[7] All these powers increase the risk of corruption and revenue loss, most recently manifested with respect to the PSA for Exploration Area 2 when the Minister of Finance was purported to have exempted Tullow Oil Company

[5] Interview with member of the Parliamentary Advocacy Forum on Oil, Kampala.
[6] Section 8, Petroleum (Exploration, Development and Production) Act 2013.
[7] Ibid.

from payment of capital gains taxes. On the strength of this provision, Tullow Oil claimed exemption from payment of taxes on gains realized from the sale of its assets to Total and the China National Offshore Construction Company (CNOOC). The claim was denied by the Uganda Revenue Authority (URA), which prompted Tullow Oil to challenge the tax assessment before the Tax Appeals Tribunal (TAT), albeit unsuccessfully. In its ruling, the TAT found that the minister did not have the mandate to give the tax exemption.[8] The TAT's finding was based on Article 152 of the Ugandan Constitution, which states that only the legislature can impose taxes. This was interpreted by the TAT to include the power to grant tax exemptions.[9]

By vesting in the minister overwhelming discretion in sector regulation and licensing, the law as passed contradicts the Oil and Gas Policy of 2008. The policy stipulates that licensing and negotiation of all petroleum agreements shall be vested in the Directorate of Petroleum under the Ministry of Energy. In addition, all aspects of sector regulation must be handled by the Petroleum Authority of Uganda. The third institution envisaged by the policy is the National Oil Company, whose mandate is to manage all commercial aspects of oil. It should be noted that these policy suggestions were borrowed from the highly acclaimed Norwegian tripartite model (Kyepa, 2012; Kjaer, 2013).

The risks associated with giving the minister this overwhelming mandate were raised by different actors during the debate and passage of the law by Parliament, but they were ignored and, in some cases, vigorously opposed by members of the ruling elite. Prominent among the critical voices were opposition-leaning members of parliament and a small number of outspoken members of the ruling party. Together they formed a pressure group known as the Parliamentary Forum on Oil and Gas (PFOG). They acted collectively to vigorously challenge the provisions of the draft law that gave the Minister of Energy broad discretion in negotiation of PSAs and licensing of international oil companies on the grounds that this would facilitate executive interference and encourage corruption in the sector (Lumu, 2012; Imaka, 2012b). In its quest the PFOG was supported by a coalition of non-governmental organizations (NGOs) under the umbrella of the Civil Society Coalition on Oil and Gas (CSCO) in Uganda.[10] The efforts of the PFOG were further backed by donor groups who supported several

[8] *Tullow Uganda Ltd & Tullow Operational Pty Ltd v. Uganda Revenue Authority* TAT Application No. 4 of 2011.

[9] Ibid.

[10] Interview with Coordinator of the Civil Society Coalition on Oil and Gas, Kampala.

capacity-building sessions for its members.[11] As a result of these engagements, members of the PFOG emerged as an outspoken group of parliamentarians who opposed the Bill. This made the PFOG and civil society and donors that supported it key players in the petroleum sector legislative process.

However, this was short-lived, as the ruling elite was determined to pass the law for its own benefit. At the height of the parliamentary debate and opposition to the Bill, the NRM summoned its members to party caucuses where they were urged to vote for passage of the Bill. The President, who is the party chairman, is reported to have made personal phone calls to NRM party-leaning members of parliament to persuade them to pass the Bill (Lumu and Kakaire, 2012). The ruling party thus used its numerical strength in Parliament to pass the problematic Bill into law in December 2012 (Biryabarema, 2012; Imaka, 2012c). The politics of the day and the desire for the executive to control the resource ensured that the minister enjoyed powers that were initially reserved for the Petroleum Authority. The result has been increased personalization and micromanagement of oil by the executive. It is thus unsurprising that the President has been quoted on several occasions referring to the resource as 'my oil' and its discovery as 'an NRM achievement' (Salama, 2014; Patey, 2015).

From a revenue-bargaining perspective, the vesting of huge discretionary powers in the minister has strengthened the ruling elite's leverage in negotiations with international oil companies. It is in a better position to influence many aspects of licensing and regulation compared to, for example, Parliament and the established petroleum institutions. The ruling elite is also able to influence the size of fees and other revenues paid by international oil companies. This approach has been extended to the taxation of the sector, which is discussed next.

8.3 Bargaining in the context of petroleum sector taxation legislation

8.3.1 Robust taxation of petroleum income

At the time of the commercial oil discovery, Uganda did not have a dedicated framework for taxation of sector activities, and income from petroleum

[11] Interview with member of Parliamentary Forum on Oil and Gas, Kampala.

operations was taxed in the same manner as that from other businesses.[12] Companies involved in petroleum operations were entitled to almost the same tax allowances in the form of deductions of business expenses as those accruing to taxpayers in other sectors.[13] However, following the confirmation of the existence of commercial oil, the position of the law began to change.

In 2008, the Ministry of Finance introduced an amendment to the Income Tax Act with an objective of establishing a specialized regime for the taxation of petroleum activities.[14] Stringent restrictions were imposed on business expenses (allowable deductions), so that oil companies could only recover expenses incurred in the contract area from which the income subject to tax was derived.[15] This meant that expenses incurred by the same company in a less profitable contract area could not be offset from income realized from a more profitable contract area. Although this approach is a common industry practice known as ringfencing, the timing of its introduction in the law illustrates the enhanced bargaining power of the ruling elite as well as its determination to maximize sector revenues at the earliest opportunity. It should be noted that the provisions were introduced very early in the exploration phase and before the companies could realize tangible profits. While this move could ordinarily have discouraged investment in the sector, the ruling elite was much more confident in taking this approach after the existence of commercial reserves had been confirmed.

New amendments to the law on taxation of petroleum income in 2015 and 2016[16] only clarified the extent of allowed business expenses and did not result in substantial changes.[17] Nonetheless, they expanded the scope of allowed deductions to include exploration and development expenditure as well as decommissioning costs. While these benefited international oil companies, they are common in the industry and cannot be said to reflect entirely enhanced company bargaining power.

Further amendments to the Income Tax Code in 2017 limited the total amount of deductible expenses recoverable by international oil companies to the amount of cost oil (the amount of oil companies are entitled to keep as part of cost recovery) realized from a specific contract area.[18] Total business expenses and other allowable deductions that exceed value of the

[12] Section 18, Income Tax Act cap. 340. Business income includes gains made from the disposal of capital assets, proceeds of trading stock, interest, consideration received in return of trade restriction, and the value of any gift derived in the course of business.
[13] Ibid., Section 22.
[14] Income Tax (Amendment) Act, no. 2 of 2008.
[15] Ibid.
[16] Income Tax (Amendment) Act, no. 11 of 2015.
[17] Ibid. See also Income Tax (Amendment) Act, no. 20 of 2016.
[18] Income Tax (Amendment) Act, no. 10 of 2017.

cost oil were not allowed but could be carried forward.[19] This presents a differential approach to taxation of the oil sector. Other businesses outside the petroleum sector may deduct all business expenses without similar restrictions (Kakembo, 2017).

Overall, the amendments to the income tax code show that the approach of the government of Uganda has been to tax the petroleum sector in a rigorous manner compared to other sectors. Arguably, this is a result of the enhanced bargaining power of the ruling elite following the discovery of commercial oil in 2006, and it is done with the objective of maximizing tax revenues from the sector for the elite's own benefit.

8.3.2 Stringent administration and enforcement of taxation in the petroleum sector

In 2014, a separate tax procedural law was enacted,[20] among other things to regulate tax administration and enforcement processes.[21] However, the timing and the potential impact of its provisions point towards another deliberate strategy to aggressively tax revenues in the hands of international oil companies.

It is quite clear that the passing of the new procedural law was partly informed by informed by the difficulty encountered by the Uganda Revenue Authority in collecting capital gains taxes from a transaction involving two major international oil companies.[22] In 2010, Heritage Oil and Gas Ltd (Heritage Oil) sold its stake in petroleum exploration areas 1 and 3A to Tullow Uganda Limited (Tullow Oil). Under the sale and purchase agreement signed by the two companies, Heritage was responsible for payment of all non-transfer taxes, and Tullow for transfer taxes.[23] With full knowledge of the transaction, the Uganda Revenue Authority (URA) issued two separate assessments totalling USD 404,925,000 in capital gains taxes. The assessments were issued to Tullow Oil since it had not yet made the payment, and Heritage, which was responsible for payment of the tax, was in the process of exiting the country. In issuing the assessments, the URA relied on Section 108 of the Income Tax Code, which gave the Commissioner powers to require any person in possession of assets (including money) belonging to a non-resident taxpayer to pay tax due on behalf of such taxpayer.

[19] Ibid.
[20] Tax Procedure Code Act, 2014 (as amended).
[21] Ibid. Long Title to the Act.
[22] Interview with Prof. David Bakibinga, Kampala, 5 November 2018.
[23] Ibid.

The assessments were fiercely contested by both Heritage and Tullow. Heritage Oil challenged the assessment before the TAT because it contravened the stabilization clause contained in the PSA signed with the government of Uganda. It was argued that under that PSA, the government was not permitted to change the terms of the agreement to the detriment of the company. Heritage further argued that the PSA dictated that all disputes (including tax disputes) be determined through arbitration, and that the assessments could not be enforced unless the arbitration process was complete. However, these arguments did not find merit before the TAT, and the tax assessments were upheld.[24] The TAT's decision was confirmed by the High Court of Uganda following an appeal by Heritage.[25] Heritage initiated arbitration proceedings against the government of Uganda in London, which they lost, as is discussed in the following paragraphs.

Tullow took a different approach, with the objective of delaying the imminent tax collection until all disputes had been resolved. They sent delegations to meet and lobby officials at the tax body as well as high-level politicians including the President. All these efforts were futile, and the government of Uganda put further pressure on the company to remit the assessed tax to the URA. The Ministry of Energy also declined to renew Tullow's licence until the tax was fully settled. In the end, Tullow opted to honour the agency notice and sue Heritage for recovery of taxes paid on its behalf before the High Court of England and Wales.[26] After full consideration of the evidence presented by both parties, the High Court entered judgment in favour of Tullow Oil on grounds that the URA assessment was valid under Ugandan law and that Tullow oil was justified to act on it.[27]

The ruling of the High Court of England and Wales, as well as the tedious experience of the URA in collecting the taxes due on the transaction, greatly inspired the enactment of the Tax Procedures Code Act, 2014. The law, which was passed a year after the court decision, clarified the power of the Commissioner of the URA to recover full taxes due through third parties.[28] Under the law, it is immaterial whether the tax is already due at the time of recovery or whether it will fall due later.[29] In this respect, the Tax Procedures Code Act is much more rigorous than Section 108 of the Income Tax Act on which the URA had relied in issuing the assessment on the Tullow/Heritage transaction. The new law thus gave the Commissioner of the URA the power to

[24] *Heritage Oil and Gas v. Uganda Revenue Authority*, TAT Application No. 26 of 2010.
[25] *Heritage Oil and Gas v. Uganda Revenue Authority*, High Court Civil Appeal No. 14 of 2011.
[26] *Tullow Oil Uganda Ltd v. Heritage Oil and Gas Ltd & Heritage Oil Plc* [2013] EWHC 1656 (Comm).
[27] Ibid.
[28] Ibid. See Section 31.
[29] Ibid.

initiate collection of the full tax payable solely based on their belief that the taxpayers will incur tax liability in the future.

It is important to note that the power of the Commissioner to issue third-party agency notices was one of the most contentious issues raised in the case filed by Tullow against Heritage before the High Court of England and Wales. It was argued on behalf of Heritage that the assessment notice was invalid (in which case Tullow should not have complied) since it had been issued prematurely (before the transaction could be completed), and that the tax assessed was not final since it was disputed by Heritage. In response, Tullow argued that it was required by law to effect full settlement of the tax assessed on behalf of Heritage, and that it had taken all steps to avoid effecting payments to the URA in vain. To determine whether full settlement of the tax was required the moment the notice was received, the court examined the difference in the terms 'due' and 'due and payable' as used in the income tax code at the time. After careful consideration of the evidence and the term 'due' as used in Section 108 of the law, the court found that Tullow was justified to remit the full tax assessed by the URA the moment the assessment was raised, irrespective of whether the URA's actions were premature or not. In effect, Section 108 of the Income Tax Act made full payment of the assessed tax mandatory regardless of any outstanding disputes and objections filed by the taxpayer (in this case Heritage). For this reason, Tullow was entitled to recover the full amount paid to the URA on behalf of Heritage.[30] With the enactment of the Tax Procedures Code, the URA can now compel third parties, including international oil companies, to make tax payments on behalf of taxpayers to whom they owe money. This can be done on the sole basis of the Commissioner's belief that such taxpayers are likely not to pay the tax on the date it falls due.

From a revenue-bargaining perspective, there are several points to highlight. First and notably, in most cases, tax-related legislative amendments with implications for the petroleum sector were initiated by the executive arm of government, and Parliament's role was to debate and enact laws. Even then, parliamentary debates about tax-related bills were not as heated or intense as those about the enactment of petroleum-sector regulatory legislation. It is not clear why this was the case, but some have attributed it to the capacity limitations of majority members of parliament to debate taxation matters since they are considered too technical.[31] This same reasoning has been applied to explain the absence of civil-society groups in legislative processes

[30] Ibid.

[31] Interviews with members of Parliament and officials from civil society, Kampala.

for enactment of taxation legislation with implications for the petroleum sector.[32] In the end, the process of formulation of taxation laws was initiated and dominated by the executive arm of government based on advice from technocrats from mainly the Ministry of Finance and the URA.[33] This strengthened the ability of the ruling elite to introduce reforms for the stringent enforcement of tax laws against international oil companies. Secondly, the elite, led by the President, declined to interfere with tax assessments issued by the URA notwithstanding intensive lobbying by international oil companies. Due to this strict approach, Uganda has to date been able to collect close to USD 1 billion (most of it in capital gains taxes) from international oil companies.

The strict taxation of international oil companies raises other points of interest. First, it contradicts the executive's long-known practice of granting tax concessions to foreign investors and businesspeople with political connections and influence (Tangri and Mwenda, 2013; Ladu, 2016; Kafeero, 2018; SEATINI, 2019). The varying tax treatment accorded to international oil companies shows that, unlike other businesses that have benefited in the past from tax concessions, they have not gained much. This has been attributed to the fact that the political cost of strict enforcement of taxation against international oil companies is minimal compared to the cost where more influential taxpayers are involved (Kjaer et al., 2021). More critically, the strict taxation of international oil companies has ensured that the ruling elite has raised additional revenues necessary to protect its power.

In 2011, the government of Uganda almost depleted its foreign exchange reserves, in a hurried decision to purchase fighter jets and other military equipment from Russia at an estimated cost of USD 744 million (Bariyo, 2011). The procurement was not sanctioned by Parliament, nor was it urgent since the country was not facing threat of war. The purchase was thus purely intended to enhance the strength of the military—an establishment that was critical in the NRM's annexation of power in 1986, and one that has been relied on to crack down on political dissent and maintain political power (Kabumba et al., 2017). According to the Governor of the Central Bank, the decision to utilize the funds for the purchase was reached following President Museveni's personal assurances that his government would allow the bank to utilize early oil revenues to replenish the reserves (Imaka, 2011; Mwesigwa, 2017). Using this strategy, the ruling elite succeeded in spending oil revenues to enhance the military without parliamentary approval.

[32] Interview with a member of the Civil Society Coalition on Oil and Gas, Kampala.
[33] Interview with Officials from the Ministry of Finance and the Uganda Revenue Authority, Kampala.

Moreover, the ruling elite has been accused of utilizing oil revenues to fund its electoral campaign activities. During the 2011 general election campaigns, the NRM-dominated Parliament passed a supplementary budget of UGX 602 billion of which UGX 85 billion were allocated to the presidency. The ruling elite insisted that the funds were necessary to cover budgetary shortfalls, but there was no sufficient linkage between the expenditure and public services provided under the budget. Reports emerged to support the view that a significant share of the funds could have been deployed to further the political interests of the ruling NRM during the campaigns (European Union Election Observation, 2011). It is also imperative to note that the supplementary budget was passed at a time when the government of Uganda had succeeded in collecting large revenues in the form of capital gains taxes from international oil companies. The realized taxes were deposited in the oil revenue account (the petroleum fund had not been established at the time), which was controlled by the ruling elite. Since it is not clear what the funds were spent on, there is a very high likelihood that they were spent as part of the 2011 supplementary budget and for the benefit of the ruling elite.

Finally, it is observable that following the discovery of commercial oil, the ruling elite has used the country's improved revenue prospects to borrow massively in order to undertake expensive infrastructure projects (Looney, 2015; State House, 2016; Muhumuza, 2017). In launching such projects using oil revenue-backed loans, the ruling elite has succeeded in delivering on key election campaign promises and appeasing its core political support base without having to increase their tax burden. Parliament and civil-society groups had little influence on these decisions about spending and borrowing.

Lastly, the successful taxation of multinational oil companies has been used by the ruling NRM to claim political mileage and to align its strict approach with national interests. Consequently, during election campaigns, the President and other members of the ruling elite attribute the successes registered in the sector so far to the ruling NRM party.

8.4 Conclusion

In this chapter, I have used the political settlements theory to untangle the power and interests of different categories of groups involved in the formulation and passage of Uganda's petroleum regulatory and taxation laws. I have shown that international oil companies initially leveraged their financial muscle, technical capacity, and experience to negotiate favourable terms in the PSAs signed with the government of Uganda. However, this began to change with the discovery of commercial oil in 2006, at a time when the prevailing commodity prices were high. In the aftermath of this development, the ruling elite gained confidence to push a hard deal against the companies and to initiate far-reaching sector regulatory and taxation legislative reforms for its own benefit. Although other actors like members of parliament, foreign donors, and civil society were critical of some of the proposed legislative reforms because they gave the executive unfettered powers over the sector and increased the risk of corruption, the ruling elite used its numerical strength in Parliament to ensure that the law passed. The implication is that the ruling elite has enhanced its control over sector regulation and licensing processes, and has used its enhanced bargaining power to introduce provisions for robust taxation of international oil companies. As a result of all these efforts, the government of Uganda has realized close to USD 1 billion from the sector, even before the commencement of commercial oil production. Of this, close to USD 777.4 million has been spent on activities that give the ruling elite political mileage and enhance its military machinery—a critical feature in its more than 30-year period in power. The strict enforcement of taxation laws on the less politically significant international oil companies has also ensured that the ruling elite maintains a low tax burden on politically influential groups *and* is able to provide critical goods and services and undertake expensive infrastructure projects.

Acknowledgements

I am deeply grateful to Prof. David Bakibinga, Prof. Anne Mette Kjær, Ole Therkildsen, Marianne Sandvad Ulriksen, Ane Karoline Bak, and two anonymous reviewers for their review and feedback on the initial drafts of this chapter. All errors and omissions remain entirely mine.

References

Bank of Uganda. 2017. *Annual Report 2016/17*. 30 June. https://www.bou.or.ug/bou/bouwebsite/bouwebsitecontent/publications/Annual_Reports/All/Annual-Report-2016-2017.pdf.

Bank of Uganda. 2021. *Annual Report 2020/21*. https://bou.or.ug/bouwebsite/bouwebsitecontent/publications/Annual_Reports/All/Annual-Report-2021-for-upload-on-website-1.pdf.

Bariyo, N. 2011. 'Uganda Buys Fighter Jets'. *Wall Street Journal*. 7 April. https://www.wsj.com/articles/SB10001424052748704013604576248094099823846.

Biryabarema, E. 2010. 'US Diplomat Believed Eni Bribed Uganda Ministers: US Cable'. *Reuters*. 10 December. https://www.reuters.com/article/wikileaks-uganda-oil-idUKLDE6B911I20101210.

Biryabarema, E. 2012. 'Uganda Lawmakers Pass Oil Bill, Worry about Corruption'. *Reuters*, 7 December. https://www.reuters.com/article/uganda-oil-idUSL5E8N7AJH20121207.

Bukenya, B., and J. Nakaiza. 2020. 'Closed but Ordered'. In *Oil Wealth and Development in Uganda and Beyond*, edited by Arnim Langer, Ukoha Ukiwo, and Pamela Mbabazi, pp. 103–124. Leuven University Press.

Daily Monitor. 2015. 'Museveni on Oil Production'. 27 December.

Directorate of Petroleum—Uganda. 2013. 'Petroleum Exploration History'. https://www.petroleum.go.ug/index.php/who-we-are/who-weare/petroleum-exploration-history.

European Union Election Observation Mission. 2011. 'Final Report of the Uganda General Elections'. 10 March. https://www.eods.eu/library/FR%20UGANDA%2010.03.2011_en.pdf.

Global Witness. 2014. 'A Good Deal Better? Uganda's Secret Oil Contracts Explained'. 24 September.

Golooba-Mutebi, F., and S. Hickey. 2013. 'Investigating the Links between Political Settlements and Inclusive Development in Uganda: Towards a Research Agenda'. *ESID Working Paper No. 20*. https://www.effective-states.org/wp-content/uploads/working_papers/final-pdfs/esid_wp_20_goloobamutebi-hickey.pdf.

Goodfellow, T., and K. Titeca. 2012. 'Presidential Intervention and the Changing "Politics of Survival" in Kampala's Informal Economy'. *Cities* 29(4): pp. 264–270.

Hickey, S., and A. Izama. 2017. 'The Politics of Governing Oil in Uganda: Going against the Grain?' *African Affairs* 116(463): pp. 163–185.

Hickey, S., and A. Izama. 2020. 'The Politics of Governing Oil after "Best-Practice" Reforms: Can "Pockets of Effectiveness" Survive within Uganda's Political Settlement?' *The Extractive Industries and Society* 7(4): pp. 1200–1210.

Imaka, I. 2011. 'Mutebile Reveals Oil Deal with Museveni'. *Daily Monitor*. 16 November.

Imaka, I. 2012a. 'MPs Insist Tullow Oil Gave Bribes for Contracts'. *Daily Monitor*. 12 April.

Imaka, I. 2012b. 'Move to Cut Ministers' Powers Stands in Way of Passing Oil Bill'. *Daily Monitor*. 11 October.

Imaka, I. 2012c. 'Oil Bill Passed amidst Protests'. *Daily Monitor*. 8 December.

Kabumba, B., D. Ngabirano, and T. Kyepa. 2017. *Militarism and the Dilemma of Post-colonial Statehood.* Kampala: Development Law Publishing Company Limited (DLP).

Kafeero, S. 2018. 'Taxes: Who Is Exempted, Why?' *Daily Monitor.* 5 May. https://www.monitor.co.ug/uganda/news/national/taxes-who-is-exempted-why-1754534.

Kagenda, P. 2009. 'Secrecy, Woes, War over Uganda's Oil'. *The Independent.* 9 July.

Kakembo, D. 2017. 'Why Uganda Should Reconsider Oil Tax Amendment'. *New Vision.* 10 November. https://www.newvision.co.ug/news/1465456/uganda-reconsider-oil-tax-amendment.

Kangave, J., and M. W. Katusiimeh. 2015. 'Tax Bargains: Understanding the Role Played by Public and Private Actors in Influencing Tax Policy Reform in Uganda'. *UNRISD Working Paper No. 2015-2.* United Nations Research Institute for Social Development, Geneva. https://www.econstor.eu/bitstream/10419/148733/1/861116208.pdf.

Kasimbazi, E. B. 2012. 'Environmental Regulation of Oil and Gas Exploration and Production in Uganda'. *Journal of Energy & Natural Resources Law* 30(2): pp. 185–221.

Kiiza, J., L. Bategeka, and S. Ssewanyana. 2011. 'Righting Resource-Curse Wrongs in Uganda: The Case of Oil Discovery and the Management of Popular Expectations'. *Mawazo: The Journal of Humanities and Social Sciences, Makerere University* 10(3): pp. 183–203.

Kjær, A. M. 2013. 'Foreign Investments in Uganda's Oil Sector: Linkages and Issues for the Local Economy'. *DIIS Working Paper 2013:24*, Danish Institute for International Studies. ReCom: Copenhagen. https://www.econstor.eu/bitstream/10419/122287/1/780313763.pdf.

Kjær, M., O. Therkildsen, L. Buur, and M. W. Hansen. 2021. 'When "Pockets of Effectiveness" Matter Politically: Extractive Industry Regulation and Taxation in Uganda and Tanzania'. *The Extractive Industries and Society* 8(1): pp. 294–302.

Kyepa, T. 2012. 'Integrating the Proposed National Oil Company of Uganda into the Corporate Governance Discourse: Lessons from Norway'. *Journal of Energy & Natural Resources Law* 30(1): pp. 75–89.

Ladu, M. I. 2016. 'Uganda: Govt Loses Shs 1 Trillion in Tax Exemptions Annually—Report'. *Daily Monitor.* 23 June.

Lay, T., and M. Minio-Paluello. 2010. *Contracts Curse: Uganda's Oil Agreements Place Profit before People.* London: Platform. https://www.platformlondon.org/carbonweb/documents/uganda/Cursed_Contracts_Uganda_PLATFORM_CSCO_Tullow_Heritage_2010_February.pdf.

Looney, R. 2015. 'In Uganda, It's Bust before Boom: Uganda Picked the Wrong Time to Mortgage Its Future to Oil'. *Foreign Policy*. 12 February. https://foreignpolicy.com/2015/02/02/in-uganda-its-bust-before-boom-oil-prices-east-africa/.

Lumu, D. T. 2012. 'My Amendments Will Keep Away Oil Sharks'. *The Observer*. 16 October.

Lumu, D. T., and S. Kakaire. 2012. 'Oil Bill: NRM's Winning Formular'. *The Observer*. 9 December. https://www.observer.ug/news-headlines/22553-oil-bill-nrms-winning-formular.

Ministry of Energy and Mineral Development. 2008. *The National Oil and Gas Policy for Uganda*. https://www.pau.go.ug/download/the-national-oil-and-gas-policy-for-uganda-2018/.

Muhumuza, M. K. 2017. 'Where Is Uganda's Oil Money?' *Daily Monitor*. 15 January.

Mwesigwa, A. 2017. 'Shs. 2.3 Trillion from Oil Disputes Already Spent'. *The Observer*. 30 October. http://observer.ug/news/headlines/55683-shs-2-3-trillion-from-oil-disputes-already-spent.html.

Oloka-Onyango, J. 2019. 'Courting the Oil Curse or Playing by the Rules?' In *Oil Wealth and Development in Uganda and Beyond*, edited by Arnim Langer, Ukoha Ukiwo, and Pamela Mbabazi, pp. 49–74. Leuven: Leuven University Press.

Parliament of Uganda, Republic of Uganda. 2011. *Resolution of Parliament in Respect of Regulation of the Oil Sector and Other Matters Incidental Thereto*.

Patey, L. 2015. *Oil in Uganda: Hard Bargaining and Complex Politics in East Africa*. Oxford: Oxford Institute for Energy Studies.

Private Sector Foundation Uganda. 2009. *Widening Uganda's Tax Base and Improving Tax Administration*.

Salama, V. 2014. 'Museveni's Oil Bet: Letter from Kampala'. *Foreign Affairs*. 20 February. https://www.foreignaffairs.com/articles/africa/2014-02-20/musev–enis-oil-bet.

SEATINI Uganda. 2019. *Impact of Harmful Tax Incentives and Exemptions in Uganda*. https://seatiniuganda.org/wp-content/uploads/2020/06/impact-of-harmful-tax-incentives-and-exemptions-in-uganda-2019.pdf.

Shepherd, B. 2013. *Oil in Uganda: International Lessons for Success*. London: Chatham House.

Ssekika, E. 2017. 'CSOs Call for End of Secrecy in Oil Deals in a Petition to Parliament'. *Oil in Uganda*. 9 March.

State House. 2016. 'Uganda Will Not Spend Oil Revenue on Consumables—President Museveni'. 22 November.

Tangri, R. K., and A. Mwenda. 2013. *The Politics of Elite Corruption in Africa: Uganda in Comparative African Perspective*. London and New York: Routledge.

Wass, G., and C. Musiime. 2013. *Business, Human Rights, and Uganda's Oil*. Kampala: IPIS.

9

Campaign financing and revenue bargaining in Tanzania and Uganda

Moses Khisa, Jamal Msami, and Ole Therkildsen

9.1 Introduction

'Is there clear evidence—as distinct from surmise—that political donations have significant effects on public policy?' This pertinent question was posed by Pinto-Duschinsky (2012, xiii). Surprisingly, research on the influence of campaign financing on sector-specific policymaking and rent-seeking in Africa is limited. 'Money in politics' research mainly focuses on the influence of money on the quality of democratic governance (Arriola, 2013; Weghorst, 2015; Bleck and van de Walle, 2019; Collord, 2019). Inspired by Pinto-Duschinsky's question, and with a focus on Tanzania and Uganda, we therefore ask the following questions: Do campaign finance contributions strengthen the revenue-bargaining power of campaign finance donors more than paying tax? Is there a link between campaign finance donations and revenue bargaining?

Tanzania and Uganda provide interesting country contexts for analysing the impact of campaign funding on revenue policies. Like many other countries in Africa, the two are not beacons of democracy but rather competitive authoritarian regimes (Kjær and Therkildsen, 2012), with elections becoming more competitive during the 2000s (Khisa et al., 2022) as their ruling coalitions have grown more fragmented—more so in Uganda than in Tanzania (Whitfield et al., 2015). Absent oppression and election fraud, these trends amplify the need for funds to win elections and build coalitions.

In line with the analytical framework for this book (as outlined in Chapter 2), we define *revenue bargaining* as the direct and indirect negotiations between ruling elites and revenue providers about revenue payments. We define *campaign financing* as money and other resources used by parties and candidates during elections, which relates directly to winning an electoral contest (Khisa et al., 2022, 7). Our main focus is on the possible

Moses Khisa, Jamal Msami, and Ole Therkildsen, *Campaign financing and revenue bargaining in Tanzania and Uganda.* In: *The Politics of Revenue Bargaining in Africa.* Edited by: Anne Mette Kjær, Marianne S. Ulriksen, and Ane Karoline Bak, Oxford University Press. DOI: 10.1093/oso/9780192868787.003.0009 revenue-bargaining power of major private donors who contribute to the presidential election campaigns, the (often indirect and opaque) bargaining processes involved, and the outcomes of such bargaining. However, campaign financing for the elections of the president and members of parliament (MPs) are often intertwined. Where relevant, MP campaign financing is, therefore, included in the analysis.

The information in this chapter is based on original fieldwork done between 2017 and 2019. It covers the 2010 and 2015 general elections in Tanzania, and the 2011 and 2016 elections in Uganda. Among the major sources of information are official party documents, newspaper material, and interviews with active and retired politicians as well as people in academia, the media, and civil society—especially those engaged in election monitoring. However, due to the sensitive nature of campaign financing, we also rely on informal sources, circumstantial evidence, and deductions in seeking to trace the revenue-bargaining processes (for details on methods, see Khisa et al., 2022).

The Tanzanian case study focuses on Vodacom's successful revenue bargaining. The company is one of Tanzania's largest and has developed very close relations with the ruling-party elite. The Ugandan case analyses the quid pro quo relations between the ruling party and two prominent businessmen who fund the former and are beneficiaries of a range of government rents.

We do not focus on the impact of campaign financing on election results, nor on the use of soft power, ideational resources, group organization, or group links to the ruling elite—all of which may also be important bases of power and influence during election campaigns (see Golooba-Mutebi and Hickey, 2016; Khisa, 2016; Bleck and van de Walle, 2019). Our main argument is that campaign financing, especially to the incumbent presidential campaigns, provides more bargaining power for campaign donors than tax paying does, for three reasons. First, increased electoral competition (absent oppression of the opposition) makes the ruling party more dependent on private campaign funding and on the use of the government budget to run effective campaigns.

Second, such dependency relations between recipient and campaign finance donors enhance the bargaining power of the latter. Moreover, unlike tax payment, campaign funding can be targeted on those ruling party politicians—especially the presidential candidate—that are able to influence the allocation of government rents due to their position in the party or in parliamentary committees. Finally, campaign costs are—relative to the government budget—much smaller, so that a private donation to a presidential election campaign makes a relatively bigger addition (and hence, buys relatively more influence) than an equivalent tax payment to the government's general budget does.

Among the main findings that support these arguments are that: (a) presidential campaign costs in Uganda, where elite fragmentation is considerable and where presidential elections are much more personalized than in Tanzania, increased significantly in the election cycles of the 2010s, but remained stable in Tanzania; (b) the expenditures in both countries are higher for the incumbents than for the opposition candidates; (c) the government budget is a much more important source of funding for the presidential elections in Uganda than in Tanzania; and (d) private sources of campaign financing for the ruling party are mainly individuals and domestic companies with links to the ruling party, and these have—as the case studies from both countries indicate—clearly bargained for reduced taxation with some success.

The next section provides an analytical framework for the subsequent empirical analyses. Methodology, estimates of campaign costs, and findings on the sources of funding are explained in section 9.3. Case studies of bargaining processes involving major campaign donors are presented in section 9.4, while some broad theoretical implications are given in section 9.5.

9.2 Framework for analysing campaign finance bargaining

Quid pro quo is a common theme in research on campaign financing in both poor and rich countries. Major private donations to a party or a candidate are often exchanged for expected access to rents (e.g. import licences, tax exemptions, and land titles), changes in (specific) government policies, or simply to maintain the ruling party in power. This can result in undue influence, back-door cronyism, and favours for sale, which distort democratic governance (see e.g. Butler, 2010; Mendilow, 2012; Norris et al., 2015). For poor countries, this exchange is often taken for granted rather than substantiated theoretically and empirically. An attempt to do so is presented in this chapter.

Campaign contributions—especially to the incumbent party and its candidates—can be strategically important for both the recipient and the donor. For the recipient ruling elite, this directly targeted and often covert money can be used to legitimize and build ruling coalitions among competing factions that are important for winning elections. Such money can also be used to run individuals' election campaigns. For the private donor, money contributions can provide some bargaining power vis-à-vis the recipient parliamentary candidates or the party/president, thereby helping to establish a basis for quid pro quo bargaining and exchanges (see Chapter 2). Elements of the theoretical framework outlined in Chapter 2 are useful for analysing campaign finance-induced bargaining in Tanzania and Uganda. Consequently, the following case studies focus on holding power, triggers, processes, and outcomes.

However, some differences in the political economy of paying taxes and contributing campaign finances are important and will be worth highlighting here. First, the *trigger* for campaign finance contributions is, obviously, parliamentary and presidential elections. Although candidates may often seek to amass 'war chests' in advance, it is during the run-up to elections that their search for money intensifies. Such efforts, which sometimes include state/ruling party coercion and extortion (Morse, 2018), may increase donors' inclinations to contribute. Second, *holding power*, a key concept in political settlement analyses (Khan, 2010) and in this book's framework, assumes that donors who contribute significant amounts of 'strategic' money to the party/candidate and are better organized have more bargaining power than poorly organized minor contributors.

Given the magnitude of money involved in running campaigns (see section 9.3), some of the private donors must be found among the richest individuals and firms in the country. Foreign individuals and companies are less likely to be among major party donors because multinationals (MNCs) have higher capabilities and better access to capital than local firms do. Relations of foreign capitalists to host country ruling political elites are typically also less 'embedded' compared to those of domestic capitalists (Amsden, 2009). The latter are typically much more dependent on state rents to thrive than MNCs are. Hence, campaign funds in exchange for such rents are based on mutual interests between domestic capitalists and ruling elites (Whitfield et al., 2015).

The bargaining processes induced by major private campaign financing contributions have some common characteristics that differ from bargaining induced by paying taxes. The provision of campaign financing is—in principle—voluntary (absent coercion),[1] while it is compulsory to pay statutory taxes. Tax-based bargaining may take the form of lobbyism, understood as concerted efforts to affect government policy through legal, rule-based means (see Chapter 6). Some MPs may be important in getting such tax exemptions passed in parliament, but so may the ruling party/president.

[1] Many minor private donations to the ruling party (or its candidates) are typically given to avoid harassment by the tax authorities according to some of our interviewees.

Campaign finance-based bargaining typically takes place outside the public arena. Each donor negotiates rents and influence independently of others. Bargaining in this regard is implicit and indirect (Prichard, 2015, 29). It is individualistic and depends on personal contacts and networks. Under such circumstances—unlike tax-based bargaining—neither collective action among campaign finance providers nor a fiscal contract with respect to campaign financing is likely to emerge.[2] Obviously, tax-based and campaign finance-based bargaining may be intertwined and occur simultaneously—especially when a company is a major contributor to both (as our case study on Tanzania illustrates). However, the relative bargaining power of campaign finance donors is typically larger.

Outcomes of campaign finance bargaining obviously depend on the donors and recipients involved and on the types of rents negotiated. Bargaining—what Moore (2008, 37–38) calls 'a sort of reciprocal haggling'—may also result in no outcome (see also Chapter 2). The case studies on Tanzania and Uganda presented here illustrate some of such variation. From a campaign financing perspective, the interesting question is this: Does political financing of especially the ruling party and its candidate give donor(s) a stronger (or different) bargaining position on rent access and policy influences than paying taxes to the state? There are three main reasons why the answer to that question is affirmative.

First, a growing need for campaign finance money weakens politicians' bargaining power vis-à-vis financiers. The realignment of holding power relations is likely in the context of increasing demand and supply of campaign financing. The growing demand for campaign financing reflects the fact that the dominant (ruling) party in both Tanzania and Uganda has become more fragmented and more clientelist over time (Whitfield et al., 2015). As the opposition has gained seats in recent elections (Collord, 2019), life as a politician has become more uncertain and precarious. Competition for political power has increased both within and between parties. There is very high turnover of parliamentarians—more than 60% in the case of Uganda in the two election cycles considered here.[3] What is more, lower-level factions in particular have gained strength in both Tanzania's and Uganda's ruling coalitions since political liberalization (Hickey and Golooba-Mutebi, 2013; Kjær, 2015; Whitfield et al., 2015). Consequently, ruling elites have

[2] Ulriksen, Bak, and Kjær (Chapter 2) define a fiscal contract as 'agreements between ruling elites and revenue providers related to revenue provision'.

[3] The margin of victory for both parliamentary and presidential elections in Tanzania declined significantly in the last two electoral cycles prior to 2020, despite enjoying a comparatively lower parliamentary turnover rate of 8% between 2010 and 2015.

become more vulnerable over time, and this increases the need for political financing to keep the Chama Cha Mapinduzi (CCM) and the National Resistance Movement (NRM) in power in the respective countries.

Second, campaign finance donations can be targeted directly to specific parliamentary or presidential candidates. This improves the funder's bargaining power vis-à-vis the recipient for specific rent and/or policy outcomes. Direct financing also makes it easier for the funder to ascertain whether the recipient is complying with a bargaining deal. In the presidential systems that are the predominant feature of African states, a key target is the president and the presidency who, as the head of state,[4] singularly wields enormous policy power. In contrast, almost all tax payments are used to finance the general government budget. Revenues are not earmarked for specific purposes.

Nonetheless, revenues are relevant for winning elections as they help the government to finance a range of public or club goods (including pork-barrel spending) appreciated by voters, such as law and order, social services, and infrastructure (Kjær and Therkildsen, 2012). In addition, the ruling party can mobilize voters by using state resources in election campaigns, such as civil servants, government vehicles, and the police. However, these routes to gain votes and reward major taxpayers require the cooperation of many government agencies to allocate bargained rents and implement policy changes to specific (typically larger) tax-paying individuals and firms.

Finally, buying influence through campaign financing is likely to be more cost effective from the financier's point of view than buying influence through tax payments. Party/candidate campaign budgets are simply much smaller than government budgets. Recipients of campaign funding therefore become more dependent on donors for lesser amounts of money than politicians are on large taxpayers for their contributions to the government budget. This means more direct reciprocity and quid pro quo in a campaign finance-based relationship than in a tax-payment relationship—simply 'a bigger bang for the buck'.

Summarizing, the cost of electioneering is growing in many African countries. To meet this need, large domestic firms and rich individuals are becoming very important. Incumbent politicians in particular are increasingly dependent on private capitalists for running election campaigns. Contributing campaign funds gives donors stronger bargaining power vis-à-vis incumbents than paying the equivalent sum of money in tax. In the next section, we provide estimates of the magnitudes and sources of money involved in electioneering in Tanzania and Uganda.

[4] In hybrid systems like Tanzania, the winning candidate has also gone on to be the party chair, further consolidating political power in the party and beyond.

9.3 The magnitudes and main sources of campaign financing in Tanzania and Uganda

We define campaign financing as money and other resources used by parties and candidates during a period of five months prior to the general/presidential elections, which relates directly to winning the electoral contest.[5] This money is a part of political financing—income generated by parties and politicians for political purposes including campaign financing (Nassmacher, 2003, 34). Separating 'money for electioneering' from routine party organization expenses is difficult. Moreover, the ruling party's use of state resources, as well as money spent by, for example, legally distinct NGOs, foreign aid agencies, media, lobbyists, and other organizations to support specific parties or candidates are part of political-cum-campaign financing too but are difficult to quantify (Pinto-Duschinsky, 2002, 70).

Non-compliance with the country-level rules and regulations of campaign financing is a major obstacle for accurate mapping of the size and sources of campaign finances. Major campaign finance contributions in countries like Tanzania and Uganda are typically not officially recorded because of poor compliance with campaign financing regulations. On the Perceptions of Electoral Integrity Index, Tanzania ranks as number 23 out of 46 African countries (excluding North African). Uganda ranks as number 37 (Norris and Grömping, 2019, fig. 2).[6] Campaign finance is part of the ranking. Tanzania scores 23 on the integrity index. Uganda's score is 14. This indicates that official[7] sources of information on campaign finances are not reliable.[8] In what follows, we provide some estimates and order of magnitude of campaign costs as well as the major sources, drawing from a combination of our own primary fieldwork and a range of secondary sources.

9.3.1 Election campaign costs and sources

The incumbent CCM presidential candidate in Tanzania spent slightly less in 2015 compared to 2010, measured in constant dollars and purchasing power

[5] Methodology and additional results are available in Khisa et al. (2022). See also https://www.idea.int/data-tools/data/political-finance-database.

[6] The index scores on 11 elements covering the entire cycle for elections held during the 2012–2018 period (see Norris and Grömping, 2019, table A3).

[7] By 'official' we refer to information filed by individual political candidates and parties to bodies tasked with overseeing election expenses. This definition can also be extended to refer to subjective responses collected from candidates who may feel compelled to ensure a tallying of filed and surveyed figures.

[8] See also http://www.idea.int/data-tools/data/political-finance-database.

parity according to estimates we obtained (Table 9.1). There are two explanations for this. First, the former Prime Minister, Lowassa, who defected to the opposition, decamped with his campaign donors and electoral machinery (key party officials including regional chairs), which meant the CCM had to look elsewhere and even requested more money from the donors with which it was left. Second, the timing and unexpectedness of Lowassa's defection, occurring three months before the election date, left the CCM scrambling to mobilize resources and votes. It is also worth noting that in 2015, the main opposition presidential candidate spent only around half as much on campaigns as the CCM candidate did.

Much more money is spent in the Ugandan presidential campaigns than in the Tanzanian ones. There are several reasons for this. First, it is possible that the figures for Uganda overstate how much was actually spent. In the past, other analysts like Tangri and Mwenda (2013) have come up with figures for the 2011 elections that ranged from USD 30 and 50 million to USD 100 million, the latter dismissed by NRM officials as inaccurate. By contrast, it is also possible that the figures for Tanzania somewhat underestimate the actual expenses incurred by especially the incumbent presidential candidate, owing to the difficulties of quantifying non-monetary state support and the absence of audited party expenses.

Second, the Alliance for Campaign Finance Monitoring (ACFIM), whose figures we rely on for the Ugandan case, claims to have tracked campaign expenditure in real time for the six months preceding the 2016 elections. Much of the focus and tracking was on expenditures out of the national budget, which the incumbent president leveraged for campaign purposes, as well as direct expenditures by the NRM and its presidential candidate. On the other hand, figures for Tanzania come from data collected from party officials who may not have taken into consideration campaign expenses using official government budgets, and only correspond to spending in the three months leading up to the elections. In other words, it is possible that Tanzania's presidential campaign estimates do not capture the full breadth of money expended for CCM's campaign purposes, except for that borne directly by the party, its candidate, or the array of financiers footing specific costs of the campaign process.[9] Third, Uganda's higher presidential campaign expenditure is

[9] For example, the budgets for state security organs and local governments do increase during electoral cycles. There have been documented instances of these very same organs supporting the party by, among others, the provision of vehicles, offices, and stationery, and even state officials pursuing partisan politics while in office. It is difficult to accurately quantify the extent of such support.

Table 9.1 Estimated costs of presidential campaigns

Campaign costs per main candidate	Tanzania				Uganda			
	2010	2015			2011	2016		
	Total	Total	Incumbent	Opposition	Total	Total	Incumbent	Opposition
Cost in local currency (million)	14.629	33.135	21.175	11.960	75.000	857.000	790.000	67.000
Cost in USD (million)	10	17	11	6	30	251	231	20
Cost in constant 2010 local currency (million)	14.629	20.972	13.402	7.570	65.147	549.691	506.716	42.975
Cost in constant 2010 USD (million)	10. 15	14. 55	9. 30	5. 25	29.92	25.245	23.271	19.74
Cost in PPP dollars (million)	29	41	26	15	88	707	652	55
Cost per capita USD	0.24	0. 32	0. 21	0.12	0. 84	6.26	5.82	0.49
Cost per capita PPP dollars	0.66	0.79	0.51	0.29	2. 49	17.68	16.42	1.39
(Cost/capita)/(GDP/capita) in PPP dollars (%)	0.03%	0.03%	0.02%	0.01%	0.12%	0.85%	0.79%	0.07%

in part due to the competitive clientelist and personalist nature of Ugandan politics under Museveni, rife with factional contestations and needing more patronage resources to buy continued stay in power. The longer Museveni has stayed in power, the more resources he needs to oil his patronage machinery and meet campaign time pledges and money handouts on the campaign trail.

The average campaign expenditure per candidate for the *general parliamentary elections* for 2016 in Uganda was some USD 56,100 (USD 51,060 in constant 2010 dollars, as shown in Table 9.2). Compared to 2011, this is an increase of 60% measured in constant 2010 dollars. Extrapolated, the total estimated expenditure in 2016 for all the 427 MPs was some USD 24 million in 2016 dollars. These figures are comparable to what the consortium of election-observation NGOs, the Alliance for Campaign Finance Monitoring (ACFIM), found in a survey of 113 MPs during the 2016 elections, namely an average of 9% higher than the figure in Table 9.2. These figures are, however, lower than those of Golooba-Mutebi (2016), which ranged from USD 43,000 to 143,000, and Wilkins (2016, 630) who, from 'six knowledgeable sources', gave estimates averaging USD 162,000.

For Tanzania, the average campaign expenditure per candidate for the 2015 general elections was USD 40,600 (some USD 37,300 measured in constant 2010 dollars as indicated in Table 9.2). Compared to the 2010 elections, this is an increase on some 24% (a much smaller growth than in Uganda). Extrapolated for all the 264 MPs in 2015, it amounts to some USD 10.7 million in 2015 dollars, far exceeding the parliamentary expenditure ceiling defined by the 2015 revisions of Tanzania's Electoral Expenses Act.[10] The figures underscore the ineffectiveness of electoral expense laws in contexts with limited

Table 9.2 Average campaign finance costs per elected candidate for parliamentary[a] elections

	Tanzania		Uganda	
	2010	2015	2011	2016
All elected MPs, constant 2010 USD	30,007	37,325	32,009	51,063
USD PPP	84,248	100,645	96,290	158,432

[a] The campaign costs of primaries in Tanzania were around 5 to 6% of parliamentary campaign costs during the 2010 elections. In Uganda, they amounted to some 8% in 2011 and 12% in 2016.
Source: Khisa et al., 2022.

[10] Tanzania's Election Expenses Act defines an expenses cap that ranged from TZS 33 to 88 million (i.e. USD 16,600–44,200) as a result of Tanzania's vast geography. The low end of the expenses range caters for some 60 constituencies, while only 12 constituencies fall under the higher end of the scale.

enforcement capacity (TEMCO, 2016). They demonstrate the costly nature of competitive and clientelistic elections in two poor countries whose Gross National Income per capita (at PPP) in 2016 was USD 1,800 for Uganda and USD 2,740 for Tanzania.[11]

9.3.2 Campaign finance sources

Interviews with well-informed Tanzanian observers indicate that local businesses funded around 60% of the ruling party's presidential campaign in 2015. Other local supporters contributed around 30%, some 5% comes from the government budget, and another 5% from MNCs.[12] No official information about the identity of the private donors exists. However, given the volume of money involved, some of the larger domestic companies must be important sources of campaign funds. Interviews confirm that this is indeed the case. They also confirm that some of the large firms have close ties to CCM. Yet, these large domestic companies are not on the list of Tanzania's 15 largest corporate taxpayers. This was already noted by Parliament in 2011 when parliamentarians asked for explanations but did not get them (Hoffman, 2013).

Taxation of the telecom sector is a case in point. Airtel, with 28% of the mobile market, was the eighth-largest taxpayer during the 2005–2011 period, while Vodacom, with a market share of 43%, was not on the list at all. Airtel had no significant local ownership, but Vodacom did (Hoffman, 2013). Vodacom is, therefore, selected here as a case study to gain insights into the campaign finance–revenue bargaining relationship.

In Uganda, likewise, public information about the relative importance of the main sources of incumbent presidential campaign financing is not available. However, based on field interviews and secondary materials, it is possible to identify two key sources of funding for the NRM and President Museveni: official budget allocations and funding from the business community (with minor amounts coming from foreign companies and local supporters). Thus, analyses of budget cycles show spikes in the total national budget during or preceding the election year. The most revealing aspect of

[11] A detailed comprehensive and comparative analysis of these parliamentary campaign costs and their sources is in Khisa et al. (2022). Here, we have provided only a simplified picture to underscore the fact that parliamentary and presidential elections in Tanzania and Uganda are intertwined and that bargains on revenue collection and expenditure involve both the legislature and the executive.

[12] Local supporters include overt and anonymous contributions by local individuals who directly contribute to individual parties and their candidates. These also include friends, colleagues, and families. They are distinguishable from local businesses by virtue of not directly owning legally registered trading entities or identifying as trading entities when contributing.

this is the supplementary budgets passed on the eve of general elections (ACFIM, 2016, 8–9; Flynn et al., 2017). For example, with only few weeks to go until the 2011 general elections, Parliament retrospectively passed a staggering 30% supplementary budget, ten times the legal threshold of 3%. Among the main beneficiaries were State House and the defence and security dockets, all with classified expenditures (Helle and Rakner, 2014, 164; Khisa, 2015, 183).

In 2015—one year prior to elections—Uganda's budget dramatically increased from UGX 14 trillion in the previous fiscal year to almost 24 trillion for the electioneering year. Curiously, while government did not allocate money to domestic debt payment in 2014, it assigned an unprecedented 20% of the budget for this purpose in 2015, the year leading up to the 2016 elections, a move interpreted as meaning that domestic creditors were one channel through which the NRM 2015/2016 secured campaign funds (ACFIM, 2016, 7). What is more, since the early 2000s, the budget for State House has growly exponentially and tends to take a huge chunk of supplementary budgets passed closer to election time. The bulk of the State House budget goes towards meeting presidential pledges and donations.

The other major source of campaign funding is large domestic companies. Like in Tanzania, most of these are absent among Uganda's large taxpayers. Between 2006 and 2016, the list of the top taxpayers is dominated by foreign corporations. There was no wholly Ugandan-owned company among the top ten taxpayers in 2006, and there was only one in 2016. Missing from the top ten, and even the top 20, are indigenous Ugandan and Asian-Ugandan businesses such as the Madhvani Group, the Imperial Group, the Ruparelia Group, the Mukwano Group, the Haba Group, and others owned by individuals who are known—as our own interviews and other sources show—to be the leading donors to Museveni and the NRM.

In sum, the nature of the ruling coalition has implications for competitive politics both intra- and inter-party. Uganda's ruling coalition is more fragmented than Tanzania's. Consequently, rent allocation is more decentralized in Uganda than it is in Tanzania. This helps to explain the higher campaign costs in the former than the latter. However, Tanzania too has lately experienced factional struggles with the ruling CCM and the fight for control over access to rents. The trend is likely to continue as elections continue to serve as avenues for patronage distribution and elite haggling over rent allocation.

Getting accurate and reliable campaign finance estimates is difficult. Through primary and secondary sources, we were able to compile comprehensive enough aggregates of individual campaign-related activities, which, in the final analysis, suggest that the ruling parties in both Tanzania and

Uganda rely heavily on private funders and official government budgets to finance their election-related expenses. In that regard, the respective ruling parties engage in bargaining at the level of revenue —bargaining between political and economic elites on one hand and intra-political elite bargaining at the level of revenue expenditure on the other. The next section takes up this aspect.

9.4 Bargaining for rents and influence in Tanzania and Uganda

The central claim we advance is that donors that contribute campaign finances to the ruling party candidates—especially the presidential candidate—gain more bargaining power with respect to *policy decisions* and *rent-seeking* (tax reductions, tax avoidance, land, licences, etc.) than individuals/firms that pay the same amount of money in taxes. In both countries, the combined effect of competitive elections, decentralized rent management, and the need to distribute increased levels of patronage in order to maintain the ruling CCM or NRM coalition increased the amount of political financing required (Whitfield et al., 2015). We now discuss a few cases and individuals that illustrate the relationship between campaign finance supply and revenue-related outcomes. We focus on specific individuals, given the personalist nature of political bargaining and patronage-based political processes in both countries.

9.4.1 Micro-level evidence: Party, kingmaker, taxpayer, and taxing mobile financial services in Tanzania

Despite being one of the oldest and longest-governing independence parties, Tanzania's ruling CCM has remained largely dependent on contributions and other handouts from private donors to run the party. In recent years, private contributions have accounted for two-thirds and three-quarters of the party's revenue in non-election and election years, respectively (Lugongo, 2017).[13] Such dependence has left the party (and by implication, executive decisions) vulnerable to influence by private donors, particularly in election

[13] Macro-evidence from Tanzania shows that both tax exemptions and smuggling of sugar (which generate substantial rents to major domestic traders) are cyclical and peak in election years (Andreoni and Tasciotti, 2019; Therkildsen and Bak, 2019).

cycles. The party's inability to self-finance has seen it entangled with prominent local businesses, members of whom have proceeded to assume party, parliamentary, and cabinet positions in recent years.

Despite links with many of the country's wealthiest business elites, the CCM private capital links have been most pronounced in its association with Rostam Aziz. Aziz served as the CCM National Treasurer (and financier of elections) from 2005 to 2007, an MP for the Igunga constituency in Western Tanzania (1994–2011), and member of the Central Committee of the CCM from 2006 to 2011. He was once considered the most powerful business and non-cabinet individual in Tanzania, generally referred to as the 'kingmaker' by supporters and opponents alike (Cooksey, 2011).

Prior to September 2019, Aziz was also a minority shareholder in Tanzania's largest telecom provider, Vodacom.[14] Along with long-time associate Peter Noni,[15] Aziz owned 35% of Vodacom (Ubwani, 1999; Nsehe 2018; 2019). Fieldwork suggests that both Aziz and Noni made substantial contributions and channelled contributions from other members of the business elite to the CCM between 2004 and 2015, until the decamping of their long-time ally, Edward Lowassa, in August 2015. Certainly, Aziz's shareholding in Vodacom shows an important case of revenue bargaining involving the CCM and private business centred on the government's attempted taxation of one of Vodacom's core businesses: mobile financial services (MFS).[16]

MFS began in Tanzania in 2008 and currently boast over 22 million registered users (TCRA, 2019), who constitute a substantial tax base. On average, some 242 million transactions worth TZS 7.8 trillion (USD 3.4 billion) a month are conducted using MFS in Tanzania (ibid.). Of the six mobile telecoms providing MFS, none is bigger than Vodacom Tanzania, whose M-PESA platform accounts for 41% of the market share (ibid.). Currently, MFS account for approximately 30% of Vodacom's annual revenues. In 2016, an effective tax rate of 28%, comprising 18% VAT and a 10% excise duty on money transfers, was levied on the sector (GSMA, 2017).

However, rather than targeting the telecoms, the Government allowed the telecoms to pass the tax burden onto users of MFS in a move seen as conciliatory to the politically powerful telecoms lobby, especially as the Government had initially promised not to burden users of MFS (Wainaina, 2016). The

[14] With an annual turnover of USD 458 million, Vodacom was ranked as the 283rd largest company in Africa. It had a 33 per cent share of the domestic telecom's voice market as of June 2019 (TCRA, 2019) and has been among the top ten largest taxpayers in Tanzania since 2013.

[15] Noni was a high-ranking official with the central bank between 1995 and 2006, and later the head of the Tanzania Investment Bank from 2008 (Cooksey, 2011).

[16] That is, the use of a mobile phone to access financial services and execute financial transactions.

telecoms responded through their Mobile Operators' Association of Tanzania (MOAT), which successfully lobbied the CCM to impose a whip on its parliamentarians to water down tax regulations. With a third of the domestic market share (TCRA, 2019), Vodacom wields considerable power within the MOAT and has long been known to leverage its political connections in protection or advancement of commercial interests, including through the appointment of a then speaker of Parliament as a chairperson of its board of directors (Brümmer, 2007).

MOAT embarked on a combination of intense lobbying of key party and Government officials and a public information campaign to secure the backing of the chairs of all parliamentary select committees and the Executive. MOAT appealed to CCM elders, many of whom had directly benefitted through the telecoms' financing of past electoral campaigns (Sambaiga et al., 2018). The tactic soon paid off, when some party stalwarts began to voice fears that the taxes could harm the ruling party's unity in the immediate aftermath of what had been a bruising election.

The 2016 MFS tax reforms and associated revenue bargaining mirror many of the dynamics that have historically defined the taxation of the sector.[17] Though Aziz was able to deflect the tax burden, analysts argue that a reduction, suspension, or complete withdrawal of the taxes might have been possible had he overtly backed the Magufuli campaign in 2015 or had Lowassa not defected in anger. Despite limited consultations between the Government and telecom operators over MFS tax, the lobby group's past contributions to the CCM ultimately assisted in it receiving tip-offs from party sources. These historical connections are also evident in how the Tanzania Revenue Authority (TRA) has contrived to create deliberate ambiguities in the MFS regulations that have aided the transfer of the tax burden onto MFS consumers. For example, the 2016/2017 Finance Act levies a 10% excise duty on mobile transfers and mobile payments without offering explicit definitions of what these services are or what they entail.

Similar to his business partner, Noni is known to have played a key role in financing the CCM's campaigns prior to a falling out believed to have been precipitated in part by an equally generous contribution to the campaign of the opposition's Edward Lowassa in 2015, who had also been a friend and business associate. While both Noni and Aziz exacted economic rents from their political contributions through tax exemptions enjoyed by Vodacom, the former also enjoyed promotion within the civil service.

[17] Multiple interviews.

The case of Noni is instructive as his wealth and prominence in ruling circles both rose with his progress, from civil servant, to senior director with the central bank, and later to being the head of the Tanzania Investment Bank. Noni had also served as a prosecution witness to the infamous External Payments Arrears (EPA) affair that involved improper payments worth some USD 131 million to 22 local firms, some with close ties to the ruling CCM (Gray, 2015). Nine of the implicated firms had received some USD 42 million without lodging a single document (*The East African*, 2009). A reversal in political fortunes suffered by both Aziz and Noni in the post-2015 election period gives credence to insider reports of severed political ties following their covert support for the opposition.

9.4.2 Micro-evidence, Uganda: NRM/Museveni business ties

Several media reports underscored that some of the indigenous Ugandan entrepreneurs like Charles Mbire, Patrick Bitature, and Hassan Basajjabalaba, with strong ties to the first family, are among the leading funders of the NRM and the campaign activities of its candidates (Mufumba, 2010; Muhwezi, 2012; Matsiko, 2016). On the eve of the 2016 elections, in a long public statement that included appeals for campaign funds, incumbent Yoweri Museveni lauded the 'big contributors', noting that they have 'solely carried the burden' (*Daily Monitor*, 2016). Some of these are from Western Uganda, Museveni's home area, which has the highest regional average campaign expenditure for MPs from our survey data.

The NRM-allied businesspeople use their resources to campaign for Museveni in presidential elections and for individual NRM candidates in parliamentary races (ACFIM, 2016; Tangri and Mwenda, 2019). These same individuals and their companies form the bulk of a select group of businesses that have consistently benefited from tax waivers and other forms of rent reward from the government (ACFIM, 2016, 13; Tangri and Mwenda, 2019). The owners of the companies in question are known to be close to the President and have provided financial support during campaign times. Two individuals (and their respective companies) stand out and are worth detailed analysis: Sudhir Ruparelia and Hassan Basajjabalaba.

Sudhir Ruparelia emerged in a relatively short period as arguably Uganda's richest man, with a chain of businesses across sectors, from hotels and horticulture to banking, education, and real estate. He previously owned Crane Bank, which in 2016 officially ranked as the third-largest commercial bank. Despite this, it was ranked 28th taxpayer, while the top-ranked bank Stanbic (foreign owned) was the fifth-largest taxpayer. In what appears to have been a political falling out, shortly after the 2016 elections, the central bank went after Crane Bank, declaring the bank insolvent. Crane Bank's closure remained shrouded in mystery. It is somewhat bewildering that a bank with a clean bill of health before the 2016 elections would suddenly become distressed soon after. Informal interviews with political actors and media sources suggested that Sudhir hedged his bets in the 2016 elections by funding both the NRM and the opposition.

Given his many businesses, Sudhir would ordinarily be a leading taxpayer but for his connections to the ruling party and especially direct access to the President. Thus, as of 2008, Sudhir's Meera Investments Limited had accumulated tax arrears to the tune of USD 12 million, which were cancelled on the directives of President Museveni, and earlier, the Government had sunk USD 32 million into Sudhir's Munyonyo Commonwealth Resort, a deal fraught with controversy (Tangri and Mwenda, 2019, 6). Earlier, in 2006, the President ordered the Uganda Revenue Authority to stop collecting tax arrears and investigating his financial affairs (Tangri and Mwenda, 2013, 111). As part of the evidence for payback, in 2015, on the eve of the 2016 election, Sudhir was among a long list of business actors involved in a fundraiser for the ruling party and contributed UGX 3 billion (approximately USD 1 million at the time) ostensibly towards building the headquarters for the ruling party (Kaaya, 2015).

Like Sudhir, Basajjabalaba has been a major beneficiary of rents at the same time as being a long-standing financier of the NRM and party candidates, especially in his home district of Bushenyi in Western Uganda. He was the Chairman of the Entrepreneurs' League in the NRM (a group of businesspeople allied to the ruling party) and was responsible for mobilizing funds from businesspeople to finance the NRM during elections (Tangri and Mwenda, 2019, 12). From the other end of the equation, Basajjabalaba has been the recipient of many questionable payments and compensations from the Government. One such payment caused the forced resignation of two cabinet ministers, Syda Bumba and Khiddu Makubuya, in 2012 following a parliamentary probe into a USD 60 million payment scandal (BBC, 2012).

In 2005, the President instructed the Ministry of Finance to waive taxes (estimated worth USD 6.8 million) on building materials for the construction of the Ishaka Teaching Hospital in Bushenyi, Western Uganda, part of Kampala International University owned by Basajjabalaba. He also received a controversial UGX 20 billion grant from the central bank, again on the instruction of the President, to pay debts and taxes and to subsidize his Kampala International University. As payback, Bassajabala donated to the

NRM's 2011 election coffers and also funded the campaigns of at least two dozen MPs (Tangri and Mwenda, 2013, 113; 2019, 11).

While Basajjabalaba and other indigenous business actors have been key funders of the NRM, anecdotal evidence suggests that the biggest source of funds from the business community is from the Asian-Ugandans, who exchange donations for preferential treatment. Resident Asian business tycoons like Karim Hirji, Sudhir Ruparelia, and Nitin Madhvani are among the individuals known to give large sums to Museveni's campaigns (Tangri and Mwenda, 2019, 6). In return for financial and other transfers for his election campaigns, President Museveni rewards Asian firms after the elections in various ways.

According to Tangri and Mwenda (2013, 110), State House (which is in essence the President) has, over the years, instructed the Uganda Revenue Authority not to pursue and penalize substantial tax evasions and tax arrears by Asian-Ugandan-owned business. Other rents granted to this group have included Museveni's unilateral giveaway to the Madhvani Group, a licence for sugar farming in the Butamira Forest Reserve, and the decision to direct the Ministry of Lands to give the Mehta Group one-third of Mabira Forest Reserve for sugar cultivation (Tangri and Mwenda, 2019, 6). However, the latter move did not materialize in the face of violent protests in Kampala that led to death of an Indian national. This may point to the fact that it is becoming more difficult for the NRM and Museveni to provide land to favoured businesspeople, resulting in a possible switch towards less visible rents such as tax breaks and import privileges.

9.4.3 The campaign finance–revenue bargaining nexus

The case studies illustrate the role and holding power of private-sector actors as sources of campaign financing and their influence on electioneering in Tanzania and Uganda. Local tycoons and domestically owned business have acquired leverage in their close relations with the political class, particularly as power monopolies in the two countries have increasingly been challenged within and beyond party lines. Factional fights contribute to the realignment of relations between campaign finance donors and the political elites, as happened in Tanzania during the 2015 elections. These weaken the revenue-bargaining positions of ruling parties while strengthening the holding power of local elites.

Overall, the higher the cost of campaigns, the more the bargaining powers of campaign finance providers grow as does the dependence of the political class on the providers. In practice, some notable contributors of campaign finance in Tanzania and Uganda have been beneficiaries of a range of revenue concessions from the Government, both directly and indirectly, in quid pro quo relations. In the final section, we summarize these findings and draw out some implications.

9.5 Conclusion

'The future of democracy in Africa will mean more money in politics, more patronage and clientelistic offers thrown around, and for a while increasing use of violence as a strategy to influence the [election] outcome' (Ham and Lindberg, 2015, 26). For Tanzania and Uganda, this statement is perhaps too sweeping, although the tendencies outlined in the quote certainly exist. The competitive nature of elections in both countries, under conditions of clientelism and weak institutions, triggers the need for mobilizing campaign funds. Electoral competition and the demand for campaign financing shape bargaining-power relations between political elites and business actors. One key area in which these relations play out is in the realm of revenue collection and expenditure and in the allocation of state rents more generally.

We have shown in this chapter that: (a) campaign costs increased in the election cycles of the 2010s in both Uganda and, to a lesser extent, Tanzania; (b) these expenditures are higher in Uganda than Tanzania for both parliamentary and presidential elections, and they are higher for the incumbents than for the opposition; (c) the volume of tax exemptions is higher—and the total revenue as a percentage of GDP lower—around election years, indicating a clear causal relationship between taxation and elections (such evidence is only available for Tanzania at present); and (d) sources of campaign financing for the ruling party are mainly domestic private individuals and companies, and these have—as the case studies suggest—engaged in bargaining for reduced taxation, with some success.

We argue that campaign financing is likely to provide more bargaining power for donors (arguably than tax-paying does), for three reasons. Increased electoral competition (absent oppression of the opposition) makes the ruling party more dependent on private campaign funding to run effective campaigns. Moreover, unlike tax payment, campaign funding can be targeted to those politicians—especially the presidential candidate—that are able to influence the allocation of government rents due to their position in the party or in parliamentary committees. Finally, campaign costs are—relative to the government budget—much smaller so that a private donation to a campaign makes a relatively bigger addition (and hence, buys relatively more influence) than an equivalent taxpayment to the government's general budget.

More specifically, the Tanzanian case shows the influence of a key CCM campaign finance donor, Rostam Aziz, on the taxation of the major company in which he had a considerable share. Thus, while the tax on mobile phones was not reduced, the Aziz–CCM links enabled the telecom companies (including Vodacom in which Aziz had major shares) to transfer the tax burden onto end users of MFS, contrary to the Government's earlier promises of not taxing end users. Further, these links have allowed the status quo to remain unchanged since then, despite MFS users feeling the pinch. This case suggests that revenue bargaining need not result in reductions or waivers of revenue decisions. Governments can respond to pressures from non-state power-holders by transferring the burden of policy change through concealment of target groups.

The Ugandan case shows continuity in the ruling NRM party's reliance on opaque sources of campaign financing, it having no known finance sources of its own that are legal and transparent yet increasingly needing more finances to pay for a vast patronage network and material handouts to buy support. The fact that leading local businesspeople, allied with the ruling party, tend to benefit from generous tax exemptions and are not among the top taxpayers suggests a possible quid pro quo and bargaining over revenue and rents.

By many accounts, including from our own field interviews as well as secondary sources, running for Parliament in Uganda has become very costly, while the campaign expenses for president are astronomical compared to Tanzania. This is in part due to the weakness of Uganda's ruling party and the fragmentation of the ruling coalition, necessitating more resources to oil the patronage machinery, especially during election campaign time. In both countries, the ruling party far outspends the combined opposition, pointing to a hugely skewed campaign finance landscape. This has grave implications for the struggle for democracy, the quality of elections, and the state of good governance among African countries.

References

ACFIM (Alliance for Campaign Finance Monitoring). 2016. *Extended Study of Campaign Financing for Presidential and Member of Parliament Races, 2015–2016 in Uganda*. Kampala: ACFIM.

Amsden, A. 2009. 'Nationality of Firm Ownership in Developing Countries: Who Should "Crowd Out" Whom in Imperfect Markets'. In *Industrial Policy and*

Development: The Political Economy of Capabilities Accumulation, edited by M. Cimoli, D. Giovanni, and J. E. Stiglitz, pp. 409–423. Oxford: Oxford University Press.

Andreoni, A., and L. Tasciotti. 2019. *Lost in Trade: Towards a Red-Flag System to Target Trade Misinvoicing and Tax Evasion in Tanzania.* Working Paper 019. London: SOAS University of London.

Arriola, L. R. 2013. *Multiethnic Coalitions in Africa: Business Financing of Opposition Election Campaigns.* Cambridge: Cambridge University Press.

BBC. 2012. 'Uganda Ministers Bumba and Makubuya Resign after Probe'. 16 February. https://www.bbc.com/news/world-africa-17069545.

Bleck, J., and N. van de Walle. 2019. *Electoral Politics in Africa since 1990: Continuity and Change.* Cambridge: Cambridge University Press.

Brümmer, S. 2007. 'Vodacom's Elite Network'. *Mail and Guardian.* 13 April. https://mg.co.za/article/2007-04-13-vodacoms-elite-network.

Butler, A. ed. 2010. *Paying for Politics: Party Funding and Political Financing in South Africa and the Global South.* Dunkeld: Jacana Media and the Konrad Adenauer Foundation.

Collord, M. 2019. *The Political Economy of Institutions in Africa: Comparing Authoritarian Parties and Parliaments In Tanzania and Uganda.* Oxford: University of Oxford.

Cooksey, B. 2011. 'Marketing Reform? The Rise and Fall of Agricultural Liberalisation in Tanzania'. *Development Policy Review* 29(1): pp. s57–s81.

Daily Monitor. 2016. 'Only Few Rich Funding NRM—Museveni'. 25 January. https://www.monitor.co.ug/uganda/oped/commentary/only-few-rich-funding-nrm-campaigns-museveni-1638140.

Flynn, S., I. Aziz, K. Khasiani, F. Sheik Rahim, B. Robinson, and A. Tripathi. 2017. *Uganda: Fiscal Transparency Evaluation.* IMF Country Report No. 17/130. Washington, DC: International Monetary Fund.

Golooba-Mutebi, F. 2016. *The Cost of Politics in Uganda.* London: Westminster Foundation for Democracy Background Paper.

Golooba-Mutebi, F., and S. Hickey. 2016. 'The Master of Institutional Multiplicity? The Shifting Politics of Regime Survival, State-Building and Democratisation in Museveni's Uganda'. *Journal of Eastern African Studies* 10(4): pp. 601–618.

Gray, H. 2015. 'The Political Economy of Grand Corruption in Tanzania'. *African Affairs* 114(456): pp. 382–403.

GSMA. 2017. *Taxation and Mobile Money in Tanzania.* GSM Association. https://www.gsma.com/mobilefordevelopment/wp-content/uploads/2017/10/Taxation-and-Mobile-Money-in-Tanzania-October-2017.pdf.

Ham, C. v., and S. I. Lindberg. 2015. *Vote Buying Is a Good Sign: Alternate Tactics of Fraud in Africa 1986–2012.* V-Dem Working Paper 2015:3. Gothenburg: University of Gothenburg. https://doi.org/10.2139/ssrn.2613854.

Helle, S.-E., and L. Rakner. 2014. 'Grabbing an Election: Abuse of State Resources in the 2011 Elections in Uganda'. In *Corruption, Grabbing and Development: Real World Challenges*, edited by T. Søreide and A. Williams, pp. 161–171. London: Edward Elgar.

Hickey, S and F. Golooba-Mutebi. 2013. *Investigating the Links between Political Settlements and Inclusive Development in Uganda: Towards a Research Agenda.* ESID Working Paper No 20. Manchester: University of Manchester.

Hoffman, Barak. 2013. *Political Economy of Tanzania.* Washington, DC: Center for Democracy and Civil Society, Georgetown University.

Kaaya, S. K. 2015. 'Sudhir Gives 3bn for NRM House'. *The Observer*. 29 June. https://observer.ug/news-headlines/38495-sudhir-gives-shs-3bn-for-nrm-house.

Khan, M. H. 2010. *Political Settlements and the Governance of Growth-Enhancing Institutions.* London: SOAS University of London.

Khisa, M., 2015. 'Political Uncertainty and Its Impact on Social Service Delivery in Uganda'. Africa Development 40 (4): pp. 159–188.

Khisa, M. 2016. 'Managing Elite Defection in Museveni's Uganda: The 2016 Elections in Perspective'. *Journal of Eastern African Studies* 10(4): pp. 729–748.

Khisa, M., J. Msami, and O. Therkildsen. 2022. *The Demand and Supply of Political Campaign Financing in Tanzania and Uganda during the 2010s.* DIIS Working Paper, 2022:10. Copenhagen: Danish Institute for International Studies.

Kjær, A. M. 2015. 'Political Settlements and Productive Sector Policies: Understanding Sector Differences in Uganda. *World Development* 68: pp. 230–241.

Kjær, A. M., and O. Therkildsen. 2012. 'Elections and Landmark Policies in Tanzania and Uganda'. *Democratization* 20(4): pp. 1–23.

Lugongo, B. 2017. 'CCM Seeks Electronic System to Administer Revenues Better'. *Daily News*. 19 December.

Matsiko, H. 2016. 'Fight over Museveni Business Bailout'. *The Independent*. 19 July. https://www.independent.co.ug/fight-musevenis-business-bailout-money/.

Mendilow, J. ed. 2012. *Money, Corruption, and Political Competition in Established and Emerging Democracies*. Plymouth: Lexington Books.

Moore, M. 2008. 'Between Coersion and Contract: Competing Narratives on Taxation and Governance'. In *Taxation and State-Building in Developing Countries: Capacity and Consent*, edited by D. Bräutigam, O.-H. Fjeldstad, and M. Moore, pp. 34–64. Cambridge: Cambridge University Press.

Morse, Y. L. 2018. *How Autocrats Compete: Parties, Patrons, and Unfair Elections in Africa*. Cambridge: Cambridge University Press.

Mufumba, I. 2010. 'Who Funds NRM'? *The Independent*. 8 September. https://www.independent.co.ug/who-funds-nrm/.

Muhwezi, W. 2012. 'Who Is Who in Bushenyi's Rich Club'. *The Observer*. 26 August. https://www.observer.ug/index.php?option=com_content&view=article&id=20576:who-is-who-in-bushenyis-rich-club&catid=38:business.

Nassmacher, K.-H. 2003. 'The Funding of Political Parties in the Anglo-Saxon Orbit'. In *Funding of Political Parties and Election Campaigns*, edited by R. Austin and M. Tjernström, pp. 33–54. Stockholm: International IDEA.

Norris, P., and M. Grömping. 2019. *Electoral Integrity Worldwide*. Sydney: University of Sydney.

Norris, P., A. A. van Es, and L. Fennis. 2015. *Checkbook Elections: Political Finance in Comparative Perspective. Executive Report*. Sydney: University of Sydney.

Nsehe, M. 2018. 'Tanzania's Former Richest Man Rostam Aziz to Earn More than $200 Million from Selling Vodacom Shares'. *Forbes*. 1 July. https://www.forbes.com/sites/mfonobongnsehe/2018/07/01/tanzanias-former-richest-man-rostam-aziz-to-earn-more-than-200-million-from-selling-vodacom-shares/?sh=4b6a943f4cf7.

Nsehe, M. 2019. 'Tanzanian Tycoon Rostam Aziz Sells Last Tranche of Vodacom Shares for $220 Million'. *Forbes*. 23 September. https://www.forbes.com/sites/mfonobongnsehe/2019/09/23/tanzanian-tycoon-rostam-aziz-sells-last-tranche-of-vodacom-shares-for-220-million/

Pinto-Duschinsky, M. 2002. 'Financing Politics: A Global View'. *Democratization* 13(4): pp. 69–86.

Pinto-Duschinsky, M. 2012. 'Introduction: Political Finance, Corruption, and the Future of Democracy'. In *Money, Corruption, and Political Competition in Established and Emerging Democracies*, edited by J. Mendilow, pp. 1–16. Plymouth: Lexington Books.

Prichard, W. 2015. *Taxation, Responsiveness, and Accountability in Sub-Saharan Africa: The Dynamics of Tax Bargaining*. Cambridge: Cambridge University Press.

Sambaiga, R. F., C. Baez-Camargo, and L. Koechlin. 2018. *Informal Governance and Corruption—Transcending the Principal Agent and Collective Action Paradigms Dismantling Networks of Corruption: Challenges and Opportunities in Reforming Informal Governance in Tanzania*. Basel: Basel Institute on Governance.

Tangri, R., and A. M. Mwenda. 2013. *The Politics of Elite Corruption in Africa: Uganda in Comparative African Perspective*. London: Routledge.

Tangri, R., and A. M. Mwenda. 2019. 'Change and Continuity in the Politics of Government–Business Relations in Museveni's Uganda'. *Journal of Eastern African Studies* 13(4): pp. 678–697.

TCRA. 2019. *Quarterly Communications Statistics, April–June 2019 Operators' Submissions*. Tanzania Telecommunications Regulatory Authority.

TEMCO. 2016. *The 2015 Tanzania General Elections: Report of the Tanzania Election Monitoring Committee*. Dar es Salaam: Tanzania Election Monitoring Committee.

The East African. 2009. 'EPA Scandal Dominated 2008, Shook Kikwete'. 03 January. https://www.theeastafrican.co.ke/tea/news/east-africa/epa-scandal-dominated-2008-shook-kikwete--1293244.

Therkildsen, O., and A. K. Bak. 2019. *Democratisation in Tanzania: No Elections without Tax Exemptions.* ICTD Working Paper 98. Brighton: International Centre for Tax and Development, Institute of Development Studies (IDS).

Ubwani, Z. 1999. 'Planetel to Invest $90m in Tanzania'. *The EastAfrican.* 17 August. https://allafrica.com/stories/199908170035.html.

Wainaina, E. 2016. 'Tanzania's 10% tax on Mobile Money Transactions Criticized'. *The Citizen.* 13 June.

Weghorst, K. R. 2015. *Losing the Battle, Winning the War: Legislative Candidacy in Electoral Authoritarian Regimes.* (Ph.D. Dissertation). University of Florida.

Whitfield, L., O. Therkildsen, L. Buur, and A. M. Kjaer. 2015. *The Politics of African Industrial Policy: A Comparative Perspective.* New York: Cambridge University Press.

Wilkins, S. 2016. 'Who Pays for Pakalast? The NRM's Peripheral Patronage in Rural Uganda'. *Journal of Eastern African Studies* 10(4): pp. 619–638.

10 A third party at the table

How donors and chiefs influence revenue bargaining in Togo

Rachel Beach

10.1 Introduction

Much of the fiscal sociology literature focuses on macro-level revenue bargaining, which tends to see two parties at the table: state and societal actors. Examining cases more closely, however, allows us to see other actors engaged in the bargaining process. For example, international donors, traditional authorities, or other societal intermediaries can influence bargaining over taxes between a state and its citizens. Understanding the potential avenues through which these parties influence outcomes is an important element to examine in the politics of taxation.

This chapter analyses two separate attempts at increasing tax takes in the context of Togo: one in the capital city of Lomé, the other in the remote outpost of Cinkassé. The two cases demonstrate two very different ways in which third parties were involved in the negotiations between Togolese tax officials and revenue providers. In the first case, a new semi-autonomous revenue authority and municipality fail in attempts to collect a residence tax, despite financial backing and commitments with development partners. In the second case, bureaucrats struggle to collect taxes on Togo's northern border with Burkina Faso. They concede to implicit measures of tax leniency for a local power broker in exchange for his support in their wider efforts. Both cases involve narrow revenue bargaining—with development partners in the former and a chieftain in the latter—and episodes of bargaining with the wider citizenry. The conditions and expectations arrived at within the narrow (micro-level) fiscal contracts affected the state's bargaining positions and outcomes in the broader spheres of negotiation. These important actors

Rachel Beach, *A third party at the table*. In: *The Politics of Revenue Bargaining in Africa*. Edited by: Anne Mette Kjær, Marianne S. Ulriksen, and Ane Karoline Bak, Oxford University Press. © Oxford University Press (2024).
DOI: 10.1093/oso/9780192868787.003.0010

became, in effect, third parties to the bargaining table between a poor state and its citizens.

Political economy literature on developing countries frequently observes the relevance of customary power brokers to governance, tax effort, and the political settlement in a poor state. Mamdani, Boone, and others have written at length on the complex relationships between the administration of power and traditional authorities on the African continent (e.g. Nieuwaal, 1981; Mamdani, 1996; Boone, 2003b; Lund, 2007; Logan, 2008; Gardini, 2012; Balan et al., 2020). In addition, much has been written about the role of donors as development partners who support struggling regimes but never fail to hold firm to their own agendas (e.g. Fjeldstad, 2001; Sacks, 2012; Kjær and Ulriksen, 2014; Brett, 2016; Mascagni, 2016; Cruz and Schneider, 2017). What is less explored is the role of such actors in the theatre of revenue bargaining. This chapter adds to our understanding of this role by asking: *How do third parties influence revenue bargaining between states and citizens?*

Togo is a low-income country that offers an interesting setting in which to study micro-instances of revenue bargaining. In 2014, Togo's government established a semi-autonomous revenue authority with the mandate to increase revenue mobilization. This provided an opportunity for observing a shift in the tax authority's strategic approaches to revenue mobilization. Historically, the country sustained a volatile relationship with development partners, and, at present, is highly dependent on aid (Kohnert, 2007; Nikabou, 2013; IMF, 2016). It is also a state in which traditional authority figures have held varying degrees of influence in the evolving political settlement since the early German colonial era (Knoll, 1978; Nieuwaal, 1981; Gardini, 2012). Given the strong presence and importance of donors and intermediaries in Togo, as is the case in many African countries, the country offers ample opportunity for studying the presence and influence of such third parties in revenue bargaining.

The two cases are examples of episodes of revenue bargaining in which a third party was determinant for how the negotiation processes evolved and for their outcomes. They were observed during five months of embedded fieldwork with the Togolese revenue authorities. The cases studies are informed by extensive semi-structured interviews and participatory observation of the work of revenue authorities, as well as interviews with other actors related to each identified including municipal authorities, traditional authorities, local residents, businesses, and presidential appointees. The interview data were complemented by analysis of the Togolese fiscal code, donor project agreements, and local media related to the cases in question. This chapter's contribution is two-fold. First, it is a close examination of revenue bargaining during implementation of the tax law rather than during policy formulation. The involved parties are therefore government administrators[1] and citizens, as opposed to politicians and constituencies. The case studies underscore the importance of revenue bargaining that takes place in the *de facto* implementation of a fiscal contract. Second, this chapter identifies micro-level conditions that affect revenue bargaining in the two cases. In the first case, a trigger is evident: a *shift in the state's capacity for tax enforcement.* With donor financing and technical support, government agencies initiate a plan of action for upgrading capacity to collect a neglected residence tax, triggering strong reactions from residents in the City of Lomé. In the second case, a mechanism of *leveraged organizational power* is employed. The state's revenue authorities leverage the authority of a local chief to strengthen their hand in revenue bargaining with the citizens of Cinkassé.

10.2 Introducing a third party to the revenue-bargaining table

Revenue bargaining is most often seen as a bilateral negotiation between two parties, namely the state and the revenue provider, at a metaphorical bargaining table. However, these two parties rarely sit alone at the table. Rather, they are often joined by other actors who arguably condition revenue bargaining and its potential outcomes. These actors might facilitate the negotiations, support or constrain either of the parties, or even have a direct stake in revenue bargaining and outcomes. In Togo, two kinds of actors played a determinant, albeit very different, role in revenue bargaining between state and citizens, namely donors and customary authorities. In this section, I briefly present them in turn.

In low-income states, governments continue to be highly dependent on aid from development partners and external actors (Collier, 2006; Brett, 2016). And as is widely understood, aid is generally accompanied by corresponding stipulations and conditionalities, such as China seeking privileged access to natural resources in exchange for highways and airports (Alves, 2013), or the International Monetary Fund (IMF) stipulating debt ceilings and fiscal consolidation as conditions for credit disbursements (IMF, 2018). Where aid comes in the form of grants and credits, these agreements fall within our understanding of micro-level fiscal contracts (see definition in Chapter 2), in this instance between the state and external donors as revenue providers.

[1] For example tax-collecting agencies and local authorities.

While development partners could be perceived as revenue providers in their own right, this chapter focuses on their presence and influence as third parties in revenue bargaining between a state and its citizens. External partners' support of a state can serve many broad purposes—from underwriting government policy objectives to legitimizing the authority of the state regardless of its ability to control territory (Herbst, 2000; Bierschenk, 2006). This backing can buttress the state's position vis-à-vis other revenue providers, while simultaneously weakening the state's negotiating power with donors that finance them.

Though the literature on this issue is fairly limited, there are two important studies of the role of donors in revenue bargaining. Lim et al. (2015) found empirical evidence to support a 'revenue substitution hypothesis', suggesting that governments are less sensitive to trade stipulations when foreign aid inflows are higher, with aid serving to moderate the leverage of a country's trade partner in bilateral negotiations. The presence of donor aid displaced the urgency of generating revenues from trade partners and weakened their counterparts' bargaining power. While this case centred on trade rather than fiscal affairs, it provides evidence that development partners' financial aid often affects the government's power and position in negotiating over revenue contributions. Kelsall's (2000) study of donors' (limited) role in the advent of a tax revolt in rural Tanzania points to a risk of overestimating the influence of donors. What might have been superficially attributed to the fruits of a donor 'governance agenda' in an episode of seemingly popular tax resistance was in fact largely the result of co-optation of local politics by elites. To gauge the different and potentially diverging influences, this chapter carefully traces and contextualizes donors' influence in one specific instance of revenue bargaining.

Another third party in revenue bargaining (as well as in governance more generally) is customary authorities. In many low-income states, particularly in Africa, we find synergistic relationships between traditional authorities and the state (Mamdani, 1996; Boone, 2003a). As Boone and Kwame Duku (2012) found in Ghana, political regimes have often intentionally reinforced the position and autonomy of chiefly and customary authorities in their rural domains, in exchange for allegiance. Customary authorities and poor states lean on each other for legitimation, vote whipping, tax mobilization, and control in local political arenas (e.g. Nieuwaal and Dijk, 1999; Labonte, 2012). Chiefs have often played an important role in tax-collection efforts given their authority and organizational power. They are therefore well-placed to play an intermediary role in revenue bargaining between a state and its citizens. As the second case study will show, this puts chiefs in an exclusive position, allowing them to include their own narrow interests as revenue providers in the broader revenue bargaining with the state.[2]

10.2.1 Case 1: Residence revenue bargaining in the City of Lomé

This first case examines an episode of revenue bargaining surrounding a residence tax (known in French as the *taxe d'habitation*) in an urban setting: Togo's capital city of Lomé. Theoretically, the tax base included all residents, whether renters or property owners, citizens and foreigners living in Togo. It was a tax intended to finance local governments' public service provision.[3] The case offers a rare glimpse of an explicit public debate over fiscal reciprocity. Donors underwrote both the efforts undertaken to mobilize this tax and the enhancement of the public services the tax was eventually intended to finance. The government ultimately failed to impose the residence tax, following a public outcry. Ironically, there is some evidence to suggest that the development partner's support may have undermined the government's bargaining position in this broad-based bargaining arena.

The government agencies of relevance include the semi-autonomous Office Togolais des Recettes (OTR) and the City of Lomé municipal authorities. These local authorities, referred to as the 'Special Delegation', were not elected officials but rather appointed by President Gnassingbé (Kohnert, 2017).[4] Taxpayers relevant to this case are the residents of Lomé (the residence tax of interest is imposable upon all residents regardless of ownership status and excludes only 'indigent persons'[5]). The capital city is inhabited by the politically disenfranchised Ewé people. The Ewé have maintained a persistent but weak opposition throughout the fifty years of brutal rule by this Kabiyé patriarchy from the North (Seely, 2006; Tobolka, 2014). These facets together characterized a dynamic in which local residents had very limited power or political avenues to ensure that their local government was responsive and accountable to them.

The third party of relevance in this case is the development partners—the French Development Agency (AFD) (together with the European Union (EU), African Development Bank (AfDB), IMF, and World Bank). While the

[2] This argument is similar to the one elaborated in Chapter 12 on brokers in the informal economy in Senegal.

[3] See Arts 1440–1448 of the Code Général des Impôts, Edition 2016 du République Togolaise.

[4] Officer from Kara Municipality, President's appointee; manager from Mayor's office, financial affairs; Prefect (Presidential Appointee) in northern Togo.

[5] Code Général des Impôts, Edition 2016 du République Togolaise, 2016, Art. 1444

partners did not explicitly engage in debates and the public exchange between citizens and the public authorities, donor agreements with the government (i.e. the City of Lomé and the OTR) played a key role in the City and the OTR's actions in this episode of revenue bargaining.

In 2011, the Togolese Republic signed the Urban Environment Project of Lomé II (PEUL II) with the AFD.[6] The AFD had agreed to provide financing to the city for two related components: urban development and local resource mobilization. The funds were transferred from the Ministry of Finance to the City of Lomé. The first component centred on infrastructure improvements including a new landfill site and the rehabilitation of sewage, waste, and drainage systems, which posed significant problems in the rapidly urbanizing capital. The second component was intended as a pilot project to augment municipal capacity and serve as a model for supporting eventual decentralization and devolvement of state fiscal capacity and functions across Togo. For the City of Lomé, it would support the development of a 'fiscal' cadastre and address system to identify city residents, updating government records on renters and property owners. This data would facilitate the imposition of the residence tax (together with property and business taxes). A specific objective within the revenue agreement with the AFD was an improvement in local resource mobilization. This arrangement suggested a three-way affair in which the City's obligation to one (narrow) revenue provider, its development partner, was the collection of revenue from another (broad-based) revenue provider, the city's inhabitants.

A convention was signed between the City of Lomé and the General Directorate of Taxes (DGI, the antecessor to the OTR).[7] The convention and two related protocols focused on fiscal capacity-building and supporting local resource-mobilization efforts, in particular in carrying out a fiscal census and collecting residence taxes[8] on behalf of the city. This agreement was intended to facilitate the city's fulfilment of its (revenue) agreement with the AFD. However, little demonstrable progress was evident in efforts to impose the residence tax under this collaboration.[9]

The revenues the residence tax could generate would theoretically finance local service provisions such as rubbish collection, water, electricity, and road

[6] Convention No. CTG 1124 01T.

[7] Direction Générale des Impôts, the former revenue agency in Togo.

[8] The local government collects other types of fees independently.

[9] Official at headquarters, OTR, Lomé, Togo, 16 August 2016; senior official at headquarters, OTR, Lomé, Togo, 31 August 2016; senior official at headquarters, OTR, Lomé, Togo, 20 September 20 2016; interviews with field staff from OTR, Badou, Togo, 27 September 2016, and Pagouda, Togo, 4 October 2016. Also: observation memo from discussions with residents of Lomé re. their observations at customs and tax authorities, Togo, 14 August 2016

maintenance. This aspect is important, as it provides a clear link between a tax and public service delivery provision, which the tax is intended to finance—as evidence of a fiscal contract. Given the need for major infrastructure rehabilitation, both the EU and France had contributed significantly to improving these same local public service provisions since 2006.[10] Roughly USD44 million had been poured into the city for lagoon dredging, road rehabilitation, and overhauling the city's outdated sewage and drainage systems. In a sense, one narrow, important group of revenue contributors—the development partners—were underwriting the achievement of obligations the city would be expected to deliver to its residents, if the residence tax were imposed.

With the creation of the OTR, a third protocol was signed in relation to PEUL II, this time between the head of the new semi-autonomous revenue agency and the City of Lomé.[11] The convention between the OTR and the city would remain in place as long as necessary to allow for 'experimentations' in trying to augment local tax collections. The OTR was also directly financed by donors, including the IMF, World Bank, and African Development Bank (2016; Beach, 2018). The OTR had been established under a five-year contract as an experiment in improving revenue mobilization in Togo and thus faced considerable pressure in delivering on its mandate. Perhaps emboldened by its own pressure from donors to improve revenue performance, coupled with increasing revenue pressure facing the Government of Togo that year, the OTR began to send out letters in early 2016 to the city's main employers requesting specific residence information about their employees. (Neither the OTR nor the City of Lomé had yet made any formal announcement regarding the plan to impose the residence tax.)

The evident trigger in this case was the fact-finding mission by the tax authority, which was not legally mandated to enforce collections of the resident tax. Moreover, the local authorities collaborating in the effort did not represent the interests of local inhabitants. Legally, this tax was to be collected by the municipality itself, but municipal elections had failed to take place for two decades. As letters went out to business establishments throughout Lomé, inquiring as to the residence details of company employees, the government encountered significant backlash from the city's residents and opposition leaders—writ large in local newspapers. Rumours and speculation spread through local media and social media platforms citing the letters

[10] From France: PEUL, an urban renewal project for the city of Lomé and Maritime region, 2011, 5 million EUR; from the EU: PAUT, rehabilitation of the city, initiated in 2013, 39 million EUR.

[11] Convention de Partenariat entre La Ville de Lomé et L'Office Togolais des Recettes Pour La Mobilisation des Ressources Fiscales de la Commune de Lomé.

received by firms in the city, and suggesting that the OTR was intending to impose a 'new' residence tax—despite its legal existence for over 15 years (e.g. K.B., 2016; Lawson, 2016; *Veille Economique*, 2016). A former presidential candidate (an opposition politician) denounced the rumoured plan in an interview with a local newspaper as an 'aberration' of the mandate of the OTR (Telli, n.d.). Local radio stations such as the Press Club hosted by Kanal FM and newspapers decried the tax as 'one tax too many' for an economically disenfranchised citizenry already facing a heavy tax burden (A.G., 2016a; Faria, 2016; Mensah, 2016a; K.B., 2016; Lawson, 2016; Mensah, 2015). A civil society organization (CSO), *Veille Economique* (2016) (English: Business Intelligence), released a white paper analysing both the nature of the residence tax and the current economic and fiscal position of Togo. It then organized a public forum to debate the legality and public reception to this tax (A.G., 2016b).

Newspapers, radio stations, individual citizens (referenced above), and civil society organizations such as the Togo Workers' Synergy (STT) protested against the imposition of this new tax, on several counts. First, the tax was legally intended as a tax to be imposed by municipalities. However, there had been no elections of municipal authorities since 1987, and the city was run by the presidential appointees. The opposition leader, Gerry Tamaa, and local newspaper op-eds protested against the imposition of the tax by authorities who were not legitimately elected local authorities as well as the involvement of the central government's revenue authority (OTR) in the tax-collection plan (M. K., 2016b; Telli, n.d.). The Ewé had little say in how their own city was ruled. These factors affected the relative bargaining positions of each party, including the fact that the state's political appointees were running a city inhabited by the Ewé (opposition) ethnic group, and the regime had been perpetually delaying promised elections. These factors reinforced the citizens' bargaining position and weakened the state's claims.

Second, the OTR, with major financial backing from the IMF, AfDB, and World Bank, had replaced the former Direction Générale des Impôts (DGI) and brought the customs authority under its direction. The two former agencies were reputed to be among the most corrupt within the Gnassingbé regime's government.[12] The OTR had been working purposively to establish a new, positive, and constructive rapport with the citizens, to correct for the reputation and behaviour of the former agency, build good will, and improve

[12] Author interviews, August–December, 2016: multiple interviews with mid-level and senior officials at OTR headquarters, OTR; OTR field staff. Author's participatory observation memos in Togo and Benin, August–December, 2016: two meetings between the OTR's Fiscal Control Unit and a field office in rural Togo, OTR; memo from discussions at social gathering with prominent figures in Bénin.

tax compliance.[13] However, the sincerity in their new approach, including more stringent and broad-based imposition of existing taxes, came as a surprise and concern to citizens who were coming under the scrutiny of the tax-collection agency, but were now unable negotiate their way out of tax liabilities with a bribe.[14] In such an environment, this new tax was depicted by local media as the latest instrument in the hands of a newly empowered mafia (i.e. the OTR, who now enjoyed larger salaries thanks to donor support and a semi-autonomous status) to further impoverish the residents of the capital (Faria, 2016; Lawson, 2016; Mensah, 2016b; Beach, 2018, 244).

Third, the costs of living in the capital were rising, urbanization rates increasing, and the housing deficit had reached 100,000 by 2016 (Atcha, 2016; Kohnert, 2017). In contrast, jobs and incomes had remained stagnant over the preceding decade: a third of the city's residents lacked stable employment, over half lived in poverty, and 14% in absolute poverty. More than half of all the capital's residents still lacked sufficient (if any) running water, and many areas lacked paved roads, electricity, and suffered from flooding in the advent of rains due to dysfunctional drainage and sewage systems (which were in the process of being rehabilitated). Accordingly, citizens, CSOs, and newspaper editors resented the imposition of a tax which, from their perspective, was intended as a fiscal exchange for the provision of these non-existent or undersupplied public services. The *Veille Economique*'s (2016) white paper declared that the OTR's plan failed on three counts: fiscal ethics, fiscal justice, and fiscal reciprocity. They decried the government's lack of fiscal transparency; its high indebtedness and consequential high levels of pressure from development partners to repay debt (which consumed 24% of the state's budget); its overdependence on citizen's taxes and under-dependence on revenues from mineral resources; and the lack of a social housing plan and sufficient available, affordable housing for the city's residents.

The onus was now on the state and its locally appointed representatives to legitimate their claims and deliver on their part of the fiscal contract. Where electricity, water, drainage, and other services were still lacking in quality and extension to large portions of the city, they found these new tax claims unjustified.

Following the public outcry, the OTR and the City of Lomé halted any forward movement on the fiscal census activities to update the local cadastre

[13] Field staff from Togolese Revenue Authority (OTR); follow-up discussion with fiscal control official after observing meeting with a field office, OTR; participatory observation memo of meeting between fiscal control unit and a field office in northern Togo, OTR.

[14] Informal discussions with citizens during fieldwork, including neighbourhood residents, guests at local social events, taxi drivers, etc.

and residential records.[15] According to media outlets, a spokesperson for the OTR stated that there was a misinterpretation of the immatriculation operation underway, and that there was 'no question' of the OTR imposing this residence tax (A.G., 2016; Telli, 2016; Lawson, 2016).

The OTR and the City of Lomé regrouped to develop a new strategy. To gain credibility and improve the legitimacy of their negotiating position, they proposed imposing the tax first on officials implicated in the collection of the tax.[16] This strategy was a non-starter, however, among the staff of the OTR. As a mid-level OTR official explained to me, they themselves, even with improved salaries, still often lacked electricity and running water, paved roads, and internet access from the state-run agency, and endured the frequent flooding of their streets. They were frustrated with the government's persistent lack of service delivery (despite significant inputs from development partners) and, like their fellow citizens in Lomé, did not find the imposition of the residence tax justified. The OTR and city were left with limited options for proceeding.

The city and OTR embarked upon another strategy of engaging local community leaders in sensitization and an overall campaign citywide to articulate the OTR's approach and citizens' fiscal civic duties in paying taxes. However, this manoeuvre was undermined by a lack of government movement on action points demanded by Lomé's citizens. No local elections had been organized. Urban renewal projects financed by the AFD, EU, and AfDB advanced, but slowly, with insufficient improvements in public-service delivery. Electricity and adequate drainage systems were still absent across wide swathes of the city. As of late 2017, the entire affair remained at a standstill, and the government had yet to find effective bargaining leverage.[17]

In the City of Lomé, the trigger for this round of protests and haggling over revenue contributions was the evidenced shift in the state's enforcement capacity and intentions and engagement by actors whom Lomé residents felt did not have legitimate claims to impose the residence tax. The PEUL II project agreement with the AFD and related protocol between the City of Lomé and the OTR outlined financial and technical capacity-building efforts to enhance the municipality's revenue-mobilization efforts. (The residence tax would be collected by the OTR on behalf of the city, with support provided by development partners to facilitate necessary information-gathering

[15] Manager of financial affairs, Mayor's office; Director of Togolese Revenue Authority, OTR; OTR official, Lomé, Togo; OTR official (dates retained for confidentiality).

[16] Customs official, Port de Lomé, OTR, 2016

[17] Observation memo from follow-up interview, OTR official, date retained for confidentiality.

activities such as the rollout of a fiscal census, address-creation programme, and residence registry for the city.) Though as mentioned the tax had legally existed for more than 15 years, when city residents and opposition leaders recognized the state's manoeuvres to augment the city's ability to effectively impose the tax, they reacted with fear and alarm. It was not the creation of the fiscal policy that elicited a political reaction and resistance. The fiscal policy was largely ignored until development partners' revenue contributions galvanized government efforts to impose the tax. Even the initial protocols between the DGI and the City of Lomé, intended to enhance the city's capacity to collect these taxes, did not create such an impetus. It was not until a new, semi-autonomous agency—also underwritten by donors and contractually obligated on revenue performance—signed a protocol with the City of Lomé and began the actual process of fiscal data-collection efforts, that residents of the capital city pronounced their fears of yet another tax and claims of illegitimacy of the tax imposition. Backed by donor financing, contractual objectives, and concrete efforts towards enhancing local resource mobilization, the two agencies' actions together presented a credible 'threat' of enforcement—enforcement, moreover, perceived to be illegitimate given the lack of local elections and the central agency collecting a locally mandated tax.

The government's bargaining strategies ultimately failed to move the negotiations towards a productive agreement. In the end, the tax-collection plan was halted. The conclusion of this round of revenue bargaining was to the advantage of an important group of revenue contributors—the City of Lomé's residents.

The City of Lomé case illustrates a scenario where the outcome of this three-way revenue-bargaining process was *no change* in revenue contributions from the residents of the City of Lomé. In other words, no revision of the residents' contributions under the existing fiscal contract between the city and its residents. It is an excellent example of a broad-based tax effort improving the accountability of the state—in that citizens were not willing to contribute to a tax (for which the state had already received development partners' revenue contributions) until there was demonstrable improvement in the delivery of public services. That said, this outcome did weaken society's obligations to the state, as well as the state's authority and legitimacy of its claims on citizen's assets. The case also likely reinforced the notion that citizens' contributions to the state for this public service provision had been displaced by development partners' revenue contributions to finance this same public service, despite the state's claims. This case illuminates the complex state–society dynamics that can arise in securing donor support to underwrite both public service delivery and the tax-enforcement capacity that is intended to finance this public service delivery.

10.2.2 Case 2: Power and rural revenue bargaining in Cinkassé

The second case of revenue bargaining concerns the residents and customary chief of Cinkassé, a small city crowning Togo's northernmost tip, on the border with Burkina Faso. Many of the residents of Cinkassé are Burkinabé. Moreover, the *Chef du Canton* of Cinkassé, Chief Nagnango Abdoulaye, is himself of the lineage and customary power hierarchy of the ancient Mossi people.[18] The Mossi are largely based in Burkina Faso and enjoyed a resurgence in their politically dominant position after the fall of Thomas Sankara, the former Burkinabese dictator (McKenzie, 1998; Konkobo, 2015). A small finger of this Mossi people group stretches into Cinkassé.

This case examines two intersecting spheres of revenue-bargaining and tax-collection efforts in Cinkassé. While the previous revenue-bargaining arena was the state's broader efforts of taxation among the town's general population carried out by the agents of the newly established OTR, this second bargaining arena involved the tacit negotiating and explicit engagement between Chief Nagnango himself and these same OTR field agents—a classic example of a narrow sphere of revenue bargaining.

The OTR's agents assigned to this remote outpost self-described as 'strangers'[19] in a region dominated by Burkinabé. Their agency had only recently established these administrative bureaus. Prior to this time, 98% of Togo's taxes were collected in the capital city. However, in its hunt for revenues, the OTR challenged the notion that taxing 'the interior' was not fruitful and established field offices in 2015–2016.[20] This new push proved difficult. The agents' lack of local social capital and 'foreignness' weakened their bargaining position vis-à-vis local inhabitants. They faced many challenges in efforts to impose taxes across the district, with villagers frequently running away, refusing to comply, or even attacking tax collectors.

[18] Prefect (Presidential Appointee) in northern Togo; Chef du Quartier, city in northern Togo.

[19] Author's participatory observation of meeting between fiscal control unit and field office agents in Cinkassé, Togo, 6 October 2016; and interviews with OTR field officer, Cinkassé, Togo, 7 October 2016; OTR officer from fiscal control unit, Cinkassé, Togo, 6 October 2016; observation memo, 6 October 2016.

[20] Official from OTR headquarters, 31 August 2016. Lomé, Togo; OTR official, Daopong, Togo, 10 October 2016.

Understanding the authority Chief Nagnango commanded in a largely Burkinabé-dominated rural district, the OTR field agents sought his assistance and soon began to witness striking changes in the behaviour of the villagers. The state's agents would arrive at ostensibly empty villages, only to find the entire village gathered in a communal space and Chief Nagnango, who was also the administratively appointed *Chef du Canton*, standing there at the head of the gathering, inviting the OTR's agents to his side. He would then turn to his people and command them to pay the taxes owed to the central regime. According to the OTR agents, the villagers complied. The agents explained that their work in the region would be all but futile without the backing of Chief Nagnango. In addition to reinforcing their direct efforts to press for tax compliance, he would at times provide them with material resources, such as vehicles, as needed, to carry out their work. With his support, the new agents were able to make some gains in revenue contributions from the town of Cinkassé.

Conversely, when it came to the *Chef du Canton*'s own tax assessments, it emerged that his revenue contributions were much lower than the amounts formally owed.[21] The chef would fill out tax declaration forms, sometimes even in collaboration with the tax agents, and there would be a cordial agreement on how much was officially owed. However, no sincere efforts were made to assure that his taxes were actually paid. The field agents were very reluctant to press for his compliance, as they were dependent on his authority to reinforce and effectuate broader compliance. He, himself, while explicitly acknowledging the formal tax obligations, was less than forthcoming in paying taxes owed on a business operation worth roughly a quarter of a million dollars in revenues annually. There appeared to be a form of tacit agreement that the field agents would refrain from coercive enforcement of his tax obligations in exchange for his continued backing of their wider efforts of tax collection and enforcement across his district.[22]

When representatives from the OTR's fiscal control unit (FCU) toured the Cinkassé field office's operations and held meetings with the locally posted OTR team to understand the local situation and field agents' achievements in implementing the fiscal code, they pressed the local field agents to rectify the situation with the chief.[23] The field agents, however, explained to the FCU how critical Chief Nagnango was to the success of their mission in this region. Regardless of pressure from the headquarters, the revenue negotiations between the OTR's agents and the Chief would likely continue in a

[21] Ibid.
[22] Ibid.
[23] Ibid.

diplomatic and lenient fashion to ensure his continued reinforcement of the agents' efforts.

These arrangements between the state's tax-collection agents and the *Chef du Canton* reflected macro-level dynamics between President Faure himself and Chief Nagnango.[24] The president, according to at least one source, greatly depended on the chief for vote whipping. In exchange, or in passive recognition of his political dominance in the region, Chief Nagnango was apparently left to manage the affairs of Cinkassé and its surrounding district largely as he pleased. This power dynamic closely parallels the relationships described in the works of Nieuwaal, Mamdani, and Boone, between states and customary authorities (Nieuwaal, 1981; Mamdani, 1996; Boone and Duku, 2012). Chief Nagnango's nephew, who held him in great esteem, was appointed as the regional prefect.[25]

Officials from the revenue authority's headquarters engaged in evasive actions to avoid a personal encounter with the chief (and made efforts, in vain, to prevent the author's visiting him) (Beach, 2018, 256). From the author's observations and the statements of the OTR officials from the Lomé headquarters, it was apparent that they were wary of Chief Nagnango's dominating power in the region, feeling uneasy and wanting little to do with him. This dynamic reinforces the notion that the chief's power eclipsed the state's in this region, and that any interactions with such a figure would be conducted on his terms, not the OTR's.

In summary, there was strong evidence that the chief enjoyed the balance of organizational power in the region—with the implication that the wealthier canton chief paid little in the way of taxes, while (generally poorer) citizens were compelled into tax compliance. Citizens of this rural outpost were antagonistic in their relations with the OTR's field agents but acquiescent to their Chief. It was evident that the OTR's agents would need to leverage this power to succeed in revenue-mobilization efforts in the region. The state's weaker position vis-à-vis this chief allowed him to obtain individual exemptions in exchange for the OTR's greater success in its broader bargaining position. Through the mechanism of *leveraged organizational power*, Chief Nagnango strengthened the state's position by directly calling on his subjects to comply with the demands of the field agents, that is, to pay their taxes. Failure to comply would mean that residents of Cinkassé would be answerable to their Chief (whom they greatly feared and revered). This suggests that it is not only the revenue contributors' organizational power

[24] OTR customs official, Lomé, Togo, 25 October 2016.
[25] Prefect (Presidential Appointee), Cinkassé, Togo, 7 October 2016.

that is important to consider in the analysis of revenue-bargaining positions, but also that of the state. Due to the Chief's intervention, the state's bargaining position among the inhabitants of Cinkassé shifted from a weaker position to an enforced one.

This case also speaks to the particular dynamics of revenue bargaining between the state and customary authorities. It appears that traditional authorities are not necessarily treated as a special class *en masse*. Instead, we find a state calibrating the power balance between itself and each local customary figure, a perspective that resonates with Boone's analysis of the political topographies of the African state (Boone, 2003b). The OTR's agents certainly did not always lean on customary authorities in other field offices, but the case was not isolated. In instances where they relied on support from other (less powerful) traditional leaders, the corresponding negotiations surrounding that chieftain's own taxes never matched the fairly substantial disregard for the chieftain's tax obligations as witnessed in this case. From this behaviour, we can understand that where greater political legitimacy and influence lie with a customary figure, on balance, one might expect the state to place greater value on the backing of a chieftain in broader spheres of bargaining than on compliance with their own tax obligations. Where the balance of legitimacy and power sways in the other direction, we would expect lower degrees of leniency as the traditional authority figure commands weaker organizational capacity, and the state finds diminished usefulness in leveraging a chief's authority.

10.3 Conclusion

This chapter's case studies of revenue bargaining in rural and urban settings in Togo provide fruitful terrain for exploration of the conditions under which such bargaining emerges, evolves, and leads to fiscal contracts—that is, conditions where third parties are present. First, we find evidence to support the proposition that revenue bargaining is often a three-way affair in the poorest states. States are rarely sitting alone at the metaphorical negotiating table. The development partners' agreement with and revenue contributions to the City of Lomé and the OTR impacted on citizens' perceptions at the outset of the residence tax episode and the state's bargaining position. The OTR's agents in Cinkassé found that they could not operate in this local arena without engaging a local power broker in the bargaining process.

Second, the process of revenue bargaining at the level of implementation is likely to be just as important as (perhaps more relevant than) fiscal policy negotiations, to actual outcomes regarding who contributes revenue in a poor state. From a rule-of-law perspective, the tax-collection efforts presented in Lomé and Cinkassé had little to do with the formal arenas of fiscal policy negotiations between various tax groups and the state. But in the context of Togo in 2016, as in many low-income states on the African continent, the full enforcement of that fiscal mandate was far from a given. In Lomé, the residence tax in question had been passed into law sixteen years prior to the episode in question. However, the legal mandate was seemingly irrelevant to taxpayers until the revenue agency and the city demonstrated a credible 'threat' of imposing the tax with augmented enforcement capacity. In Cinkassé, taxpayers often physically exited the bargaining arena, hiding or running from the OTR's field agents, refusing to entertain discussions of contributing to the state coffers from their earnings. The bureaucrats had to develop a bargaining strategy to achieve even a limited portion of their tax-collection mandate in Cinkassé.

Third, as we see in both cases, the terms of a third party's intervention in episodes of revenue bargaining can invert both the bargaining power and position of the state. In the first case, in the City of Lomé, the development partners' role shifted both components of the state's position in the bargaining arena. Their support enhanced the OTR and the city's enforcement capacities, which presented a credible threat of enforcement and triggered protests. Their financial aid, however, likely played a role in weakening the legitimacy of the city's claims on citizens' tax contributions, where the city (1) had not been able to achieve demonstrable, consistent improvements in public service delivery (despite revenue support from donors) and (2) could not credibly deny the substitution of residence tax revenues with donor funding.

These findings nuance Sacks' analysis of Afrobarometer data, which suggested that donor and non-state actors' provision of public services tends to reinforce the relationship between the state and citizens (Sacks, 2012) as well as Beach and van den Boogaard's argument (2022) that a 'services-first' approach could be part of the solution to low-tax, low-capacity traps. In this case, the act of donors underwriting public-service provision does not appear to reinforce the state's claims on tax revenues intended to finance these services in the medium term, nor strengthen positive state–society engagement around relevant taxes, but it did put pressure on the state for accountability and addressing issues of legitimacy—which was ultimately constructive. It also challenges Fjeldstad's (2001) finding that the presence of donors is likely to swing the balance of power in favour of local governments in the revenue-bargaining arena. In the case of Lomé, despite donor funding to support improvements in public-service delivery, citizens were ultimately successful in making their case—claiming that the state had failed to deliver on local elections and public-service provision—and blocking the imposition of the residence tax. The lack of a fiscal contract emerging from this bargaining episode strengthened the accountability challenge to the government but weakened citizens' sense of obligation to the state.

These outcomes reinforce the central tenet of this book—the importance of looking into the micro-dynamics of revenue-bargaining processes. They also offer some nuance to the conventional wisdom on tax governance, which would suggest that outcomes in broader arenas of revenue bargaining are likely to lead to stronger state–society relations, building accountability and improved governance (Prichard, 2015). In the case of Cinkassé, it was the narrow agreement with a powerful local broker that strengthened the state's bargaining position among local residents at large. These negotiations did not strengthen the accountability of the state to its citizens in this northern region. Nor did they offer the townspeople a platform to challenge the legitimacy of the state's claims. The mechanism of leveraged organizational power rendered inhabitants weaker but compliant in tax negotiations, as they could not escape their local chief.

In summary, third parties can alter the outcomes of broad-based revenue bargaining—in specific, sometimes counterintuitive, ways.

Acknowledgements

I am deeply grateful to Professor Anne Mette Kjær, Associate Professor Marianne Sandvad Ulriksen, and Assistant Professor Ane Karoline Bak for their review and feedback on the initial drafts of this chapter. All errors and omissions remain entirely mine.

References

A.G. 2016a. 'L'OTR dément l'application de la taxe d'habitation'. *Ici Lome*. 2 February. https://news.icilome.com/?idnews=818516&t=l-otr-dement-l-application-de-la-taxe-d-habitation

A.G. 2016b. 'Togo "Veille économique" revient sur l'inopportunité de la taxe d'habitation société'. *Ici Lome*. 23 August. https://news.icilome.com/?idnews=819716.

African Development Bank. 2016. 'Tax Governance Support Project (PAGFI)'. Appraisal report.

Alves, A. C. 2013. 'China's "win-win" cooperation: Unpacking the impact of infrastructure-for-resources deals in Africa'. *South African Journal of International Affairs* 20(2): pp. 207–226. https://doi.org/10.1080/10220461.2013.811337.

Atcha, E. 2016. 'The housing sector booming in Togo'. *Africa News Agency*. 5 August.

Balan, P., A. Bergeron, G. Tourek, and J. L. Weigel. 2020. 'Local Elites as State Capacity: How City Chiefs Use Local Information to Increase Tax Compliance in the D.R. Congo'. *CEPR Discussion Paper No. DP15138*. London.

Beach, R. 2018. *The Hunt for Revenues in a Poor State*. Aarhus: Politica.

Beach, R., and V. Van Den Boogaard. 2022. 'Tax and governance in the context of scarce revenues: Inefficient tax collection and its implications in rural West Africa'. *ICTD Working Paper No. 139*. Brighton.

Bierschenk, T. 2006. The Local Appropriation of Democracy: An Analysis of the Municipal Elections in Parakou, Republic of Benin, 2002–03. *The Journal of Modern African Studies* 44(4): pp. 543–571.

Boone, C. 2003a. Decentralization as political strategy in West Africa. *Comparative Political Studies* 36(4): pp. 355–380.

Boone, C. 2003b. *Political Topographies of the African State: Territorial Authority and Institutional Choice*. Cambridge studies in comparative politics. New York: Cambridge University Press.

Boone, C., and D. K. Duku. 2012. 'Ethnic Land Rights in Western Ghana: Landlord–Stranger Relations in the Democratic Era'. *Development and Change* 43: pp. 671–693. https://doi.org/10.1111/j.1467-7660.2012.01778.x.

Brett, E. A. 2016. 'Explaining Aid (In)Effectiveness The Political Economy of Aid Relationships'. *LSE International Development Working Paper, No. 176* (16).

Collier, P. 2006. 'Is Aid Oil? An Analysis Of Whether Africa Can Absorb More Aid'. *World Development* 34(9): pp. 1482–1497. https://doi.org/10.1016/j.worlddev.2006.01.002.

Cruz, C., and C. J. Schneider. 2017. 'Foreign Aid and Undeserved Credit Claiming'. *American Journal of Political Science* 61(2): pp. 396–408. https://onlinelibrary.wiley.com/doi/abs/10.1111/ajps.12285.

Faria, A. 2016. 'Taxe d'habitation: La nouvelle trouvaille de l'OTR du couple Rwando-Togolais Gapéri-Ayassor pour appauvrir encore plus les Togolais'. *Liberté*, 26 January.

Fjeldstad, O-H. 2001. 'Taxation, coercion and donors: local government tax enforcement in Tanzania'. *The Journal of Modern African Studies* 39 (2): pp. 289–306.

Gardini, M. 2012. 'Land Transactions and Chieftaincies in Southwestern Togo'. *Africa Spectrum* 47(1): pp. 51–72.

Herbst, J. 2000. *States and Power in Africa: Comparative Lessons in Authority and Control.* Princeton studies in international history and politics. Princeton, NJ: Princeton University Press.

IMF. 2016. *Togo Aide Memoire: Evaluation de la Mise en Oevre Operationnelle de l'Office des Recettes et Poursuite des reformes d'Administration Fiscale et Douaniere—Rapport de Mission.* Lomé.

IMF. 2018. 'West African Economic and Monetary Union'. *IMF Country Report, No. 106* (18). Washington, DC: IMF.

K. B. 2016. 'Mobilisation des recettes fiscales pour l'Etat—La taxe de trop'. *Togo Matin.* 25 January.

Kelsall, T. 2000. 'Governance, Local Politics and Districtization in Tanzania: The 1998 Arumeru Tax Revolt'. *African Affairs* 99(397): pp. 533–551.

Kjær, A. M., and M. S. Ulriksen. 2014. 'From Consensus to Contention Changing Revenue and Policy Dynamics in Uganda'. *UNRISD Politics of Domestic Resource Mobilization Working Paper No. 21.*

Knoll, A. J. 1978. *Togo under Imperial Germany 1884–1914: A Case Study in Colonial Rule.* Stanford, CA: Hoover Institution Press.

Kohnert, D. 2007. 'Togo: Failed election and misguided aid at the roots of economic misery'. GIGA Institute of African Affairs, Hamburg. *MPRA Paper No. 5207.* 8 October.

Kohnert, D. 2017. 'Togo: Political and Socio-Economic Development (2015–2017)'. GIGA Institute of African Affairs, Hamburg. *MPRA Paper No. 81176.*

Konkobo, L. 2015. 'Mogho Naba: Burkina Faso's mediator monarch'. BBC News. 23 September.

Labonte, M. T. 2012. 'From patronage to peacebuilding? Elite capture and governance from below in Sierra Leone'. *African Affairs* 111(442): pp. 90–115.

Lawson, K. 2016. 'La taxe d'habitation, c'est du faux et usage de faux selon l'OTR'. *Africa RDV.* 1 February.

Lim, S., L. Mosley, and A. Prakash. 2015. 'Revenue Substitution? How Foreign Aid Inflows Moderate the Effect of Bilateral Trade Pressures on Labor Rights'. *World Development* 67: pp. 295–309.

Logan, C. 2008. 'Traditional Leaders in Modern Africa: Can Democracy and the Chief Co-Exist'. *Afrobarometer Paper No. 93.*

Lund, C. 2007. *Twilight Institutions: Public Authority and Local Politics in Africa.* Malden, MA: Blackwell.

Mamdani, M. 1996. *Citizen and Subject: Contemporary Africa and the Legacy of Late Colonialism.* Princeton studies in culture/power/history. Kampala: Fountain.

Mascagni, G. 2016. 'Aid and Taxation in Ethiopia'. *Journal of Development Studies* 52(12): pp. 1744–1758. https://doi.org/10.1080/00220388.2016.1153070

McKenzie, G. 1998. 'Ancient Mossi Dynasty Coexists With Modern Trappings in Burkina Faso'. *Associated Press*, pp. 1–3. 14 June.

Mensah, K. 2015. 'Réactions de Nicodème Habia sur l'éventualité d'une taxe sur l'habitation et du lynchage d'un ivoirien'. *KOACI*. 7 August. https://www.koaci.com/article/archive/2015/08/09/togo/politique/togo-interview-reactions-de-nicodeme-habia-sur-leventualite-dune-taxe-sur-lhabitation-et-du-lynchage-dun-ivoirien_90213.html.

Mensah, K. 2016a. 'Pression fiscale sur les citoyens, Gapéri et compagnie tiennent les contribuables par le cou'. *L'Alternative*. January 22.

Mensah, K. 2016b. 'Affaire de taxe d'habitation: L'OTR pris en flagrant délit de mensonge'. *L'Alternative*. 5 February.

Nieuwaal, E. A. B. van Rouveroy van. 1981. 'La chefferie du Nord-Togo. La position ambiguë d'un chef supérieur des Anufom à N'zara (Sansanné Mango)'. *State and Society in Black Africa. French Review of Overseas History* 68(250): pp. 204–212.

Nieuwaal, E. A. B. van Rouveroy van, and R. van Dijk. 1999. *African Chieftaincy in a New Socio-political Landscape*. Hamburg: Lit Verlag.

Nikabou, L. J. 2013. *Les conventions ACP–EU et les sanctions économiques de l'Union européenne contre les États ACP: le cas du Togo*. Strasbourg: Strasbourg University.

Prichard, W. 2015. *Taxation, Responsiveness, and Accountability in sub-Saharan Africa: The Dynamics of Tax Bargaining*. Cambridge: Cambridge University Press.

Sacks, A. 2012. 'Can Donors and Non-State Actors Undermine Citizens' Legitimating Beliefs?'. *Policy Research Working Paper No. 6158*. Washington, DC: World Bank.

Seely, J. C. 2006. 'The unexpected presidential election in Togo'. *Electoral Studies* 25(3): pp. 611–616.

Telli, K. 2016. 'Togo: Supposée collecte de la taxe d'habitation: les responsables de l'OTR se disent "surpris"'. *A Free Press*. 3 February.

Telli, K. n.d. 'La prochaine taxe d'habitation de l'OTR fait réagir: Gerry Taama conteste à l'OTR cette prérogative'. *Togo Actualité*.

Tobolka, R. 2014. Togo: Legislative Elections of July 2013. *Electoral Studies* 35: pp. 389–394.

Veille Economique. 2016. 'Taxe d'Habitation ou l'Aggravation de l'Injustice Sociale au Togo'.

11

Who should pay?

Government and donor bargaining over social protection funding in Tanzania

Marianne S. Ulriksen, Flora Myamba, and Constantine George

> Every year the government has been budgeting for the PSSN . . . however, disbursement is another thing.
>
> **Government official**

11.1 Introduction

As in many other lower- to middle-income countries in Africa, the World Bank along with other donors initiated and funded a social protection programme in Tanzania, called the Productive Social Safety Net (PSSN).[1] The donor agencies envisaged that, in time, the Tanzanian government would fund the programme. However, the government has contributed only a small share of the required budget, and the question of who should finance the PSSN has been a recurring issue of bargaining between the international donor agencies and the Tanzanian government.

As is the focus in this volume, we explore the micro-level revenue-bargaining process between a specific group of revenue providers (here, the international aid agencies—the current revenue providers of the PSSN) and the Tanzanian government. We complement other theoretical and empirical contributions in this volume by paying specific attention to the preferences of negotiating parties and how the parties seek to maximize their own interests in the negotiations. Specifically, we ask how policy design and funding are negotiated in a setting of diverging preferences and what the outcomes are.

[1] See Ulriksen (2019) and Porisky (2022) on the development of the PSSN. The programme is implemented on both the Tanzania mainland and Zanzibar. For more information on social protection in Zanzibar, see Seekings (2016).

Marianne S. Ulriksen, Flora Myamba, and Constantine George, *Who should pay?*. In: *The Politics of Revenue Bargaining in Africa*. Edited by: Anne Mette Kjær, Marianne S. Ulriksen, and Ane Karoline Bak, Oxford University Press.
 DOI: 10.1093/oso/9780192868787.003.0011

We show how the policy preferences of the donors and the Tanzanian government, with respect to the PSSN, are clearly conflicting: the international donors want to continue the PSSN although with increasing budgetary commitment by the Tanzanian government, whereas the government is sceptical of the programme and does not consider it a clear priority area. We find that, throughout the negotiations, each party seeks to push through their agenda. In talks over the design of the programme, the Tanzanian government tries to downscale the cash transfer element, which is, however, a key element for the donors. In negotiations over disbursements, the government tries to limit payments even if it has agreed with donors to contribute. The fiscal contract outcome remains unresolved, as the donors continue to pay the lion's share of the programme. Our findings speak to a general conclusion of this volume: that even revenue providers with substantial financial muscle have limited revenue-bargaining power vis-à-vis the ruling elite (see Chapter 13 in this volume).

Our analysis focuses on the years 2016–2018, as during this time, there were negotiations over the continuation and funding of the PSSN. We interviewed and have had continued conversations with at least 20 persons close to the process, who we label in three general and neutral categories: *government officials*, which covers bureaucrats working at implementation as well as decision-making levels in the government; *donor representatives*, being officials working for donor agencies; and *experts*, who represent people working for other organizations and research institutions in or outside government that are particularly knowledgeable about social protection and politics in Tanzania. None of the interviews were recorded. Instead, to ensure reliability, two of us strived to be present at the interviews, and we transcribed the interviews immediately afterwards. The quotes included are based on our notes from the interviews.

11.2 Bargaining over funding responsibility

In this chapter, we explore negotiations around who should take responsibility for funding a social programme. The *revenue providers* in this case study are international donor agencies who have initiated and are funding the PSSN in Tanzania. The international donors would like the government to take over the funding of the programme to ensure its long-term sustainability. The government, for its part, can be seen as a *revenue maximizer*—seeking to ensure the best utility of its resources and prioritizing policies that best achieve its political and developmental goals. Through this lens, the government may not jump at the opportunity to fund the PSSN. Consequently, the parties bargain over whose revenue to use for the continued funding of a social programme supporting poor and vulnerable Tanzanians. In the following, we elaborate on the rise of social protection and why it is an interesting case of bargaining between governments and international aid agencies in Africa. We draw from recent aid literature and the theoretical framework presented in Chapter 2 to hypothesize the possible policy and funding preferences of the government and international aid agencies that inform our subsequent case analysis.

Few would question that there has been a 'global rise of social cash transfers' (Leisering, 2019) since the 'quiet revolution' of social protection expansion started in middle-income Latin American countries around the new millennium (Hanlon et al., 2010). Social protection programmes—conditional or unconditional cash transfers, public works, feeding schemes, or combinations of these—have spread across the Global South. Even in low-income countries, there has been a rapid expansion: in the past decade, social protection spending in low-income countries has increased from one to about three per cent of GDP (Klugman et al., 2017).

In many of the lower-income countries in Africa, the 'primary and most consistent advocates of social protection appear to be global actors' (Rudra, 2015, 468). It is the international donor agencies—multilateral agencies like the World Bank and the UN, as well as bilateral ones such as the Department for International Development (DFID)—who have been the most enthusiastic about the poverty-reducing potentials of social protection, and it is largely through their encouragement that national governments have adopted social protection programmes (Deacon, 2007; McCord, 2009; Hickey and Seekings, 2017; Hickey et al., 2019). In low-income African countries, the World Bank has been particularly instrumental in the rise of conditional cash-transfer programmes (Simpson, 2017).

While many poorer African countries have, in time, committed themselves to the adoption of social protection programmes, many governments have been rather unenthusiastic about programmes they perceive to have the potential of creating dependency and which they deem to fit poorly with their 'productivist development ideology' (Hickey and Seekings, 2017, 23). International aid agencies have not necessarily been deterred by such reluctance as it has been suggested that such hesitation can be overcome by the 'consistent engagement by progressive social policy advocates . . . to seize opportunities, and ensure continued investment in . . . social protection systems' (Koehler and Mathers, 2017, 351). Advice of this nature illustrates the continued unequal power relations that come with giving and receiving development aid, as donors tend to push through their agenda with limited regard for, or understanding of, the political dynamics and policy preferences of recipient countries (Aubert et al., 2018). In fact, the disregard for recipient countries' ideas and policy preferences is also a problem in the scholarly literature where '[a]cademic studies of aid to Africa have typically asked how "we" in the West can get "them" in Africa to adopt [specific] economic and political systems' (Whitfield and Fraser, 2010, 342).

The theoretical framework of this volume (see Chapter 2) highlights how fiscal and organizational resources shape the relative bargaining positions of governments and revenue providers. International aid agencies have substantial fiscal clout but may be of less value for the ruling elite in ensuring its legitimacy and maintaining its ruling coalition. There are thus good reasons to question the actual strength of international aid agencies in shaping domestic public policy in recipient countries, and recent studies from Africa suggest that the influence of donors in pushing for social protection has been overrated (Cherrier, 2020). Donors can support programme design, implementation, and evaluation, and have the means to transfer knowledge and expertise, but domestic decision-makers need to gain an interest in social protection to be willing to support its long-term implementation (Hickey et al., 2019; Lavers and Hickey, 2021). For instance, in Zambia, international aid agencies played a critical role in developing and promoting social protection, but the programme operated as a pilot for ten years before the national government was willing to expand it. Although there was an ideational shift towards a pro-poor agenda in Zambia, it is argued that the main impetus came due to changes in the political settlement, with new political stakeholders seeing a value in social transfers for rent-allocation purposes (Pruce and Hickey, 2019). Similarly, the Livelihood Empowerment against Poverty programme in Ghana was largely pushed by donors, and only when the programme aligned with the interests of the political elite was it expanded and institutionalized (Abdulai, 2021). In Ethiopia, the government was only willing to reform the emergency relief system and introduce the Productive Safety Net Programme when the government faced a political crisis; at this point, social protection became useful as an element in the national development plans and as a mechanism to retain political power (Lavers, 2019).

Consequently, there are good reasons to open the 'black box' of policy bargaining between governments and international donor agencies (Bourguignon and Sundberg, 2007). There are several useful studies that acknowledge the bargaining power of recipient governments and explore how negotiations unfold, but they generally focus on the macro level. Whitfield (2009) and Whitfield and Fraser (2010) study aid negotiations across a range of

African countries on a structural level, focusing on the macro-level resources of national governments vis-à-vis the donor agencies. Feyissa (2011) explores how the Ethiopian governing party EPRDF effectively used its negotiating capital to ensure a consistent flow of development aid despite conflicting interests between the government and the international aid agencies. Aubert et al. (2018) include in their analysis of aid negotiation in Ethiopia both structural and actor-level analyses, but the latter analysis centres primarily on changes in the institutional settings of negotiations rather than the direct policy negotiation between government and development partners. We are, however, interested in exploring the micro-level bargaining between international aid agencies and the Tanzanian government over the funding of the PSSN. To understand how this bargaining unfolds, we need to focus on the possible divergent preferences of the negotiating parties, as we explain the following.

Swedlund and Lierl (2020) come closer to the actual bargaining processes in their case studies of Rwanda and Tanzania, where they highlight the different preferences with which each party enters the negotiations. International aid agencies want to determine how their own money is spent, but they also want influence on broader matters given that aid is fungible. Recipient governments, for their part, value donor support and expertise but also want to maintain political autonomy. Following this, they argue that 'differences in preferences between donor agencies and recipient countries mean that aid policy is always negotiated' (Swedlund and Lierl, 2020, 54). Whereas Swedlund and Lierl (2020) focus on negotiations over budget support with implications for a broader spectrum of policies and development plans, we are interested in micro-level negotiations around the financing of a specific social protection programme. Nevertheless, to study revenue bargaining, we take as a starting point the possible divergent preferences of international aid agencies and recipient governments.

Although international aid agencies also pursue less altruistic objectives (Lancaster, 2007), their *raison d'etre* is to promote development. Poverty reduction is a central objective on the development agenda with this being the first of the UN's 17 Sustainable Development Goals. In fact, one of the reasons for the donor enthusiasm for social protection is precisely because of its proven ability to reduce poverty (von Gliszczynski and Leisering, 2016). Consequently, we expect poverty reduction to be an important preference of the international aid agencies and hence this to be their argument for promoting social protection. At the same time, they would want social protection to become a sustainable part of a recipient country's policy framework and therefore would want the recipient government to take over the funding.

Following the insights from the social protection literature, we expect that the recipient government will only be interested in (partly) financing a social protection programme if the programme fits the government's development priorities. At the same time, one could expect the recipient governments to be revenue maximizing in the sense that they will seek to maintain donor commitment to programmes that donor agencies value and instead prioritize government funding of policy areas that the government values and/or where donor funding is less likely.

In our analysis of revenue bargaining between the Tanzanian government and international aid agencies over the funding of social protection, we start by investigating the preferences of the negotiating parties, which we find to be divergent. Next, we explore how this conflictual standpoint caused substantial bargaining over programme design and funding. Before this, however, we present the social protection programme in Tanzania and how it has been funded.

11.3 The case: Productive Social Safety Net Programme in Tanzania

Tanzania represents a lower- to middle-income African country where the national government ambivalently committed to implement a nationwide social protection programme, the PSSN (Ulriksen, 2019). In the early 2000s, social protection was not a key priority of the national government in Tanzania. However, the government agreed in 2012 to roll out the PSSN Phase I following intense advocacy by the World Bank and the TASAF (the Tanzania Social Action Fund, an implementing government agency placed within the President's Office). While the programme was initially funded by international aid agencies (primarily the World Bank), it was agreed in 2015 that the government would gradually take over the funding of the programme. In the following, we briefly explain the background to the PSSN and the main features of the programme as well as its funding. Table 11.1 presents an overview of the events.

Prior to the PSSN, the World Bank funded and the TASAF implemented the pilot project CB CCT (Community-Based Conditional Cash Transfers) starting in 2009. Based on positive evaluations of achievements, emphasizing the project's poverty-reducing effects as well as increases in educational attainment and health outcomes, the World Bank and the TASAF argued for the project to become nationwide as the PSSN. To convince government to implement the PSSN, the World Bank and the TASAF highlighted

Table 11.1 Timeline of events

2000	TASAF (Tanzania Social Action Fund) created as a social fund for poverty alleviation
2009	CB CCT (Community-Based Conditional Cash Transfers)—pilot programme initiated
August 2012	PSSN Phase I launched[a]
2012–2017	Envisaged implementation period for PSSN I[b]
2015	The fourth government commits to gradually take over funding, with full government financing envisaged for 2020[c]
2015	After elections in October, President Magufuli becomes the fifth president of Tanzania
2016–2018	Discussions on PSSN Phase II (as analysed in this chapter)
September 2018	TASAF presents programme design document for PSSN II[d]
December 2019	End of implementation of PSSN I[e]
February 2020	Start of PSSN II[e] (with the aim of reaching 1.4 million households)
2023	Official end of PSSN II[e] (with possibility of extension beyond 2023)

[a] TASAF (2015).
[b] project document shared by the World Bank (for official use only).
[c] as informed to authors by TASAF in 2016.
[d] URT (2018).
[e] TASAF (2021).

the 'productive' aspects of the programme to be in line with the development ideology of the government. By presenting the programme as a means of raising 'productivity', 'community development', 'self-reliance', and 'co-responsibility', the social protection advocates spoke to concepts prevalent in the government's Development Vision and Five-Year Development Plans, and this way, the PSSN was made more acceptable to the government (Ulriksen, 2019).

The government's commitment was probably also eased by the fact that it had a clear champion in the Ministry of Finance (Klugman et al., 2017). Hence, while social protection in Tanzania was initially driven by the World Bank and the TASAF (Jacob and Pedersen, 2018; Ulriksen, 2019; Porisky, 2022), the fourth Tanzanian government (2010–2015) took an increasing interest in the programme. In one account, the government's relationship with the TASAF improved over time, and they took ownership of the PSSN as the domestic elite saw it as fitting domestic political priorities (Porisky, 2022). In another account, Jacob and Pedersen (2018) argue that the political elites also used the programme for electoral purposes. They make this claim because, as they observe, the speed and scale of programme implementation accelerated tremendously in 2015, which was also an election year—and had the most competitive election in Tanzanian political history. In 2015 the fourth Tanzanian government committed to gradually take over the funding of the PSSN so that the programme would be fully government funded by 2020. As will be discussed later, the subsequent fifth government has been reluctant to live up to its financial commitments.

The PSSN programme is administered by the TASAF.[2] The programme targets the extremely poor, which is calculated to be about 10% of the population. The aim was to reach 1.3 million extremely poor households by the end of the initial phase closing in 2019. The PSSN programme has four main components: cash transfer, public works, livelihood enhancement, and targeted infrastructure. The cash-transfer component has both unconditional and conditional elements. All programme households receive a basic (unconditional) transfer, while certain qualifying members, such as pregnant women and children, in addition become eligible for conditional cash transfers on meeting educational and health requirements. Able-bodied members of the targeted households qualify and are encouraged to participate in the public works programme, although it is not mandatory. The livelihood-enhancement programme is aimed to improve livelihoods and graduate beneficiaries out of extreme poverty by encouraging beneficiary households to make regular savings as members of community savings groups. The fourth component of the PSSN is targeted infrastructure development, which is geared to support livelihood-related activities by facilitating good infrastructure for the smooth provision of health, agricultural inputs, micro-finance, and similar activities. The conditional cash transfer (CCT) component is by far the largest in terms of funding and targeted beneficiaries, covering about 80% of the programme costs, although, as will be discussed later, this is also the component receiving the most criticism from the fifth government.

11.3.1 Funding of the PSSN programme

While the PSSN started off by being largely funded by the World Bank, other donors subsequently came on board, most strongly the DFID and the Swedish International Development Cooperation Agency (Sida), the aid agencies of the United Kingdom and Sweden respectively (see Figure 11.1). UN agencies have been actively involved in social protection in Tanzania for years, but most of their support is in kind rather than financial, such as

[2] This information about the PSSN was provided by the TASAF and a social protection expert in July 2017.

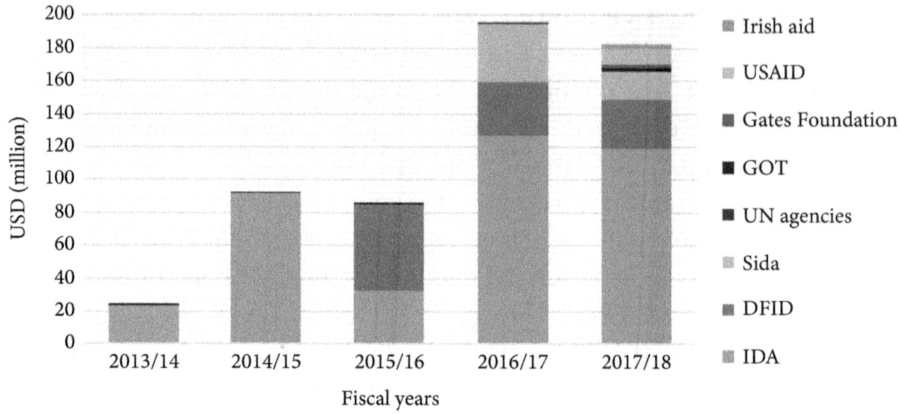

Figure 11.1 PSSN financing trends by donors.
Source: TASAF.

expertise, technical assistance, and facilitation. Finally, the funding by the World Bank (IDA[3] in the figure) is largely through loans (Ulriksen 2019).

As mentioned, although the PSSN and the precedent pilot programmes were donor funded from the beginning, it was decided that the PSSN should be fully government financed by 2020 when a new phase of the programme (PSSN II) would be implemented. In the meantime, it was agreed in 2015 that the government should cover around a third of the budget per year—the financial requirements were estimated at USD 300 million per year, with the obligations divided between the government (USD 100 million), development partners (USD 100 million), and credit from the World Bank (USD 100 million).[4] In practice, the financial requirements as well as the government's actual contribution were downscaled. For instance, the estimated amount required for the operation of the PSSN between July 2015 and June 2016 was set to approximately USD 170.7 million. Of this, the government initially committed to pay out USD 44 million (TZS 70 billion) to the PSSN from the 2015/2016 national budget, thereby covering 25.7% of the estimated programme costs for that period. However, in the end, the government only contributed USD 7 million, which represents only 4.1% of the overall programme costs and only 15.9% of the government's initial commitment (URT et al., 2016). Thus, in 2016, the government's contributions were lower than anticipated. Moreover, at the time, there was much uncertainty about the government's long-term financial commitments as the government did

[3] IDA, short for the International Development Association, is part of the World Bank and has the objective of fighting extreme poverty.
[4] As informed by TASAF in 2016.

Table 11.2 PSSN—funding requirements and available funds 2016–2020.

	2016/17	2017/18	2018/19	2019/20
FUNDING REQUIREMENTS				
CCT costs	126,720,000	126,720,000	126,720,000	126,720,000
PW costs	26,285,714	26,285,714	26,285,714	26,285,714
Livelihoods	660,000	713,000	713,000	713,000
Inst. strengthening and op. costs	12,503,000	12,503,000	12,503,000	12,503,000
TOTAL	**166,168,714**	**166,221,714**	**166,221,714**	**166,221,714**
AVAILABLE FUNDS				
Balance from previous year	12,156,607			
IDA-Additional financing	100,263,388	99,736,612		
DFID	28,000,000	26,000,000	18,000,000	17,000,000
Government of Tanzania	7,000,000			
Sida	17,200,000	17,500,000	17,500,000	17,500,000
Gates Foundation	893,720	1,966,620	908,860	
UN Agencies	655,000			
USAID		5,000,000	5,000,000	5,000,000
TOTAL	166,168,714	150,203,232	41,408,860	39,500,000
Financing Gap		***(16,018,482)***	***(124,812,854)***	***(126,721,714)***

Source: URT et al. (2016, 10–11)—joint review conducted by the United Republic of Tanzania (URT), World Bank, UNDP, UNICEF, ILO, DFID, and Sida.

not provide its implementing body (TASAF) with any clear indication of its financial support of the PSSN programme (see Table 11.2), other than committing to 2016/2017 the same (low) funds as for the previous budget year.

During our fieldwork, it was notoriously difficult to get a clear picture of the financing of the PSSN programme. This was in part because there were several new donors contributing in a variety of ways. However, in 2017, the estimates received suggested that the government's own financial contribution still amounted to about only 4% of the full programme costs.[5] Thus, around 2017, the Tanzanian government had not lived up to its financial

[5] According to TASAF officials, the end of 2017 (predicted) financing for the full PSSN programme implementation stands at USD 749.3 million. The government of Tanzania will contribute USD 30 million (= 4%). The rest of the funding will come from the following sources: IDA: USD 420 million (original credit USD 220 million, additional financing USD 200 million); DFID: USD 170 million; SIDA: USD 85 million; Organization of Petroleum Exporting Countries (OPEC): USD 16.5 million; USAID: USD 10.0 million; Irish Aid: USD 10 million; Bill and Melinda Gates Foundation: USD 4.01 million; and UN Agencies: USD 3.6 million.

commitments, and there were good reasons to doubt that it would do so in the future. As an anonymous government official informed us:

> The government was expected to gradually take over the funding by 100% in 2020. I do not see that happening. Every year the government has been budgeting for PSSN . . . however, disbursement is another thing.

The donors continued to push the government to increase its financial commitments, and the negotiations became particularly heated around 2017 and 2018 when the new phase (PSSN II) was on the table. Negotiations were difficult, in part due to the conflicting preferences of the Tanzanian government and the development partners, as we explain in the following section.

11.4 Conflicting preferences

In 2015, the Tanzanian government agreed to gradually take over funding of the PSSN, partly because key politicians and bureaucrats in government were persuaded that the programme could reduce poverty (Ulriksen, 2019). That was also the year that a new president (still for the ruling party, CCM) was elected. Late[6] President John Magufuli became known for his productivist ethos and centralization of decision-making (Cheeseman et al., 2021), which changed the government's position on the social protection programme. The new President emphasized hard work and had a strong dislike for 'handouts' (Paget, 2021). In addition, with the President's centralization of power, the policy coalition of domestic technocrats and development partners that had initially driven the introduction of the PSSN (Ulriksen, 2019) became less influential. Instead, the discourse in the government at large swung in favour of those sceptical of cash transfers and away from the proponents of the programme (Jacob and Pedersen, 2018). These developments make our case study even more interesting and relevant. During the period in focus, 2016–2018, the contrasting position of the government vis-à-vis the donor agencies became even more pronounced, the negotiations consequently more difficult, and the ability to find a compromise even more remarkable. However, as presented in the following, the two parties' preferences differed at the outset. The Tanzanian government did not regard the PSSN as a priority, whereas the donors were, unsurprisingly, supportive of it. These contrasting preferences played into the negotiations of the new phase of the programme (PSSN II) as explored in section 11.5.

[6] President Magufuli died in March 2021, after our period of analysis.

11.4.1 The preferences of the Tanzanian government

Although the Tanzanian government had agreed to the PSSN programme, there was a feeling that the programme fitted poorly with the fifth government's development priorities. The CCT component in particular was criticized, and the condemnation became more pronounced under President Magufuli, who came to power in November 2015. As one source explains:

> The CCT does not match with the ideology of the ruling party and the philosophy of economic development. Providing free money to the market economy must create friction, and the majority did not agree it was the right way to go. This [the programme] raises the question of sustainability and dependency. This project design was not from inside but driven by the thinking of the funder [the World Bank].
>
> **(Government official)**

The hesitation towards the CCT came largely from a general belief that cash transfers will not help people out of poverty. There had been complaints that even beneficiaries of the public works component found it hard to improve their situation because the daily wages are very low. Many did not feel they saw tangible results.

> The feeling is that there is so much money given with little or no impact. This creates resistance. I know of a Regional Commissioner who said very openly that he doesn't want TASAF people at his office. But I also think such people are less informed about the programme.
>
> **(Expert)**

There was also scepticism towards handing out 'free money', and negative stories on the misuse of cash transfers flourished. The media revelations of 'ghost beneficiaries'—that some PSSN beneficiaries were not poor (enough) to be part of the programme—raised even more public misgivings about the PSSN.[7] Although the numbers of 'ghost beneficiaries' were determined to be small (around 55,000 out of 5.4 million), the public attention magnified this scepticism among politicians. President Magufuli, who came to power on an anti-corruption stance (Paget, 2021), was particularly vocal regarding his reservations about the PSSN programme.

Cash transfers fitted poorly with the President's slogan '*hapa kazi tu*', which roughly translates to 'here is only work'. The President was concerned with poverty, but in achieving development, he emphasized the importance of

[7] Kennedy (2016); Makene (2016); *The Guardian* (2017b).

productivity and infrastructure where people must lift themselves out of poverty through entrepreneurship and hard work. As one source explains:

> I don't think the government will take over the World Bank support for the PSSN given the *hapa kazi tu* ideology. To support this [claim], one may recall the recent drought scenario whereby the current government refused to support [give free food to] people who were starving.
>
> **(Expert)**

Furthermore, as may be remembered, when the government committed itself to the PSSN programme, there were champions in the government that successfully advocated for the programme despite some scepticism about cash transfers and long-term sustainability (Ulriksen, 2019). With the administration under President Magufuli, these champions were either no longer in government or silenced:

> To a large extent, the President's stance is likely to influence other government leaders. When a president like Magufuli says no to putting money into the PSSN programme, who are you to say yes or vice versa? It is obvious his interest is more on construction. He is, therefore, limiting any champions, particularly within the government, who would have raised their voices on behalf of the poor beneficiaries.
>
> **(Expert)**

Thus, although there had been reservations towards cash-transfer programmes in Tanzania in the past, the scepticism increased and become more vocal. This may, in part, explain the government's limited financial commitment. Another issue is the general constraint of financial resources, which caused the government to afford the programme low priority in terms of financial disbursements.

Being a lower-middle-income country, Tanzania has limited financial resources and many urgent needs and policy areas that require attention. Consequently, it is not surprising that all stakeholders we interviewed mentioned resource constraints as a general challenge facing all sectors. This is also supported in government documents; for example, in the Five-Year Development Plan 2016/17–2020/21 (URT, 2016, 15) it is stated that inadequate financing (underfunding and delay of disbursements) is a key challenge impacting negatively on the implementation of development plans in the country. However, the Tanzanian government also spends less on social protection compared to other countries in the region (Ajwad et al., 2018). The resource envelope was further tightened by loan repayments and high recurrent costs. Thus, some interview sources explained that Tanzania was obliged to repay several World Bank/IMF loans that were taken around 2012/13, and that about one third of government revenue was for repaying loans. Another priority named through interviews was to pay salaries to public servants (at both central and local levels, as well as within the social services, e.g. to teachers), which absorbs a large bulk of the budget. Nevertheless, even within the existing funds available, other areas took priority. For instance, one interviewee argued that the government was particularly resource constrained because the country had to fully fund the general elections in 2015 (donors have, in the past, funded large parts of the election costs), which impacted directly on the PSSN programme:

> There was a time where the budget for PSSN was taken off due to election expenses. Nevertheless, this has not largely impacted the programme because PSSN components were not rolled out at one time but rather gradually.
>
> **(Government official)**

The government, even more so with the new President, also prioritized infrastructure and construction, and if World Bank loans were to be taken, it should be for such areas and not for the PSSN where the World Bank had already committed funds. As a source explained:

> The government is still in a high need of soft loans to be taken for the construction, infrastructure, and other productive and economic activities. If the World Bank is willing to give loans for investment in infrastructure, then we will take [them]. Those are the loans we are looking for.
>
> **(Government official)**

Within the social sector, the recently introduced provisions of free education to ensure that children from poor families get an education, and free health provision for children under five and the elderly above 70 years, were priority areas for the President. Some sources argued that this made the PSSN even less relevant than before:

> Evidence from the TASAF [pilot cash-transfer programme] showed increased school enrolment, but the government is now advocating that there is fee-free education and says this is a more effective way to improve education than the TASAF programme.
>
> **(Government official)**

> The new government has come with the policy of free education and [is] pushing for free mandatory health insurance especially for the poor and aged, which were the main arguments for the creation of the TASAF. Now, what is the separation between the two [PSSN and education and health services]?
>
> **(Government official)**

In fact, the previously mentioned scepticism towards cash transfers clearly played a role, not just in terms of giving the PSSN lower priority than other policy areas but also in arguing that *other* programmes would be more effective in addressing poverty. A centrally placed government official within the Ministry of Finance's Poverty Eradication Department went to great lengths to explain to us the advantages of savings and investment schemes that could encourage poor citizens to do 'productive' activities:

> I wish I could promote the savings programmes. I think the CCT is not sustainable; I don't think it is the right way to go. If we get more money from donors, we can continue with the CCT but minimize it while putting more focus on productive programmes.
>
> **(Government official)**

In sum, the Tanzanian government was sceptical of the PSSN, particularly the cash-transfer component, and found other social programmes more fitting to their development plans. This contrasted with the donors' prioritizing the PSSN and desiring for the government take ownership.

11.4.2 The preferences of the donors

The donor community in Tanzania, as in many other low-income African countries, had high regard for social protection programmes such as the PSSN:

> PSSN is one of the most effective and largest social protection programmes in Africa. It is well managed and is making a huge impact. The programme is also strong in that it is implemented through the government system rather than through a parallel donor system.
>
> **(Donor representative)**

Whereas the World Bank initiated the PSSN, other donors started to support the programme due to its poverty-reducing potential. In a written communication, a donor representative provided this explanation, following this question from the authors:

> Authors: Is your rationale for supporting the PSSN due to its ability to reduce poverty or (/and) as part of [your country's] strategy to expand social protection/social security/social rights?
>
> Donor representative: It is mainly the first rationale, that is to reduce poverty and also that we believe it will contribute to better learning outcomes for children, not least girls (as you may know, the programme has conditions related to school attendance), and also that it will contribute to employment and income among the poorest (through the public works component)—these are results that are emphasized in our country strategy.

While aid agencies see the value of the PSSN, they wanted the government to take ownership to ensure its long-term sustainability. It was also argued that the PSSN would be affordable:

> The financial commitment should be for the long term, and we believe that domestic financing is possible in the long run. They can afford it but need to make the right decision and over time gradually take over from the donors.
>
> **(Donor representative)**

However, as explained, the Tanzanian government was hesitant to prioritize funds to the PSSN, and this put the donor agencies in a tricky position. While wanting to ensure that the programme was not donor dependent, and therefore wanting the government to take over the programme, the aid agencies were also aware that it would be difficult to (threaten to) pull out, given the support that poor and vulnerable households receive:

> We have continued with the support even if we don't see much coming from the government's side, because we understand that pulling out our financing has a direct effect on the poor and vulnerable people who benefit from the programme.
>
> **(Donor representative)**

Thus, the government and aid agencies had conflicting preferences with respect to the PSSN, which caused difficult negotiations. As one donor representative put it: 'The relationship is not always easy. Both sides have their own vision, mission, and priorities for social protection'. Given the government's limited interest in the PSSN as compared to other issues, one might ask why it then committed to the programme in the first place. One source offered an explanation:

> It is a tradition for the government to commit when donors ask it to do so. The government says yes, and they just default; this goes across all sectors. The government doesn't feel any liability to that.
>
> **(Expert)**

Whatever the reasons, the status in the period of our study (2016–2018) was that the Tanzanian government was unsteadily to live up to its financial commitments to the PSSN programme. In the following, we explore how the government and donor community sought to push through their preferences. This engagement became especially heated during 2018 where the design and future financing of the PSSN II were negotiated.

11.5 Revenue bargaining: Who should pay?

The following analysis explores the bargaining between the Tanzanian government and international aid agencies over the programme design of the PSSN II and the disbursement of funds. We show how the Tanzanian government sought to influence the design of the programme to better fit its priorities, particularly by reducing the importance of the cash-transfer element. While the international donors were able to maintain a strong cash-transfer element in the PSSN II, they were unable to hold the government to its earlier commitments regarding disbursement of funds.

11.5.1 Programme design

The first phase of the PSSN programme was set to run through to 2019. Thus, for our period of analysis, bargaining increasingly revolved around the continuation of the programme (i.e. PSSN II). As mentioned, President Magufuli had been highly sceptical about the cash-transfer element of the PSSN, and his strong public reactions affected the relationship between the government and the development partners.

For instance, in July 2017, the President harshly criticized cash transfers, and he went so far as to order an immediate stop to the provision of cash transfers to refugees in Tanzania.[8] Although, he did not mention any

[8] *The Guardian* (2017a).

specific names, his criticism seemed to be pointed at organizations offering humanitarian aid to refugees in Tanzania, including the World Food Programme and the United Nations High Commissioner for Refugees.[9] In another incident, towards the end of 2017, the government refused at the eleventh hour to sign a memorandum of understanding (MoU) with Irish Aid that would otherwise have secured additional funds for the PSSN. The reason given was that the government preferred finances to be directed to the new PSSN II, with more 'productive' components, than to the existing programme dominated by the CCT (interview with government officials). The turn-around caused confusion in the donor community and left several Tanzanian government officials embarrassed as they were involved in the lengthy process of developing the MoU and keenly aware of donor funding cycles that encouraged disbursements to be made within the calendar year.

The President subsequently directed the TASAF to review the PSSN and to consider some revisions to the design of the PSSN II (interview with government officials). Consequently, in August 2018, an alternative programme design document for the PSSN II was circulated. In the alternative design, the cash-transfer component was almost entirely removed and the focus was instead predominantly on public works and productive inclusion (i.e. training and coaching to enhance participants' savings and productive activities).[10] In government discourse, the alternative design was not a change of the entire PSSN but merely a change in priorities of the different programme components so that the focus was less on the 'wasteful' cash transfers and more on the other 'productive' components (interview with government officials). This was, however, in strong contrast to the development partners' views of the PSSN II in which they regarded cash transfers as essential:

> In case there will be huge changes within the PSSN, we will need to reassess the programme and our commitment to financing it. Our interest is to keep the percentage ratios [of the programme components] as they are currently. . . . Donors would resist money going away from the cash transfer as it is essential for the other components, at least as a start-up.
>
> **(Donor representative)**

At this point, in August 2018, a possible compromise between the government and development partners seemed unlikely. However, in the months that followed, the government slowly came around and seemed to accept

[9] Ibid.
[10] As we have been informed through conversations with stakeholders.

that cash transfers should be included. What exactly changed is hard to state firmly, but it seems that key government officials had a change of heart:

> We know that a select number of Parliament Members made deliberate visits to beneficiaries' households in several districts. The TASAF may have played a key role in this move. The report and the positive evidence from the visits reached key persons in government . . . and it made a huge change in the attitude, which [had been] based on wrong assumptions. The field visits and evidence made a big turning point. We are only glad that PSSN did not die prematurely.
>
> **(Donor representative)**

As observed in earlier studies (Ulriksen, 2019; Porisky, 2022), it seems evident that technocrats can influence domestic decision-makers through field visits and the presentation of evidence. However, international aid agencies also on their side accepted some revisions to the programme design. The cash-transfer component remains but has been modified to only cover specific groups such as children, people with disabilities, and the elderly. Households with so-called productive capacity will receive a 'productive transfer' but only until the public works programme has been rolled out.

Thus, despite a difficult environment for negotiations, a compromise was reached in the programme design. Still, the future financing of the PSSN II remained uncertain, and there was little to indicate that the government had increased its financial commitment.

11.5.2 Disbursements

Several informants suggested that the government was keenly aware of the donors' enthusiasm for the programme and that this was taken into consideration when making budget priorities in that the PSSN already had an alternative financial source, whereas other projects and policies were solely dependent on domestic sources:

> The government knows there are already donor funds, and the PSSN programme is therefore an easy target when priorities need to be made. The government's lack of disbursements should not be linked to lack of commitment or the PSSN [being] of less priority but rather general budget challenges and opportunities across all programmes.
>
> **(Government official)**

Others doubted whether the government was really committed. According to some informants, the PSSN might have been recognized as a 'good programme', but the priority for some government officials was to run the CCT programme until its current (PSSN I) period came to an end and then find the best way to exit it and build more productive assets.

I don't see the future of government giving money to CCT, and there is no sustainability. The government can continue up to 2022 if they get money from donors. (Government official)

In part, this criticism was subsequently met in the design of the new programme, where the cash-transfer component was modified, as discussed. Nevertheless, although the government had agreed to make some disbursements, it had largely failed to do so, and on the donor side there was some frustration with the government's unwillingness to prioritize the PSSN:

> You wish the government could take pride in how big and reputable the PSSN is. Others outside of Tanzania are taking notice of this programme. All assessments have been positive thus far, but on the other hand, for how long can the donor keep this going without contribution from government?
>
> **(Donor representative)**

Donors tried in various ways to pin down the government to make the agreed contributions, for instance by asking the government to come up with financial disbursement plans and by threatening to provide less funding themselves. However, as the following two quotes exemplified, this was to no avail:

> By that time [start of PSSN Phase I], it was agreed that a financial sustainability strategy plan should be developed in 2016 to ensure the financial sustainability of the programme in the long term; but it didn't happen.
>
> **(Donor representative)**

> We signed an agreement with the government that committed more contributions for PSSN. This additional amount was on [the] condition that the government would contribute what it had committed. We have received no formal feedback from the government yet, but we have had some informal feedback, not on the condition but on the nature of the cash transfer where the President has a problem with transferring cash to adults that can work. As yet, the additional amount has not been paid as the government has not contributed with its share.
>
> **(Donor representative)**

In the interviews with government officials, they argued that the government was already contributing to the programme as the PSSN has largely been funded through loans from the World Bank, which must be repaid. Consequently, as the argument follows, the Tanzanian government was excused for not providing (additional) funds. In this, the development partners seemed to have accepted a broader concept of what may constitute government contributions to the programme:

> We have now agreed that the government can contribute in many other ways, including in-kind contribution, particularly made through the local government authorities that are the primary implementing units, and through the World Bank contribution which is coming as a loan to the government.
>
> **(Donor representative)**

Certain compromises in the programme design and in the understanding of what constitutes government contributions have been made. However, in terms of financing, the donor community continues to fund the lion's share of PSSN II. The latest mid-term review of the programme (TASAF, 2021) indicates that of the actual funds received, the Tanzanian government has financed less than three per cent. The World Bank continues to be the main contributor, its financial input amounting to 75% and the rest being paid by several different donor agencies. In terms of committed funds, there is a financing gap of 26.5%. Hence, it seems, bargaining over who should pay will continue.

11.6 Conclusion

Social protection has spread across Africa, and even many low-income countries have introduced programmes, often (at least partly) due to strong advocacy by international donor agencies (Hickey et al., 2019). As many social protection programmes in Africa continue to be funded by external donors, the long-term sustainability of the programmes is a concern to those who advocate for social protection expansion. It is, therefore, surprising that little attention has been paid to how donors are (un)able to shift the financial responsibility of social protection to the national governments of developing countries. This chapter contributes to filling this gap.

We explore the bargaining between the Tanzanian government and international aid agencies over the design and funding of the Productive Social

Safety Nets (PSSN) programme. To understand the dynamics of the negotiations, we pay particular attention to the diverging preferences of government and donors. Donors were strongly in favour of the programme, whereas the Tanzanian government was more sceptical and prioritized other policy areas. In this context, the government tried to limit its own contributions with tactical delays based on the knowledge that the donor community has high regard for the programme and would want its continuation, and with the supporting arguments that the government is a primary contributor to the PSSN anyway given that it is financed in large part through World Bank loans. Concurrently, the government tried to modify the new programme to have stronger 'productivist' elements, which they perceive as more fitting to the government's development vision. While a compromise was reached with respect to the design of PSSN II, the bargaining over funding continues.

By studying revenue bargaining between the ruling elite and a revenue provider with substantial financial means, we make important findings that speak to the overall arguments of this volume. We show that although the international aid agencies are of financial importance to the government, they cannot push the government to take over funding responsibility of just any programme—probably because the PSSN is not seen as critical in maintaining political legitimacy among Tanzanians. Thus, in our case study, the government may concede in terms of programme design, but the government induces the international aid agencies to remain the main revenue providers.

References

Abdulai, A.-G. 2021. 'Competitive Clientelism, Donors and the Politics of Social Protection Uptake in Ghana'. *Critical Social Policy* 41(2): pp. 270–293. https://doi.org/10.1177/0261018320945605.

Ajwad, M. I., M. Abels, M. Novikova, and M. A. Mohamed. 2018. *Financing Social Protection in Tanzania*. Washington, DC: World Bank.

Aubert, P.-M., M. Brun, P. Agamile, and S. Treyer. 2018. 'From Aid Negotiation to Aid Effectiveness: The Case of Food and Nutrition Security in Ethiopia'. *Third World Quarterly* 39(1): pp. 104–121. https://doi.org/10.1080/01436597.2017.1368379.

Bourguignon, F., and M. Sundberg. 2007. 'Aid Effectiveness—Opening the Black Box'. *American Economic Review* 97(2): pp. 316–321. https://doi.org/10.1257/aer.97.2.316.

Cheeseman, N., H. Matfess, and A. Amani. 2021. 'Tanzania: The Roots of Repression'. *Journal of Democracy* 32(2): pp. 77–89. https://doi.org/10.1353/jod.2021.0020.

Cherrier, C. 2020. 'Domestic Resource Mobilization for Social Transfers in Sub-Saharan Africa: Can Foreign Aid Act as a Catalyst?' In *The Politics of Domestic Resource Mobilization for Social Development*, edited by K. Hujo, pp. 75–108. Geneva: Palgrave Macmillan.

Deacon, B. 2007. *Global Social Policy and Governance*. London: SAGE.

Feyissa, D. 2011. 'Aid Negotiation: The Uneasy "Partnership" between EPRDF and the Donors'. *Journal of Eastern African Studies* 5(4): pp. 788–817. https://doi.org/10.1080/17531055.2011.642541.

Hanlon, J., A. Barrientos, and D. Hulme. 2010. *Just Give Money to the Poor: The Development Revolution from the Global South*. Sterling, VA: Kumarian Press.

Hickey, S., T. Lavers, M. Niño-Zarazúa, and J. Seekings. 2019. 'The Negotiated Politics of Social Protection in East and Southern Africa'. In *The Politics of Social Protection in Eastern and Southern Africa*, edited by S. Hickey, T. Lavers, M. Niño-Zarazúa, and J. Seekings, pp. 1–41. Oxford: Oxford University Press. https://doi.org/10.1093/oso/9780198850342.003.0001.

Hickey, S., and J. Seekings. 2017. 'The Global Politics of Social Protection'. WIDER Working Paper No.2017/115. Helsiniki: United Nations University World Institute for Development Economics Research. https://www.wider.unu.edu/sites/default/files/wp2017-115.pdf.

Jacob, T., and R. H. Pedersen. 2018. 'Social Protection in an Electorally Competitive Environment (1): The Politics of Productive Social Safety Nets (PSSN) in Tanzania'. ESID Working Paper No. 109. Manchester: University of Manchester. https://www.effective-states.org/wp-content/uploads/working_papers/final-pdfs/esid_wp_109_jacob_pedersen.pdf.

Kennedy, N. 2016. 'Tanzania: Verification Finds 32,456 Households Unfit for TASAF'. *Daily News*. 16 August.

Klugman, J., M. Selowsky, J. Zhou, and A. Abrams. 2017. *The IMF and Social Protection: Seven Low-Income Country Cases*. Washing, DC: IEO, Independent Evaluation Office of the International Monetary Fund.

Koehler, G., and N. Mathers. 2017. 'Forum Introduction: Dynamics of Social Protection in Fragile Contexts: Nepal and Myanmar'. *Global Social Policy: An Interdisciplinary Journal of Public Policy and Social Development* 17(3): pp. 347–352. https://doi.org/10.1177/1468018117729914.

Lancaster, C. 2007. *Foreign Aid: Diplomacy, Development, Domestic Politics*. Chicago: University of Chicago Press.

Lavers, T. 2019. 'Distributional Concerns, the "Developmental State," and the Agrarian Origins of Social Assistance in Etiopia'. In *The Politics of Social Protection in Eastern and Southern Africa*, edited by S. Hickey, T. Lavers, M. Niño-Zarazúa, and J. Seekings, pp. 68–94. Oxford: Oxford University Press. https://doi.org/10.1093/oso/9780198850342.003.0003.

Lavers, T, and S. Hickey. 2021. 'Alternative Routes to the Institutionalisation of Social Transfers in Sub-Saharan Africa: Political Survival Strategies and Transnational Policy Coalitions'. *World Development* 146 (October): 105549. https://doi.org/10.1016/j.worlddev.2021.105549.

Leisering, L. 2019. *The Global Rise of Social Cash Transfers: How States and International Organizations Constructed a New Instrument for Combating Poverty.* Oxford: Oxford University Press.

Makene, P. 2016. 'TASAF Measures to Root out Undeserving Households Ongoing'. *The Guardian.* 31 August.

McCord, A. 2009. *Cash Transfers and Political Economy in Sub-Saharan Africa.* Project briefing no. 31. London: Overseas Development Institute. https://cdn.odi.org/media/documents/4612.pdf.

Paget, D. 2021. 'Tanzania: The Authoritarian Landslide'. *Journal of Democracy* 32(2): pp. 61–76. https://doi.org/10.1353/jod.2021.0019.

Porisky, A. 2022. *From Program to Policy: The Localization of the Community-Based Conditional Cash Transfer in Tanzania, 2010–2018.* Paper prepared for the Midwest Empirical Political Science (MWEPS) VIII Workshop, 29 April. Michigan State University.

Pruce, K., and S. Hickey. 2019. 'The Politics of Promoting Cash Transfers in Zambia'. In *The Politics of Social Protection in Eastern and Southern Africa*, edited by S. Hickey, T. Lavers, M. Niño-Zarazúa, and J. Seekings, pp. 176–201. Oxford: Oxford University Press. https://doi.org/10.1093/oso/9780198850342.003.0007.

Rudra, N. 2015. 'Social Protection in the Developing World: Challenges, Continuity, and Change'. *Politics & Society* 43(4): pp. 463–470. https://doi.org/10.1177/0032329215602884.

Seekings, J. 2016. *The Introduction of Old Age Pensions in Zanzibar.* CSSR Working Paper No. 393. Cape Town: Centre for Social Science Research, University of Cape Town.

Simpson, J. P. 2017. 'Do Donors Matter Most? An Analysis of Conditional Cash Transfer Adoption in Sub-Saharan Africa'. *Global Social Policy: An Interdisciplinary Journal of Public Policy and Social Development* 18(2): pp. 143–168. https://doi.org/10.1177/1468018117741447.

Swedlund, H. J., and M. Lierl. 2020. 'The Rise and Fall of Budget Support: Ownership, Bargaining and Donor Commitment Problems in Foreign Aid'. *Development Policy Review* 38(S1): pp. O50–O69. https://doi.org/10.1111/dpr.12463.

TASAF. 2015. *Fourth Quarter Implementation Progress Report, April–June 2015.* Dar es Salaam: TASAF.

TASAF. 2021. *Tanzania Social Action Fund. The Second Productive Social Safety Net Program. PSSN II. Mid-Term Review Report. January 2020–December 2021.* Dodoma: TASAF.

The Guardian. 2017a. 'JPM tells Burundian refugees to "go home"'. 21 July.

The Guardian. 2017b. 'TASAF in line for overhaul as JPM eyes another "boil"'. 13 January.

Ulriksen, M. S. 2019. 'Pushing for Policy Innovation: The Framing of Social Protection Policies in Tanzania'. In *The Politics of Social Protection in Eastern and Southern Africa*, edited by S. Hickey, T. Lavers, M. Niño-Zarazúa, and J. Seekings, pp. 122–147. Oxford: Oxford University Press. https://doi.org/10.1093/oso/9780198850342.003.0005.

URT. 2016. *National Five-Year Development Plan 2016/17–2020/21: Nurturing Industrialization for Economic Transformation and Human Development*. Dar es Salaam: Ministry of Finance and Planning.

URT. 2018. *Tanzania Social Action Fund, Productive Social Safety Net, Phase Two (PSSN II): Program Design Document*. Prepared by Government Project Preparation Team. Dar es Salaam: United Republic of Tanzania, President's Office.

URT, World Bank, UNDP, UNICEF, ILO, DFID, and Sida. 2016. *Final Aide Memoire of the Joint Review and Implementation Support Mission Conducted in October 2016 on the Tanzania Productive Social Safety Net Project (PSSN)*. Dar es Salaam: Government of Tanzania.

von Gliszczynski, M., and L. Leisering. 2016. 'Constructing New Global Models of Social Security: How International Organizations Defined the Field of Social Cash Transfers in the 2000s'. *Journal of Social Policy* 45(2): pp. 325–343.

Whitfield, L., ed. 2009. *The Politics of Aid: African Strategies for Dealing with Donors*. Oxford and New York: Oxford University Press.

Whitfield, L., and A. Fraser. 2010. 'Negotiating Aid: The Structural Conditions Shaping the Negotiating Strategies of African Governments'. *International Negotiation* 15(3): pp. 341–366. https://doi.org/10.1163/157180610X529582.

12

Brokered fiscal contracts

Shifting bargaining positions of Senegal's informal commercial sector

Ane Karoline Bak

12.1 Introduction

In this chapter, I trace three decades of revenue bargaining in Senegal's informal commercial sector. Drawing on the literature on the integral role of brokers in Senegal (e.g. Boone, 1992; Blundo, 2006; Beck, 2008; Gottlieb, 2017, 2022), I focus on brokers' influence on revenue-bargaining processes and specifically their outcomes. I find that what essentially become brokered fiscal contracts[1] can be explained by shifts in the relative bargaining positions of the ruling elites vis-à-vis the informal commercial sector and their brokers, in particular *Union Nationale des Commercants et Industriels du Sénégal* (UNACOIS).[2]

During the 1990s, recurring attempts at taxing the informal sector were resisted by actors in the informal commercial sector, organized by UNACOIS, and aided by a fragmented ruling coalition and weak ruling elites. In the 2000s, support of the informal commercial sector was politically important for President Abdoulaye Wade's effort to (re)consolidate the ruling coalition. While an informal sector tax was installed, it largely remained a tax on paper and not in practice. However, an organizational fragmentation of the informal commercial sector in the 2000s weakened its bargaining position vis-à-vis the ruling elites in the 2010s, and therefore, in the past decade, informal commercial actors' fiscal burden has increased with several new tax instruments and tentative expansions in tax collection.

[1] That is, fiscal contracts where an intermediary is *sine qua non* in the negotiation and upholding of the contract terms.

[2] UNACOIS changed its name in 2007 to UNACOIS-JAPPO. I refer to the organization as UNACOIS in the beginning of the chapter and to UNACOIS-JAPPO when discussing the later period.

Ane Karoline Bak, *Brokered fiscal contracts*. In: *The Politics of Revenue Bargaining in Africa*. Edited by: Anne Mette Kjær, Marianne S. Ulriksen, and Ane Karoline Bak, Oxford University Press. © Oxford University Press (2024).
DOI: 10.1093/oso/9780192868787.003.0012

I show that to understand the *relative* bargaining positions of the ruling elite and revenue providers (as theorized in the theoretical framework in Chapter 2), we should study their changing bargaining powers *in parallel.* In Senegal, fluctuations in the ruling coalition shape the resources and bargaining power of the ruling elites. On the other side, the bargaining power of UNACOIS as a broker is conditioned on its ability to organize and represent both small and large traders in the informal commercial sector, but its political influence is also conditioned by ruling coalition fluctuations creating political openings. The chapter demonstrates the instrumental value of a long-term historical approach and the importance of recognizing the distinct role of brokers when studying revenue bargaining in clientelist political settlements, in Senegal and beyond.[3]

The analysis is based on data collected from several field research stays between 2017 and 2022, including a survey of informal street vendors, tax-collection data, newspaper articles, interviews with former and current employees in the tax administration and representatives from the formal and informal economy, and reports and analyses of Senegal's informal commercial sector.

12.2 Senegal's informal commercial sector

After the agricultural sector, the commercial sector is perhaps Senegal's most important economic sector. Including both formal and informal businesses, it accounts for 40.3% of the economic turnover and employs 32.8% of all workers (ANSD, 2017, 33, 42). Focusing on the informal (non-agricultural) sector, trade and commerce provide primary employment to more than one million Senegalese across urban and rural areas (ANSD, 2019, 121). The *informal* commercial sector provides 66% of the informal economy's turnover (ANSD, 2017, 24, 34), but the tax contributions of the informal commercial economy are limited. Between 2004 and 2007, the informal commercial sector contributed on average 16.4% of total direct business income taxes (Benjamin and Mbaye, 2012, 60). More recently, a report stated that Senegal's entire informal economy contributes around 3% of tax revenues (DPEE, 2018).

Informal businesses are defined by the absence of formal account-keeping due to lack of either skill or will. While economic actors are not registered under the dominant central government tax schemes such as company

[3] Brokers here is arguably comparable to the third parties that Beach (Chapter 10) describes to be involved in revenue bargaining in Togo.

income tax, value-added taxation (VAT), or withholding taxes for employees, even the smallest vendors pay a range of taxes, fees, and levies (Bak, 2019; ILO, 2020) as elsewhere in Africa (Moore, Prichard, and Fjeldstad, 2018, ch. 7).

Senegal's informal commercial sector is incredibly diverse, comprising street-level vendors and trade business owners (in French, respectively *marchands ambulants* and *commercants*), all with some sort of fixed structure (Mbaye et al., 2014). Some have a table on the side of the road, some have a proper shop (in a structured market or in a building), and some large informal traders import and sell to smaller informal retailers. The former mostly function on a day-to-day basis, the latter group is registered and each has a business identification number (*Numéro d'Identification Nationale des Entreprises et Associations*, henceforth NINEA) which gives access to administrative procedures, banking, and, not least, import and export.

There are vast overlaps between Senegal's formal and informal economies. Most formal businesses engage in some informal activities (Marfaing and Sow, 1999; Greven, 2017; Mbaye, Benjamin, and Gueye, 2017; Ekomié et al., 2020), which is made possible by poor coordination and limited cross-referencing between the NINEA database, Senegal's tax authorities (*Directorate Générale des Impôts et Domaines*, henceforth DGID), and Customs (ILO, 2020, 30). For a long time, Customs did not differentiate between formal and informal business (Benjamin and Mbaye, 2012, 59), making it possible to be a registered business without paying taxes, and to import goods, pay customs, and sell the goods in large retail networks while remaining effectively informal, that is, not registering as taxpayers or declaring profits to the DGID. This is a key reason why large, rich traders can reside outside the tax net.

It is thus difficult, and not very useful, to apply a narrow definition to the informal sector, nor to draw a hard conceptual distinction between the formal and the informal economies. Instead, it is imperative to unpack and understand the sector's dynamics empirically and, especially, the role and influence of brokers in revenue bargaining.

12.2.1 Informal sector brokers and the implications for fiscal contracts in Senegal

Senegal's informal commercial sector includes small and large revenue providers with diverse trades and often diverging interests. Therefore, unionization and membership of business associations are vital sources of organizational and fiscal bargaining power. When unions and business associations, or effectively their leaders, sit down at the imaginary negotiation table, they bring the organizational bargaining power given by the potential mobilization of the revenue providers they represent, as well as political and social capital that many of their members often do not enjoy. The organizations and their leaders negotiate or *broker* on behalf of their members regarding issues such as tax. As shown in this chapter, one business association, UNACOIS, has been central in revenue bargaining on behalf of Senegal's informal commercial sector (see also Thioub, Diop, and Boone, 1998). Conceptualizing UNACOIS's role as broker helps us understand its varying influence on revenue-bargaining outcomes over the years, which, I argue, is a central explanatory factor of the evolution in informal sector taxation.

Brokers are defined as third-party intermediaries who utilize their power, often given by a large network and good connections, to facilitate an exchange between two other parties. Some scholars see brokers as central actors in vote buying who provide exclusive access to goods and services in countries where citizen–politician linkages are more clientelist than programmatic (see e.g. Kitschelt and Wilkinson, 2007; Stokes et al., 2013; Gottlieb, 2017; Berenschot, 2019). Others see brokers as significant actors positioned at the fault lines between state and citizens, aiding in needs translation and policy implementation in weak states (Mosse and Lewis, 2006; Blundo and Le Meur, 2008; Bierschenk and Olivier de Sardan, 2014). I focus on so-called organizational brokers (Holland and Palmer-Rubin, 2015), which are comparable to interest groups but differ in their control over what is exchanged between members and state actors (Scott, 1972, 95; Blundo and Le Meur, 2008).

Brokers balance interests in what is essentially a three-way relationship and negotiation. First, they have to consider state actors' interests; responding to and accommodating them is imperative for brokers to maintain their privileged access and potential influence. Second, organizational brokers in particular have to care for their members' social, collective, and organizational interests (Holland and Palmer-Rubin, 2015). Brokers may represent collective interests for altruistic reasons or to keep members satisfied, and if they fail to do this, members could sanction them, for example by stripping them of their power or by leaving the organization. Third, brokers have interests and can exploit their exclusive position to gain rents, patronage, or other goods (Stokes et al., 2013). For business associations, leaders are often successful businesspeople and are likely to bring their personal business interests to the negotiation table, which could conflict with those of their members.

The act of balancing these interests implies that brokered fiscal contracts, which sometimes result from revenue bargaining, might serve diverse sets of, sometimes conflicting, interests. Brokers may exploit their exclusive position to profit more than their members, who may receive limited information. However, there is a strong element of interdependence between brokers and the revenue providers they represent. While brokers can provide large groups of revenue providers with organizational power and political voice, the strength of brokers' bargaining position vis-à-vis ruling elites is largely dependent on the extent of their network and the ability to mobilize it. If brokers fail in balancing interests and leave their members dissatisfied, their organizational bargaining power and their bargaining position can be undermined. The following sections describe UNACOIS's balancing act in revenue bargaining regarding taxation of Senegal's informal commercial sector, how it changed over time, the consequences for UNACOIS and the broader group of revenue providers, and the outcomes of revenue bargaining.

12.3 Three decades of revenue bargaining

The following analysis includes case studies of the attempts in the 1990s to generalize VAT to the informal sector; the adoption of the informal sector tax, *contribution globale unique* (CGU) in 2004 and its reforms in 2006, 2012, and 2019; and the adoption of advance payments on imported goods in 2012 and 2019 targeting large informal importers. These cases represent initiatives that were implemented with the key objective to increase taxation of the informal commercial sector.

12.4 The 1990s: Attempts at generalizing taxation

Economic changes in the 1970s and 1980s caused an informalization of Senegal's economy.[4] First, there was a strong move towards a Senegalization of commerce to compete with long-established, foreign-owned firms, while the formerly fairly well-functioning productive formal sectors suffered under poor and increasingly centralized political management (Thioub, Diop, and Boone, 1998, 70–71). The mid '80s were characterized by economic recession, which only worsened as the international financial institutions (IFIs)

[4] I rely here on Thioub et al. (1998), who traced changes in Senegal's political economy in the wake of economic liberalization, including how it manifested in instances of revenue bargaining (though not conceptualizing as such).

pushed through structural adjustment programs (SAPs). As economic liberalization provided new rent opportunities, and capital in the informal sector grew competitive, a new group of self-made capitalists emerged, and the business class broadened (Thioub, Diop, and Boone, 1998). Combined, the informalization and liberalization of the economy narrowed the tax base considerably. The IFIs pressured the Senegalese government led by President Abdou Diouf to expand taxation of the informal economy, which became a key reason for the government's continuous attempts at generalizing VAT to the informal sectors.

The government's first attempt was in late 1989, when VAT and custom duty rates together increased by 5–6%. In reaction, traders in Dakar closed their shops and stopped all business activity in the capital (Boone, 1994; Thioub, Diop, and Boone, 1998). In the wake of this successful action, UNACOIS formed with the purpose of representing this new, largely informal business class to protect informal economy interests, and UNACOIS came to lead the organized opposition against the government's following attempts to increase taxation of the informal economy. The second attempt, in 1991, to apply VAT to the informal commercial sector met similar opposition. In 1993, UNACOIS reacted to negotiations regarding VAT and distribution monopolies by threatening, among other things, to stop import and export. In response to the final attempt in 1995–1996, UNACOIS called for the well-known *operation villes mortes* (operation dead cities). The shut-down of commerce in all major cities failed, but the operation demonstrated the potential organizational power of UNACOIS, its capacity of collective action, and its geographical reach. Ultimately, the traders succeeded in countering the regime's attempts at taxing the informal economy.

12.4.1 A fragmented ruling coalition and the creation of a strong broker

The instances of revenue bargaining in the 1990s did not end in a brokered fiscal contract: they did not establish a positive exchange of informal sector taxation for public services, nor did they seem to end in a devil's deal where non-taxation was exchanged for political support (Tendler, 2002; see also Chapter 2). If anything, non-taxation was exchanged for maintenance of commerce, economic activity, and social order. As elaborated in what follows, two conditions arguably explain this outcome: a poor and increasingly fragmented ruling coalition, and the making of UNACOIS as broker for an organized informal commercial sector.

The Parti Socialiste de Sénégal (PS) had been in power since independence in 1960 based on a ruling coalition built around close relations between the political and economic elites. The ruling coalition was characterized by a domestic business class that was deeply dependent on rent opportunities given by the ruling elites and a wide-reaching political machine securing election victories (Boone, 1992; Thioub, Diop, and Boone, 1998). This domestic business class remains largely tied to the structures of religious brotherhoods, especially the Mourides, whose wealth and capitalist strength were built during colonial times (Cruise O'Brien, 1971; Diop and Diouf, 1990; Boone, 1992; Villalón, 1995; Golub and Hansen-Lewis, 2012; Koter, 2021). The SAPs and economic liberalization coupled with poor political management diminished the economic resources of the ruling elites. Though President Diouf had made strides to centralize and consolidate his power during the 1980s and 1990s (Diop and Diouf, 1990), the structural economic changes limited the resources available to distribute patronage and maintain the religious groups' function in the political machine (Boone, 1990; Young and Kanté, 1991; Schaffer, 1998; Koter, 2021). Hence, the foundation of the ruling coalition withered, and the coalition became fragmented as elsewhere in Africa during these years (Whitfield et al., 2015).

Among revenue providers in the informal commercial sector, the instances of revenue bargaining prompted mobilization and organization. Under the conditions of an increasingly fragmented ruling coalition, potential revenue providers in the informal commercial sector became an important support group. Moreover, UNACOIS was able to utilize its organizational power to position itself as a broker between the two and increase its political influence. This established a relatively strong bargaining position of the revenue providers vis-à-vis the ruling elites (see Table 2.1, Chapter 2). Therefore, when protests and strikes paralyzed Senegal's economy, the Diouf regime was pressured to accommodate the potential revenue providers and abandon its attempts at expanding its tax effort.

12.5 The 2000s: Installation and reform of the informal sector tax

In 2004, a tax reform was passed, which included the installation of the *contribution globale unique* (CGU), an annual tax on informal economy activities applied to traders with a turnover below 50 million XOF (approx. €76,000), and service providers with a turnover below 25 million XOF (approx. €38,000).[5] The CGU substituted and synthesized several taxes, including income tax on industrial and commercial profits, VAT, and the business tax, *patente*. The CGU was calculated based on estimated turnover with fixed amounts for payments according to 20 turnover brackets. The tax brackets varied between the trade and service sectors. For traders, the effective tax rates varied between 1.5 and 9% and increased progressively with the level of turnover (UNACOIS, 2012).[6]

The motivation for the unified tax scheme was to ease the act of paying taxes, create a first fiscal acquaintance between informal economic actors and tax authorities, and promote tax compliance.[7] The CGU is an informal economy tax because, although declarative, it does not require provision of financial statements. Business owners need to register, make yearly declarations, and pay accordingly. It is primarily declarative in theory, though. For the most part, the tax is collected by a group of officials who tour the markets once a year (tax inspector 3, Dakar, 26 February 2018; municipal employee, Dakar, 1 March 2018). They assess turnovers based on vendors' goods and collect the relevant amount of tax. Hence, the CGU is effectively as much a presumptive as a declarative regime.

The CGU represents a first brokered fiscal contract between the informal commercial sector and the ruling elites, facilitated by UNACOIS, who, according to the narrative of the CGU, proposed it. This has been stated publicly by the DGID (APS, 2013) and in interviews with a UNACOIS representative (Dakar, 23 February 2018) and a DGID representative (Dakar, 20 February 2018). Although fighting generalization of VAT in the early '90s, UNACOIS had proposed an instrument that promotes informal sector taxation, at least on paper. However, in the wake of the adoption of the CGU in 2004, UNACOIS criticized the tax brackets for being out of sync with the traders' means (*Sud Quotidien*, 2004; Barry, 2004) and claimed that it had not been consulted in the formulation of the final tax brackets (ibid.). Nothing came of these protests in 2004, but the tax brackets became the focal point of subsequent revenue bargaining and several reforms of the CGU. In 2006, following consultation with UNACOIS (UNACOIS, 2012), the fixed amounts were lowered for the 15 highest brackets but increased for the fourth- and fifth-lowest.[8] For the highest bracket, the reduction was notable: from 4,200,000 XOF (approx. €6,407) to 1,500,000 XOF (approx.

[5] Loi no. 2004-12 du 6 février 2004 modifiant certaines dispositions du Code Général des Impôts.
[6] See Appendix, Table 12.A1 for overview of the CGU calculus and its reforms.
[7] Expose des motifs, Loi no. 2004-12 du 6 février 2004.
[8] See Appendix, Table 12.A1 for overview of CGU reforms.

€2,290). Furthermore, the tax scale was split in two: one for traders dealing in food products and cement, and one with markedly lower taxation for all other traders. Further reforms of the CGU in 2013 and 2018 will be discussed later.

12.5.1 The balancing act

During its first decade, the CGU was but a contract on paper, and very few businesses were enrolled. In 2004, 2,663 firms were effectively subject to the CGU, and in 2007, the number was 4,970 (Benjamin and Mbaye, 2012, 60f) compared to 281,000 informal economic entities in 2003 in Dakar alone (DPS, 2003) and an estimated 774,000 (non-agricultural) entities across Senegal (ANSD, 2013, 16). While the total revenue collected from the CGU doubled between 2004 and 2007, the average tax collection per firm fell, and revenue from the CGU did not exceed 1.5 billion XOF (approx. €2.3 million), which equals less than 1% of total direct taxes collected (Benjamin and Mbaye, 2012, 60). By 2012, revenue collections had fallen to 0.7 billion XOF (approx. €1.1 million) (Sy, 2016). Based on its limited reach into the informal sector, the fiscal outcome of the CGU was negligible in terms of revenue collection and experienced tax burden. In addition, street-level vendors will, when asked, most likely say that they never have heard of the CGU, and that they pay the *patente* (even though their payment receipts actually say CGU).[9]

The installation and poor implementation of the CGU can be explained, at least in part, by the interests of then President Abdoulaye Wade and UNACOIS's balancing act. The fragmentation of the ruling coalition in the 1990s increased political competition leading up to Senegal's presidential election in 2000. There was real uncertainty about election results (Beck, 2008, 7), and in the country's first transfer of power, the Parti Démocratique Sénégalais (PDS) and its leader, Abdoulaye Wade, took over from PS. In the wake of his election, President Wade sustained his presidential power by catering to religious leaders and (re)creating avenues for patronage financed in part by large-scale corruption, for example around public tenders (Beck, 2008, 223ff; Mbow, 2008; Kelly, 2012). He reconsolidated the ruling coalition and ensured centralized power and control of central state institutions (Dumont and Kanté, 2019). Moreover, he openly wooed people whose basic livelihood was secured by working in or relying on the informal economy (Dankoco

[9] In a survey by Gottlieb (2022), only 6% of firms had heard about the CGU. Author's interviews and focus groups with informal actors corroborated this (e.g. focus group with presidents from five associations representing informal commercial professions, Dakar, 30 March 2022).

and Brown, 2017). Seeking to implement informal sector taxation effectively would have countered this political courtship and affected large parts of the population negatively, which might jeopardize social stability. Furthermore, administrative and state capacity suffered under Wade's use of state positions as patronage (Gellar, 2013, 125), which challenged effective implementation of the tax.

On the other side of the bargaining, it might seem curious why UNACOIS would promote taxation of the informal economy and, hence, their members. However, the CGU can be interpreted as a balancing act between the three sets of interests that UNACOIS as a broker needed to accommodate. First, UNACOIS helped the ruling elites signal a willingness to tax the informal economy towards IFIs, who had pushed for this and a general simplification of tax regimes since the 1980s (Moore and Fjeldstad, 2008). Second, in line with the interests of both small and large revenue providers among UNACOIS's members, the CGU legitimized the presence of the informal sector and, at least on paper, constrained the grounds for arbitrary or coercive taxation by reducing the number of taxes and encounters between taxpayers and state actors. Lastly, it served UNACOIS's interests well to manifest its role as representative for the informal sector while also, in principle, promoting taxation and fertilizing the grounds for long-term financing for development. The larger informal traders probably saw a benefit in the CGU's installation as a tax regime, which would be more forbearing, and hence attractive, than one taxing profit directly.[10] In turn, the process of adopting, implementing, and reforming the CGU could delay future initiatives to include these traders in the formal tax net.

Consequently, the ruling elites and UNACOIS as broker had an interest in adopting a tax regime for informal economic actors; however, neither the ruling elites, the revenue providers, nor UNACOIS had an interest in expanding tax collection. At the same time, the 2006 reform changed the terms of the brokered fiscal contract to the benefit of the larger informal traders among UNACOIS's members. It effectively decreased tax progressivity by reducing taxation for the highest turnover brackets by almost two-thirds in absolute terms; and the separate tax bracket for trade of food products lowered taxation on the type of products that some of UNACOIS's most influential members import and sell. Hence, UNACOIS seemed to utilize its exclusive position as broker to promote interests of the more influential members comprising its leadership and, hence, those sitting at the bargaining table.

[10] I thank Jessica Gottlieb for making this point.

12.5.2 A shift in UNACOIS's position as broker

Since its establishment in the late 1990s, UNACOIS has developed and demonstrated high organizational power. It progressed from being activist to entering alliances with the *patronats*, the employers' organizations, and becoming a prominent member of the Dakar Chamber of Commerce (Thioub, Diop, and Boone, 1998; Scheld, 2010). This enabled UNACOIS to promote its causes in political decision-making arenas and in meetings with members of the ruling elite, with whom UNACOIS and its influential importers grew close ties and still enjoy direct access (tax consultant, Dakar, 23 March 2022).

Nevertheless, there has always been an inherent tension within UNACOIS due to the diversity of the informal commercial sector. In the late 1990s, this tension caused a division of UNACOIS, which lasted until 2007 when a reconciliation led to the formation of UNACOIS-JAPPO.[11] Tension also emerged on several occasions during the 2000s, bringing to light the diverging interests between UNACOIS as a broker and the broader group of revenue providers in the informal commercial sector. First, it became clear that UNACOIS had been using its position to promote the interests of its leading wealthy members. In addition to the 2006 reform of the CGU, special deals and exemptions were negotiated for some of the most important importers of rice, sugar, and oil (Mbaye, Golub, and English, 2015; Mbaye, Golub, and Gueye, 2020). Second, the diverging interests showed in debates in 2007 about the presence of Chinese traders. UNACOIS deplored explicitly their presence, while Senegalese petty traders enjoyed easy and cheap market access provided by the Chinese (Marfaing and Thiel, 2013). Third, street vendors broke into violent protest in November 2007 over a sudden bout of evictions from central Dakar (Dankoco and Brown, 2017). Though UNACOIS had been informed about the imminent evictions, it had not passed the information on and failed to support the vendors. These protests led to a rupture in the organization of the informal sector (focus group, Dakar 30 March 2022), which culminated in 2009 with the formation of several new vendors' associations, organized mostly by profession, in umbrella organizations and occasional strategic platforms in response to specific challenges.[12] In this period, the UNACOIS-JAPPO membership dropped from around 100,000 in 2007 (Brown, Lyons, and Dankoco, 2010, 673) to around (self-reported) 70,000 in 2012 (UNACOIS, 2012).

[11] *Jappo* means 'togetherness' in Wolof (Scheld, 2010).
[12] Field notes, Dakar 28 and 30 March 2022.

Overall, this created a shift. UNACOIS's role as representative of the broader informal commercial sector was impaired, its position as broker weakened, and its relative bargaining position vis-à-vis the ruling elites changed. This arguably helps explain the evolution of informal sector taxation in the decade that followed.

12.6 The 2010s: Expanding the portfolio of tax instruments

The 2010s saw a continuous stream of tax reforms in Senegal in line with the global tax-reform agenda (Moore and Fjeldstad, 2008): from a complete restructuring of Senegal's tax legislation in 2012 into one *Code Générale des Impôts*, to subsequent adaptations of tax policies and the tax administration.[13] I focus on the taxes and tax instruments that target directly the informal commercial sector: the reforms of the CGU and the adoption of advance payments on imported goods.

The CGU was reformed twice in this period. The 2012 reform reduced the number of tax brackets and increased the threshold for service providers, aligning it with that of the traders, and the fixed payment amounts were substituted for tax rates as proposed by UNACOIS-JAPPO (2012).[14] However, effective tax payments did not really change until 2019 when the CGU was reformed again. At this point, the progressivity of the tax was removed completely, and the two categories of traders were abolished (see Appendix, Table 12.A1), which left two sector-based tax rates: traders and producers now pay 2% on their turnovers, and the service sector pays 5%.[15] The official motivation to remove the progressivity was to simplify the tax even more to aid the smallest taxpayers (Diaw, 2019); however, the reform is regressive on paper.

Besides the CGU reforms, two new tax instruments were adopted to capture traders who import and distribute goods for retail but manage to escape taxation. The first was a 3% advance payment on profits in the commercial and industrial sectors (in French, and henceforth, the *Acompte BIC*) adopted in 2012. The *Acompte BIC* is applicable to all importers who are not registered at the Large Taxpayers Office at the DGID and is to be paid at entry point with Customs.[16] It is not a tax per se but a payment to be deducted from

[13] Most recently, *patente*, the business tax, which still applied to formal business, was modernized into *Contribution Economique Locale* (tax consultant, Dakar, 16 March 2022).
[14] Loi no. 2012-31 du 31 décembre 2012. See Appendix, Table 12.A1.
[15] Loi no. 2019-17 du 20 décembre 2019. See Appendix, Table 12.A1.
[16] Loi no. 2012-31 du 31 décembre 2012.

tax liabilities when taxes have been declared with the DGID. As stated in the law's explanatory memorandum, the objective was to collect revenue from importers and incentivize them to register at the DGID to avoid paying up front. To be clear, the *Acompte BIC* follows closely a UEMOA directive from 2001;[17] however, the decision to target commercial and industrial sectors was not prescribed by the directive but came from the Senegalese state.

In 2019, the DGID announced another similar tax instrument, a 12% tax compliance levy (*Prélèvement de Conformité Fiscale*, henceforth PCF) on all imports by natural and legal persons (i.e. individuals or businesses) who do not regularly declare and/or pay taxes.[18] Levied in conjunction with the *Acompte BIC*, the PCF is an advance payment to be deducted from later tax liabilities, assuming the taxpayer declares their taxes later. The PCF was announced with the proposed finance law for 2020 (Republic of Senegal, 2019) and put into effect in September 2021 (tax inspectors 2 and 4, Dakar, 18 and 21 March 2022). While the DGID took the initiative to the PCF (tax inspector 2, Dakar, 18 March 2022), pressure from the IMF to expand revenue mobilization was important for its actual implementation (tax inspector 4, Dakar, 21 March 2022). The importance of securing revenue is emphasized in the law's explanatory memorandum, together with equity concerns and an expectation that the PCF will help expand the number of registered, formalized business.

UNACOIS-JAPPO reacted in similar ways to the announcements of the two tax instruments. In 2013, they described the *Acompte BIC* as an extra tax and proclaimed that it would lead to price increases (Malou, 2013). DGID officials called for dialogue by inviting UNACOIS-JAPPO to a public meeting to clarify, but they did not attend, arguing that they wanted to talk to the relevant minister or, alternatively, the Director General of the DGID. Reacting to UNACOIS-JAPPO's absence, representatives from the DGID interestingly referred to the fact that they had followed UNACOIS-JAPPO's suggestions regarding the CGU (Malou, 2013), probably as a way to emphasize the DGID's willingness to enter dialogue and follow propositions from the private sector. When the PCF was announced in 2020, UNACOIS-JAPPO similarly argued that it was yet another tax hike that would raise prices (APANEWS, 2020; Balde, 2020). This argument is curious; while the PCF is likely to influence liquidity (as also argued by a UNACOIS-JAPPO representative, Dakar, 1 April 2022), it is not an actual (new) tax, unless of course one has not paid due taxes before.

[17] Directive no. 07/2001/CM/UEMOA du 26 novembre 2001.
[18] Loi no. 2019-17 du 20 décembre 2019.

12.6.1 A weakened bargaining position of revenue providers

The reforms of the CGU can be seen as a renegotiation of the brokered fiscal contract. The DGID continued to accommodate the demands of UNACOIS-JAPPO a bit at a time, making the tax regime more regressive. However, the *Acompte BIC* and the PCF seem to have been implemented with limited dialogue or bargaining and are at odds with the interests of UNACOIS-JAPPO and the large importing traders. This mix of outcomes can be explained by changes in the bargaining resources on both sides of the table, which significantly influenced the relative bargaining positions of the two parties.

On one side, the political and administrative resources[19] of the ruling elites have increased. First, the administrative resources of the DGID appear to be improving. Besides the simplification of the tax code in 2012, attempts have been made to modernize the administration over the last decade, including organizational restructuring, simplification of administrative procedures, and, most recently, implementation of performance contracts for each DGID directorate (tax inspector 2, Dakar, 18 March 2022). Much has been done to integrate taxpayer data from Customs and the DGID (Ndiaye, 2017) (tax inspector 1, Dakar, 26 February 2018) and, very recently, with NINEA as well (tax inspector 2, Dakar, 21 March 2022). The changes have been supported by international collaboration and technical assistance (tax consultant, Dakar, 16 March 2022). Of course, it can be questioned whether administrative capacity has really increased, but the adopted tax instruments signal innovative thinking and a commitment to expanding the tax base.

Second, the ruling elites' political resources have grown in yet another bout of reconsolidation and centralization of the ruling coalition under Senegal's current president Macky Sall. Sall came to power in 2012, when a large popular movement countered Abdoulaye Wade's bid for a third (unconstitutional) presidential term. Since the turnover, he has consolidated his power through the now well-known instruments of Senegal's ruling elites: nursing relations with religious leaders, maintaining the patronage opportunities that he had promised to remove, centralizing power by co-opting important opposition figures and parties, and clamping down on other key opponents (Dumont and Kanté, 2019; Kohnert and Marfaing, 2019; Kelly, 2020).

More recently, Sall has taken actions to narrow the ruling coalition. He has centralized control by limiting the ruling elites' access to resources and power (Riedl and Sylla, 2019) and excluding formerly close allies (social

[19] As defined in Chapter 2.

activist, Dakar, 31 March 2022). The increase in administrative and political resources and, perhaps most importantly, Sall's effort to narrow the ruling coalition have strengthened the bargaining position of the ruling elites vis-à-vis revenue providers in the informal commercial sector. The *Acompte BIC* and PCF could be taken as evidence, as both were developed in cooperation with the Ministry of Finance (tax inspector 2, Dakar, 18 March 2022) and required the president's approval.

On the other side of the bargaining table, the internal fragmentation in UNACOIS-JAPPO weakened its relative bargaining position. When smaller informal traders left UNACOIS-JAPPO for other organizations in the late 2000s, it reduced the broker's organizational power and its obligations to represent the interests of that group. The effort to abolish CGU's progressivity can be seen as proof that UNACOIS-JAPPO represents the interests of smaller informal traders even less than before.

Adding to the internal fragmentation, UNACOIS-JAPPO experienced yet another division in 2017 when a group of members created UNACOIS-YEESSAL[20] due to dissatisfaction with the governance of the UNACOIS-JAPPO (representative from UNACOIS-YEESSAL, Dakar, 24 March 2022). According to an interviewee within UNACOIS-JAPPO, some politicians have used the strife to weaken the organization's ability to mobilize and influence politics.[21] Moreover, the organization was not invited to the latest relevant negotiations about the reform of the *patente* (UNACOIS representative, Dakar, 1 April 2022). All these things combined suggest a shift in UNACOIS-JAPPO's formerly exclusive political position. This can help explain the implementation of the *Acompte BIC* and the PCF in that the weakened organizational power of UNACOIS-JAPPO as broker for the broader informal commercial sector has spilled over into the bargaining position of the larger informal traders and importers. Of course, it is likely that some influential traders with very close ties to the ruling elites are still be able to negotiate exemptions from these tax instruments.

12.6.2 Recent fiscal outcomes

The expansion of the portfolio of tax instruments can be explained at least partly by the weakening of UNACOIS-JAPPO's relative bargaining position vis-à-vis the ruling elites. In the following, I present data on tax collection from the last five years that suggest an, admittedly tentative, increase in the effective fiscal burden of informal commercial actors.

[20] Though the same acronym, the name is L'Union nationale des associations de commerçants, opérateurs et investisseurs du Sénégal. Yeessal translates into 'renewal'.

[21] Written communication, 15 April 2022.

For the CGU, the number of taxpayers registered and declarations increased between 2012 and 2022. In 2013, there were 2,035 CGU declarations (Gottlieb, 2022), which almost doubled between 2012 and 2019, and then rose by more than 50% in the two following years. Between 2012 and 2019, the revenue collected from CGU likewise rose from 0.72 (Sy, 2016) to 0.89 billion XOF (approx. €1.5 billion) (Table 12.1). As shown in Table 12.1, collections rose equally within the much shorter period between 2019 and 2021 to 1.15 billion XOF (approx. €1.75 million).

The data in Table 12.1 should be complemented with data on revenue collected by teams that visit market areas once a year. In 2021, 29,372 taxpayers were reached, paying in total 1,531,197,361 XOF (approx. €2.3 million),[22] which means that many more taxpayers are reached than those registered. In fact, these tours collect more revenue than is collected through declarations, even though an average taxpayer pays 52,131 XOF (approx. €80), which is lower than the average tax payments made by registered taxpayers.[23] Still, the sum of presumptive and declarative taxpayers comprises only a small share of the informal commercial sector.

Despite an increase in taxpayers and tax revenue under the CGU, they remain low in absolute terms. The 2.68 trillion XOF (approx. €4.1 million) equals 0.1% of the projected tax collections for 2021 of 2.56 trillion XOF (approx. €3.9 billion), and in real terms, the current revenue does not exceed that of 2008 (Gottlieb, 2022). However, interviews with representatives from the informal and formal economies conducted in March 2022 suggest that both smaller and larger commercial businesses have experienced a significant increase in fiscal burden. This was mentioned, also unprompted, by several interviewees (e.g. representative CNES, Dakar, 29 March 2022; representative from UNACOIS-JAPPO, 1 April 2022).

For the *Acompte BIC*, it was only possible to obtain data for the most recent years, even though it has been in place since 2012. As shown in Table 12.2,

Table 12.1 CGU, 2019–2021

	Registered taxpayers	Declarations	Revenue collected (XOF)
2019		3,991	889,093,121
2020		5,889	1,024,570,010
2021	18,206	6,487	1,149,220,868

Source: DGID (Dakar, March 2022).

[22] Called *Paiements par Anticipation*, which means advance payments but is in practice a lump-sum payment. Data provided by the DGID (Dakar, March 2022).

[23] This can be ascribed to the legal stipulation of a maximum lump-sum payment of 100,000 FCFA.

Table 12.2 Acompte sur l'importation (XOF)

2018	7.7 billion
2019	8.4 billion
2020	9.0 billion

Source: DGID (Dakar, March 2022).

the revenue collected by this instrument increased between 2018 and 2020. As the PCF has only been in place since September 2021, it is still too early to obtain data for at the time of writing this chapter. One interviewee in the DGID called PCF 'a step' towards regulating the fiscal problem posed by the informal sector (tax inspector 4, Dakar, 22 March 2022); another said that the preliminary data suggest that the PCF is securing new revenue (tax inspector 2, Dakar, 18 March 2022), while a representative of UNACOIS argued that this was not the case (Dakar, 1 April 2022).

12.7 Conclusion

As elsewhere, taxation of the informal economy has received much political attention in Senegal. From a revenue-bargaining perspective, informal economy taxation is quite peculiar: It applies to large parts of the population but generates relatively limited tax revenues; taxed informal actors often experience a high fiscal burden compared to their means, and most often, receive a limited return of public or semi-public goods compared to actors in the formal sector (Pimhidzai and Fox, 2012; Rogan, 2022). A critical strand in the tax and governance literature questions the global effort to expand informal economy taxation by highlighting equity issues (Prichard, 2018; Dube and Casale, 2019; Rogan, 2019), questioning the potential economic gains (Moore, Prichard, and Fjeldstad, 2018; Moore, 2022), and emphasizing the complexity of historical experiences, social institutions, and power relations that such taxation plays into (Tendler, 2002; Kjær, 2009; Meagher and Lindell, 2013; Prichard and van den Boogaard, 2017; Meagher, 2018).

This chapter contributes to this strand of research in two ways. First, it illustrates how to unpack the dynamics and politics of informal economy taxation. The informal economy comprises many sectors each with their economic structures, each their organizational and political dynamic, and each their kinds and levels of taxation.[24] As theorized in Chapter 2, economic actors

[24] See e.g. Chapter 3 in this volume.

from different sectors might be of more or less fiscal and political importance to the ruling coalition. To deepen the analysis, this chapter focuses on one of Senegal's most economically important sectors: the informal commercial sector. Tracing three decades of revenue bargaining with this sector, the chapter demonstrates the explanatory power of this volume's theoretical framework: from strong and successful resistance against taxation to a brokered fiscal contract with little effective taxation, and, recently, to an expansion in the tax portfolio and an increased fiscal burden felt by the sector. The evolution is linked to the changing bargaining power and, in particular, shifts in the *relative* bargaining positions of the ruling elites vis-à-vis the revenue providers and, in particular, their broker, UNACOIS. To my knowledge, this chapter is the first long-term study of politics of taxation in Senegal, both in relation to the informal economy and broadly.

The second major contribution of this chapter is that it highlights the consequences of the brokered nature of fiscal contracts between informal economic actors and ruling elites. In clientelist settings, as with all five case countries in this volume, it is imperative to consider the influence of brokers in revenue bargaining, especially when researching taxation of the informal economy that includes a large group of small, often politically marginalized, economic actors. Here, brokers must balance the diverse and often conflicting sets of interests. Furthermore, as an inherent feature of clientelism, competition for access to rents and side deals, also internally in organizations, creates tensions and frequent organizational fragmentation, such as was the case for UNACOIS.[25] These conditions became determinant for their bargaining power, which, in turn, had consequences for the brokered fiscal contract between the ruling elites and Senegal's informal commercial sector.

[25] Thanks for Catherine Boone for pointing this out.

12.8 Appendix

Table 12.A1 Overview of CGU reforms 2004–2019

	2004	2006	2012	2019
Sub-regimes	Two sub-regimes: 1. service providers 2. traders	Three sub-regimes: 1. service providers 2. traders of food products and cement 3. traders of other products	Three sub-regimes: 1. service providers 2. traders of food products and cement 3. traders of other products	Two sub-regimes: 1. service providers 2. traders
Threshold	Service providers: XOF 25,000,000 Traders: XOF 50,000,000	Service providers: XOF 25,000,000 Traders: XOF 50,000,000	All sub-regimes: XOF 50,000,000	Both sub-regimes: XOF 50,000,000
Number of turnover brackets	Both sub-regimes: 20	All sub-regimes: 20	Service providers: 5 Both categories of traders: 3	Both sub-regimes: 1
Tax levels	Service providers: XOF 10,000–3,000,000 Traders: XOF 5,000–4,200,000	Service providers: XOF 10,000–2,000,000 Traders of food products and cement: XOF 5,000–1,250,000 Traders of other products: XOF 5,000–1,500,000	Service providers: 4–8% Traders of food products and cement: 1–2.8% Traders of other products: 2–3.8%	Service providers: 5% Traders: 2%

Acknowledgements

I am grateful for comments provided by Anne Mette Kjær, Marianne S. Ulriksen, Catherine Boone, Jessica Gottlieb, Laurence Marfaing, the Taxation in Africa panel at ASA 2020, and colleagues from Aarhus University, the University of Southern Denmark, and the Political Settlements and Revenue Bargains in Africa project. Amath Mbaye and Mohamed Seydina Mbaye provided invaluable research assistance in Senegal. Regretfully, this project did not, as initially planned, turn into a joint project with the late Professor Fatou Gueye from Université Cheikh Anta Diop de Dakar (UCAD). May she rest in peace.

References

ANSD. 2013. *Enquête Nationale Sur Le Secteur Informel Au Sénégal (Ensis 2011).* Dakar.

ANSD. 2017. Agence Nationale de la Statistique et de la Démographie *Rapport Global Du Recensement Général Des Entreprises.* Dakar.

ANSD. 2019. 181–182 Agence Nationale de la Statistique et de la Démographie Enquête Régionale Intégrée Sur l'Emploi et Le Secteur Informel (ERI-ESI) Sénégal, 2017 RAPPORT FINAL.

APANEWS. 2020. 'Sénégal: La Direction Des Impôts Dément La Hausse de l'impôt Sur Les Sociétés'.

APS. 2013. 'L'acompte BIC sans Effet Sur Les Prix à La Consommation (DGID)'. Agence de Presse Sénégalaise.

Bak, Ane Karoline. 2019. *When the Fiscal Social Contract Is Not about Tax: Understanding the Limited Role of Taxation in Social Accountability in Senegal.* Aarhus: Politica.

Balde, Osseynou. 2020. 'La DGID Vise Les Importateurs Qui Ne Payent Par La Fiscalité'. *L'AS in Seneplus.* https://www.seneplus.com/economie/la-dgid-vise-les-importateurs-qui-ne-paient-pas-la-fiscalite#:~:text=La Direction Générale des Impôts,de toutes leurs obligations fiscales.

Barry, Moustapha. 2004. 'Lutte Contre La Fraude: L'Unacois Dénonce Les Faveurs Faites à La CSS de Mimran'. *Wal Fadjri*, 12 May.

Beck, Linda J. 2008. *Brokering Democracy in Africa: The Rise of Clientilist Democracy in Senegal.* New York: Palgrave Macmillan.

Benjamin, Nancy, and Ahmadou Aly Mbaye. 2012. *The Informal Sector in Francophone Africa: Firm Size, Productivity and Institutions.* http://elibrary.worldbank.org/doi/book/10.1596/978-0-8213-9537-0.

Berenschot, Ward. 2019. 'Informal Democratization: Brokers, Access to Public Services and Democratic Accountability in Indonesia and India'. *Democratization* 26(2): pp. 208–224.

Bierschenk, Thomas, and Jean-Pierre Olivier de Sardan (eds.). 2014. *States at Work: Dynamics of African Bureaucracies*. Leiden: Brill.

Blundo, Giorgio. 2006. 'Dealing with the Local State: The Informal Privatization of Street-level Bureaucracies in Senegal'. *Development and Change* 37(4): pp. 799–819.

Blundo, Giorgio, and Pierre-Yves Le Meur. 2008. 'Introduction: An Anthropology of Everyday Governance: Collective Service Delivery and Subject-Making'. In *The Governance of Daily Life in Africa: Ethnographic Explorations of Public and Collective Services*, edited by Giorgio Blundo and Pierre-Yves Le Meur. Leiden: Brill, pp. 1–9.

Boone, Catherine. 1990. 'The Making of the Rentier Class: Wealth Accumulation and Political Control in Senegal'. *Journal of Development Studies* 26(3): 425–449.

Boone, Catherine. 1992. *Merchant Capital and the Roots of State Power in Senegal, 1930–1985*. Cambridge: Cambridge University Press.

Boone, Catherine. 1994. 'Trade, Taxes, and Tribute: Market Liberalizations and the New Importers in West Africa'. *World Development* 22(3): pp. 453–467.

Brown, Alison, Michal Lyons, and Ibrahima Dankoco. 2010. 'Street Traders and the Emerging Spaces for Urban Voice and Citizenship in African Cities'. *Urban Studies* 47(3): pp. 666–683.

Cruise O'Brien, Donald B. 1971. *The Mourides of Senegal: The Political and Economic Organisation on an Islam Brotherwood*. Oxford: Clarendon Press.

Dankoco, Ibrahima, and Alison Brown. 2017. 'Commerce of the Street in Sénégal: Between Illegality and Tolerance'. In *Rebel Streets and the Informal Economy: Street Trade and the Law*, edited by Alison Brown, pp. 165–182. London: Routledge.

Diaw, Abdou. 2019. 'Strategie de Recettes á Moyen Terme: Focus Sur Le Nouveau Dispositif de Mobilisation Des Ressources'. *Le Soleil*.

Diop, Momar Coumba, and Mamado Diouf. 1990. *Le Sénégal Sous Abdou Diouf*. Paris: Karthala.

DPEE. 2018. *Impacts d'une Amélioration de La Productivité Du Secteur Informel Surl'économie Sénégalaise*.

DPS. 2003. *Le Secteur Informel Dans l'Agglomeration de Dakar: Performances, Insertion et Perspectives*. Dakar.

Dube, Godwin, and Daniela Casale. 2019. 'Informal Sector Taxes and Equity: Evidence from Presumptive Taxation in Zimbabwe'. *Development Policy Review* 37(1): pp. 47–66.

Dumont, Gérard-Francois, and Seydou Kanté. 2019. *La Géopolitique Du Sénégal De Senghor à l'élection de Macky Sall.* Paris: L'Harmattan.

Ekomié, Jean-Jacques et al. 2020. 'The Informal Sector in Francophone Africa: Dominant Characteristics, Scope, and Trends from Our Survey Data'. In *Formal and Informal Entreprises in Francophone Africa: Moving Toward a Virabnt Private Sector*, edited by Ahmadou Aly Mbaye, Stephen S Golub, and Fatou Gueye, pp. 79–102. Ottawa: International Development Research Centre.

Gellar, Sheldon. 2013. 'The Rise of Citizen Movements and the Consolidation of Democracy under the Abdoulaye Wade Regime (2000–2012)'. In *Le Sénégal Sous Abdoulaye Wade: Le Sopi à l'épreuve Du Pouvoir*, edited by Momar-coumba Diop. Dakar and Paris: CRES–Karthala, pp. 119–151.

Golub, Stephen S., and J. Hansen-Lewis. 2012. 'Informal Trading Networks in West Africa: The Mourides of Senegal/The Gambia and the Yoruba of Benin/Nigeria'. In *The Informal Sector in Francophone Africa: Firm Size, Productivity, and Institutions*, edited by Nancy Benjamin and Ahmadou Aly Mbaye, pp. 173–194. Washington DC: World Bank and Agence Française de Développement.

Gottlieb, Jessica. 2017. 'Explaining Variation in Broker Strategies: A Lab-in-the-Field Experiment in Senegal'. *Comparative Political Studies* 50(11): pp. 1556–1592.

Gottlieb, Jessica. 2022. 'How Economic Informality Constrains Demand for Programmatic Policy'. *American Journal of Political Science.* https://onlinelibrary.wiley.com/doi/10.1111/ajps.12746.

Greven, Thomas. 2017. 'Organizing the Informal Economy in Senegal'. In *Work, Institutions and Sustainable Livelihood*, edited by Virginius Xava, Debdulal Saha, and Rajdeep Singha. Singapore: Palgrave Macmillan, 303–322.

Holland, Alisha C., and Brian Palmer-Rubin. 2015. 'Beyond the Machine: Clientelist Brokers and Interest Organizations in Latin America'. *Comparative Political Studies* 48(9): pp. 1186–1223.

ILO. 2020. *Diagnostic de l'Économie Informelle Au Sénégal.* Genève: Bureau international du Travail (BTI)–ILO. https://www.ilo.org/wcmsp5/groups/public/---ed_protect/---protrav/---travail/documents/publication/wcms_735752.pdf.

Kelly, Catherine Lena. 2012. 'Senegal: What Will Turnover Bring?' *Journal of Democracy* 23(3): pp. 121–131.

Kelly, Catherine Lena. 2020. *Party Proliferation and Political Contestation in Africa: Senegal in Comparative Perspective.* Cham: Palgrave.

Kitschelt, Herbert, and Steven I. Wilkinson. 2007. *Patrons, Clients, and Policies.* Edited by Herbert Kitschelt and Steven I. Wilkinson. Cambridge: Cambridge University Press.

Kjær, Anne Mette. 2009. 'Sources of Local Government Extractive Capacity: The Role of Trust and Pre-Colonial Legacy in the Case of Uganda'. *Public Administration and Development* 29: pp. 228–238.

Kohnert, Dirk, and Laurence Marfaing. 2019. 'Senegal: Presidential Elections 2019: The Shining Example of Democratic Transition Immersed in Muddy Power-Politics'. *SSRN Electronic Journal* (92739): pp. 1–7.

Koter, Dominika. 2021. 'Religion and Electoral Competition in Senegal'. In *The Oxford Handbook of Politics in Muslim Societies,* edited by M. Cammett and P. Jones. Oxford Academic, 1–21.

Malou, Jean Pierre. 2013. 'Contentieux DGID-Unacois Sur La Taxe de 3 %—L'acompte n'a Pas d'incidence Sur Les Prix'. *Sud Quotidien.*

Marfaing, Laurence, and Mariam Sow. 1999. *Les opérateurs économiques au Sénégal: entre le formel et l'informel.* Paris: Karthala.

Marfaing, Laurence, and Alena Thiel. 2013. 'The Impact of Chinese Business on Market Entry in Ghana and Senegal'. *Africa* 83(4): pp. 646–669.

Mbaye, Ahmadou Aly, Nancy C. Benjamin, Stephen S. Golub, and Jean-Jacques T. Ekomie. 2014. *The Urban Informal Sector in Francophone Africa: Large versus Small Enterprises in Benin, Burkina Faso and Senegal.* Development Policy Research Unit Working Paper 201405. DPRU, University of Cape Town.

Mbaye, Ahmadou Aly, Nancy Claire Benjamin, and Fatou Gueye. 2017. 'The Interplay Between Formal and Informal Firms and Its Implications on Jobs in Francophone Africa: Case Studies of Senegal and Benin'. In *The Informal Economy in Global Perspective: Varieties of Governance*, edited by Abel Polese, Colin C. Williams, Ioana A. Horodnic, and Predrag Bejakovic. Cham: Palgrave Macmillan, 213–231.

Mbaye, Ahmadou Aly, Stephen S. Golub, and Philip English. 2015. 'Policies, Prices and Poverty: The Sugar, Vegetable Oil and Flour Industries in Senegal'. In *Race to the Next Income Frontier: How Senegal and Other Low-Income Countries Can Reach the Finish Line*, Policy Research Working Papers, edited by Ali Mansoor, Salifou Issoufou, and Daouda Sembene. Washington, DC: IMF, 50. https://documents.worldbank.org/en/publication/documents-reports/documentdetail/474811468183562115/policies-prices-and-poverty-the-sugar-vegetable-oil-and-flour-industries-in-senegal.

Mbaye, Ahmadou Aly, Stephen S. Golub, and Fatou Gueye (eds). 2020. *Formal and Informal Enterprises in Francophone Africa: Moving Toward a Vibrant Private Sector*. Ottawa: International Development Research Centre.

Mbow, Penda. 2008. 'Senegal: The Return of Personalism'. *Journal of Democracy* 19(1): pp. 156–169.

Meagher, Kate. 2018. 'Taxing Times: Taxation, Divided Societies and the Informal Economy in Northern Nigeria'. *Journal of Development Studies* 54(1): pp. 1–17. https://doi.org/10.1080/00220388.2016.1262026.

Meagher, Kate, and Ilda Lindell. 2013. 'Introduction: Engaging with African Informal Economies: Social Inclusion or Adverse Incorporation?' *African Studies Review* 56(3): pp. 57–76.

Moore, Mick. 2022. 'Tax Obsessions: Taxpayer Registration and the Informal Sector in Sub-Saharan Africa'. *Development Policy Review*.

Moore, Mick, and Odd-Helge Fjeldstad. 2008. 'Tax Reform and State-Building in a Globalised World'. In *Taxation and State-Building in Developing Countries*, edited by Deborah Bräutigam, Mick Moore, and Odd Helge Fjeldstad. Cambridge: Cambridge University Press.

Moore, Mick, Wilson Prichard, and Odd-Helge Fjeldstad. 2018. *Taxing Africa: Coercion, Reform and Development*. London: Zed Books.

Mosse, David, and David Lewis. 2006. 'Theoretical Approaches to Brokerage and Translation in Development'. In *Development Brokers and Translators*, edited by David Mosse and David Lewis, pp. 1–26. Bloomfield: Kumarian Press.

Ndiaye, Ameth Saloum. 2017. *Does the Implementation of Tax-Related Reforms and Institutions-Related Reforms Offer Scope for Sustained Tax Revenue Mobilization in Senegal?* Addis Ababa. Eleventh Edition of the African Economic Conference on "Governance for Structural Transformation", Addis Ababa, Ethiopia, 4–6 December 2017. https://aec.afdb.org/sites/default/files/2019/10/08/does_the_implementation_of_tax-related_reforms_and_institutions-related_reforms_offer_scope_for_sustained_tax_revenue_mobilization_in_senegal_.pdf

Pimhidzai, Obert, and Louise Fox. 2012. 'Taking from the Poor or Local Economic Development: The Dilemma of Taxation of Small Informal Enterprises in Uganda'. CSAE Working Paper. Washington, DC: World Bank.

Prichard, Wilson. 2018. 'What Might An Agenda for Equitable Taxation Look Like?' *Policy Brief*. Brighton: ICTD.

Prichard, Wilson, and Vanessa van den Boogaard. 2017. 'Norms, Power and the Socially Embedded Realities of Market Taxation in Northern Ghana'. *African Studies Review* 60(1): pp. 171–194.

Republic of Senegal. 2019. *Projet de Loi de Finances de l'année 2020*. Dakar.

Riedl, Rachel Beatty, and Ndongo Samba Sylla. 2019. 'Aspirations and Realities in Africa: Senegal's Vigorous but Constrained Election'. *Journal of Democracy* 30(3): pp. 94–108.

Rogan, Michael. 2019. Tax Justice and the Informal Economy: A Review of the Debates. *WIEGO Working Paper No. 41*. Manchester.

Rogan, Michael. 2022. 'Taxation and the Informal Sector in the Global South: Strengthening the Social Contract without Reciprocity?' In *Social Contracts and Informal Workers in the Global South*, edited by Laura Alfers, Martha Chen, and Sophie Plagerson. Noarthampton: Edward Elgar, pp. 85–105.

Schaffer, Frederic Charles. 1998. *Democracy in Translation: Understanding Politics in an Unfamiliar Culture*. Ithaca: Cornell University Press.

Scheld, Suzanne. 2010. 'The "China Challenge": The Global Dimensions of Activism and the Informal Economy in Dakar'. In *Africa's Informal Workers: Collective Agency, Alliances and Transnational Organizing in Urban Africa*, edited by Ilda Lindell. London: Zed Books, pp. 153–168.

Scott, James. 1972. 'Patron–Client Politics and Political Change in Southeast Asia'. *American Political Science Review* 66(1): pp. 24.

Stokes, Susan C., Thad Dunning, Mercelo Nazareno, and Valeria Brusco. 2013. *Brokers, Voters, and Clientilism*. New York: Cambridge University Press.

Sud Quotidien. 2004. 'Nouvelle Contribution Globale Unique Ou Impôt Synthétique: L'Unacoisdefs Rejette La Démarche Imposée Par l'État'.

Sy, Mamadou. 2016. 'Fiscalité—Le Renforcement Des Centres de Gestion Agréés Préconisé'. *Le Soleil*.

Tendler, Judith. 2002. 'Small Firms, the Informal Sector, and the Devil's Deal'. *IDS Bulletin* 33(3).

Thioub, Ibrahima, Momar-Coumba Diop, and Catherine Boone. 1998. 'Economic Liberalization in Senegal: Shifting Politics of Indigenous Business'. *African Studies Review* 41(2): pp. 63–89.

UNACOIS. 2012. *Livre Blanc de l'UNACOIS: Moderniser Nos PME et Revitaliser Nos Regions*. Dakar.

Villalón, Leonardo Alfonso. 1995. *Islamic Society and State Power in Senegal: Disciples and Citizens in Fatick*. Cambridge: Cambridge University Press.

Whitfield, Lindsay, Ole Therkildsen, Lars Buur, and Anne Mette Kjær. 2015. *The Politics of African Indutrial Policy: A Comparative Perspective*. New York: Cambridge University Press.

Young, Crawford, and Babacar Kanté. 1991. 'Governance, Democracy, and the 1988 Senegalese Elections'. In *Governance and Politics in Africa*, edited by Goran Hyden and Michael Bratton. Boulder, CO: Lynne Rienner Publishers, pp. 57–74.

13
Conclusion
The politics of revenue bargaining in Africa

Ane Karoline Bak, Anne Mette Kjær, and Marianne S. Ulriksen

Since the turn of the millennium, domestic revenue mobilization in Africa has expanded, and as a result taxation has become more politicized. Extant research has found few signs of the emergence of society-wide macro-level *fiscal social contracts*, whereby accountability and public goods and services are provided in return for tax payments. To understand why and to deepen our knowledge of the political effects of taxation in Africa, we emphasize the importance of examining the political dynamics of revenue bargaining at the micro level. While recent research in the fiscal contract literature has offered illustrative empirical evidence of connections between taxation, responsiveness, and accountability, there is nonetheless a consensus that research has remained somewhat fragmented and insufficiently theorized (see Chapter 1 for further discussion). Furthermore, the literature has lacked a systematic approach to understanding the politics of revenue bargaining, including taking seriously the influence of revenue providers' political and fiscal importance. This volume has addressed these gaps in the literature by exploring *how and under what conditions revenue bargaining emerges, evolves, and leads to fiscal contracts.* Based on a shared theoretical framework, we have explored the politics of revenue bargaining in case studies of micro-level processes of revenue bargaining across five African countries. Hence, this volume offers two major contributions to the literature: first, it broadens the empirical knowledge of how revenue bargaining emerges and evolves, and second, it deepens the theoretical foundation for understanding the politics of revenue bargaining in Africa.

We have drawn on and contribute to fiscal contract theory and the political settlement approach to build a theoretical framework (in Chapter 2), which allows us to study the triggers, processes, and outcomes of revenue bargaining. We disaggregate state actors and revenue providers and theorize how the distribution of holding power and the relative bargaining positions shape

Ane Karoline Bak, Anne Mette Kjær, and Marianne S. Ulriksen, *Conclusion.* In: *The Politics of Revenue Bargaining in Africa.* Edited by: Anne Mette Kjær, Marianne S. Ulriksen, and Ane Karoline Bak, Oxford University Press.
© Oxford University Press (2024). DOI: 10.1093/oso/9780192868787.003.0013

negotiations around tax policy and revenue mobilization. Relative bargaining positions denote the intersection of the state and societal actors' respective organizational and fiscal importance.

Based on this shared theoretical framework, the empirical chapters (Chapters 3–12) explore, in different ways, micro-level instances of revenue bargaining—that is, bargaining between individual or groups of revenue providers and representatives of the government or the ruling elites. Our actor-centred approach, cognizant of the economic and political structures that underpin actors' power and interests, allows us to draw important findings at both the micro and macro levels.

At the micro level, we observe that revenue pressure is not enough to *trigger* revenue bargaining, but that instead the impetus often comes from either politicians (the government) or the tax administration. This finding highlights the importance of disaggregating the state to identify the preferences of politicians and tax administrators, which are sometimes diverging and sometimes conflicting, and to analyse the implications for revenue mobilization. Across the chapters, we find that revenue providers' bargaining power is important for how *processes* of revenue bargaining evolve. Analysing the sources of bargaining power, we can conclude that organizational importance is more decisive for revenue bargaining than revenue providers' importance in terms of their potential fiscal contributions. Moreover, as we disaggregate the group of revenue providers, we study how informal market vendors, big businesses, and international aid agencies engage in revenue bargaining. We show that alliance-making can increase bargaining power and allow usually less resourceful revenue providers to mobilize and promote their interests more effectively. Finally, with respect to *outcomes*, we find that revenue providers who engage in bargaining can succeed in getting the government to make concessions, although these concessions tend to be tax exemptions or reductions in tax payments rather than better public services or promises of increased accountability. Although the fiscal contracts often entail suboptimal fiscal outcomes, our micro-level findings of repeated interactions between ruling elites and revenue providers do suggest that state–society reciprocity could be emerging at the macro level.

We derive such macro-level conclusions from our micro-level case studies of revenue bargaining based on our theoretical framework. As detailed in Chapter 2, ruling elites' and revenue providers' preferences, holding power, and relative bargaining positions are shaped by the political and economic contexts within which they interact. On one hand, then, processes and outcomes of revenue bargaining are products of these macro-level structures and institutions. From this perspective, our findings indicate that revenue bargaining tends to preserve the political status quo: the more organizationally and economically resourceful are more often able to negotiate good deals of tax exemptions or favours. On the other hand, when instances of revenue bargaining contribute to new alliances or change bargaining positions, this has macro-level implications. We see several cases of revenue bargaining where the ruling elite are responsive to the wishes of revenue providers. Several of these engagements develop into repeated negotiations in formal settings (such as in parliamentary committees) based on shared understandings of mutual obligations. These instances suggest state–society reciprocity, which is likely to move policymaking further into formal, structured, and responsive settings that may build accountability in time. We elaborate on these and other findings in this chapter.

13.1 Revenue bargaining at the micro level

The empirical chapters in this book deepen our knowledge and understanding of the politics of revenue bargaining in Africa, as they unpack revenue bargaining at the micro level. They identify, theorize, and analyse what *triggers* revenue bargaining between state actors and revenue providers, how bargaining *processes* unfold, and what the *outcomes* of revenue bargaining are. The following pages summarize the book's findings on each of these three aspects.

13.1.1 Findings on triggers

Most African states will experience continuous and to some extent increasing revenue pressure. Limited economic diversification keeps the tax base limited, constrains the budget, and renders states vulnerable to the global economy. Governments need resources to provide public services and maintain political stability. Staying in power has only become more expensive as the competitiveness of elections has increased. Politicians require additional resources for campaign financing and maintain the ruling coalition (Bleck and van de Walle, 2018; Bak and Therkildsen, 2022). Accordingly, African states have expanded domestic revenue mobilization over the past two decades. Research on revenue bargaining has explored the circumstances under which such increases in tax efforts lead to revenue bargaining, with a focus primarily on the institutional conditions that might facilitate it, including for example representative institutions and accessible political channels for state–society engagement as well as meaningful transparency in tax-related information (Bräutigam, 2008; Prichard, 2015; van den Boogaard et al., 2021). These institutional conditions are mainly static and are therefore not sufficient to explain instances of revenue bargaining that occur outside governments' initiatives to reform taxes. Neither can they explain why some tax reforms lead to revenue bargaining while others do not. In this volume, we explore the wider set of immediate factors that trigger revenue bargaining. These triggers include actions and non-actions, events, or changes in circumstances that prompt state actors or the revenue providers to initiate bargaining or which cause the other side to react (see also Chapter 2).

In this book, there are many examples of revenue bargaining beginning when initiatives to increase taxation cause reactions from revenue providers. However, there are also several what one could call 'negative' cases, where revenue providers try to initiate revenue bargaining, but the government does not respond; or conversely, where governments implement a new tax without negotiation. The empirical chapters offer rich contextualized analyses of triggers. Here, we focus on findings across the chapters that highlight that revenue bargaining can be caused by three types of triggers: (1) the government who decides to introduce a new tax or to reform an existing tax regime, usually as a push to improve revenue mobilization; (2) the tax administration who, under pressure from the government or external partners to meet revenue targets, seeks to expand taxation within the existing tax legislation; and (3) revenue providers who take actions, for example to mobilize protests against certain legislations or conditions.

13.1.1.1 Trigger 1: The government introduces a new tax policy measure

Many cases of revenue bargaining start with a *government's initiative* to introduce or reform tax policies which then prompts reactions and opposition from revenue providers. Most often, the stated motivation is economic, that is, to expand revenue mobilization. For example, for the revenue bargaining with the transport and tourism sectors in Tanzania, a key economic consideration was the expressed intention of the then newly elected President Magufuli to raise government revenue by increasing taxation of numerous revenue providers (Chapter 5). This move was at least in part driven by the (now late) president's 'no nonsense' political style and hard-line attitude to taxpayer resistance. As a part of the same reform package, the government also removed exemptions linked to the security forces' duty-free shops, a move which was in fact largely motivated by consistent complaints about equity voiced by the public and business sectors. Tanzania's reform of VAT was pushed for, conversely, by external donors. Specifically, IMF experts formulated the VAT reform in collaboration with Tanzania's Ministry of Finance with the purpose of gathering and streamlining legislation on VAT and, in turn, improving revenue mobilization (Chapter 6). Similarly, in Senegal, the government's attempts to increase taxation of the informal sector in the 1990s were partly driven by pressure from external actors and partly by the need to address equity concerns raised by formal sector businesses (Chapter 12).

These examples show that even when tax reforms are initiated by officials within the Ministry of Finance, their initial formulations are often done in collaboration with revenue authorities, or international finance institutions, whereafter it is discussed, negotiated, and enacted by parliament. Whether revenue providers react to tax reforms already in the formulation phases, in parliament or parliamentary committees, or in other more closed-off negotiations, varies across the cases. This is discussed in detail in section 13.1.2. regarding the key findings on the processes.

13.1.1.2 Trigger 2: The tax administration begins to enforce tax

The second frequent trigger of revenue bargaining in our case studies is an *increased effort by tax administration to expand taxation within the scope of existing legislation*. In Uganda, several cases of revenue bargaining around agricultural taxation were triggered as technocrats discovered a lack of enforcement of a tax, such as the income tax on fresh milk sales (Chapter 7). This tax was already within the regulatory framework of the Income Tax Act, but URA officials initiated its more systematic enforcement.

The two cases in Togo were of this same kind (Chapter 10). Beach describes how, in northern Togo, tax agents engaged with local traditional authorities to make tax-collection efforts possible, demonstrating how TRA officials trying to raise taxes in the rural hinterlands found innovative ways to do so. In Lomé, the residence tax was sought implemented in part by increasing the administrative capacity of the Togo Revenue Authority.

There are of course also cases where the tax administration takes the initiative to change the tax legislation. In Uganda, an annulment of a VAT exemption on agricultural inputs was tabled by tax officials as a part of the Minister's budget speech (Chapter 7). The tax officials considered taxation of the previously lightly taxed agricultural sector a good way to increase revenues. The speech set in motion a case of revenue bargaining that might never have happened had it not been for the technocrats who developed the analysis of the situation and put the annulment on the political agenda. In

Senegal, the tax administration formulated new instruments during the 2010s to reach large informal importing traders who had otherwise been able to avoid taxation (Chapter 12).

13.1.1.3 Trigger 3: Revenue providers are empowered to protest against existing taxes

In a third group of cases, the triggers constitute *changes in either the motivation or the ability of revenue providers* who then move to react negatively to an existing tax policy. It is generally a necessary condition of revenue bargaining that revenue providers are *able* to react to changes in taxation or to protest against poor public services. Large companies or powerful individuals may protest independently, but most revenue providers need to have capacity for collective action in order for revenue bargaining to occur (Prichard, 2015).

Across the instances of revenue bargaining, we find that most of the revenue providers involved in bargaining are organized in unions or business associations. These organizations may not always represent all members equally; nevertheless, in many of our cases, they do manage to mobilize protest against a perceived unfairness in taxation. We find examples where the intervention of a trade union or NGO prompts the organization of an otherwise dispersed group of revenue providers, which in turn leads to revenue bargaining. Chapter 3 shows how Tanzanian women traders continuously experienced obstacles to working in informal markets. Their grievances were latent, and it was only with the presence of an NGO or a union that the women were able to claim better conditions or fairer taxation at the market. In Senegal, the business association UNACOIS was for many years a broker that mobilized, organized, and represented informal commercial actors vis-à-vis state actors (Chapter 12).

We see few cases in which citizens react to or mobilize against existing taxation, for instance motivated by a perceived lack of reciprocity or fairness. Some chapter contributions find that revenue providers might be dissatisfied with government services, but as they do not expect state actors to even respond to expressions of dissatisfaction, they refrain from trying (e.g. Chapter 7).

In sum, we find that in our cases, revenue bargaining occurs when new taxes are suggested or adopted, when existing taxes are reformed, when existing taxes are enforced, or when changing circumstances enable revenue providers to react where they could not before. Common for all three triggers is that they disturb the status quo, either in terms of revenue providers' (potential) tax burden or in their relative bargaining position vis-à-vis the ruling elites.

13.1.2 Findings on processes

Once revenue bargaining is set in motion, how do cases of revenue bargaining evolve? We make the following four findings that highlight how bargaining positions can change, how bargaining processes evolve, and the outcomes at which they eventually arrive: (1) organizational importance matters more than potential revenue contributions; (2) revenue bargaining can build cross-sector alliances and bargaining power; (3) elections shift the relative bargaining positions of revenue providers and ruling elites; and (4) arenas of bargaining matter for strategies and fiscal contract outcomes.

13.1.2.1 Organizational importance matters more than potential revenue contributions

In this book, we examine in tandem the influence of revenue providers' organizational and fiscal importance for their bargaining positions vis-à-vis the ruling elites. Organizational importance is tightly associated with the concept of holding power in the political settlement theory, and research has demonstrated how ruling elites' need for political support explains variations in policy outcomes across countries and within countries across sectors. The power that actors can gain based on their fiscal importance to the ruling elites has received less attention in this literature. We argue that it is necessary to add a revenue dimension to the concept of holding power and emphasize fiscal importance as an important source of bargaining power for revenue providers. This allows us to examine the importance that ruling elites ascribe to fiscal concerns in comparison with the need for political support.

What we find is that a revenue provider's potential fiscal contribution to the revenue base, even when potentially large, matters less than the revenue provider's political importance. Across the cases of revenue bargaining, ruling elites prove to be keenly aware of the role of groups of revenue providers as supporting factions in the ruling coalition. For example, the ruling parties in Tanzania and Uganda very clearly prioritized the party's own political campaigns over government revenue when they allowed big businesses tax exemptions (Chapter 9). In Tanzania, the government also avoided protests from the security forces, an important faction, by pre-emptively introducing a compensatory payout at the time when the VAT exemptions of army shops were removed (Chapter 5). While the removal of the duty-free shops' exemptions hardly improved revenue mobilization, the government was able to change an unpopular and misused benefit without upsetting the politically important security forces. In Togo, the government compromised on its revenue potential by involving the local Chief in improving tax collection in his area (Chapter 10). That the Chief assisted tax collectors from the far-away capital, considered as foreigners in the area, in taxing the citizens was an apt solution to improve tax revenue; however, in return for the permission to collect revenue, tax benefits were given to the Chief, a political actor well worth being on good terms with. Furthermore, the case study from Mozambique is an interesting, though not uncommon, example of how the fiscal base can be manipulated politically to favour municipalities led by the ruling party; though with the unintended consequence of storing up revenue efforts in municipalities led by opposition parties with potential positive effects on local governance downstream (Chapter 4).

Reinforcing the point that political clout is more important than fiscal muscle, two divergent and negative cases of fiscal contracts demonstrate what happens in a counter-scenario where revenue providers could provide large fiscal contributions but enjoy little organizational importance to the ruling coalition. In Uganda, the government stood firm against multinational oil companies (MNCs) (Chapter 8). This was possible because oil MNCs are not part of important domestic factions whose support the ruling elites depend on, while at the same time, the money retrieved from MNCs' windfall taxes could be used to maintain the ruling coalition. In Tanzania, a year-long revenue-bargaining process between international aid agencies and the government over financing the continuation of a cash-transfer programme ended with the government still not funding the main part of the programme, despite its earlier commitments to do so (Chapter 11). These findings are significant because of the tendency to assume that big financial contributors such as donors or MNCs also enjoy considerable political influence. These case studies imply that this is not necessarily the case and demonstrate the need for further research on the nexus and relative importance of international versus domestic factors in revenue bargaining.

While our observation that politics matters may appear self-evident, the finding is relevant because of the analytical basis from which it is derived. As we disaggregate actors and pay attention to the variety of political, economic, and organizational sources of revenue providers' bargaining power, we are able to analyse the comparative significance of these different sources of power. We can show not only that holding power matters for revenue bargaining, but also how it can change during the process, as we elaborate in the following section.

13.1.2.2 Revenue bargaining can build cross-sector alliances and bargaining power

In Chapter 2, we theorize that the relative bargaining positions of revenue providers vis-à-vis ruling elites influence revenue bargaining, but stress that the bargaining positions should not be assumed static. While it is necessary to assess the initial bargaining positions to understand the conditions under which revenue bargaining emerges, we suggest that bargaining power, and with it the relative bargaining positions, is likely to shift as bargaining processes evolve. This proposition is confirmed by the case studies in this book. The empirical chapters show that revenue providers' bargaining power is often strengthened as revenue bargaining progresses.

In some cases, bargaining power changed when a government's initiative to increase taxation pushed a group of revenue providers to cooperate better in order to gain a foothold in the negotiations. For instance, the actors in Tanzania's transport sector have diverse needs and demands and have often been in competition with each other, but in response to the government's push to reform taxes, they unified (Chapter 5). In the case of the 2014 VAT Act in Tanzania, business associations and other lobby groups created alliances and worked towards reshaping the VAT Act in accordance with their own interests (Chapter 6).

In other cases, bargaining power was strengthened when a targeted group of revenue providers was able to create alliances with non-sector stakeholders or got assistance from external or third parties. This happened in cases where the revenue providers proved themselves unable to mobilize sufficiently to counter or put pressure on the government. In the case of Ugandan agricultural taxes, farmers' associations initially were against the announced annulment of VAT exemptions on agricultural inputs but without much noise (Chapter 7). However, when aligning with other associations such as a larger umbrella association for civil society groups, their bargaining power was strengthened. In Tanzania, informal women traders had long held grievances but were only able to enter into dialogue with local government officials when assisted by civil society organizations (Chapter 3).

In these cases, the revenue providers are actually organized in market associations, trade unions, or other associations, which in theory bolsters capacity for collective action. However, often these organizations suffer from poor funding due to lack of paying members or low membership fees and rely heavily on funding from various domestic or external sponsors. Furthermore, it can happen that such organizations are torn by conflicts among members aiming to pursue their individual business interests. In Senegal, UNACOIS was initially a facilitator of the informal commercial sector to organize and resist taxation (Chapter 12). However, the diverging interests between, on one hand, the richest and most influential members, and on the other, street vendors led to organizational fragmentation. Eventually, this weakened the bargaining position of UNACOIS as well as the broad group of revenue providers vis-à-vis the ruling elites. This case is representative of a more general point: in competitive clientelism, the constant contest for access to rents and special deals is likely to continuously stir divisions and challenge broad sector alliances, such as those in the above-mentioned example of the Tanzanian transport sector.

13.1.2.3 Elections shift the relative bargaining positions of revenue providers and ruling elites

Elections are by now regular and institutionalized events across Africa, even in non-democratic countries. In several of our case studies, the holding of elections explicitly or implicitly affected the revenue-bargaining process. Most notably, we find that elections can shape the course of the revenue-bargaining process by shifting the relative bargaining positions of revenue providers vis-à-vis the ruling elite. For instance, elections are costly to the ruling elites, as they require revenue to run campaigns as well as to mobilize support and to deliver promised public goods (as elaborated in Chapter 2). At the same time, elections are political windows that may give disgruntled groups of citizens an opportunity to raise their grievances (as noted in Chapter 1; Bleck and van de Walle, 2018). This implies that during election times, the bargaining position of ruling elites is weakened, which may prompt them to be more willing to give in to demands raised in revenue-bargaining processes. In Uganda, for example, elections increased the relative bargaining power of agricultural revenue providers who had the capacity to mobilize votes, which meant that farmers were able to bring up grievances during election campaigns, where they were more likely to be heard (Chapter 7). In both Uganda and Tanzania, political candidates are dependent on private donations to finance their electoral campaigns, which weakens the bargaining positions of candidates vis-à-vis the revenue providers donating money. These shifting bargaining positions are likely to enable revenue providers to negotiate favourable tax deals after elections (Chapter 9).

Our findings resonate with research arguing that elections enhance the bargaining power of voters and can thus drive the suspension of taxes (Tendler, 2002; Kjær and Therkildsen, 2012; Prichard, 2018; Bak and Therkildsen, 2022). We add the important aspect that revenue bargaining around elections stirs not only voters at large, but also specific groups of revenue providers who have the means to directly profit from competitive elections.

13.1.2.4 Arenas of bargaining matter for strategies and bargaining outcomes

In this book we have sought to move away from the imaginary bargaining table by paying particular attention to the spaces in which revenue bargaining actually takes place. Revenue bargaining takes place mainly in three arenas: the political, the bureaucratic, and the public. In the following, we describe in detail what these three arenas look like, how they shape revenue-bargaining processes, and the strategies that the negotiating parties pursue to navigate them.

When we talk about *the political arena*, we refer to formal and informal spaces alike. The formal political arena includes parliament, parliamentary committees, and cabinet ministers. The informal political arena refers to more exclusive meetings (or sometimes phone calls) with politicians or with powerful individuals who may or may not have an official post. They can be members of the presidential inner circle or presidential advisors. This understanding closely follows the premise that politics in clientelist political settlements is not limited to either of the two spaces. In fact, the case studies show that revenue bargaining occurs in the two arenas in parallel, and/or moves between them. Likely because the political arena is where decision-making power lies, this is where revenue providers tend to be the most successful in promoting their demands in revenue bargaining.

In most cases, revenue bargaining occurs in the formal political arena. In the case of the 2014 VAT reform in Tanzania, the business sectors made a concerted effort to lobby MPs to maintain VAT exemptions, and succeeded to a large extent in watering down the reform by these means (Chapter 6). Another example comes from the transport and tourism sectors in Tanzania, who were only able to get government concessions once they had (re-)gained access to key political committees and task forces where they could present their case and their demands (Chapter 5). In the Tanzanian example, access to the political arena was partly ensured by building contacts in the line ministries. Hence, one way to break into the political arena was through the bureaucratic one.

Though using these official channels, revenue providers also seek to build and utilize their personal connections to powerful individuals, often in parallel. The closer to the inner circles of the ruling elite revenue providers get, the more successful they will be in promoting their interests. Many revenue providers, whether protesting against tax efforts or seeking to obtain tax exemptions, try to access the president directly. This is a priority expressed by interviewees engaged in bargaining across the cases. Often, they draw on whatever connections they have to get the president's attention, either informally or formally through forums such as the presidential round table in Uganda (Chapter 7). In the case where the Senegalese business association UNACOIS was protesting against a new tax instrument, a representative is quoted in a news article as stating that they were not interested in meeting tax inspectors (Chapter 12). Instead, UNACOIS wanted to talk to relevant ministers or, alternatively, the head of Senegal's tax administration.

As a temporary yet regular political arena, elections prove to be an important condition for revenue bargaining. First, in the tangible sense that campaign rallies and meetings give voters opportunities to access and directly confront politicians with concerns or dissatisfactions over taxation (Chapter 7). Second, in the more nebulous sense that political candidates' and the ruling elites' need for campaign funding combined with under-regulation of campaign financing provides a somewhat legitimate space for narrow, exclusive bargaining between candidates and potential campaign donors (Chapter 9).

Besides serving as a channel through which to access the political arena, as mentioned above, *the bureaucratic arena* is also a space where revenue bargaining takes place. The bureaucratic arena refers to line ministries or other state agencies. In this arena, revenue providers seek to influence their tax liabilities or to protest a certain tax. They, for example, write letters to the minister in question, or contact the authority charged with collecting a tax or fee or with the legal mandate to give individual exemptions. This was the case when Ugandan dairy farmers protested against a tax on milk sales (Chapter 7). Several of the reforms of the informal sector tax in Senegal happened through continuous consultations between the tax administration and UNACOIS, who for a time was the main representative of the informal commercial sector. It is important to note that sometimes, outcomes of bargaining that takes place in the bureaucratic arena risk being challenged and subverted as they enter the political arena. The eventual dilution of the 2014 VAT reform in Tanzania is a case in point (Chapter 6).

When revenue bargaining takes place in the *public arena*, revenue providers and state actors communicate in the media and/or at public events. This arena is the furthest away from the ruling elite. Our case studies show that such bargaining often proves unsuccessful and can quickly turn conflictual, with opposing parties hardening their standpoint in their efforts to gain public support. President Magufuli and his government's reaction to the MPs' outcry in the Tanzanian media is a clear example of this; the conflict escalated as the president took a harder line (Chapter 5). In Senegal, informal traders went on strike and 'killed the economy', first for three days and then later for an additional day, as a response to the perceived lack of state responsiveness. This was a strategic move to implicate the wider population in the revenue-bargaining process (Chapter 12). Thus, despite enhancing the distance between the bargaining parties, the public arena can be instrumental for revenue providers and state actors alike in building bargaining positions and (re)gaining a foothold in negotiations, precisely because the public arena is an avenue for influencing public opinion and gaining legitimacy. Hence, in Tanzania, the tourism and transport sectors were able to build some public support and legitimacy, not least given the size of their employee groups, while in Senegal, taking to the streets and shutting down commerce was a means of demonstrating power and thereby proving the organizational importance of this group of informal economic actors.

Besides the three main arenas, bargaining also takes place elsewhere. Chapter 8 describes how bargaining can take place in and around the courts. In this case, the Ugandan government was the actor bringing the matter to court. However, the opposite scenario, where large companies with the means and connections take a tax case to court if they feel they are being unlawfully taxed, is just as likely. The role of the judicial arena in revenue bargaining is greatly under-studied and constitutes a highly relevant future research agenda.

The case studies show that revenue providers learn from their own and others' bargaining experiences including which arenas are effective for which objectives, and this knowledge often informs their applied strategies. In other words, the choice of arena is strategic. However, this choice is also shaped by the strength of revenue providers' initial bargaining position. If it is strong, they are able to access and promote their interests in the political arena. If weak, revenue providers can attempt to adopt strategies to increase their bargaining power by building access paths to the desired arena. They can take the informal route, building contacts to networks that already enjoy access to the political arena, preferably to the president or a minister. If access is easier through such personal networks, trying to access the media may be less useful, though one strategy does not necessarily exclude the other: an actor could team up with others to arrange a common protest in the public arena, which could consequently improve their access to the political arena.

Summing up, the case studies show that revenue bargaining takes place across political, bureaucratic, and public arenas. Here, the parties pursue strategies ranging from the amicable (i.e. seeking to build relationships) to the more conflictual (i.e. mobilizing protests). While many instances of bargaining are informal and at times clientelistic in nature, we see much evidence of bargaining taking place within the established political and bureaucratic state structures. This suggests that policymaking around taxes has to an extent become institutionalized, a trend which could be explored further. The more politically resourceful and organized tend to stand in a better bargaining position vis-à-vis the ruling elite compared to the less well organized. However, the close study of the processes shows that actors' relative power and position can shift during the bargaining process. Specifically, this implies that even revenue providers with initially limited fiscal and organizational importance could eventually succeed in being heard by the ruling elites.

13.1.3 Findings on outcome

An important question in this volume is whether and under what conditions revenue bargaining leads to agreements that constitute micro-level fiscal contracts, which we define as explicit or implicit agreements between the individual and groups of revenue providers and the ruling elite (or representatives hereof) related to revenue provision (see Chapter 1).

Across our case studies, we find that most cases of revenue bargaining led to some kind of agreement between the involved parties. The cases of revenue bargaining that followed a spate of tax reforms in Tanzania in 2016 led the government to make concessions, in one case even pre-emptively (Chapter 5). After several unsuccessful attempts at increasing informal sector taxation in Senegal in the '90s, the business association UNACOIS and the Senegalese government together developed a unified tax regime targeting the informal sector in 2004 and, hence, entered what Bak calls a brokered fiscal contract (Chapter 12). In Mozambique, local governments made efforts to develop contractual relations with citizens to incentivize tax compliance (Chapter 4). In northern Togo, tax agents were able to expand broad-based taxation after negotiating with the local Chief (Chapter 10). Conversely, there were also examples of revenue bargaining that did *not* lead to fiscal contracts. In Lomé (capital of Togo), the government's effort to increase residence tax failed because of popular opposition (Chapter 10). In Tanzania, the government and international donor agencies have been unable to reach an agreement as to the funding responsibilities of the cash-transfers programme (Chapter 11).

Turning to the *kinds* of micro-level fiscal contracts, the case studies found that revenue bargaining often led to what we could term *non-fiscal exchanges* between the ruling elite and the revenue providers. They are non-fiscal in the sense that the agreements manifest in the absence of a fiscal exchange yet still significantly influence revenue provision. As noted in Chapter 2, the fiscal contract literature has been preoccupied with the circumstances under which taxation may lead to reciprocal positive exchanges of revenue and public goods and/or accountability between the two parties. However, the cases studied in this book show that the more common outcomes of revenue bargaining are agreements around tax *exemptions*. To name a few, big businesses received tax exemptions in exchange for supporting ruling parties' political campaigns in Tanzania and Uganda (Chapter 9); tax collectors in northern Togo gained access to taxpayers by making special deals with the local Chief that reduced his personal tax liabilities (Chapter 10); and in Uganda, the president appeased several groups of agricultural farmers, who in exchange ceased cross-sectoral protests, by cancelling an 18% VAT on agricultural inputs and waiving corporate income tax for cooperatives (SACCOs) (Chapter 7). Such non-fiscal exchanges manifest agreements of an exchange related to revenue provision and, hence, denote micro-level fiscal contracts even if negative in the sense that they lead to less effective revenue mobilization.

Of course, it can be difficult to determine whether revenue bargaining ends because of the establishment of an agreement or because either or both of the parties simply back down. It is quite impossible to develop generalizable, observable implications of a settled micro-level fiscal contract, not least given the variation in revenue bargaining; from open debates to discrete lobbying in relation to tax reforms, to private bargaining related to campaign financing, or institutionalized revenue bargaining around cash-transfer programmes. It is all the more difficult to do so when agreements rarely manifest in positive exchanges, which would at least be easier to observe than non-fiscal exchanges and non-actions. Ultimately, it can be difficult to draw this line. In the case of campaign financing in Uganda and Tanzania (Chapter 9), Khisa et al. found evidence that campaign donors were revenue providers who seemed to deem a private exchange of donations for political influence more effective than the public fiscal exchange around taxes (Chapter 9). However, it is difficult if not impossible to determine whether campaign donors and the electoral candidates enter a sort of contractual agreement in which the respective parties can hold each other accountable. Similarly, in the case of Tanzania's VAT reform, whether revenue providers lobbying individual MPs in fact (implicitly) enter *quid pro quo* agreements is difficult to determine (Chapter 6). In both cases, though, we can conclude that these micro-level instances of revenue bargaining bolster relations between privileged groups of revenue providers and segments of the ruling elites and, eventually, constrain public revenue and the public budget.

In cases where government does concede to revenue providers without giving tax exemptions, the agreements may entail a reduction in the proposed tax payments, constraining public revenue. This occurred for example in Tanzania, where the government agreed to set lower tax rates for MPs than those originally proposed (Chapter 5). Curiously, in none of the cases studied did revenue providers connect their contributions to demands for service delivery. Their reaction was instead to protest against the tax itself rather than to demand better services for it. For instance, in Uganda, even farmers with a relatively strong bargaining position failed to achieve their demands of agricultural public goods (Chapter 7), and their demands for improved services were not linked to tax payment.

Overall, most cases studied in this volume show that revenue bargaining does lead to micro-level fiscal contracts. Ruling elites are willing to give concessions to maintain their support base. Not surprisingly, revenue providers who are important for the ruling elites' political survival are able to negotiate revenue deals preferable to them, most often in the form of tax exemptions. At the same time, ruling elites are also responsive to groups of revenue providers who are able to mobilize to negotiate their case. The fiscal contracts reflect the kind of demands that revenue providers resort to, namely reductions in tax payments rather than a return for their taxes in the form of better public service provision or increased governmental accountability.

13.2 Macro-level implications of revenue bargaining

From our many case studies we identify two overall, macro-level implications that contribute to our understanding of politics and policymaking in African countries characterized as hybrid regimes, where formal democratic institutions coexist with authoritarian features such as concentration of executive power and an infringement of rights (Diamond, 2002). First, politics matters *also* when it comes to revenue mobilization, and those within and close to the ruling elite can negotiate better deals than those who are less favourably placed. Second, we see signs of state–society reciprocity developing, which opens the political space and holds promises for more inclusive and formalized settings for policymaking.

13.2.1 *How* politics matters

Considering the 'politics matters' argument, our findings manifest two central characteristics of the politics of taxation. First, as argued above, ensuring ruling coalition stability weighs heavily on ruling elites' agenda and, consequently, the immediate outcomes of efforts to expand domestic revenue mobilization tend to reproduce the existing structures of power in our case countries. Political settlement theory has highlighted that there can be growth–stability trade-offs when creating growth-enhancing institutions

(Khan, 2010). Our findings indicate that revenue–stability trade-offs also exist: those who already enjoy political clout and are organizationally important are able to assert influence over their tax liabilities. Therefore, as also suggested by critical strands of the fiscal contract literature (e.g. Meagher, 2018), the politics of taxation by no means disrupts existing power structures or the political settlement. On the contrary, the implication will often be higher tax burdens on those without political influence. To better understand the potential implications for economic inequality and tax equity, there is a need for more empirical research on the effects of elites' incentives to promote the stability of tax systems in general, and the tax burden of marginalized and resourceless groups of taxpayers in particular.

The second characteristic of the politics of revenue bargaining is that it generally serves to reduce tax revenue compared to the revenue initially projected. Paradoxically, efforts to expand domestic revenue mobilization and the consequent politicization of taxation seem in many cases *not* to lead to effective increases in tax revenue. The contributions to this volume show a few examples of tax reforms leading to increased revenue, though often in a compromised form whereby less tax is collected than initially anticipated. In some cases, revenue bargaining ended with a return to the status quo and taxes left unimplemented; in others, existing tax legislation was changed but implementation and expansions in actual tax collection remained limited; and finally, some efforts to effectuate existing tax regimes in fact led to formalization of waivers or tax exemptions. In all these cases, the need for political support from revenue providers overruled the potential revenue gains.

This politics of revenue bargaining is costly in two ways. First, the revenue providers who are not able to mobilize resistance end up being disproportionately highly taxed. Among these revenue providers are often economically vulnerable actors including, for example, those working in the informal economy for whom taxation can create individual grievances. Second, smaller taxpayers including informal economic actors are fairly expensive to tax, and therefore tax efforts tend to cost more than they earn (Moore, Prichard, and Fjeldstad, 2018, ch. 7). Though reducing the political costs of taxation, the politics of revenue bargaining creates suboptimal fiscal outcomes as well as, potentially, additional administrative costs.

Yet, even if the ruling elites had an incentive to respond positively to revenue providers' demands for public services, they might not be able to do so. Under latent revenue pressure and limited state capacity, the short-term administrative costs outlined above are less than those created by political instability. For the ruling elite, tax concessions are a possible way in which to be responsive to the demands of powerful groups and to maintain the ruling coalition. On the other hand, improving services is costly and requires a long-term political and administrative effort. We know from recent contributions to the literature on universal primary schooling that it is one thing to promise better education in election campaigns, but quite another to deliver on these promises. While increasing enrolment may be easily achieved, it is considerably harder to make sure that pupils receive quality learning (Hickey and Hossain, 2018). In turn, these political concerns exhibited by ruling elites in revenue bargaining shape citizens' political strategies. Past failed demands for public services will reasonably discourage citizens from making such demands in the future. Citizens may perceive it as easier to protest against taxes than to demand improved services. In this way, the status quo is also upheld by citizens with fewer political resources.

Two findings tentatively suggest the conditions under which this status quo might be disrupted. First, in our case studies, revenue bargaining did create a basis for otherwise less resourceful revenue providers to mobilize, create alliances, and negotiate with state actors. This speaks to the potential of revenue bargaining to prompt capacity for collective action (Prichard, 2015). However, in this book we have not been able to follow such alliances over time; more research is needed to evaluate the sustainability of such alliances and how they shape politics in the longer term.

Second, we find that revenue bargaining around VAT reforms is more common than might be expected. This might be surprising to those expecting that direct taxes, such as personal income tax, are the key to stimulating 'healthy' conflicts between states and citizens. Direct taxes are assumed to be relatively more visible and felt than indirect taxes such as VAT. However, in many African countries, personal income taxes are not broad-based and hence not felt. Conversely, most citizens pay VAT on consumer goods and changes in VAT on staples and basic necessities such as petrol are strongly felt. Moreover, extensive issues with VAT refunds in many African countries imply that VAT is felt not only by consumers but also by companies. Indeed, we found indications that VAT reforms might actually be central in prompting the types of broad-based alliances discussed above, because these reforms often hit revenue providers sector-wide or even across sectors. This finding indicates that it is worth exploring more how different *types* of taxes or tax policies trigger and shape processes of revenue bargaining.

It may appear paradoxical that our case studies highlight *suboptimal* tax collections, when, as we outlined in Chapter 1, there has been an increase in domestic revenue collection across our case countries. In part, this is explained by new tax reforms that broaden the tax base and taxed sectors, even if the compromise is less tax than originally proposed. In part, improved revenue mobilization may also be explained as a result of a general improved in tax capacity: the revenue authorities are generally better equipped and have newer tax handles in 2020 than in 2010 (Moore, Prichard, and Fjeldstad, 2018). Future research could provide a more systematic review to assess the level of revenue foregone, for instance by comparing estimates of revenue-collection increases between bills that are tabled and bills that are eventually adopted. Of course, a deeper layer of analysis would be needed to identify the changes between a reform proposal and the bill itself, to determine who benefits from the outcomes, and to examine which policies end up unimplemented.

13.2.2 State–society reciprocity

In Chapter 1, we discussed how an older literature on state–society relations in Africa had pointed to tendencies for citizens to exit or 'disengage' from the state as they did not experience a reciprocal relationship. Citizens would see taxation more as a foreign imposition than as a potential future benefit to them. However, since the 1980s, elections have become institutionalized and civil society organizations have grown in strength. Disengagement is no longer the default option. Our five case countries are characterized as stable African economies with some electoral competition. Politically, the countries can be classified as *hybrid* regimes (Diamond, 2002) where (some level of) competitive elections exist in conjunction with the need to use repression and/or co-optation to maintain stability and power (e.g. Svolik, 2012; Gerschewski, 2013). Ruling elites need to win elections convincingly and at the same time maintain the ruling coalition (Whitfield et al., 2015).

The extent to which citizen demands matter to the ruling elite is therefore usually driven by electoral competition, and there are plenty of examples in the literature of party leaders making promises of (and sometimes delivering) social services during election times (see e.g. Stasavage, 2005; Kjær and Therkildsen, 2012; Seeberg, 2014). In line with this research, our case studies demonstrate that elections matter for revenue bargaining by prompting changes in the relative bargaining power of ruling elites vis-à-vis revenue providers. Elections force the ruling elite to be responsive to taxpayers as voters, and election campaigns may, as we have seen, offer arenas to raise tax-related concerns. However, competitive elections—even if not free and fair—also drive up the costs of staying in power, which has negative implications for revenue bargaining.

The presence of informal, clientelistic institutions and ruling elites more concerned with maintaining the ruling coalition than winning the favour of the broad masses (Svolik, 2012) may lead to the assumption that ruling elites are only responsive to citizen demands at elections, if at all. Nevertheless, across the case studies, we find that ruling elites also respond to citizens *between* elections. Our analyses of the revenue-bargaining processes show that state actors do engage in negotiations with groups of revenue providers, spreading from informal sector workers to bigger private businesses. We observed ruling elites making concessions in their tax efforts in bargaining with MPs or big businesses, and we also observed them bargaining with and eventually giving concessions to smaller businesses, informal stakeholders, and other groups of citizens of lesser organizational and economic importance. Ruling elites also acknowledge these revenue providers' demands, enter into dialogue with them, and at times make concessions or compromises. Revenue providers on their part do engage with ruling elites too; they not only rely on protests in the streets, public outcry, or passive resistance, but also mobilize, and enter into dialogue and build relations with key state actors, where they present their case based on evidence and knowledge-sharing using official bureaucratic and political channels.

We see that state and societal actors are not only responsive to each other, but also repeat their engagements based on understandings of interdependence and mutual obligations. This demonstrates state–society reciprocity. State–society relations are reciprocal when bargaining takes place in formal democratic settings (such as parliamentary committees) which serves to institutionalize state–society relations. Consequently, and as suggested in fiscal contract theory, we should continue to think of taxation as a driver of state–society reciprocity, but we should look beyond macro-level relations. If we see a broad variety of reciprocal engagements evolving and institutionalizing during and between elections, such interactions may in time increase accountability and induce a society-wide fiscal social contract.

References

Bak, A. K., and O. Therkildsen. 2022. 'Democratisation in Tanzania: No Elections without Tax Exemptions'. *Journal of Eastern African Studies* 14(1): pp. 47–67.

Bleck, J., and N. van de Walle, N. 2018. *Electoral Politics in Africa: Continuity in Change*. Cambridge: Cambridge University Press.

Bräutigam, D. 2008. 'Introduction: Taxation and State-building in Developing Countries'. In *Taxation and State-Building in Developing Countries*, edited by

D. Bräutigam, O.-H. Fjeldstad, and M. Moore, pp. 1–33. Cambridge: Cambridge University Press.

Diamond, L. 2002. 'Thinking about Hybrid Regimes'. *Journal of Democracy* 13: pp. 21–36. https://doi.org/10.1353/jod.2002.0025.

Gerschewski, J. 2013. 'The Three Pillars of Stability: Legitimation, Repression, and Co-optation in Autocratic Regimes'. *Democratization* 20(1): pp. 13–38.

Hickey, S. and N. Hossain, eds. 2018. *The Politics of Education in Developing Countries: From Schooling to Learning?* Oxford: Oxford University Press.

Khan, M. H. 2010. 'Political Settlements and the Governance of Growth-enhancing Institutions'. *Working Paper*. London: SOAS.

Kjær, A. M., and O. Therkildsen. 2012. 'Elections and Landmark Policies in Uganda and Tanzania'. *Democratization* 40(4): pp. 592–614.

Meagher, K. 2018. 'Taxing Times: Taxation, Divided Societies and the Informal Economy in Northern Nigeria'. *Journal of Development Studies* 54(1): pp. 1–17. https://doi.org/10.1080/00220388.2016.1262026.

Moore, M., W. Prichard, and O. Fjeldstad. 2018. *Taxing Africa: Coercion, Reform and Development*. London: Zed Books. https://doi.org/10.5040/9781350222861.

Prichard, W. 2015. *Taxation, Responsiveness and Accountability in Sub-Saharan Africa*. Cambridge: Cambridge University Press.

Prichard, W. 2018. 'Electoral Competitiveness, Tax Bargaining and Political Incentives in Developing Countries: Evidence from Political Budget Cycles Affecting Taxation'. *British Journal of Political Science* 48(2): pp. 427–457. https://doi.org/10.1017/S0007123415000757.

Seeberg, M. B. 2014. 'State Capacity and the Paradox of Authoritarian Elections'. *Democratization* 21(7): pp. 1265–1285.

Stasavage, D. 2005. 'Democracy and Education Spending in Africa'. *American Journal of Political Science* 49(2): pp. 343–358.

Svolik, M. W. 2012. *The Politics of Authoritarian Rule*. Cambridge: Cambridge University Press.

Tendler, J. 2002. 'Small Firms, the Informal Sector, and the Devil's Deal'. *IDS Bulletin* 33(3): pp. 1–15.

van den Boogaard, V., W. Prichard, R. Beach, and F. Mohiuddin. 2021. 'Enabling Tax Bargaining: Supporting More Meaningful Tax Transparency and Taxpayer Engagement in Ghana and Sierra Leone'. *Development Policy Review*. https://doi.org/10.1111/dpr.12563.

Whitfield, L., O. Therkildsen, L. Buur, and A. M. Kjær. 2015. *The Politics of African Industrial Policy*. Cambridge: Cambridge University Press.

Index

For the benefit of digital users, indexed terms that span two pages (e.g., 52–53) may, on occasion, appear on only one of those pages.

P